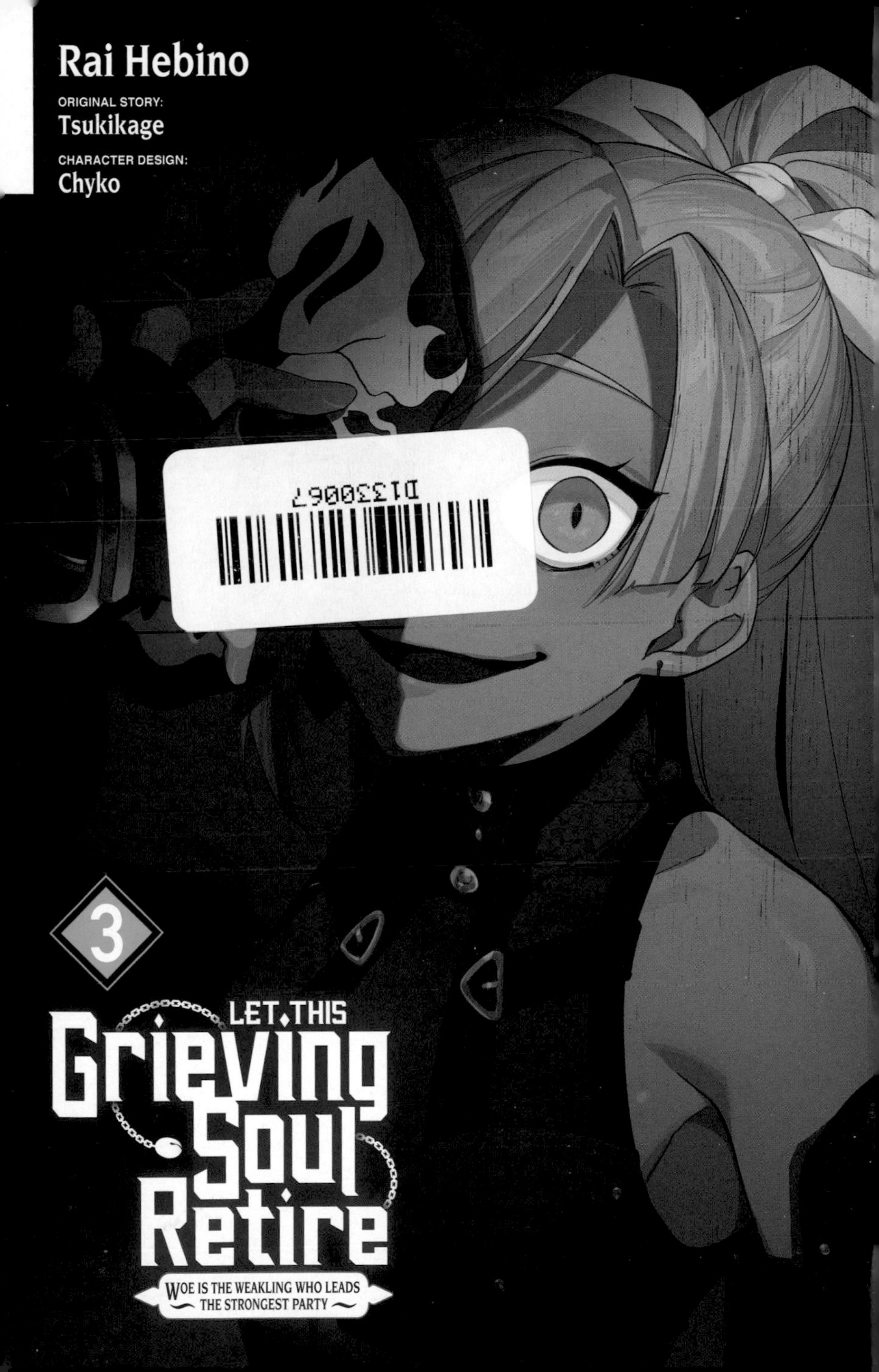
Rai Hebino
ORIGINAL STORY:
Tsukikage
CHARACTER DESIGN:
Chyko
3
LET THIS
Grieving
Soul
Retire
WOE IS THE WEAKLING WHO LEADS
THE STRONGEST PARTY

CONTENTS

Let This Grieving Soul Retire
~ Woe Is the Weakling Who
Leads the Strongest Party ~

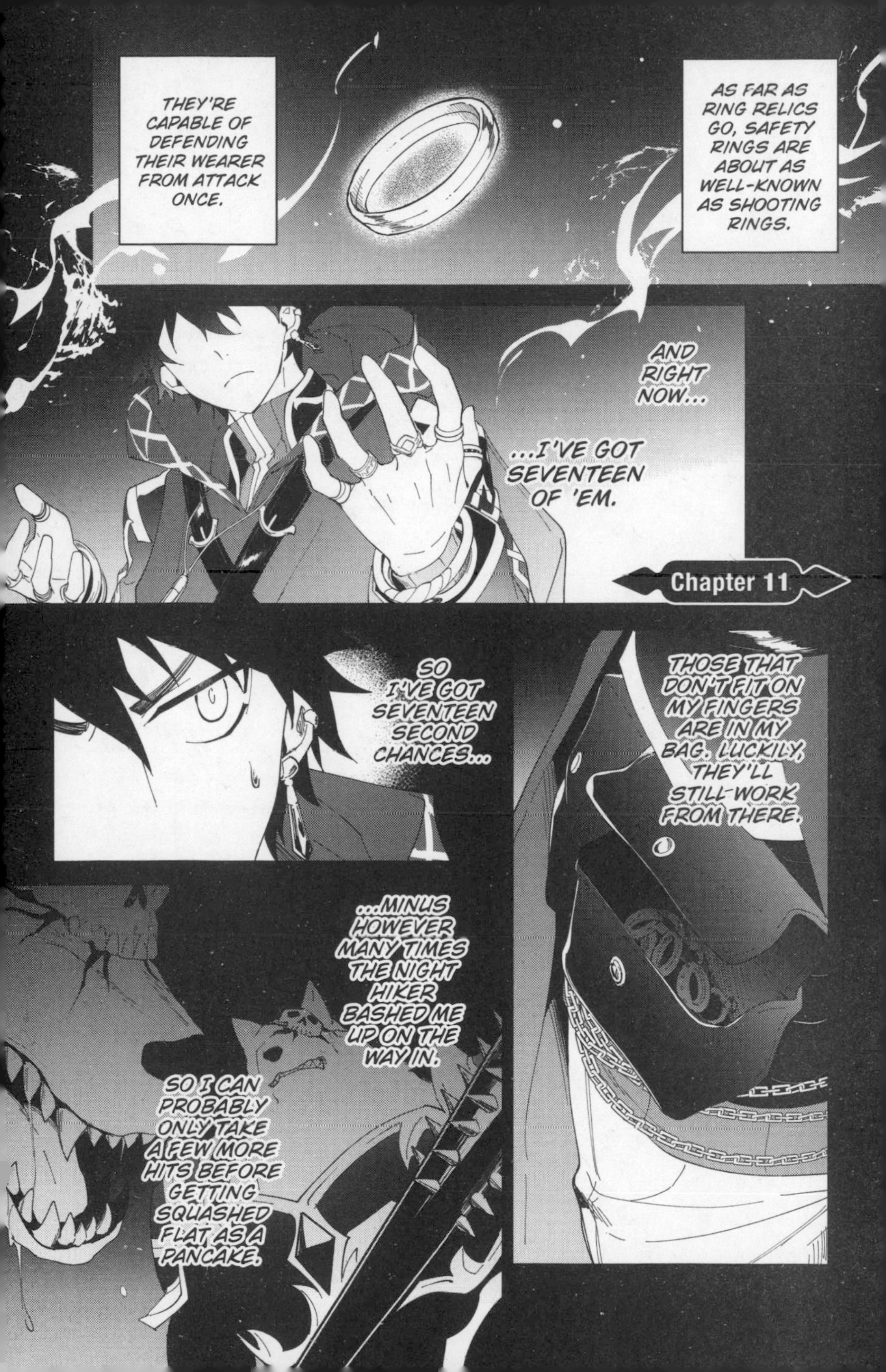
AS FAR AS RING RELICS GO, SAFETY RINGS ARE ABOUT AS WELL-KNOWN AS SHOOTING RINGS.
THEY'RE CAPABLE OF DEFENDING THEIR WEARER FROM ATTACK ONCE.
AND RIGHT NOW...
...I'VE GOT SEVENTEEN OF 'EM.
Chapter 11
THOSE THAT DON'T FIT ON MY FINGERS ARE IN MY BAG. LUCKILY, THEY'LL STILL WORK FROM THERE.
SO I'VE GOT SEVENTEEN SECOND CHANCES...
...MINUS HOWEVER MANY TIMES THE NIGHT HIKER BASHED ME UP ON THE WAY IN.
SO I CAN PROBABLY ONLY TAKE A FEW MORE HITS BEFORE GETTING SQUASHED FLAT AS A PANCAKE.

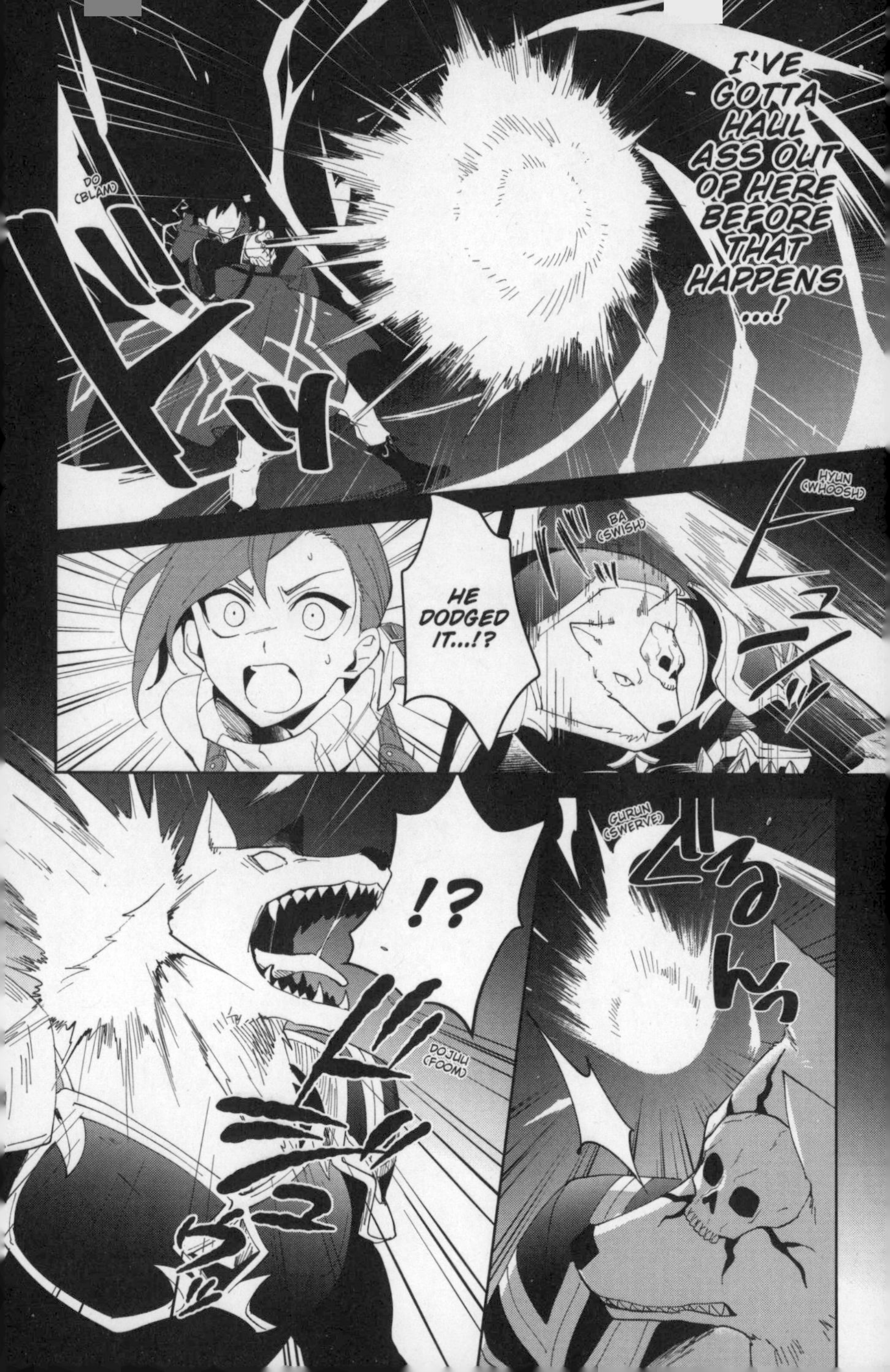
I'VE GOTTA HAUL ASS OUT OF HERE BEFORE THAT HAPPENS...!
DO (BLAM)
HYUN (WHOOSH)
BA (SWISH)
HE DODGED IT...!?
GURUN (SWERVE)
!?
DOJUU (FOOM)

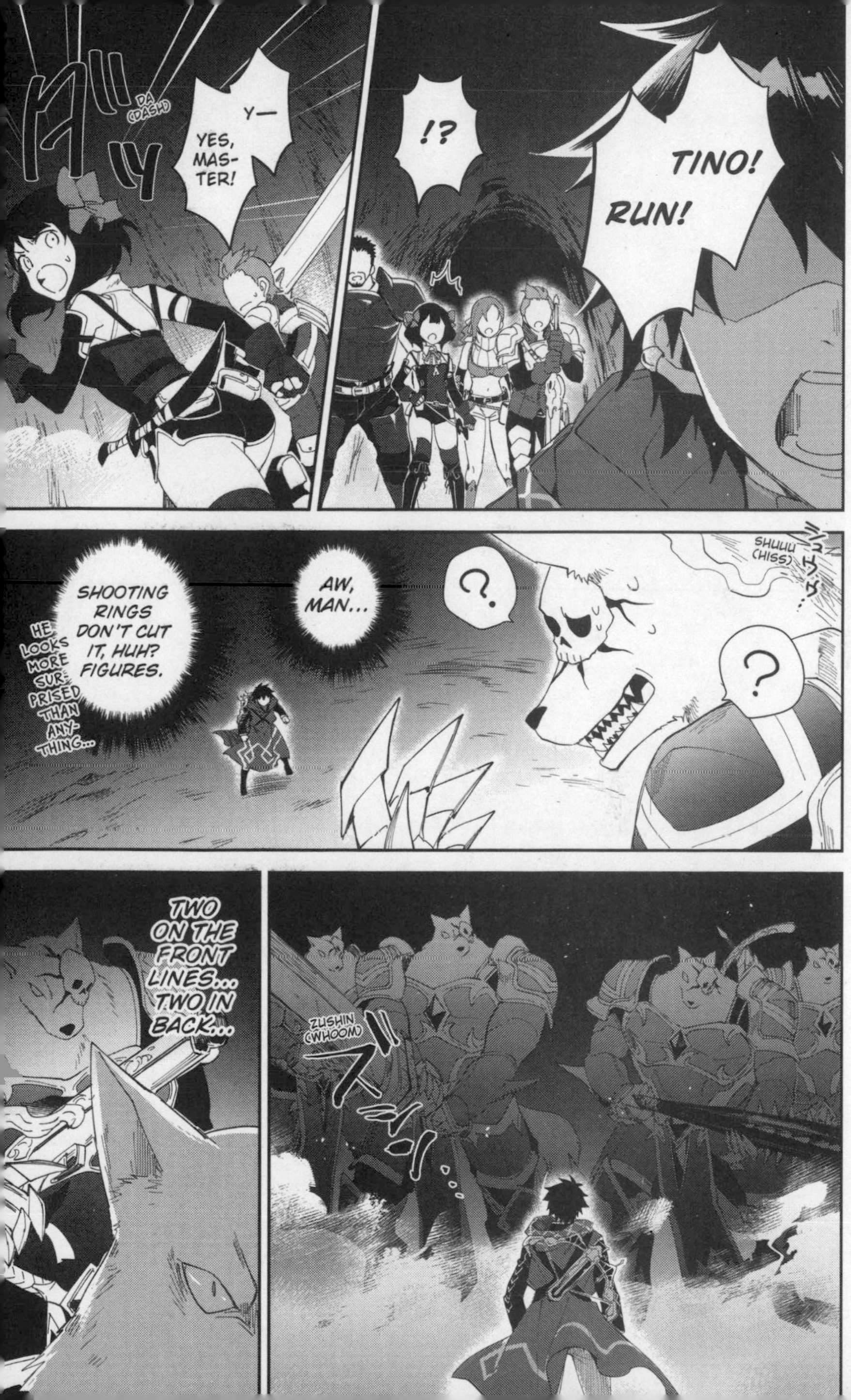
TINO!
RUN!
!?
Y—
YES, MAS-TER!
DA (DASH)
SHUUU (HISS)
?
?
AW, MAN...
SHOOTING RINGS DON'T CUT IT, HUH? FIGURES.
HE LOOKS MORE SUR-PRISED THAN ANY-THING...
ZUSHIN (WHOOM)
TWO ON THE FRONT LINES... TWO IN BACK...

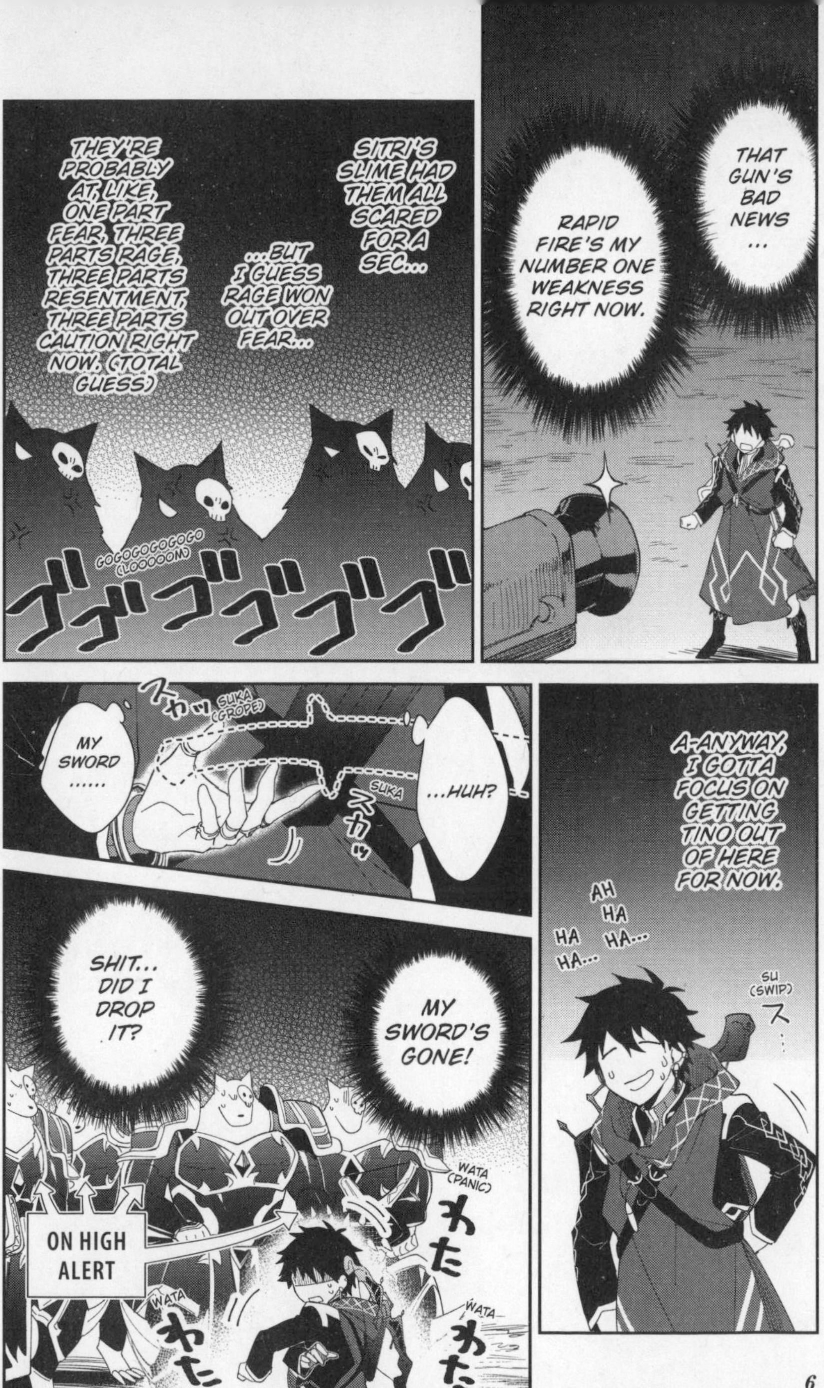
THAT GUN'S BAD NEWS...
RAPID FIRE'S MY NUMBER ONE WEAKNESS RIGHT NOW.
SITRI'S SLIME HAD THEM ALL SCARED FOR A SEC...
...BUT I GUESS RAGE WON OUT OVER FEAR...
THEY'RE PROBABLY AT, LIKE, ONE PART FEAR, THREE PARTS RAGE, THREE PARTS RESENTMENT, THREE PARTS CAUTION RIGHT NOW. (TOTAL GUESS)
GOGOGOGOGOGO (LOOOOOM)
ゴゴゴゴゴゴ
A-ANYWAY, I GOTTA FOCUS ON GETTING TINO OUT OF HERE FOR NOW.
AH HA HA...
HA HA...
SU (SWIP)
ス
SUKA (GROPE)
スカッ
...HUH?
MY SWORD......
SUKA
スカッ
MY SWORD'S GONE!
SHIT... DID I DROP IT?
ON HIGH ALERT
WATA (PANIC)
わた
WATA
わた
WATA
わた

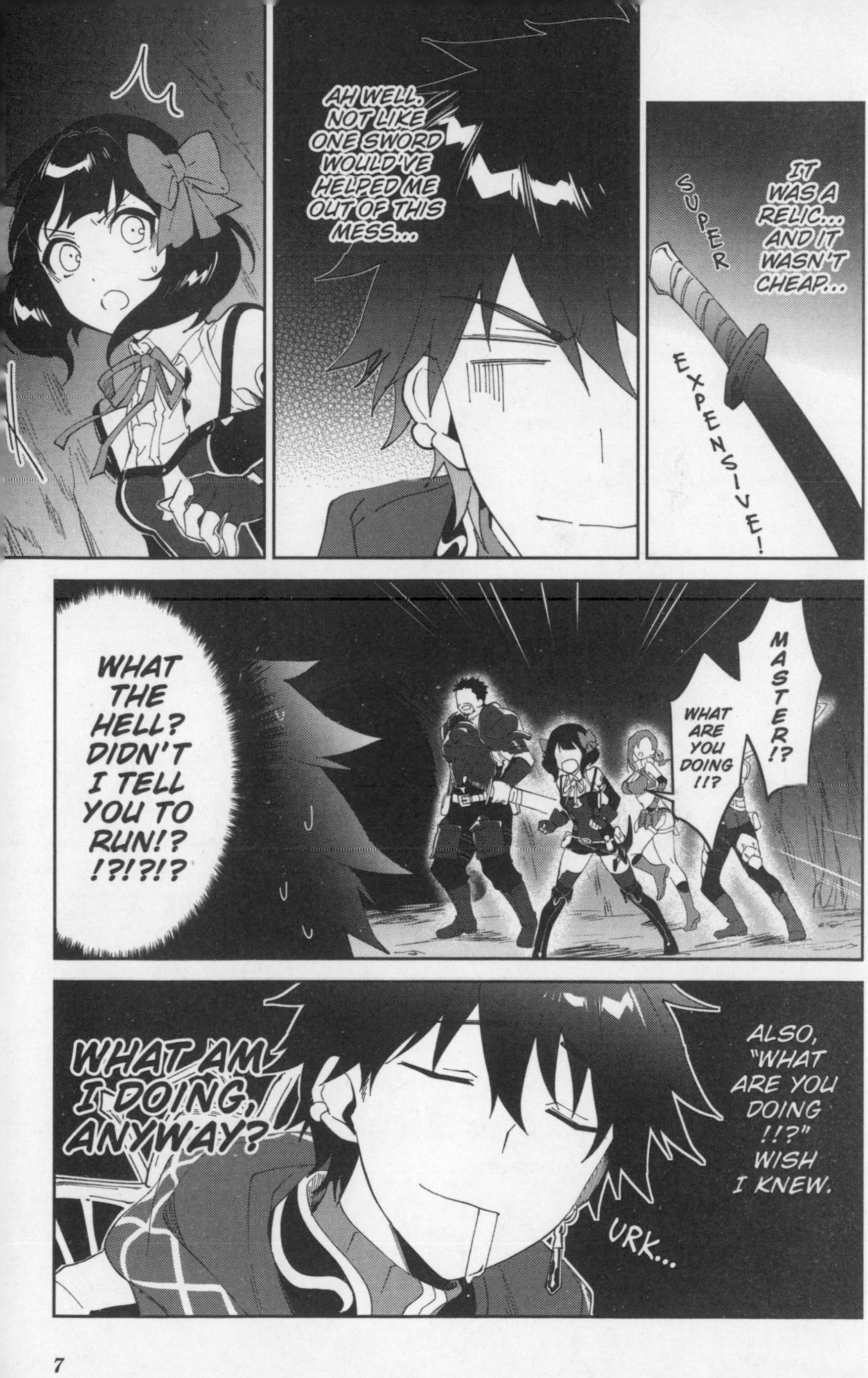
IT WAS A RELIC... AND IT WASN'T CHEAP...
SUPER
EXPENSIVE!
AH WELL. NOT LIKE ONE SWORD WOULD'VE HELPED ME OUT OF THIS MESS...
MASTER!?
WHAT ARE YOU DOING!!?
WHAT THE HELL? DIDN'T I TELL YOU TO RUN!?!?!?!?
ALSO, "WHAT ARE YOU DOING!!?" WISH I KNEW.
URK...
WHAT AM I DOING, ANYWAY?

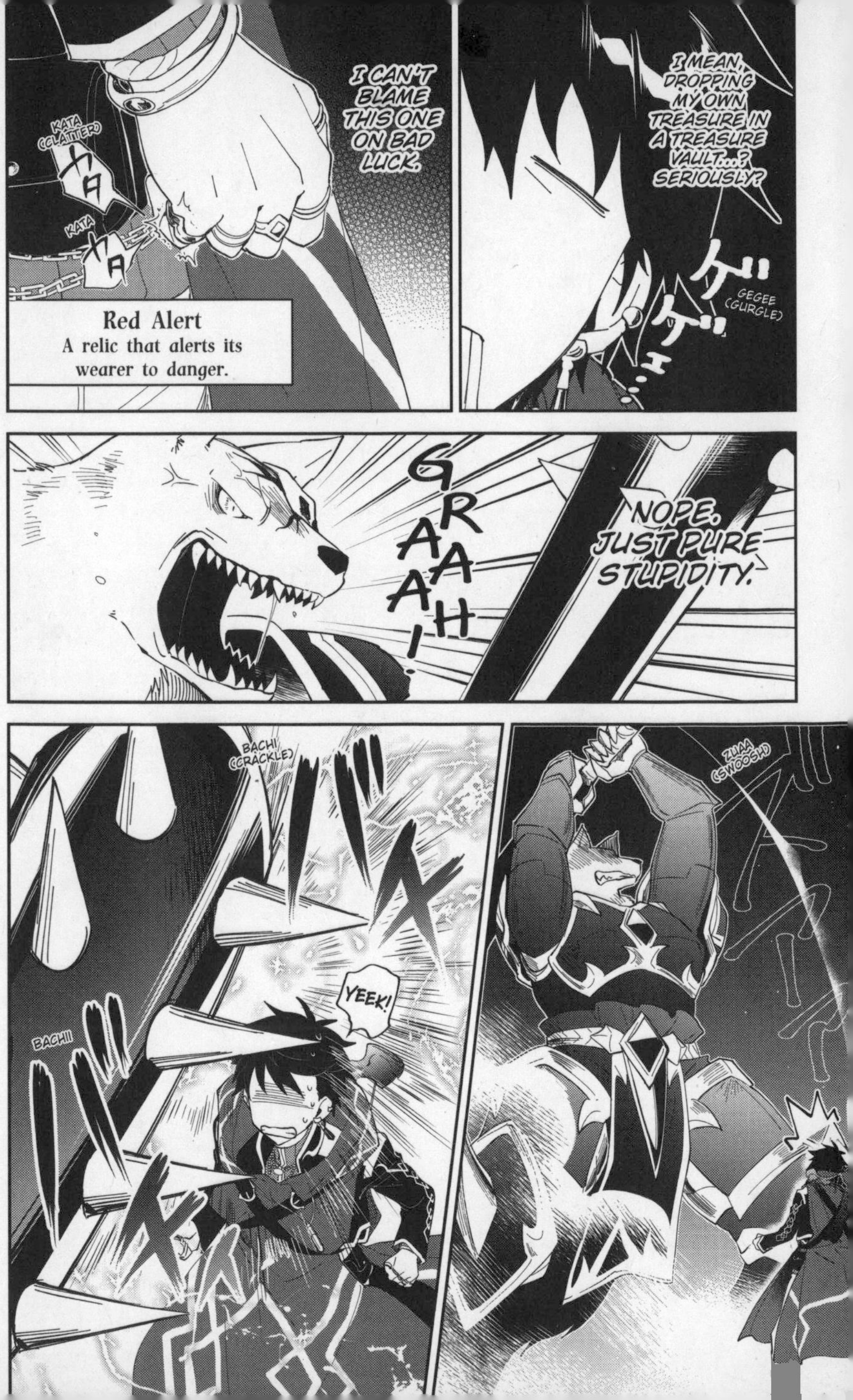
I MEAN, DROPPING MY OWN TREASURE IN A TREASURE VAULT...? SERIOUSLY?
GEGEE (GURGLE)
I CAN'T BLAME THIS ONE ON BAD LUCK.
KATA (CLATTER)
KATA
Red Alert
A relic that alerts its wearer to danger.
NOPE. JUST PURE STUPIDITY.
GRAAAH!
ZUAA (SWOOSH)
BACHI (CRACKLE)
YEEK!
BACHII

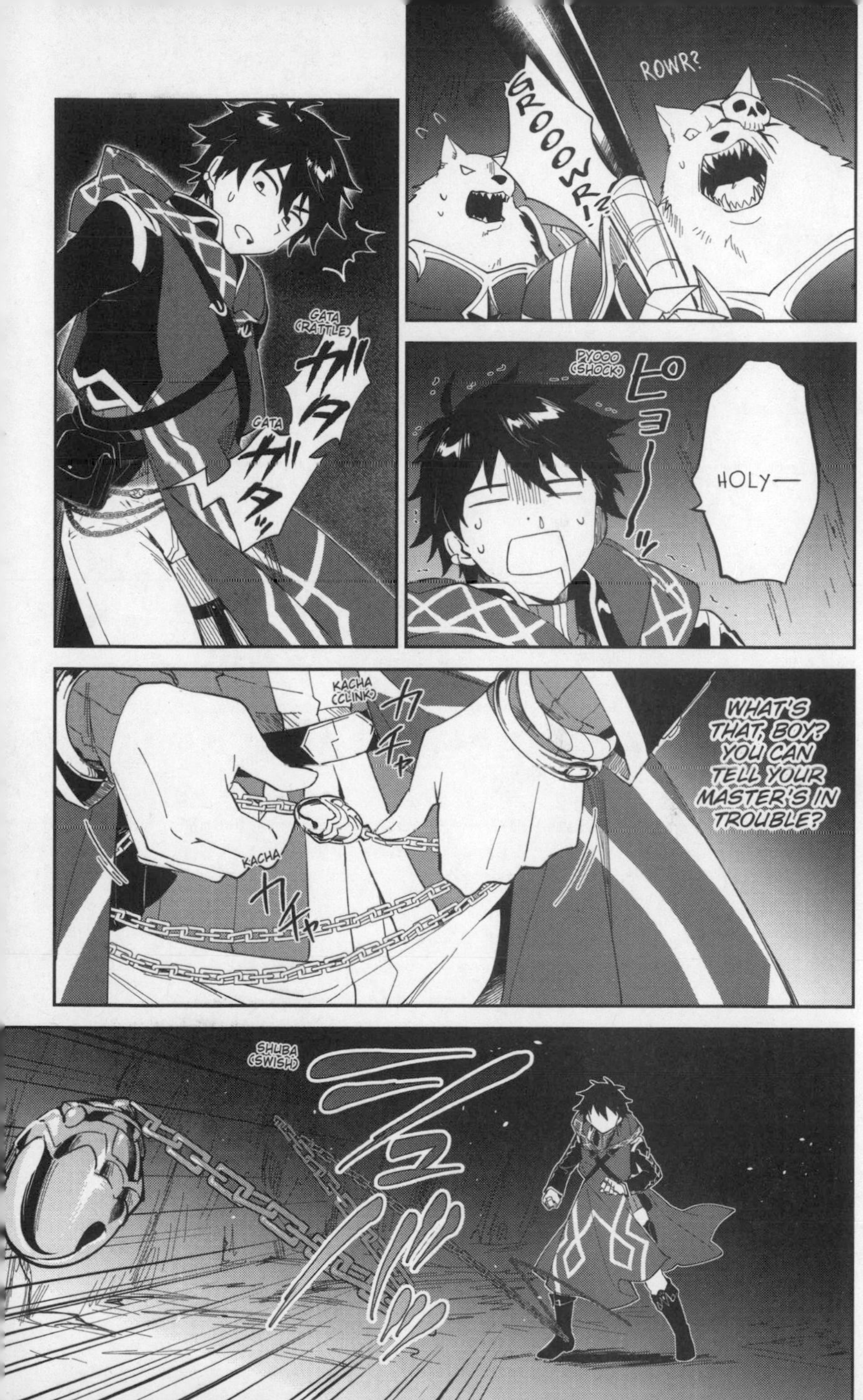
ROWR?
GROOOWR!
PYOOO (SHOCK)
HOLY—
GATA (RATTLE)
GATA
WHAT'S THAT, BOY? YOU CAN TELL YOUR MASTER'S IN TROUBLE?
KACHA (CLINK)
KACHA
SHUBA (SWISH)

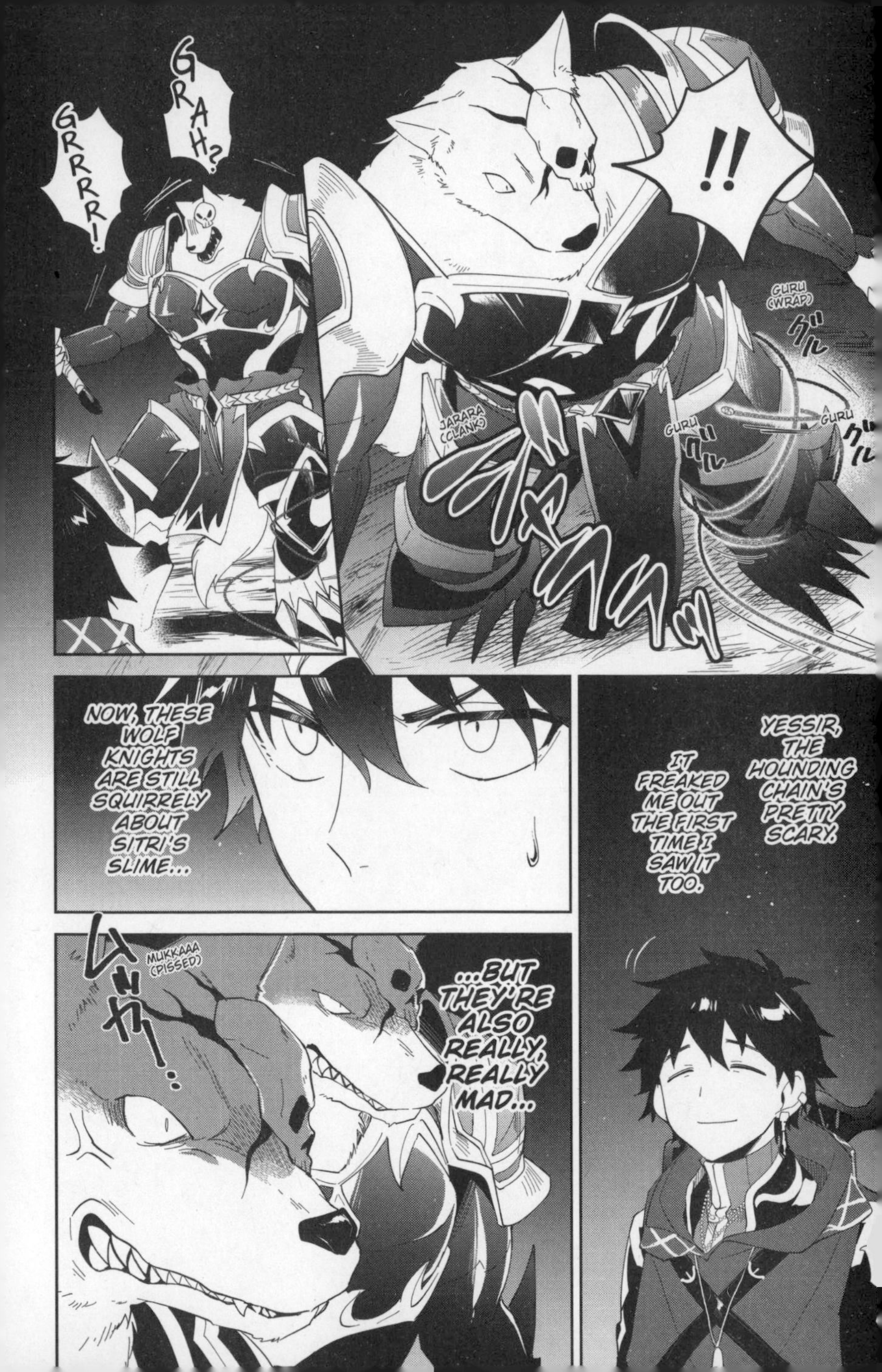
!!
GURU (WRAP)
グル
GURU
グル
GURU
グル
JARARA (CLANK)
GRAH?
GRRRRI!
YESSIR, THE HOUNDING CHAIN'S PRETTY SCARY.
IT FREAKED ME OUT THE FIRST TIME I SAW IT TOO.
NOW, THESE WOLF KNIGHTS ARE STILL SQUIRRELY ABOUT SITRI'S SLIME...
MUKKAAA (PISSED)
...BUT THEY'RE ALSO REALLY, REALLY MAD...

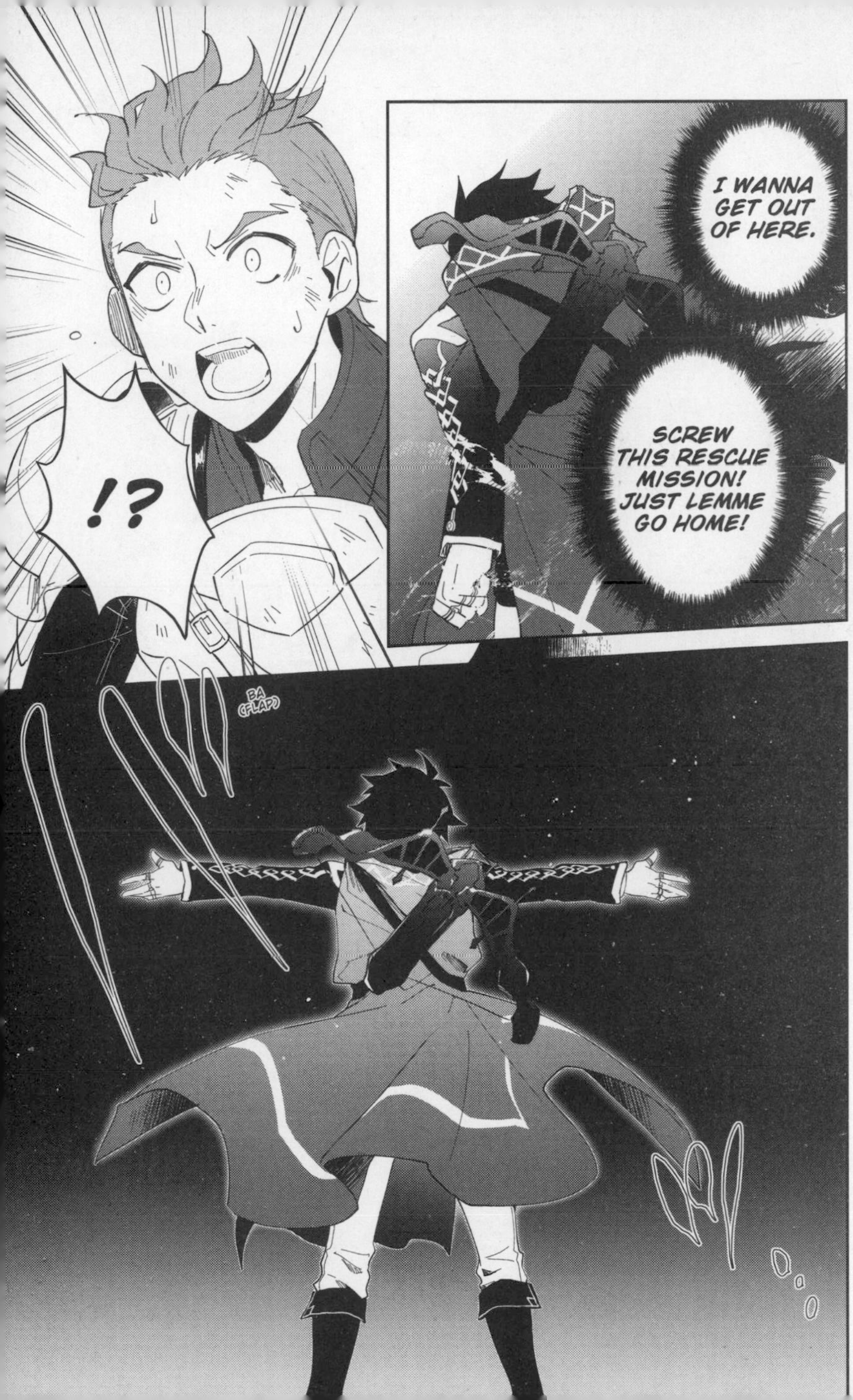
I WANNA GET OUT OF HERE.
SCREW THIS RESCUE MISSION! JUST LEMME GO HOME!
!?
BA (FLAP)

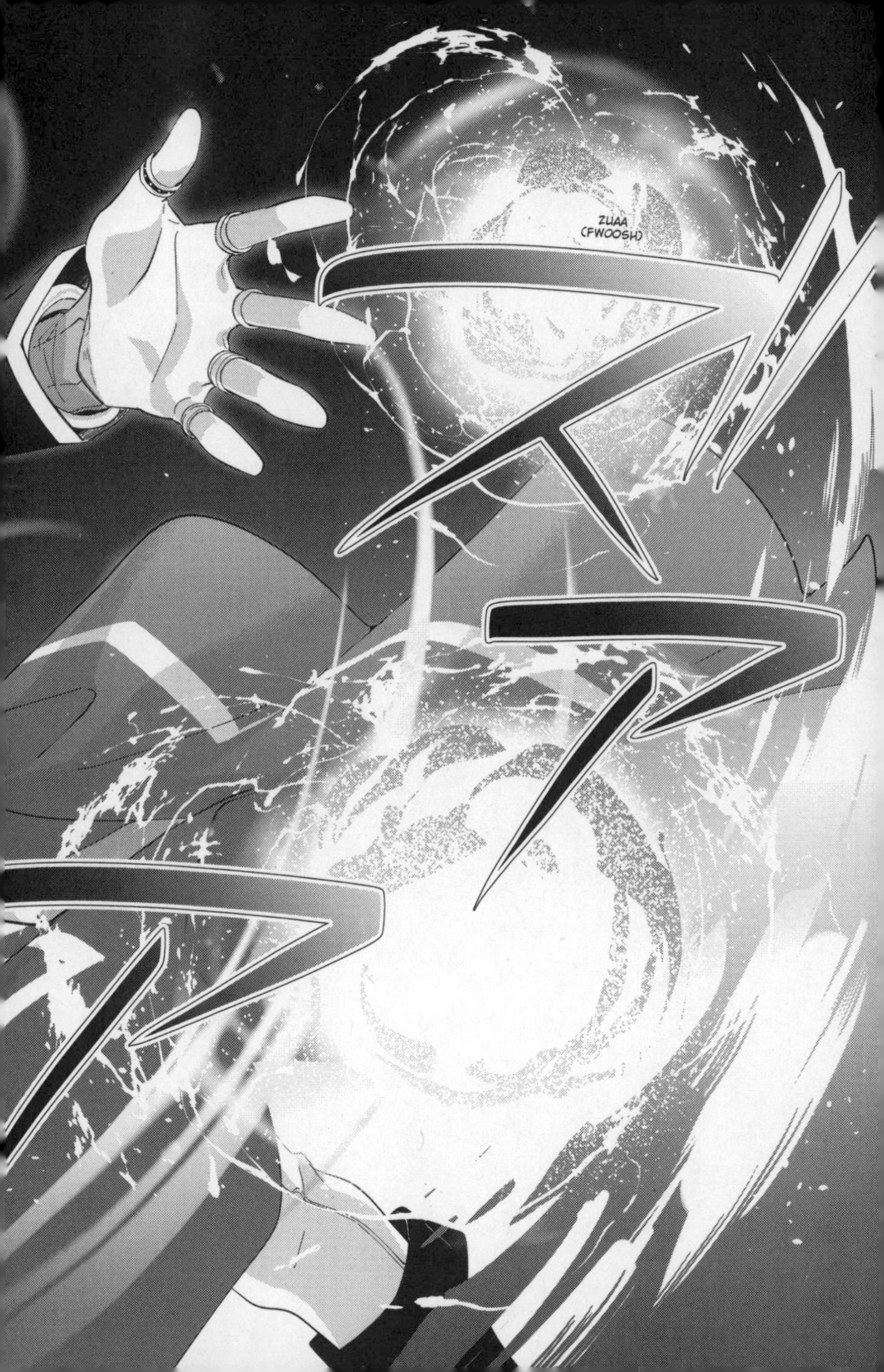
ZUAA
(FWOOSH)

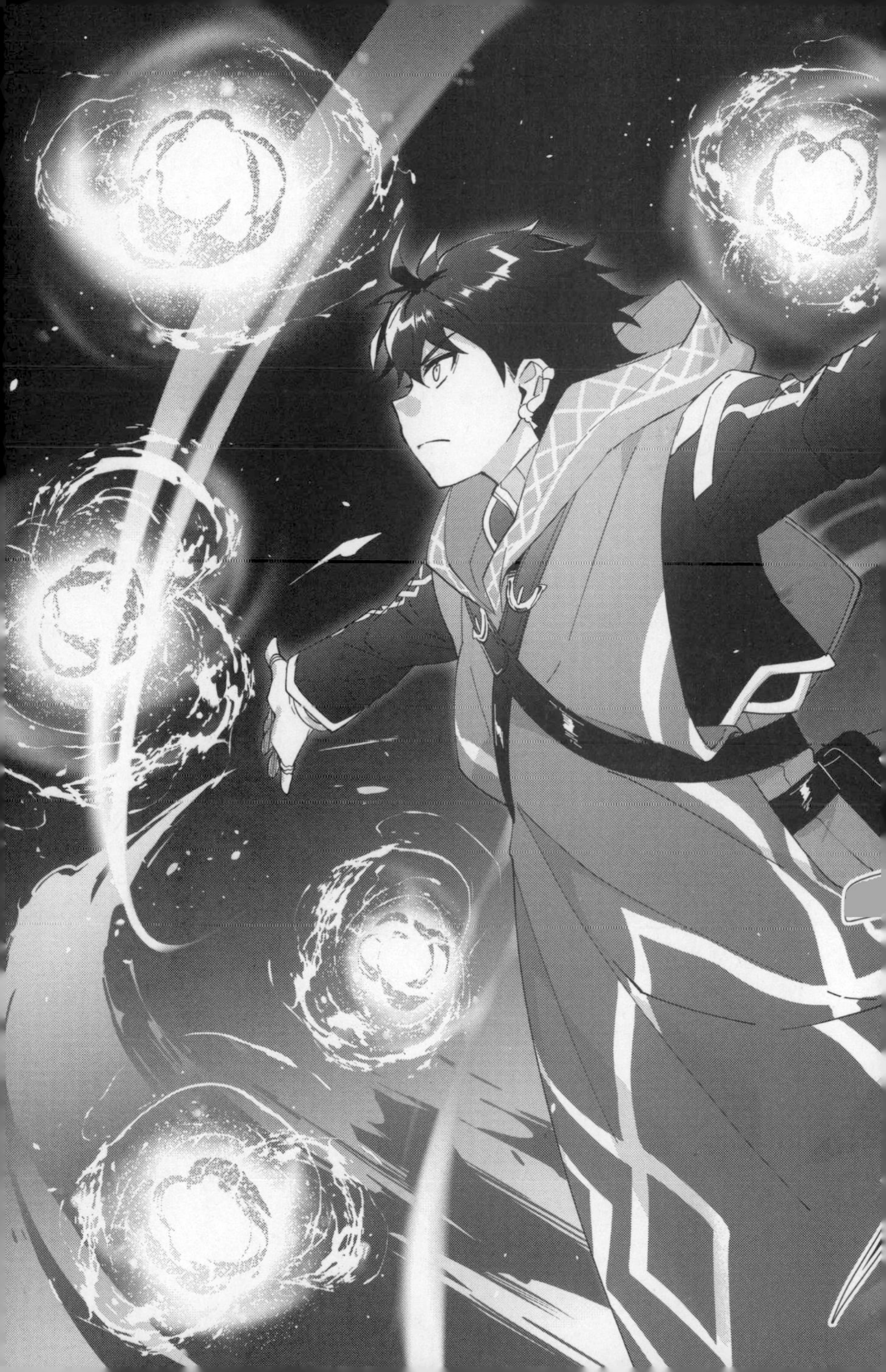

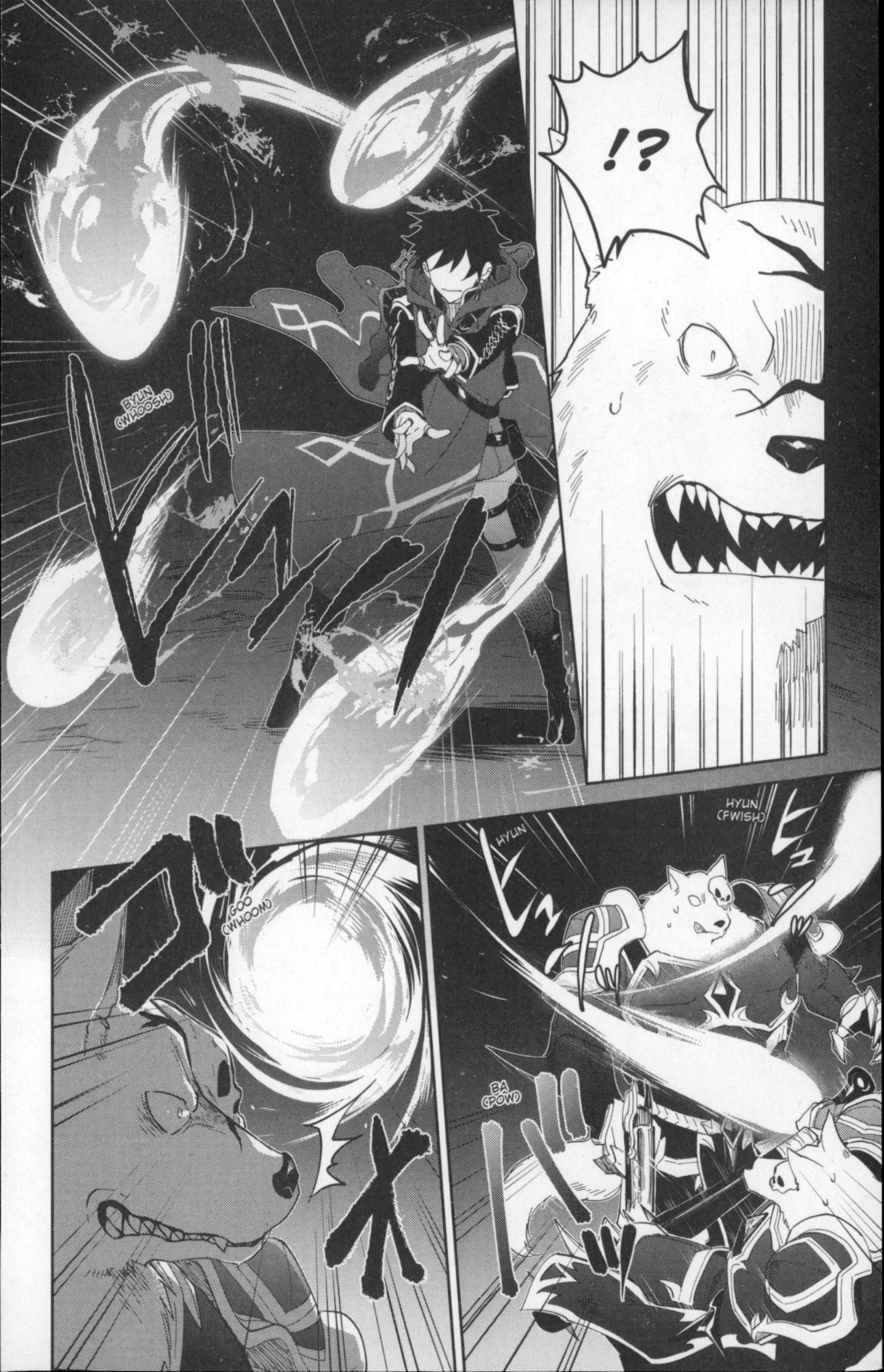
!?
BYUN (WHOOSH)
HYUN (FWISH)
HYUN
BA (POW)
GOO (WHOOM)

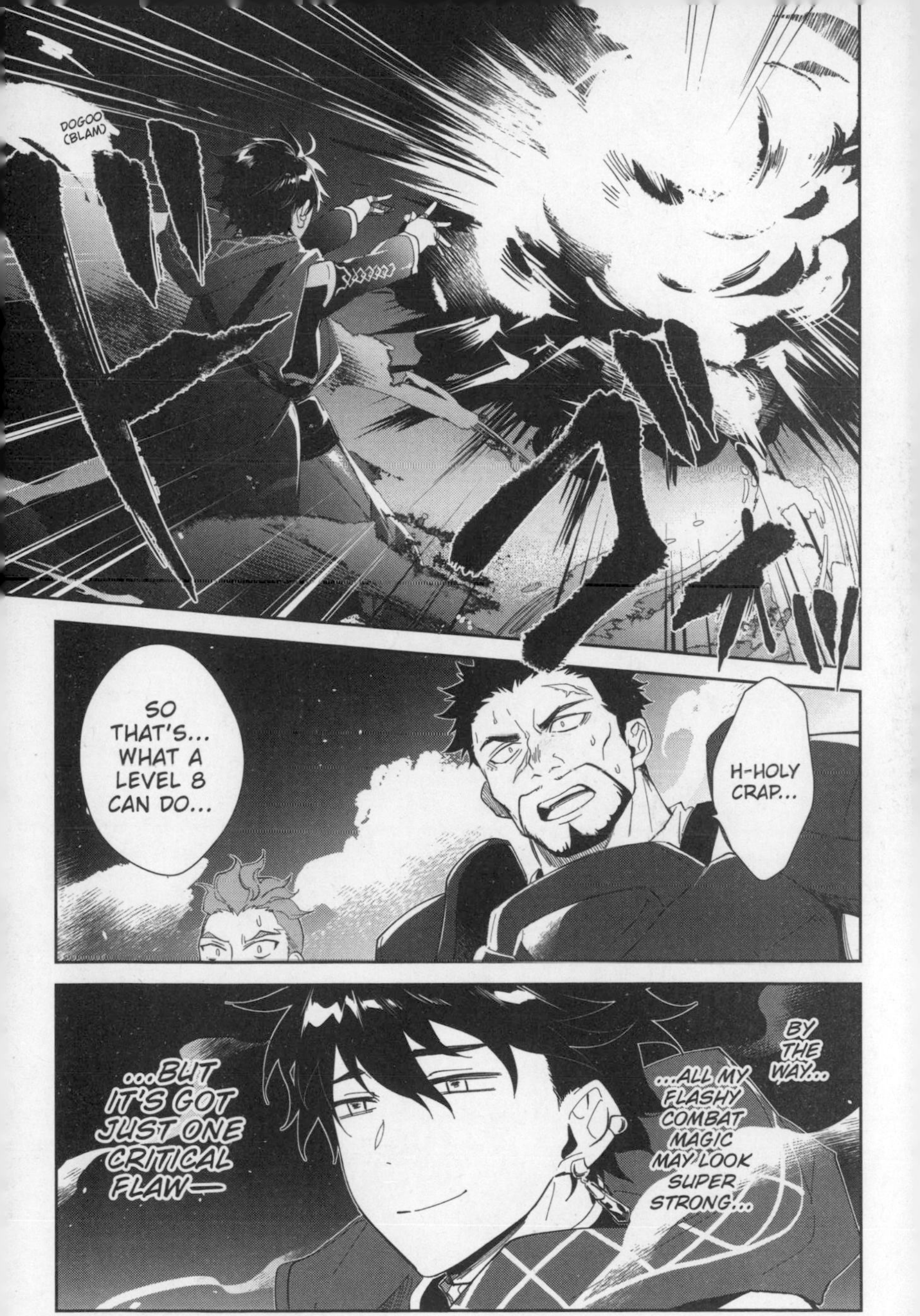
DOGOO (BLAM)
H-HOLY CRAP...
SO THAT'S... WHAT A LEVEL 8 CAN DO...
BY THE WAY...
...ALL MY FLASHY COMBAT MAGIC MAY LOOK SUPER STRONG...
...BUT IT'S GOT JUST ONE CRITICAL FLAW—

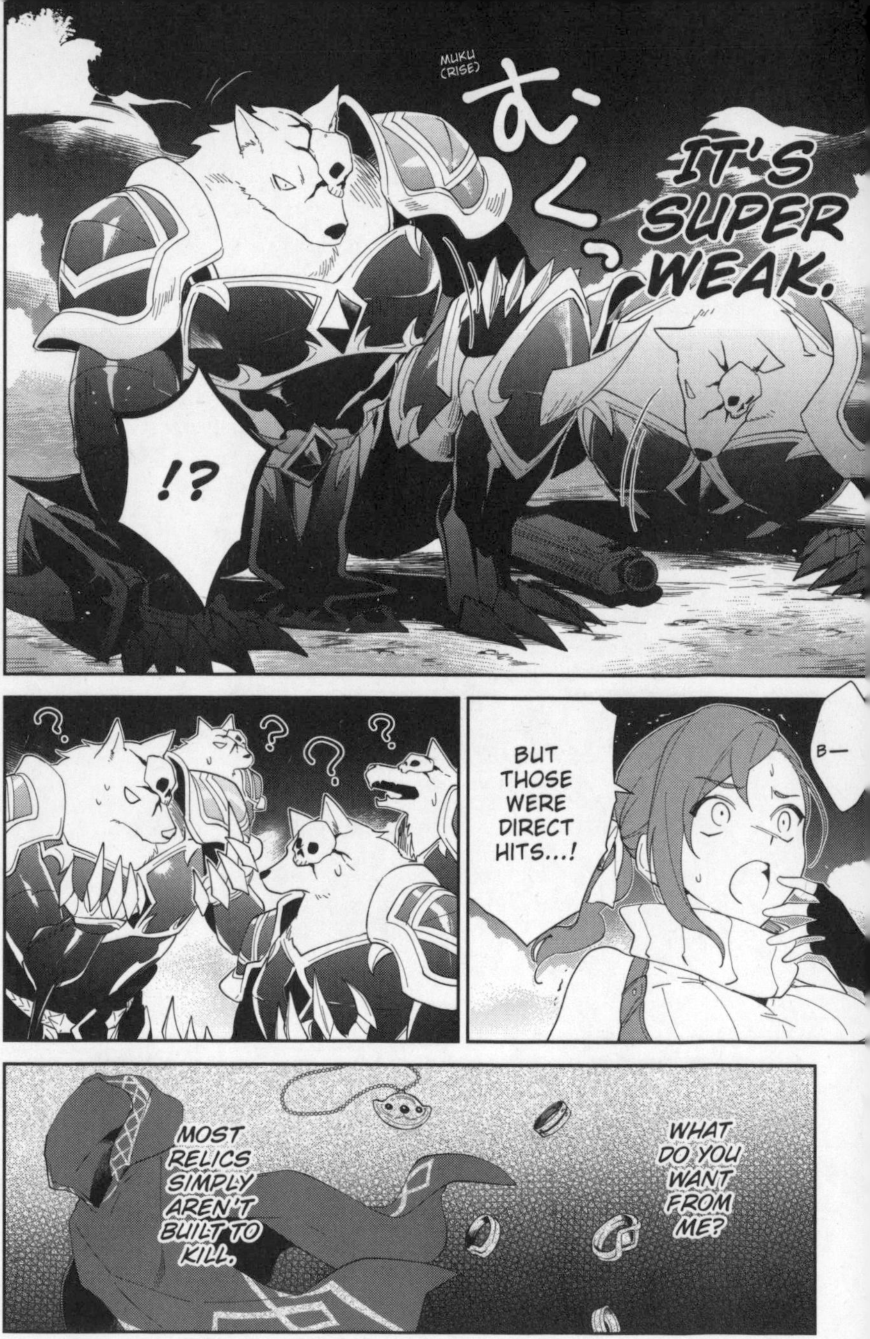
むくっ
MUKU (RISE)
IT'S SUPER WEAK.
!?
B—
BUT THOSE WERE DIRECT HITS...!
WHAT DO YOU WANT FROM ME?
MOST RELICS SIMPLY AREN'T BUILT TO KILL.

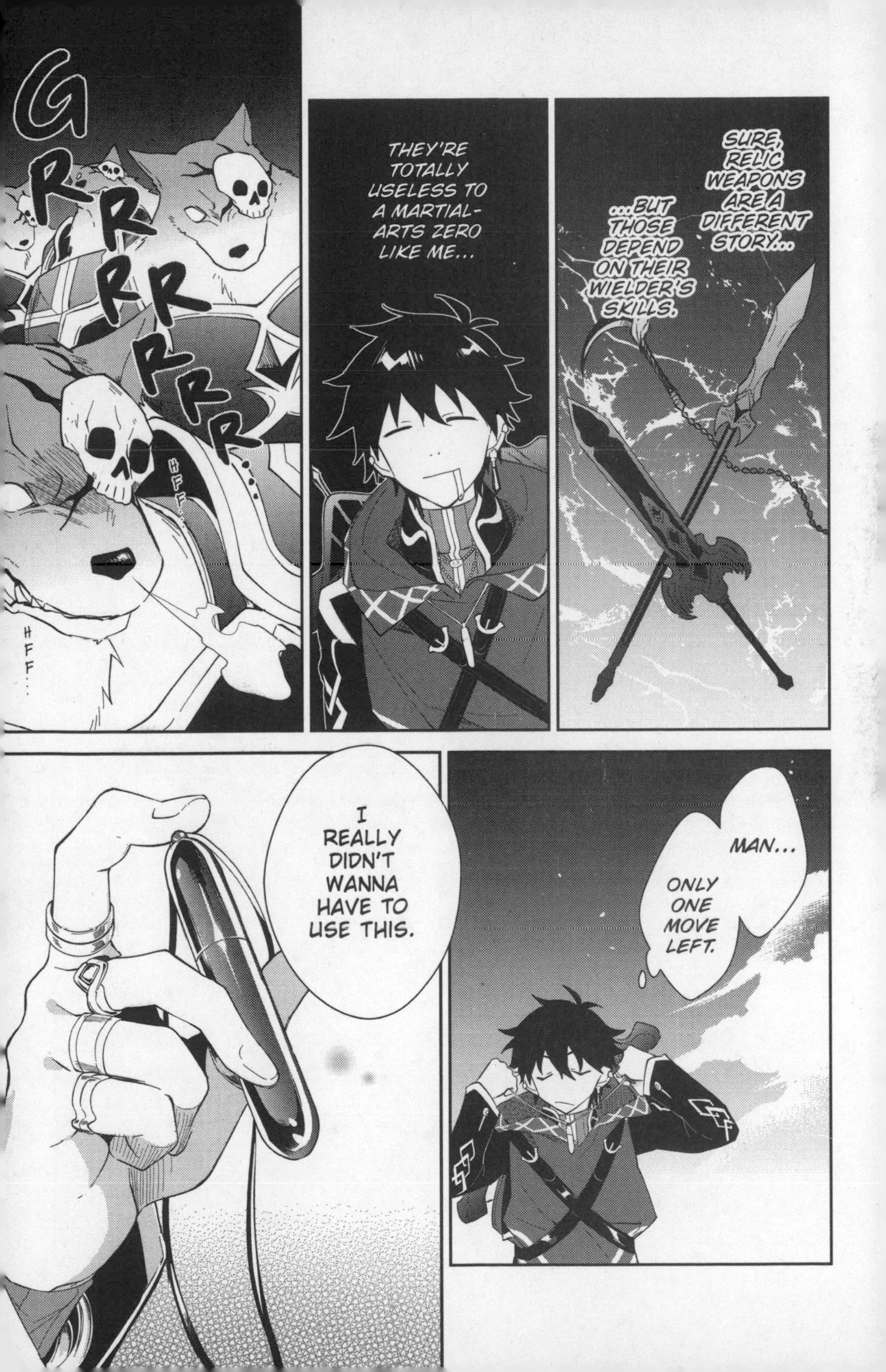
SURE, RELIC WEAPONS ARE A DIFFERENT STORY...
...BUT THOSE DEPEND ON THEIR WIELDER'S SKILLS.
THEY'RE TOTALLY USELESS TO A MARTIAL-ARTS ZERO LIKE ME...
GRRRRRR...
HFF...
HFF...
MAN...
ONLY ONE MOVE LEFT.
I REALLY DIDN'T WANNA HAVE TO USE THIS.

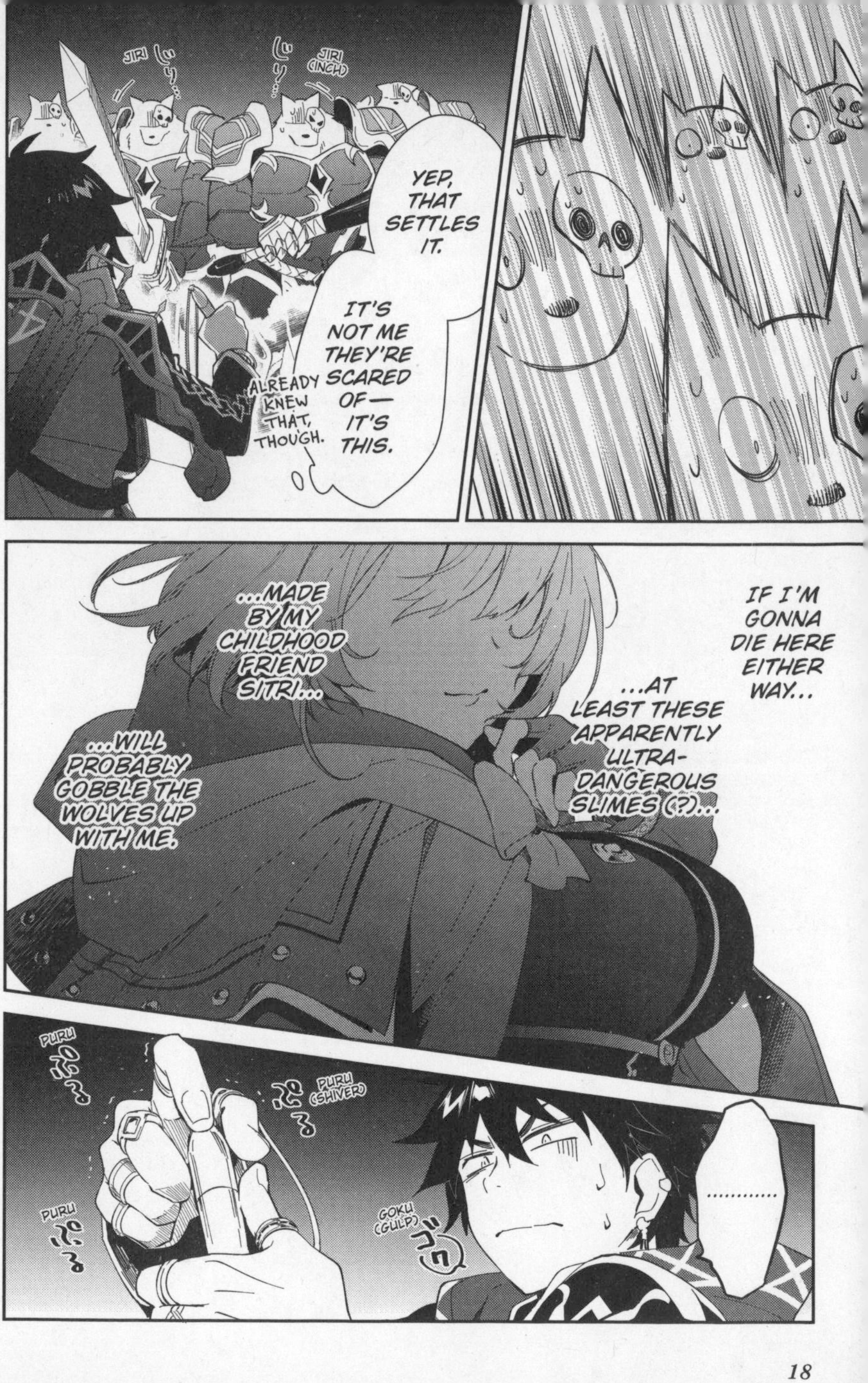
JIRI
JIRI (INCH)
YEP, THAT SETTLES IT.
IT'S NOT ME THEY'RE SCARED OF— IT'S THIS.
ALREADY KNEW THAT, THOUGH.
IF I'M GONNA DIE HERE EITHER WAY...
...AT LEAST THESE APPARENTLY ULTRA-DANGEROUS SLIMES (?)...
...MADE BY MY CHILDHOOD FRIEND SITRI...
...WILL PROBABLY GOBBLE THE WOLVES UP WITH ME.
....
GOKU (GULP)
PURU (SHIVER)
PURU
PURU

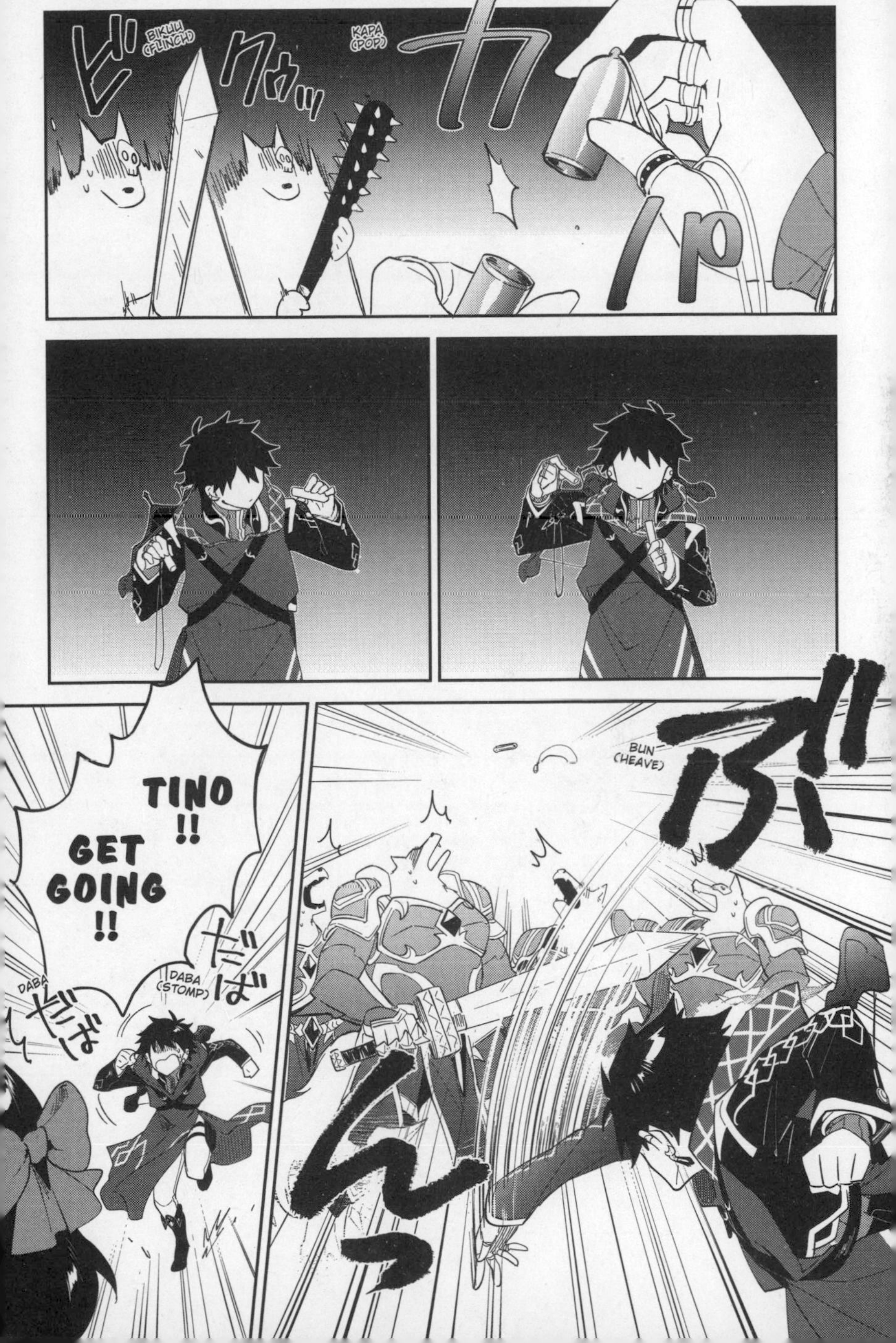
KAPA (POP)
BIKUU (FLINCH)
BUN (HEAVE)
TINO!! GET GOING!!
DABA (STOMP)
DABA

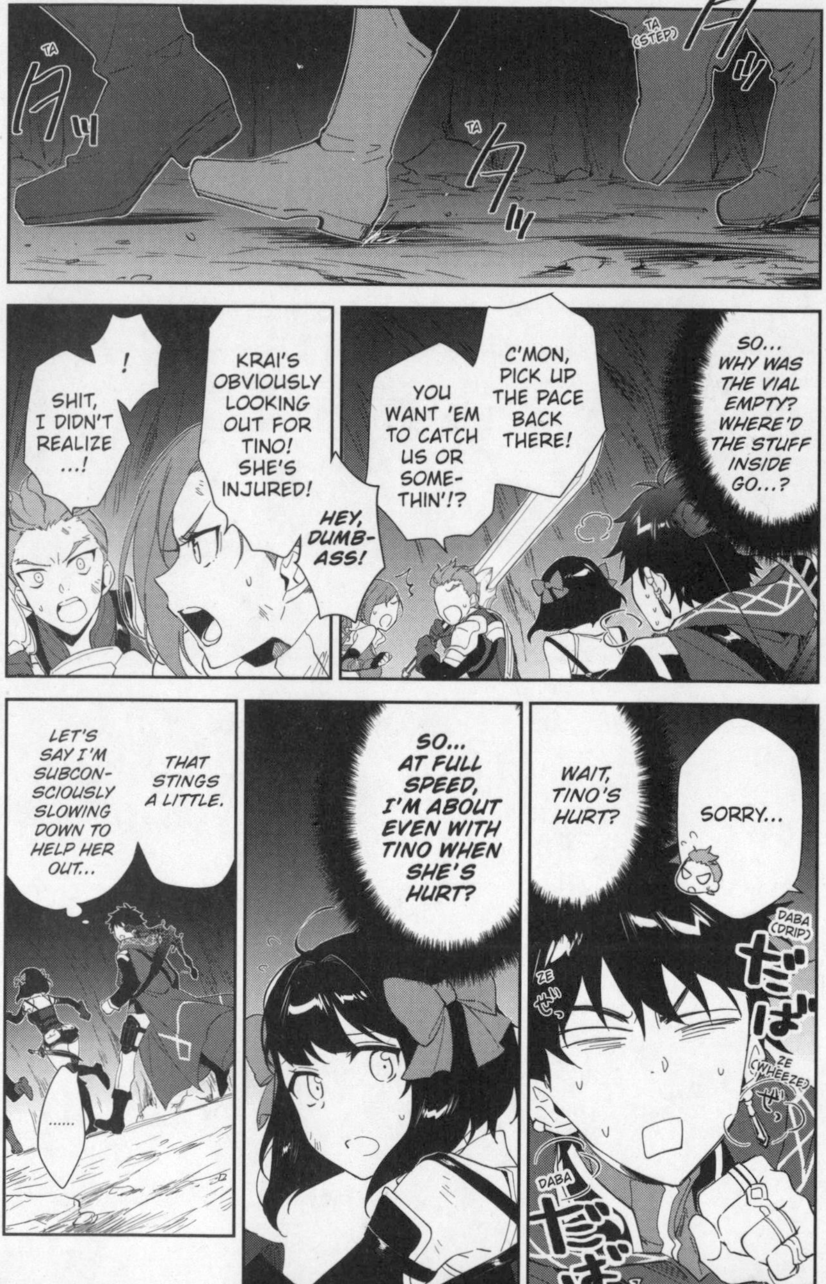
TA (STEP)
TA
TA
SO... WHY WAS THE VIAL EMPTY? WHERE'D THE STUFF INSIDE GO...?
C'MON, PICK UP THE PACE BACK THERE!
YOU WANT 'EM TO CATCH US OR SOME-THIN'!?
HEY, DUMB-ASS!
KRAI'S OBVIOUSLY LOOKING OUT FOR TINO! SHE'S INJURED!
!
SHIT, I DIDN'T REALIZE ...!
SORRY...
WAIT, TINO'S HURT?
DABA (DRIP)
ZE
ZE (WHEEZE)
DABA
SO... AT FULL SPEED, I'M ABOUT EVEN WITH TINO WHEN SHE'S HURT?
THAT STINGS A LITTLE.
LET'S SAY I'M SUBCON-SCIOUSLY SLOWING DOWN TO HELP HER OUT...
......

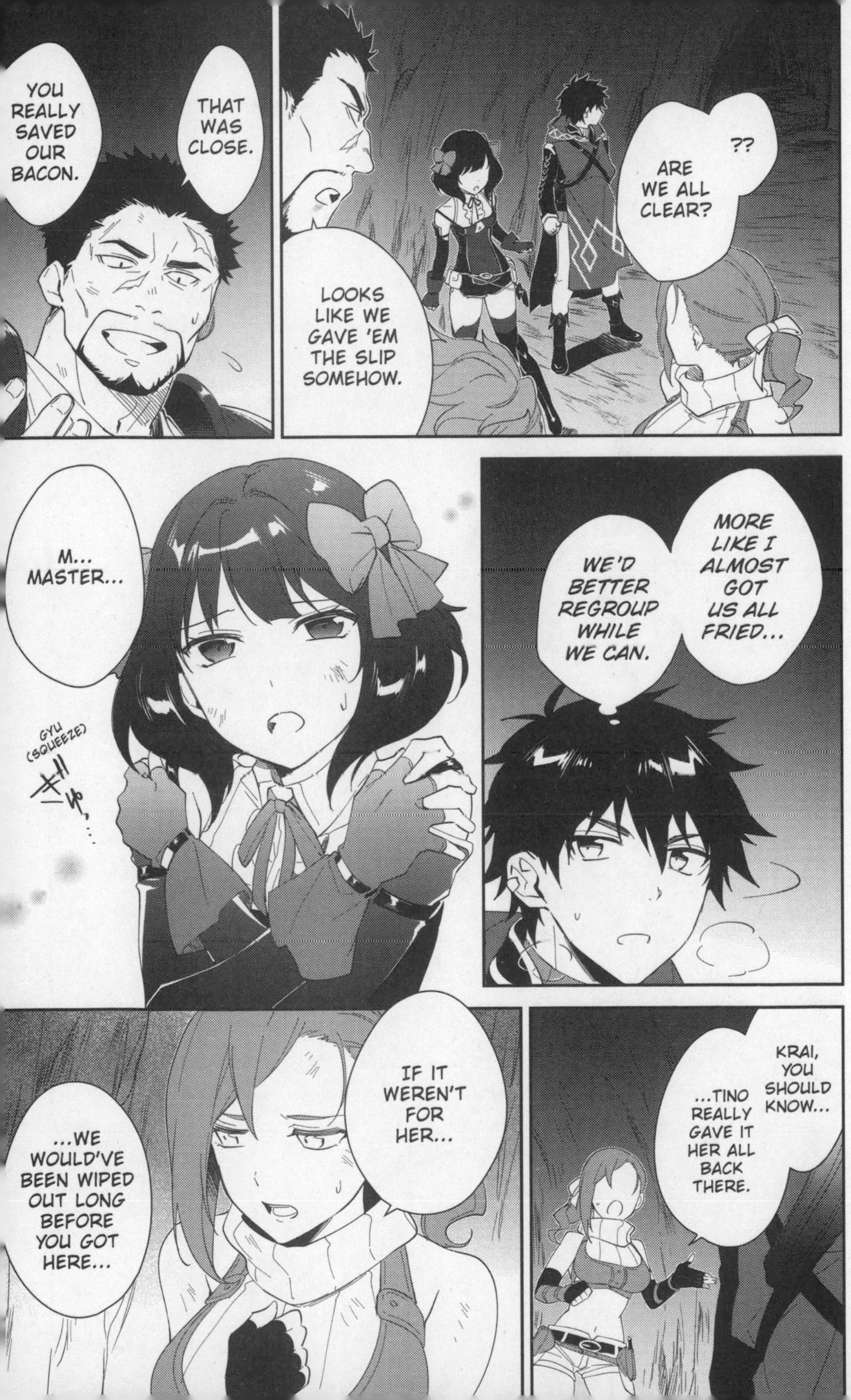
??
ARE WE ALL CLEAR?
LOOKS LIKE WE GAVE 'EM THE SLIP SOMEHOW.
THAT WAS CLOSE.
YOU REALLY SAVED OUR BACON.
MORE LIKE I ALMOST GOT US ALL FRIED...
WE'D BETTER REGROUP WHILE WE CAN.
M... MASTER...
GYU (SQUEEZE)
KRAI, YOU SHOULD KNOW...
...TINO REALLY GAVE IT HER ALL BACK THERE.
IF IT WEREN'T FOR HER...
...WE WOULD'VE BEEN WIPED OUT LONG BEFORE YOU GOT HERE...

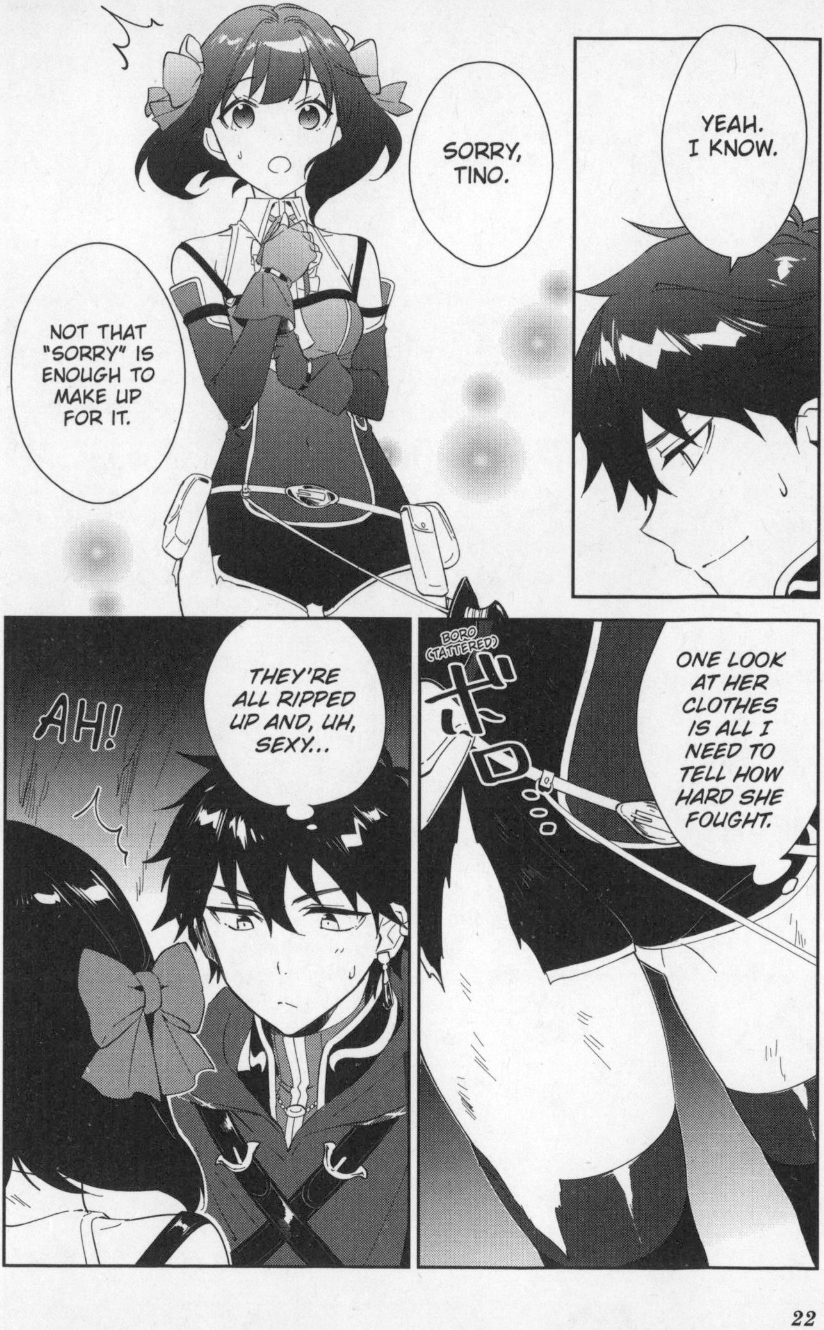
YEAH. I KNOW.
SORRY, TINO.
NOT THAT "SORRY" IS ENOUGH TO MAKE UP FOR IT.
ONE LOOK AT HER CLOTHES IS ALL I NEED TO TELL HOW HARD SHE FOUGHT.
BORO (TATTERED)
THEY'RE ALL RIPPED UP AND, UH, SEXY...
AH!

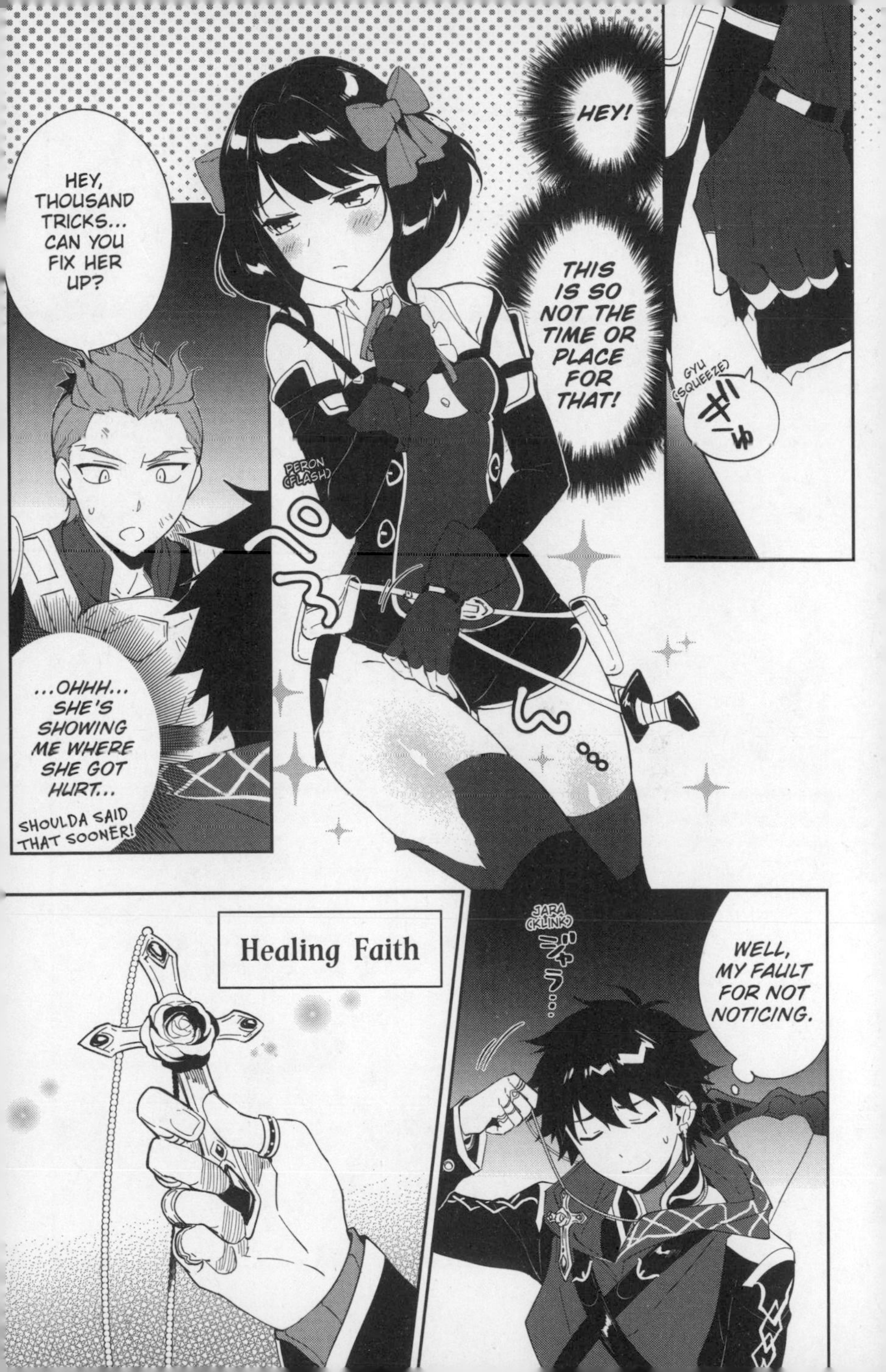
HEY!
THIS IS SO NOT THE TIME OR PLACE FOR THAT!
GYU (SQUEEZE)
PERON (FLASH)
HEY, THOUSAND TRICKS... CAN YOU FIX HER UP?
...OHHH... SHE'S SHOWING ME WHERE SHE GOT HURT...
SHOULDA SAID THAT SOONER!
JARA (KLINK)
WELL, MY FAULT FOR NOT NOTICING.
Healing Faith

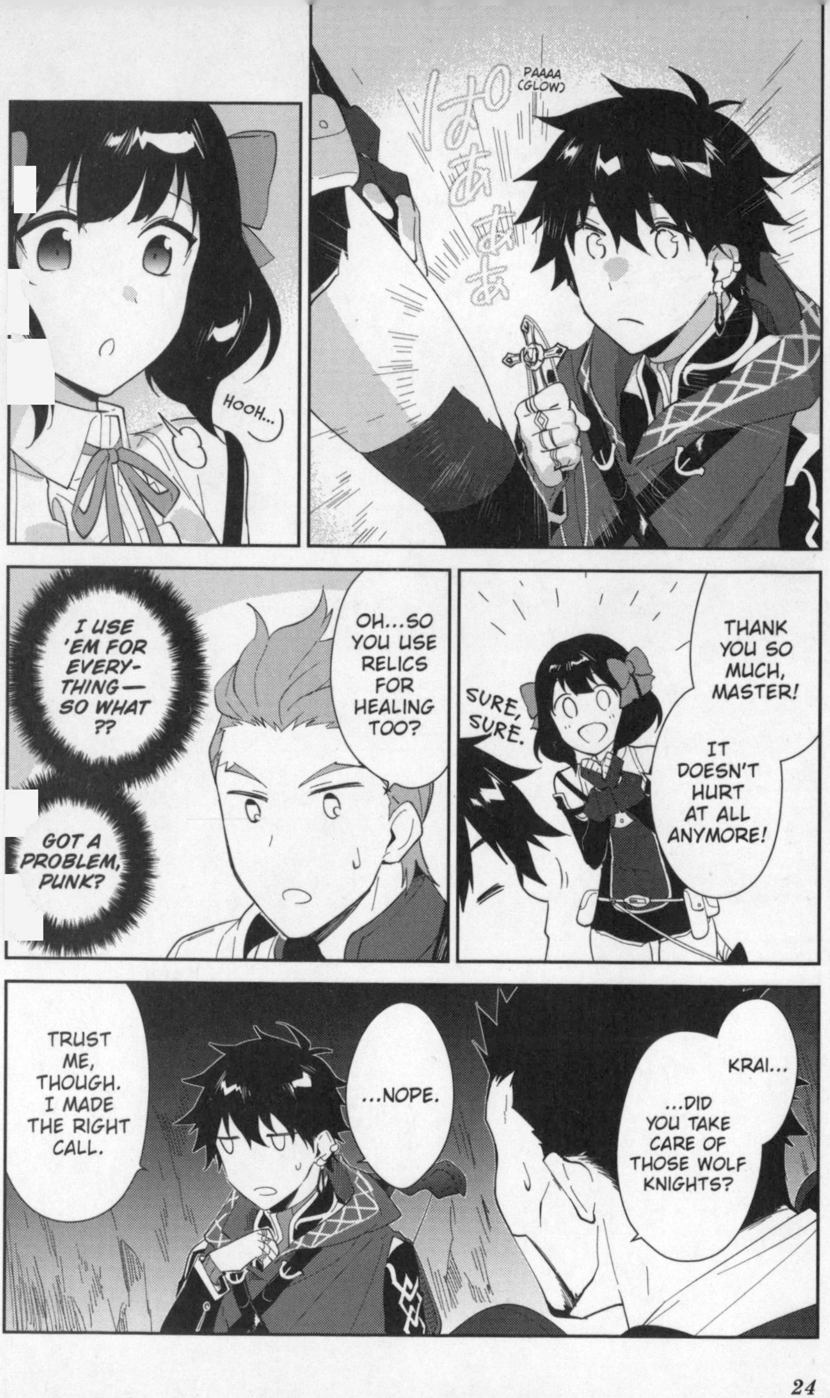
PAAAA (GLOW)
HOOH...
THANK YOU SO MUCH, MASTER!
IT DOESN'T HURT AT ALL ANYMORE!
SURE, SURE.
OH...SO YOU USE RELICS FOR HEALING TOO?
I USE 'EM FOR EVERY-THING—SO WHAT??
GOT A PROBLEM, PUNK?
KRAI...
...DID YOU TAKE CARE OF THOSE WOLF KNIGHTS?
...NOPE.
TRUST ME, THOUGH. I MADE THE RIGHT CALL.

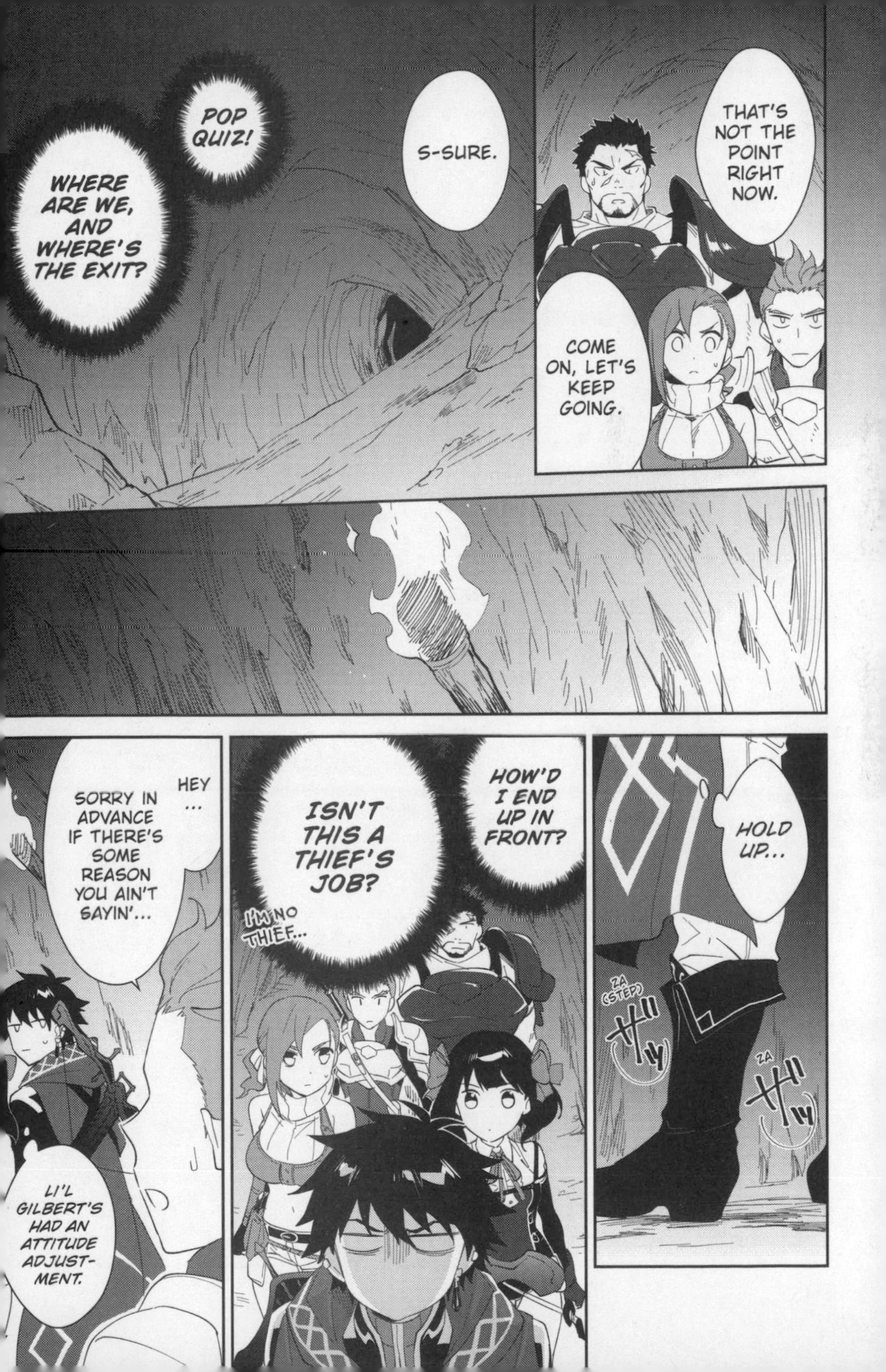
THAT'S NOT THE POINT RIGHT NOW.
COME ON, LET'S KEEP GOING.
S-SURE.
POP QUIZ!
WHERE ARE WE, AND WHERE'S THE EXIT?
HOLD UP...
ZA (STEP)
ザッ
ZA
ザッ
HOW'D I END UP IN FRONT?
ISN'T THIS A THIEF'S JOB?
I'M NO THIEF...
HEY...
SORRY IN ADVANCE IF THERE'S SOME REASON YOU AIN'T SAYIN'...
LI'L GILBERT'S HAD AN ATTITUDE ADJUST-MENT.

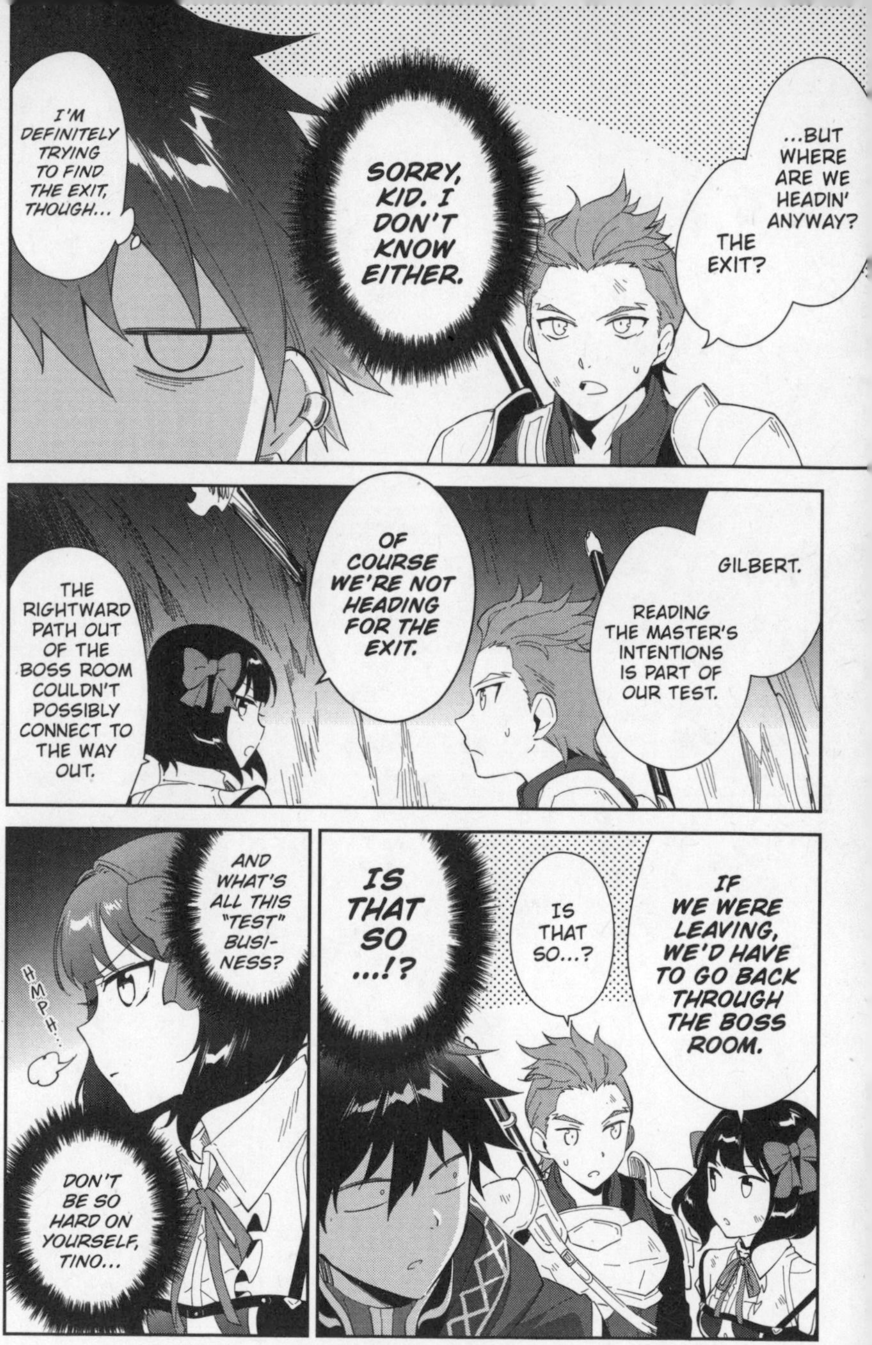
...BUT WHERE ARE WE HEADIN' ANYWAY?
THE EXIT?
SORRY, KID. I DON'T KNOW EITHER.
I'M DEFINITELY TRYING TO FIND THE EXIT, THOUGH...
GILBERT.
READING THE MASTER'S INTENTIONS IS PART OF OUR TEST.
OF COURSE WE'RE NOT HEADING FOR THE EXIT.
THE RIGHTWARD PATH OUT OF THE BOSS ROOM COULDN'T POSSIBLY CONNECT TO THE WAY OUT.
IF WE WERE LEAVING, WE'D HAVE TO GO BACK THROUGH THE BOSS ROOM.
IS THAT SO...?
IS THAT SO ...!?
AND WHAT'S ALL THIS "TEST" BUSINESS?
HMPH...
DON'T BE SO HARD ON YOURSELF, TINO...

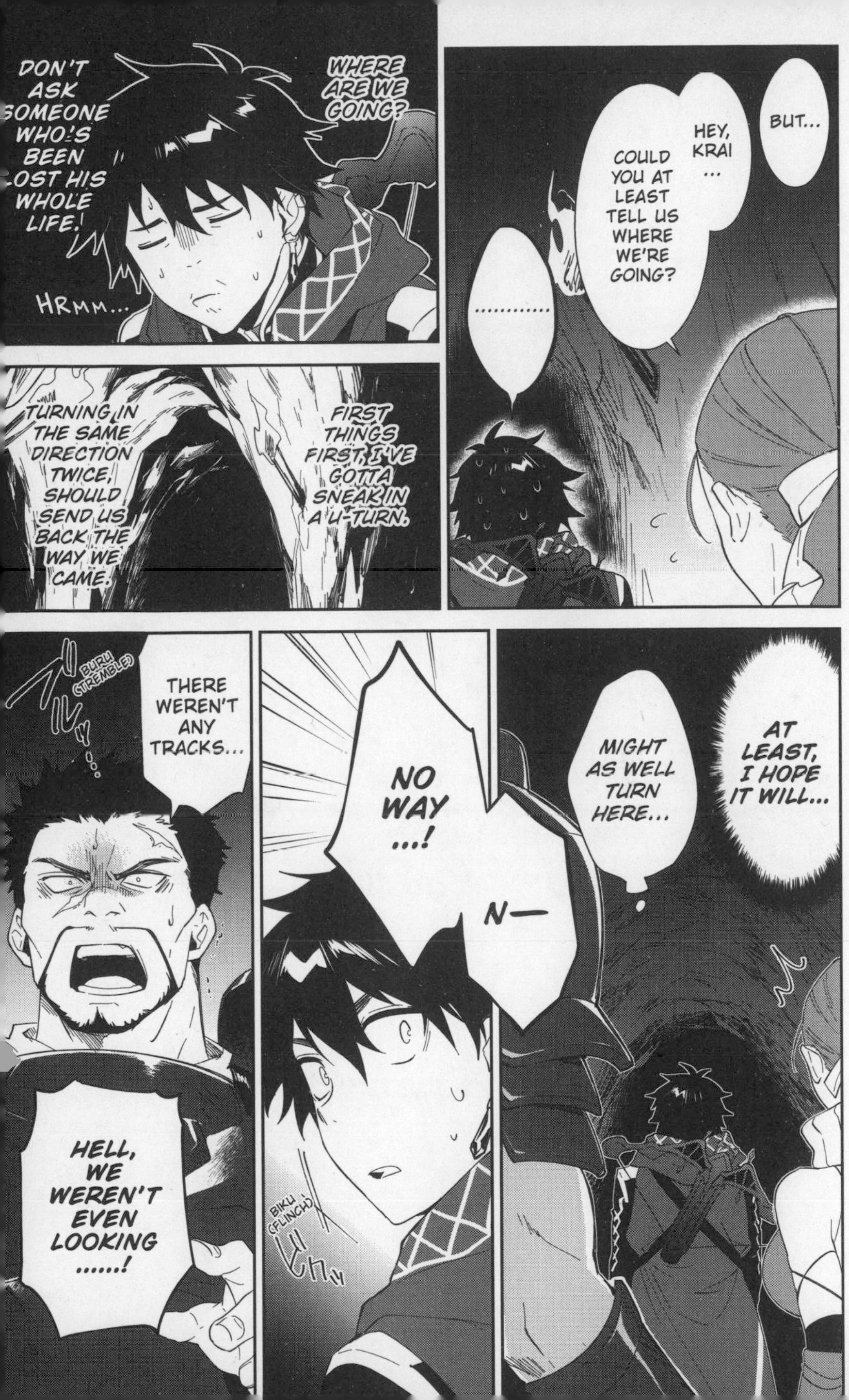
BUT...
HEY, KRAI ... COULD YOU AT LEAST TELL US WHERE WE'RE GOING?
....
WHERE ARE WE GOING?
DON'T ASK SOMEONE WHO'S BEEN LOST HIS WHOLE LIFE!
HRMM...
FIRST THINGS FIRST, I'VE GOTTA SNEAK IN A U-TURN.
TURNING IN THE SAME DIRECTION TWICE, SHOULD SEND US BACK THE WAY WE CAME.
AT LEAST, I HOPE IT WILL...
MIGHT AS WELL TURN HERE...
NO WAY ...!
N—
BIKU (FLINCH)
BURU (TREMBLE)
THERE WEREN'T ANY TRACKS...
HELL, WE WEREN'T EVEN LOOKING ......!

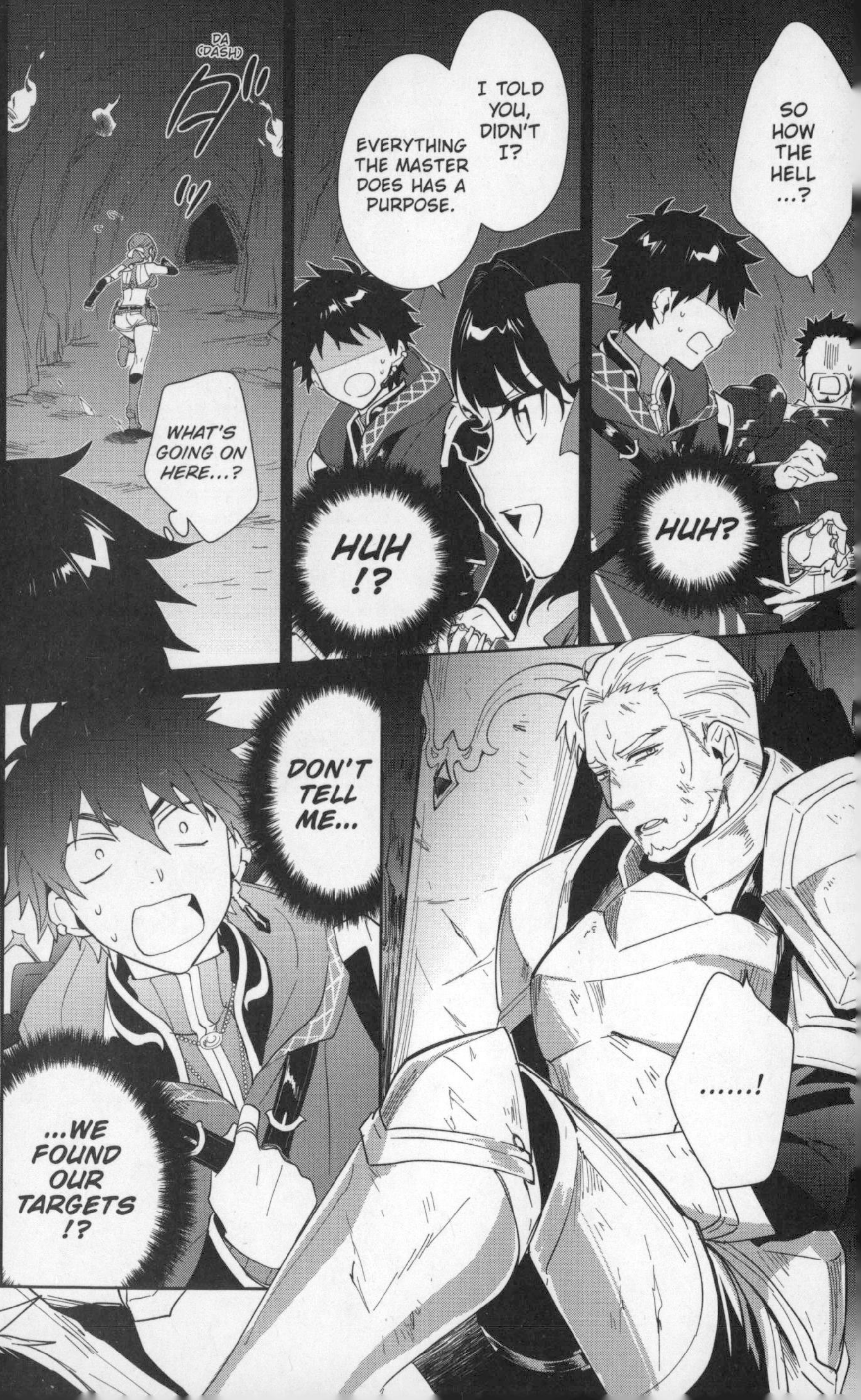
SO HOW THE HELL ...?
HUH?
I TOLD YOU, DIDN'T I?
EVERYTHING THE MASTER DOES HAS A PURPOSE.
HUH !?
DA (DASH)
WHAT'S GOING ON HERE...?
......!
DON'T TELL ME...
...WE FOUND OUR TARGETS !?

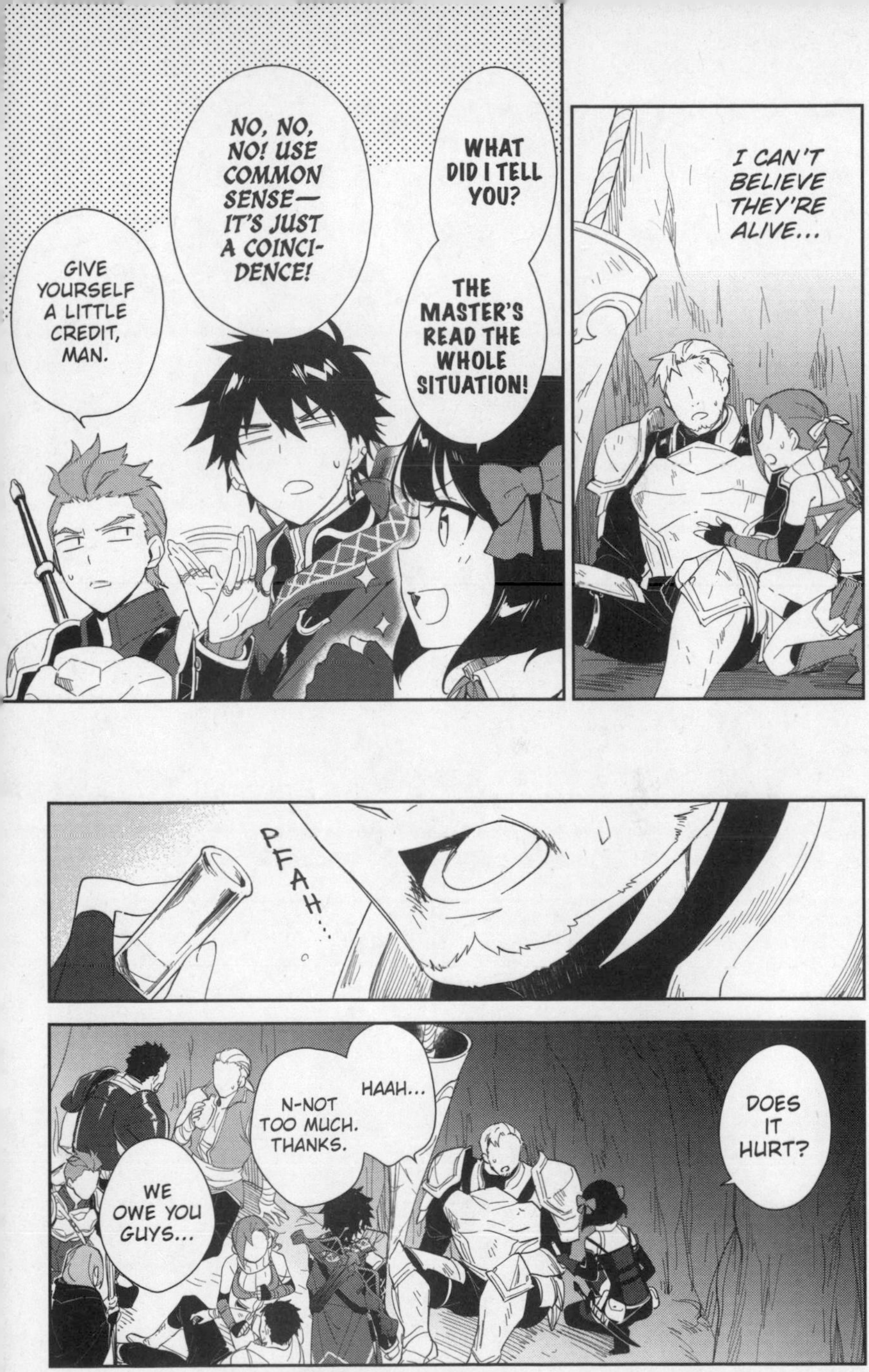
I CAN'T BELIEVE THEY'RE ALIVE...
WHAT DID I TELL YOU?
THE MASTER'S READ THE WHOLE SITUATION!
NO, NO, NO! USE COMMON SENSE—IT'S JUST A COINCIDENCE!
GIVE YOURSELF A LITTLE CREDIT, MAN.
PFAH...
DOES IT HURT?
HAAH...
N-NOT TOO MUCH. THANKS.
WE OWE YOU GUYS...

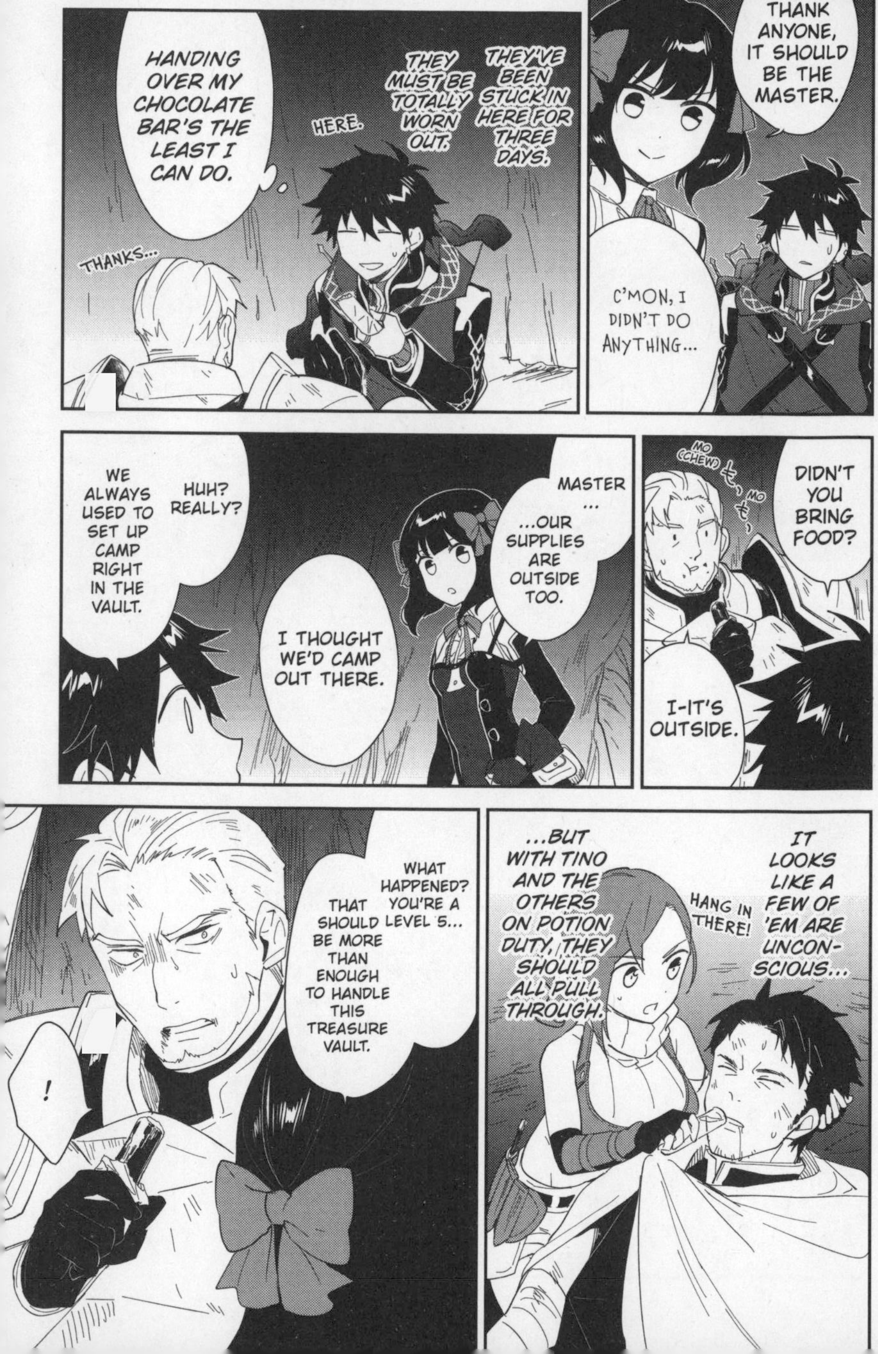
IF YOU THANK ANYONE, IT SHOULD BE THE MASTER.
C'MON, I DIDN'T DO ANYTHING...
THEY'VE BEEN STUCK IN HERE FOR THREE DAYS.
THEY MUST BE TOTALLY WORN OUT.
HANDING OVER MY CHOCOLATE BAR'S THE LEAST I CAN DO.
HERE.
THANKS...
DIDN'T YOU BRING FOOD?
MO (CHEW) も、
MO も、
I-IT'S OUTSIDE.
MASTER...
...OUR SUPPLIES ARE OUTSIDE TOO.
I THOUGHT WE'D CAMP OUT THERE.
HUH? REALLY?
WE ALWAYS USED TO SET UP CAMP RIGHT IN THE VAULT.
IT LOOKS LIKE A FEW OF 'EM ARE UNCONSCIOUS...
HANG IN THERE!
...BUT WITH TINO AND THE OTHERS ON POTION DUTY, THEY SHOULD ALL PULL THROUGH.
WHAT HAPPENED? YOU'RE A LEVEL 5...
THAT SHOULD BE MORE THAN ENOUGH TO HANDLE THIS TREASURE VAULT.
!

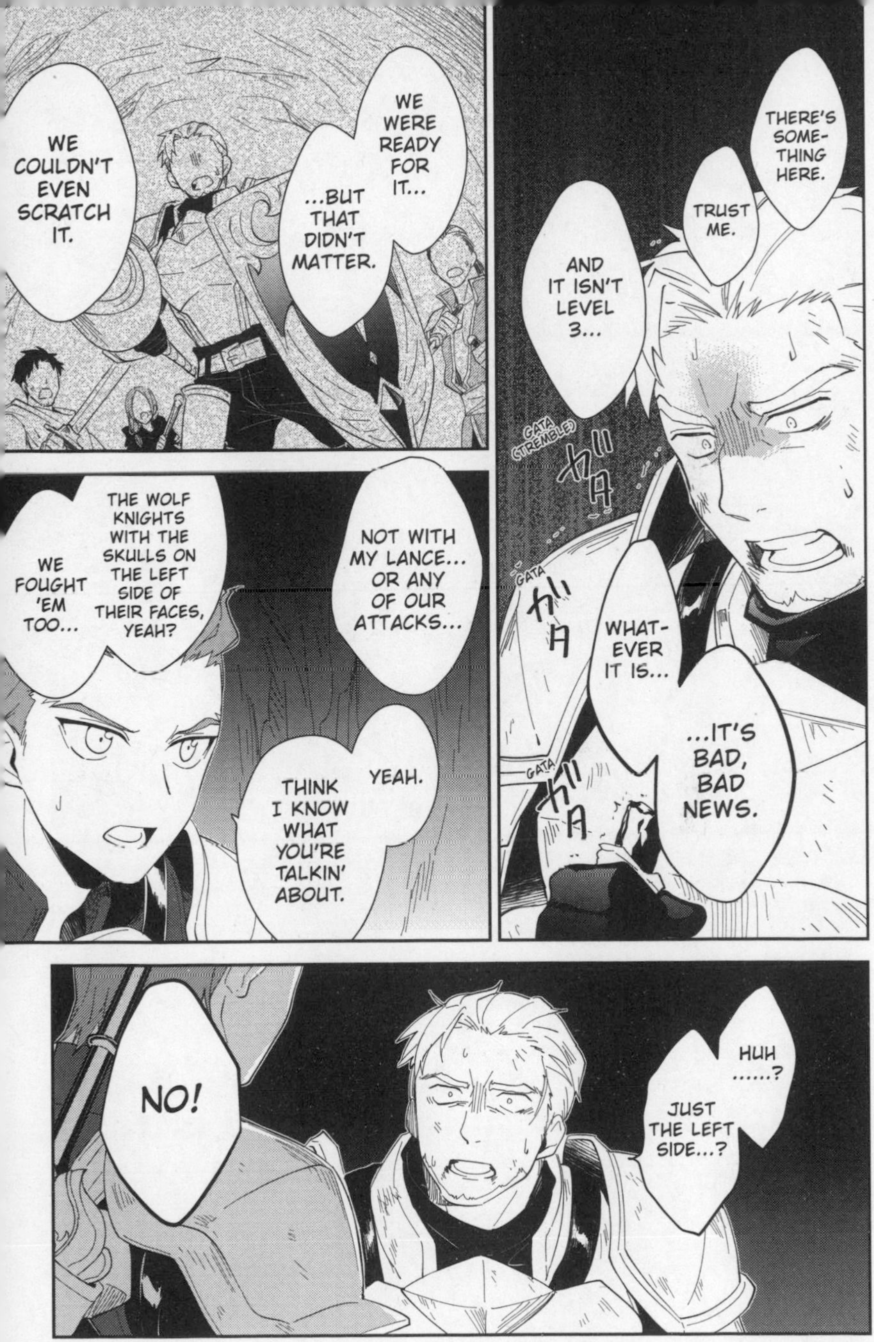

THERE'S SOME-THING HERE.
TRUST ME.
AND IT ISN'T LEVEL 3...
GATA (TREMBLE)
GATA
WHAT-EVER IT IS...
GATA
...IT'S BAD, BAD NEWS.
WE WERE READY FOR IT...
...BUT THAT DIDN'T MATTER.
WE COULDN'T EVEN SCRATCH IT.
NOT WITH MY LANCE... OR ANY OF OUR ATTACKS...
THE WOLF KNIGHTS WITH THE SKULLS ON THE LEFT SIDE OF THEIR FACES, YEAH?
WE FOUGHT 'EM TOO...
YEAH.
THINK I KNOW WHAT YOU'RE TALKIN' ABOUT.
HUH ......?
JUST THE LEFT SIDE...?
NO!

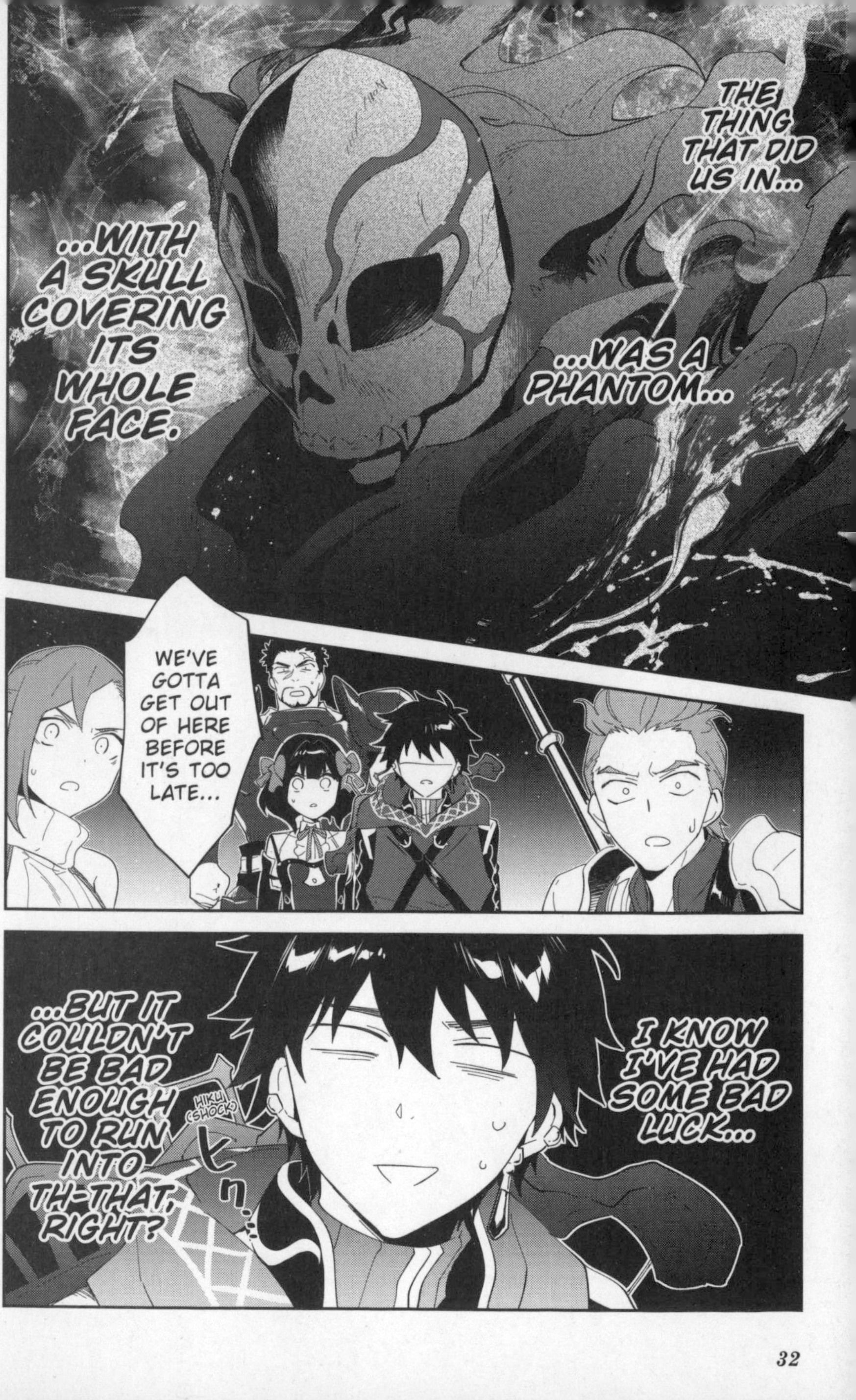
THE THING THAT DID US IN...
...WAS A PHANTOM...
...WITH A SKULL COVERING ITS WHOLE FACE.
WE'VE GOTTA GET OUT OF HERE BEFORE IT'S TOO LATE...
I KNOW I'VE HAD SOME BAD LUCK...
HIKU (SHOCK)
...BUT IT COULDN'T BE BAD ENOUGH TO RUN INTO TH-THAT, RIGHT?

LET THIS
Grieving Soul Retire

~WOE IS THE WEAKLING WHO LEADS THE STRONGEST PARTY~

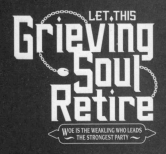

LET THIS
Grieving Soul Retire
WOE IS THE WEAKLING WHO LEADS THE STRONGEST PARTY

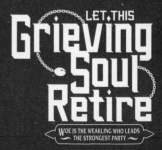

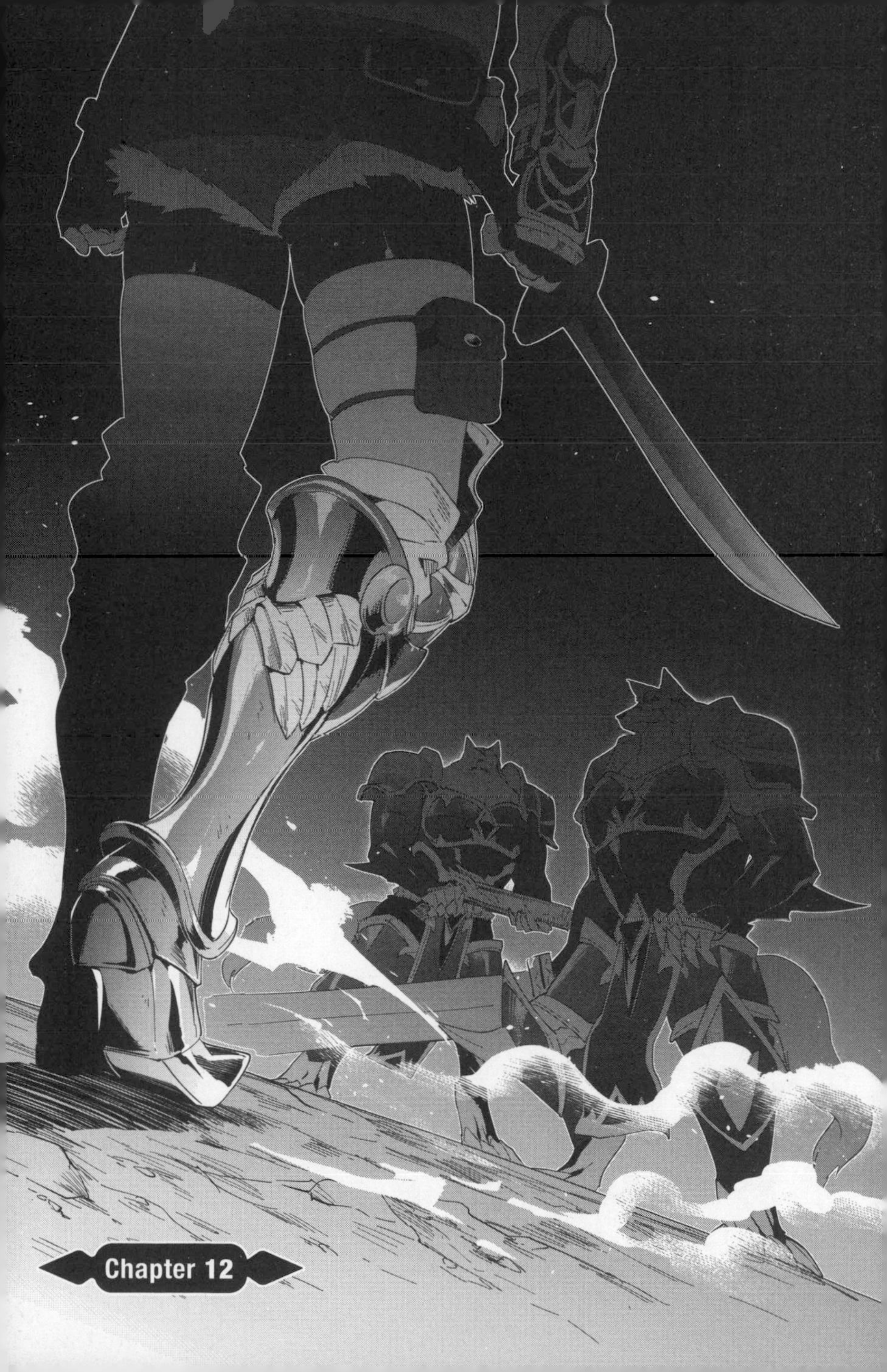
Chapter 12

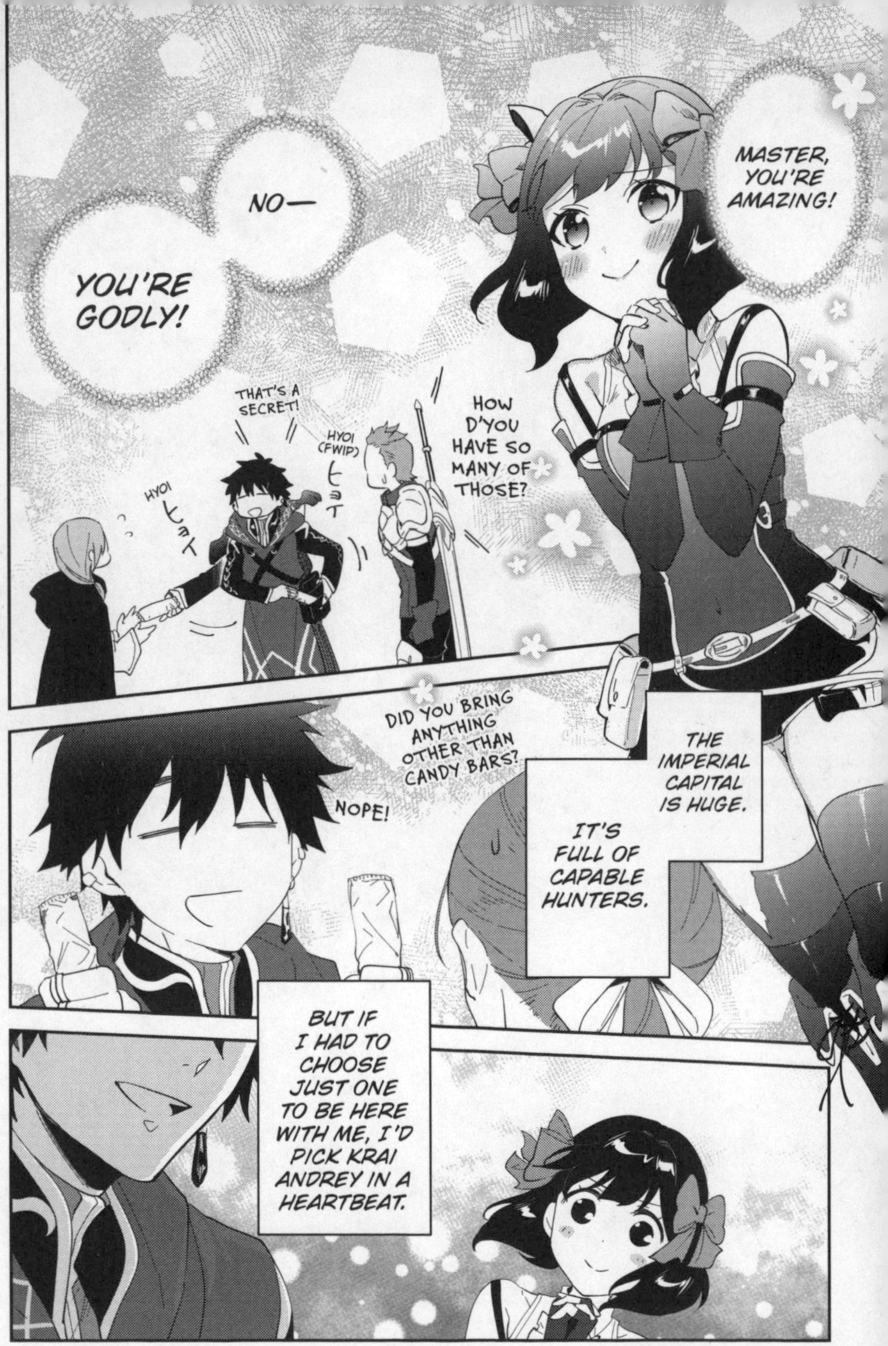
MASTER, YOU'RE AMAZING!
NO—
YOU'RE GODLY!
HOW D'YOU HAVE SO MANY OF THOSE?
HYOI (FWIP) ヒョイ
THAT'S A SECRET!
HYOI ヒョイ
THE IMPERIAL CAPITAL IS HUGE.
IT'S FULL OF CAPABLE HUNTERS.
DID YOU BRING ANYTHING OTHER THAN CANDY BARS?
NOPE!
BUT IF I HAD TO CHOOSE JUST ONE TO BE HERE WITH ME, I'D PICK KRAI ANDREY IN A HEARTBEAT.

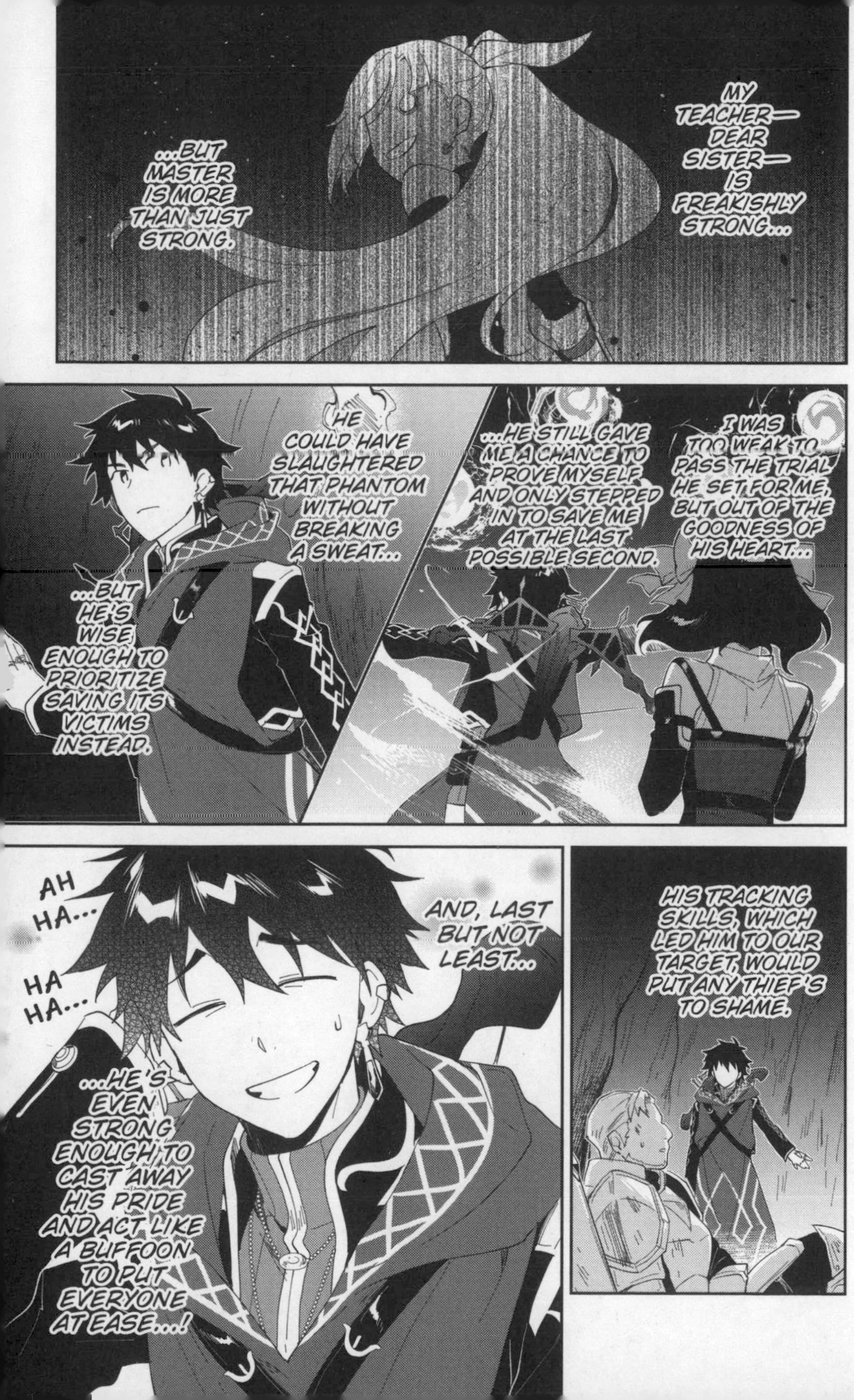
MY TEACHER—DEAR SISTER—IS FREAKISHLY STRONG...
...BUT MASTER IS MORE THAN JUST STRONG.
I WAS TOO WEAK TO PASS THE TRIAL HE SET FOR ME, BUT OUT OF THE GOODNESS OF HIS HEART...
...HE STILL GAVE ME A CHANCE TO PROVE MYSELF AND ONLY STEPPED IN TO SAVE ME AT THE LAST POSSIBLE SECOND.
HE COULD HAVE SLAUGHTERED THAT PHANTOM WITHOUT BREAKING A SWEAT...
...BUT HE'S WISE ENOUGH TO PRIORITIZE SAVING ITS VICTIMS INSTEAD.
HIS TRACKING SKILLS, WHICH LED HIM TO OUR TARGET, WOULD PUT ANY THIEF'S TO SHAME.
AND, LAST BUT NOT LEAST...
AH HA...
HA HA...
...HE'S EVEN STRONG ENOUGH TO CAST AWAY HIS PRIDE AND ACT LIKE A BUFFOON TO PUT EVERYONE AT EASE...!

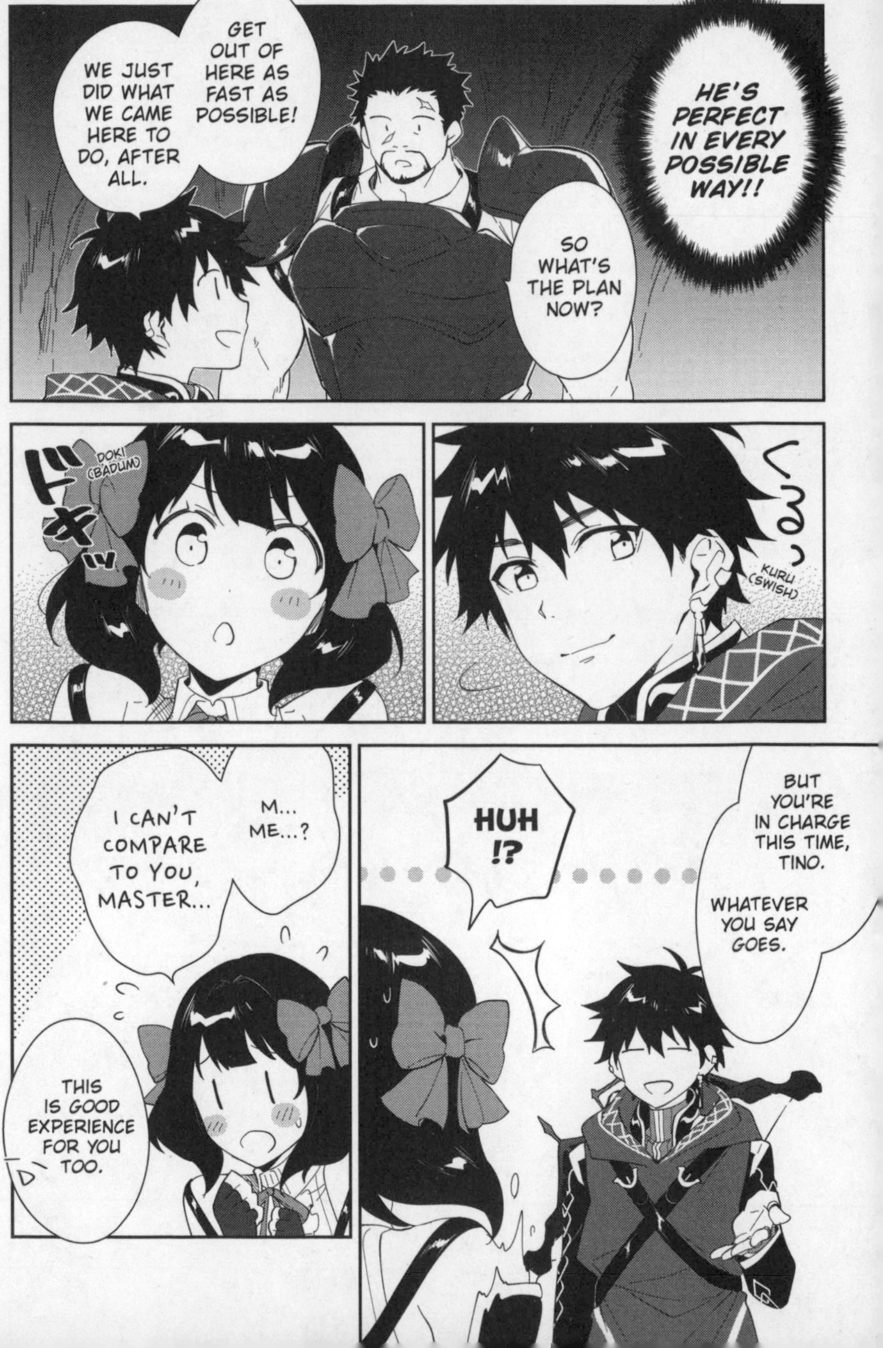
HE'S PERFECT IN EVERY POSSIBLE WAY!!
SO WHAT'S THE PLAN NOW?
GET OUT OF HERE AS FAST AS POSSIBLE!
WE JUST DID WHAT WE CAME HERE TO DO, AFTER ALL.
くるっ
KURU (SWISH)
ドキッ
DOKI (BADUM)
BUT YOU'RE IN CHARGE THIS TIME, TINO.
WHATEVER YOU SAY GOES.
HUH !?
M... ME...?
I CAN'T COMPARE TO YOU, MASTER...
THIS IS GOOD EXPERIENCE FOR YOU TOO.

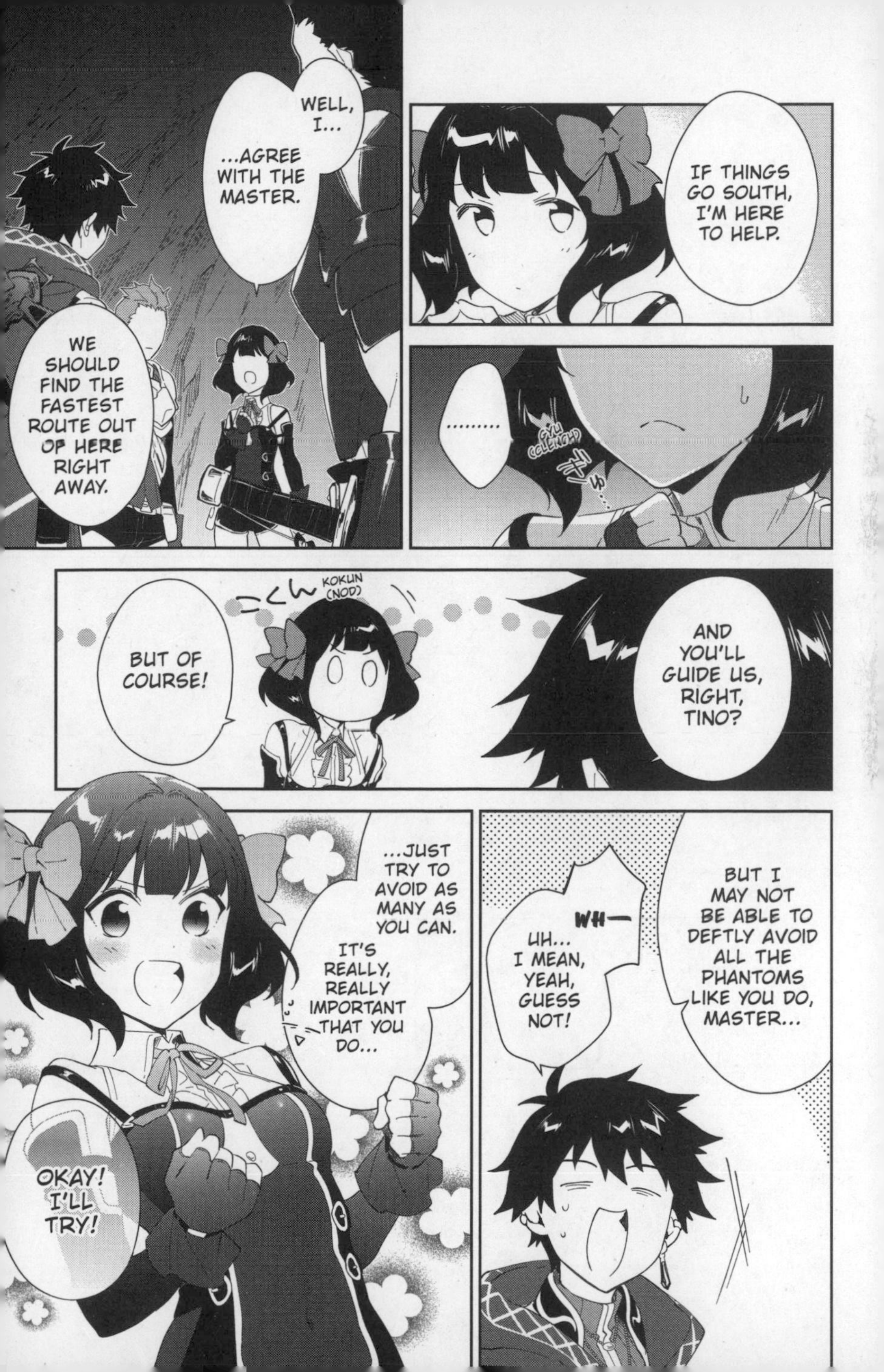
IF THINGS GO SOUTH, I'M HERE TO HELP.
....
GYU (CLENCH)
WELL, I...
...AGREE WITH THE MASTER.
WE SHOULD FIND THE FASTEST ROUTE OUT OF HERE RIGHT AWAY.
AND YOU'LL GUIDE US, RIGHT, TINO?
KOKUN (NOD)
BUT OF COURSE!
BUT I MAY NOT BE ABLE TO DEFTLY AVOID ALL THE PHANTOMS LIKE YOU DO, MASTER...
WH—
UH... I MEAN, YEAH, GUESS NOT!
...JUST TRY TO AVOID AS MANY AS YOU CAN.
IT'S REALLY, REALLY IMPORTANT THAT YOU DO...
OKAY! I'LL TRY!

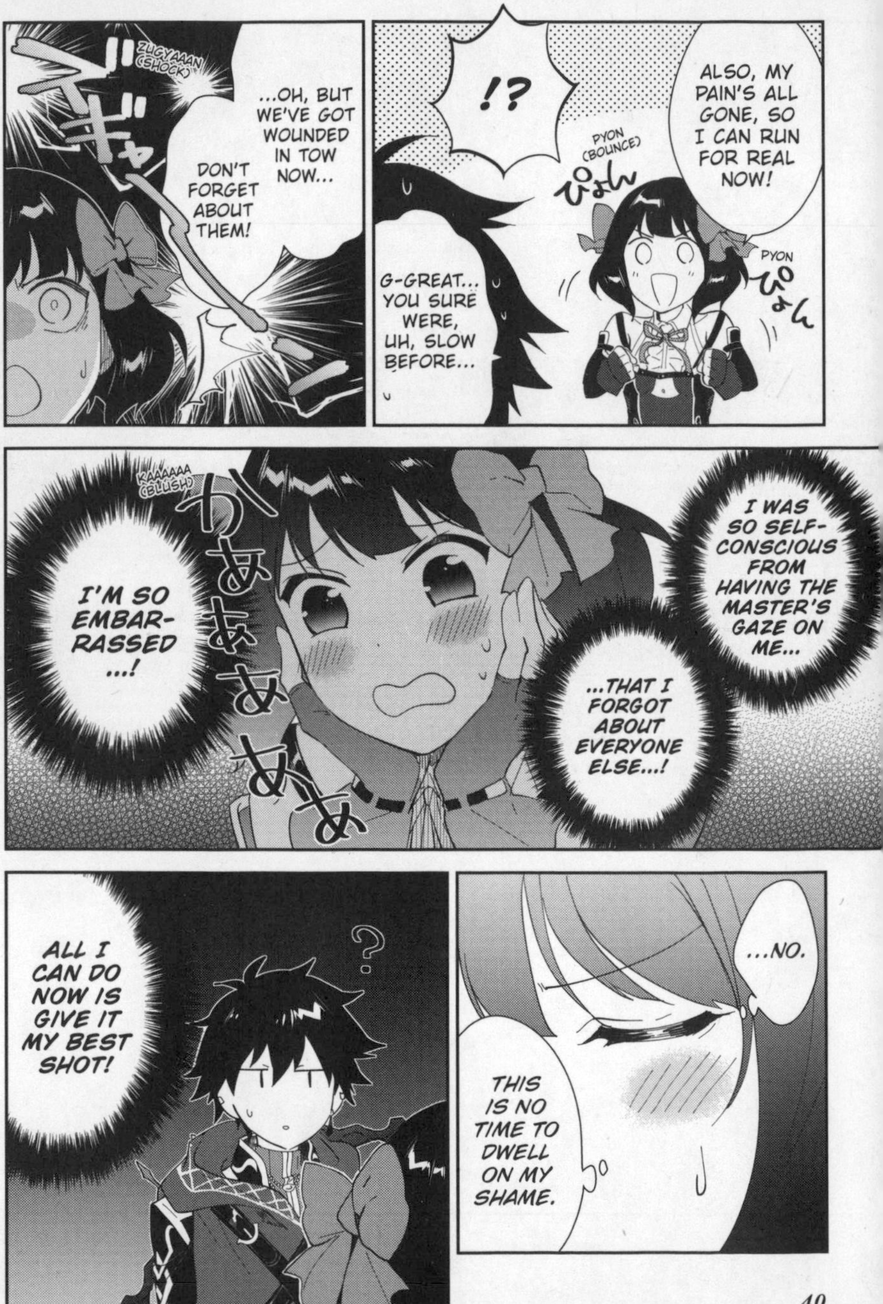

ALSO, MY PAIN'S ALL GONE, SO I CAN RUN FOR REAL NOW!
PYON (BOUNCE)
ぴょん
PYON
ぴょん
!?
G-GREAT... YOU SURE WERE, UH, SLOW BEFORE...
...OH, BUT WE'VE GOT WOUNDED IN TOW NOW...
DON'T FORGET ABOUT THEM!
ZUGYAAAN (SHOCK)
ズギャーン
I WAS SO SELF-CONSCIOUS FROM HAVING THE MASTER'S GAZE ON ME...
...THAT I FORGOT ABOUT EVERYONE ELSE...!
I'M SO EMBARRASSED...!
KAAAAAA (BLUSH)
かあああああ
...NO.
THIS IS NO TIME TO DWELL ON MY SHAME.
ALL I CAN DO NOW IS GIVE IT MY BEST SHOT!
?

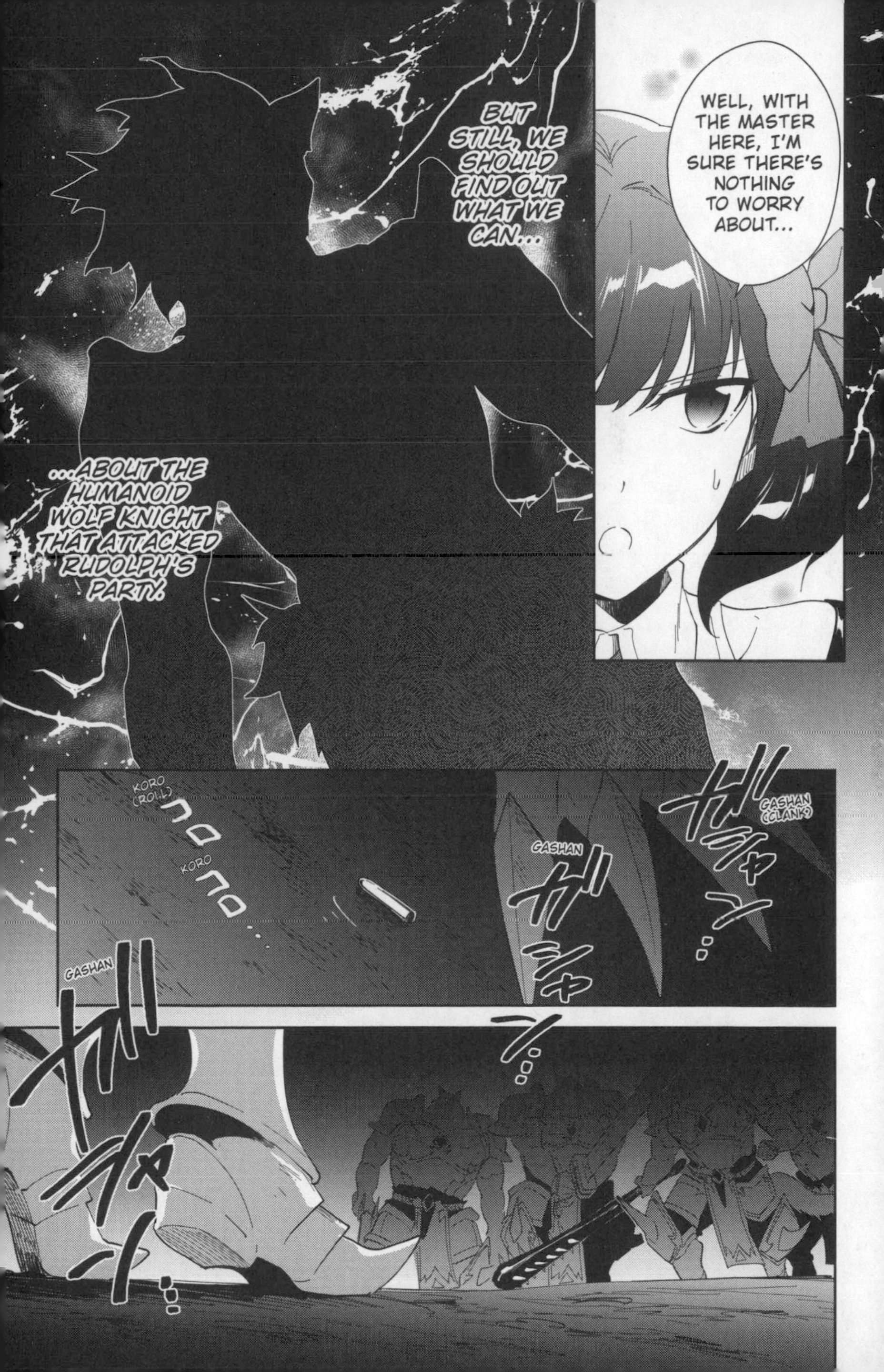
WELL, WITH THE MASTER HERE, I'M SURE THERE'S NOTHING TO WORRY ABOUT...
BUT STILL, WE SHOULD FIND OUT WHAT WE CAN...
...ABOUT THE HUMANOID WOLF KNIGHT THAT ATTACKED RUDOLPH'S PARTY.
GASHAN (CLANK)
GASHAN
KORO (ROLL)
KORO
GASHAN

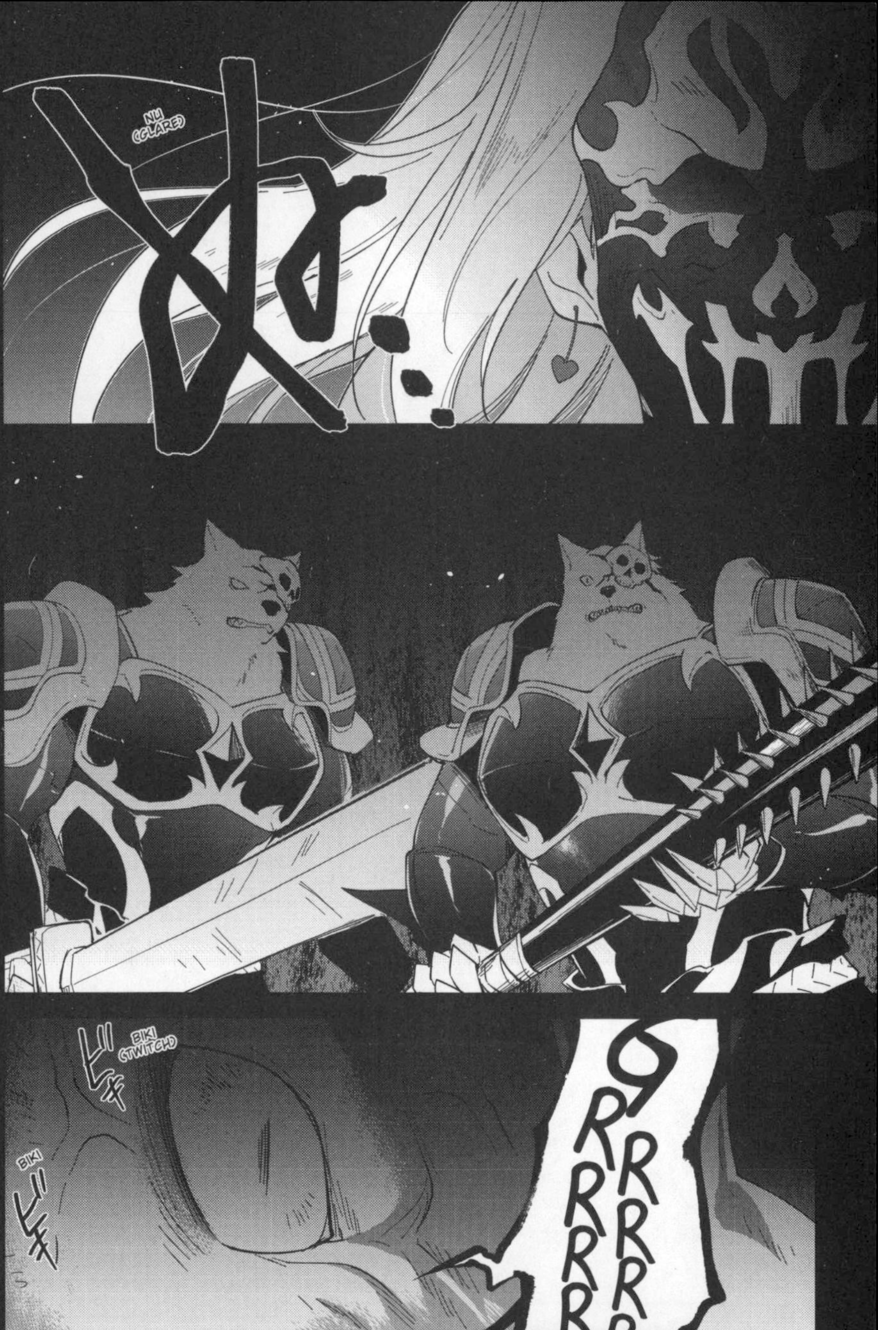
ぬっ
NU (GLARE)
GRRRRR
RRRRR
ビキッ
BIKI (TWITCH)
ビキ
BIKI

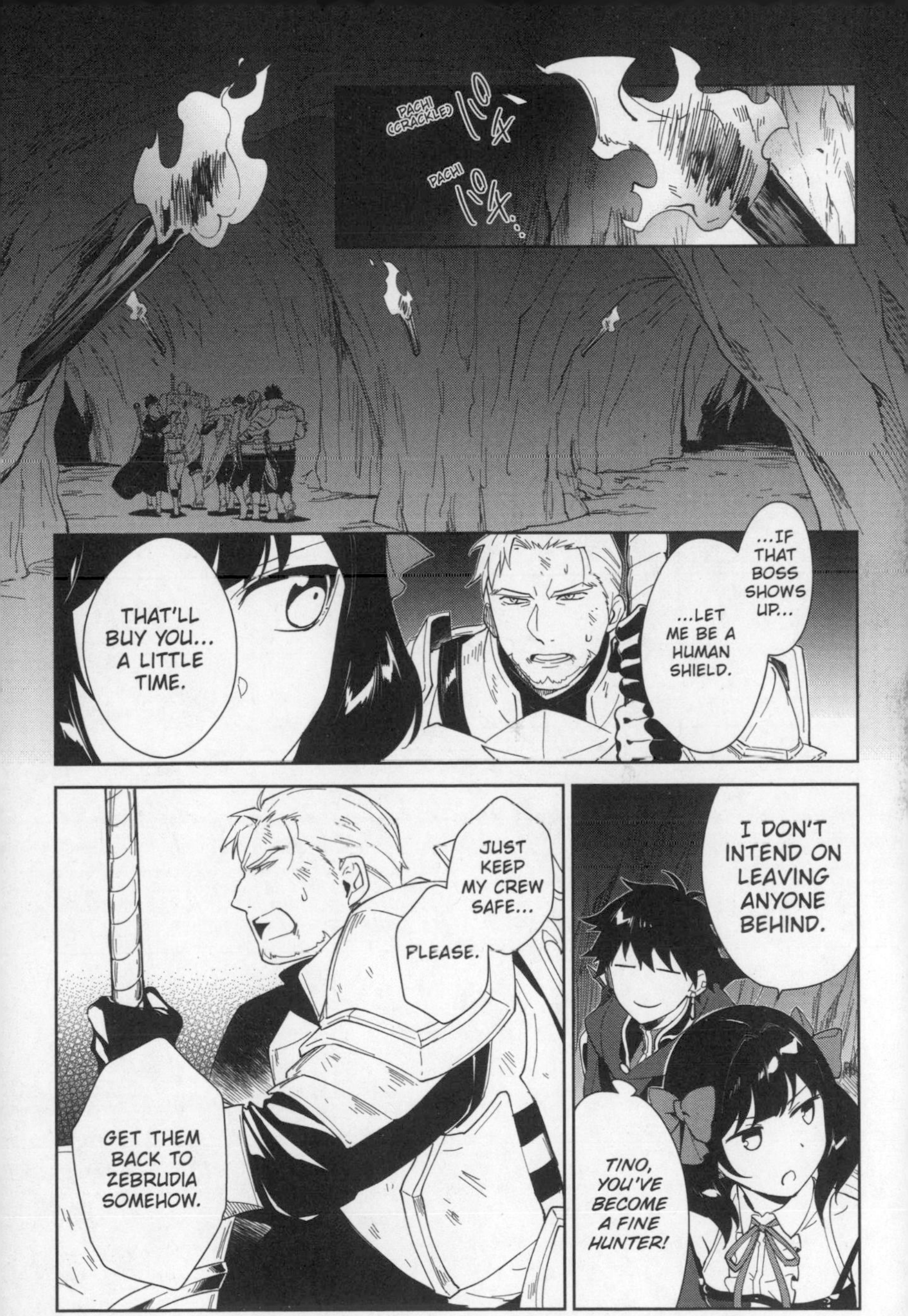
PACHI (CRACKLE)
PACHI
...IF THAT BOSS SHOWS UP...
...LET ME BE A HUMAN SHIELD.
THAT'LL BUY YOU... A LITTLE TIME.
I DON'T INTEND ON LEAVING ANYONE BEHIND.
TINO, YOU'VE BECOME A FINE HUNTER!
JUST KEEP MY CREW SAFE...
PLEASE.
GET THEM BACK TO ZEBRUDIA SOMEHOW.

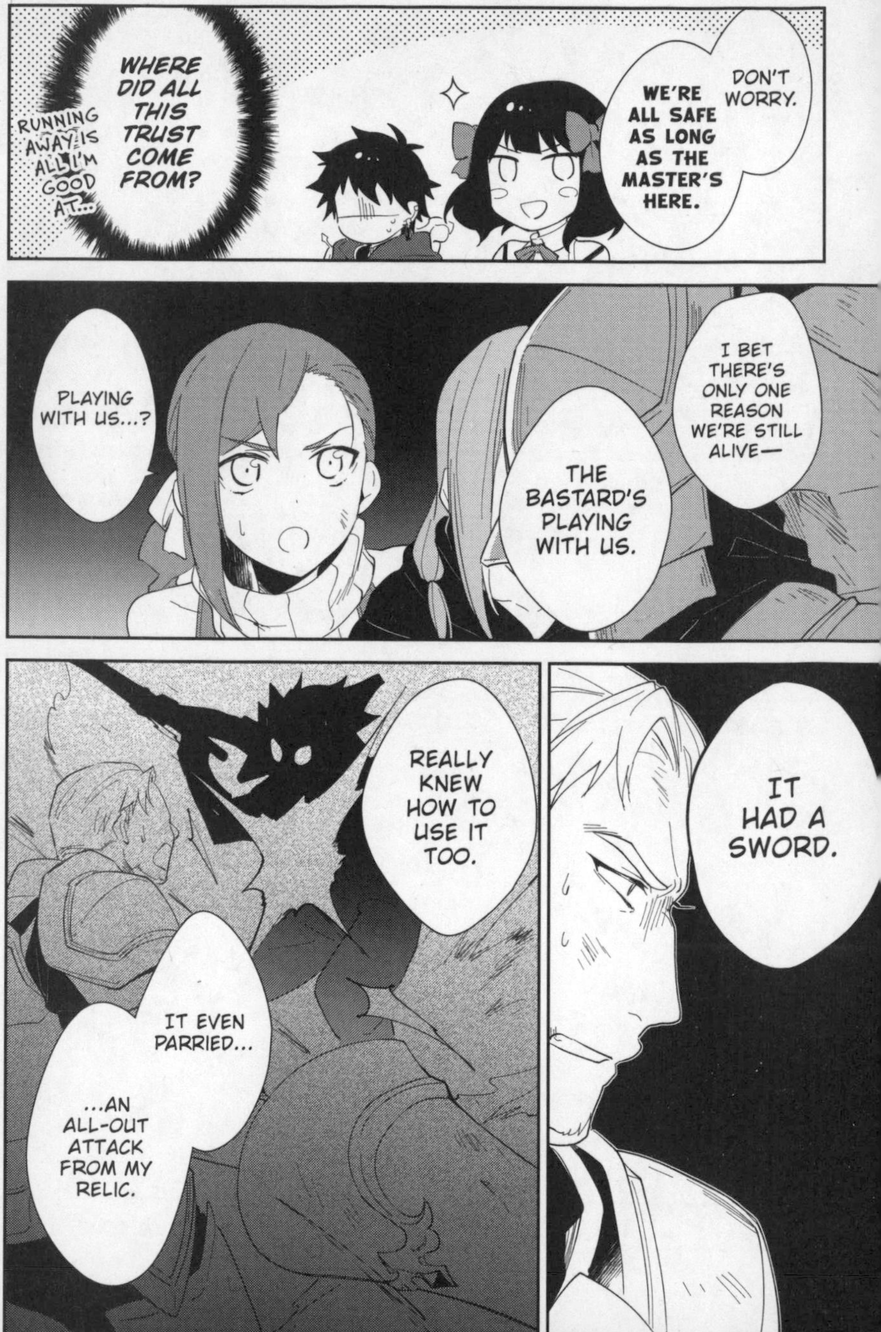
DON'T WORRY.
WE'RE ALL SAFE AS LONG AS THE MASTER'S HERE.
WHERE DID ALL THIS TRUST COME FROM?
RUNNING AWAY IS ALL I'M GOOD AT...
I BET THERE'S ONLY ONE REASON WE'RE STILL ALIVE—
THE BASTARD'S PLAYING WITH US.
PLAYING WITH US...?
IT HAD A SWORD.
REALLY KNEW HOW TO USE IT TOO.
IT EVEN PARRIED...
...AN ALL-OUT ATTACK FROM MY RELIC.

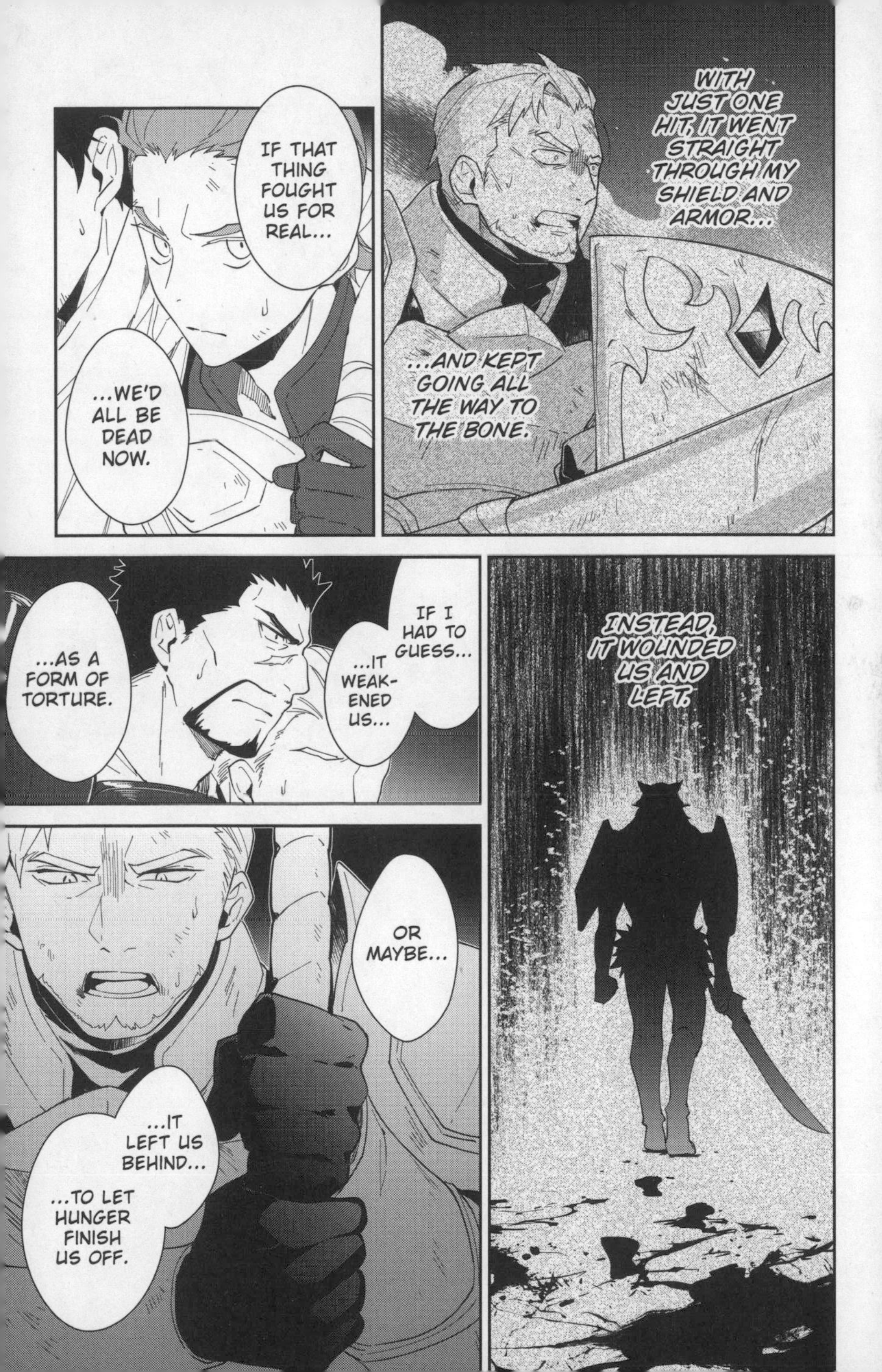
WITH JUST ONE HIT, IT WENT STRAIGHT THROUGH MY SHIELD AND ARMOR...
...AND KEPT GOING ALL THE WAY TO THE BONE.
IF THAT THING FOUGHT US FOR REAL...
...WE'D ALL BE DEAD NOW.
INSTEAD, IT WOUNDED US AND LEFT.
IF I HAD TO GUESS...
...IT WEAK-ENED US...
...AS A FORM OF TORTURE.
OR MAYBE...
...IT LEFT US BEHIND...
...TO LET HUNGER FINISH US OFF.

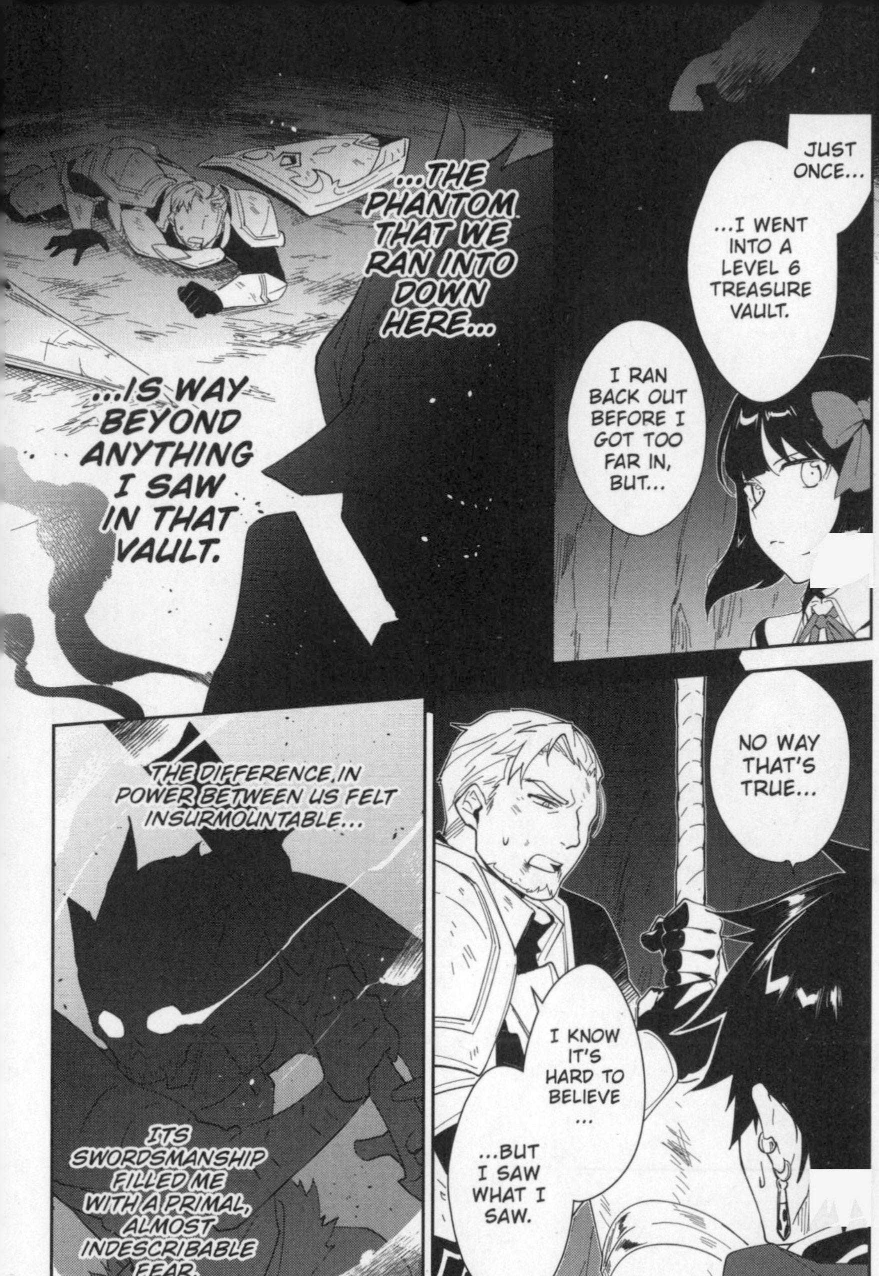
JUST ONCE...
...I WENT INTO A LEVEL 6 TREASURE VAULT.
I RAN BACK OUT BEFORE I GOT TOO FAR IN, BUT...
...THE PHANTOM THAT WE RAN INTO DOWN HERE...
...IS WAY BEYOND ANYTHING I SAW IN THAT VAULT.
NO WAY THAT'S TRUE...
I KNOW IT'S HARD TO BELIEVE...
...BUT I SAW WHAT I SAW.
THE DIFFERENCE IN POWER BETWEEN US FELT INSURMOUNTABLE...
ITS SWORDSMANSHIP FILLED ME WITH A PRIMAL, ALMOST INDESCRIBABLE FEAR.

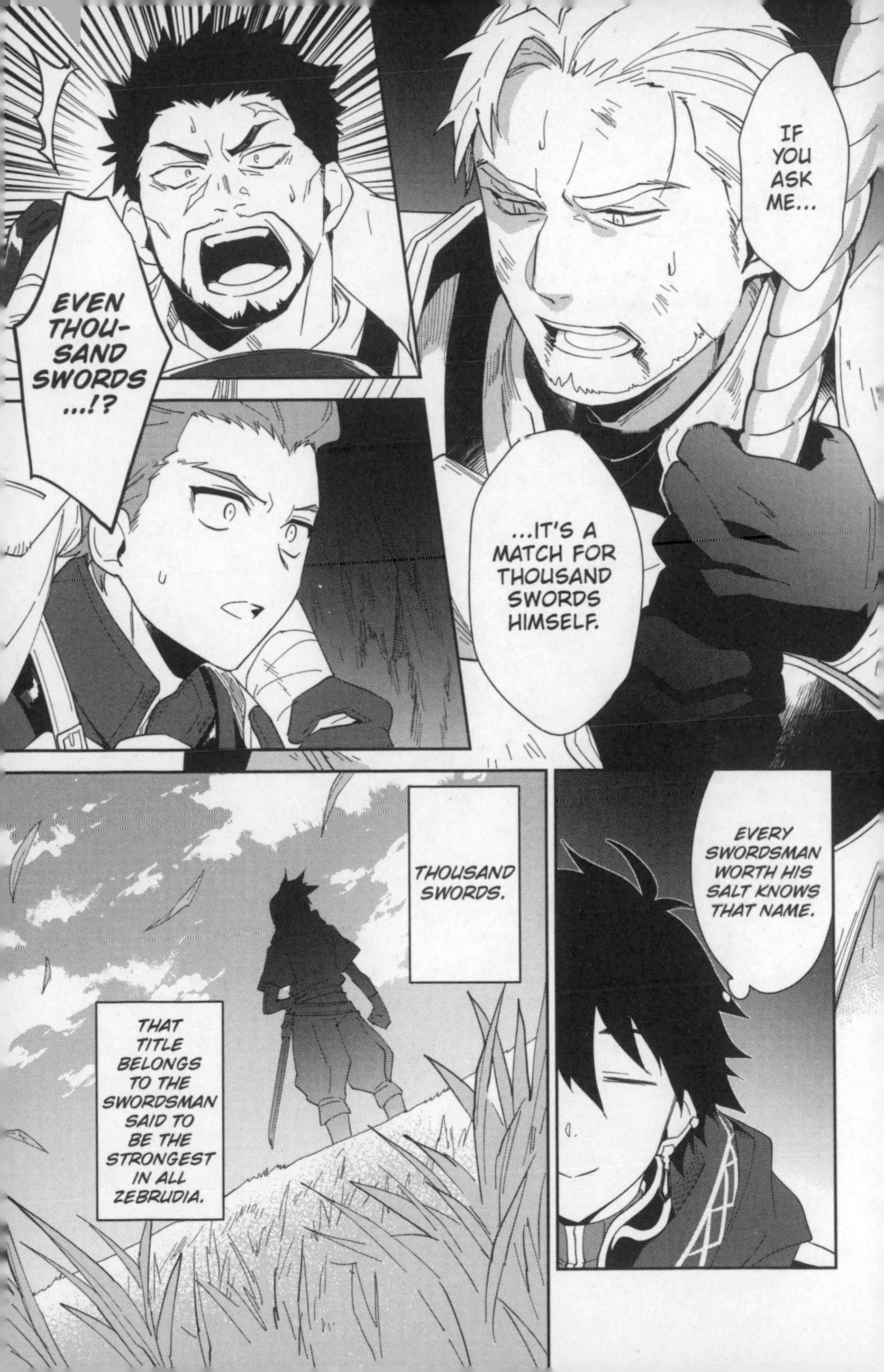
IF YOU ASK ME...
...IT'S A MATCH FOR THOUSAND SWORDS HIMSELF.
EVEN THOUSAND SWORDS...!?
EVERY SWORDSMAN WORTH HIS SALT KNOWS THAT NAME.
THOUSAND SWORDS.
THAT TITLE BELONGS TO THE SWORDSMAN SAID TO BE THE STRONGEST IN ALL ZEBRUDIA.

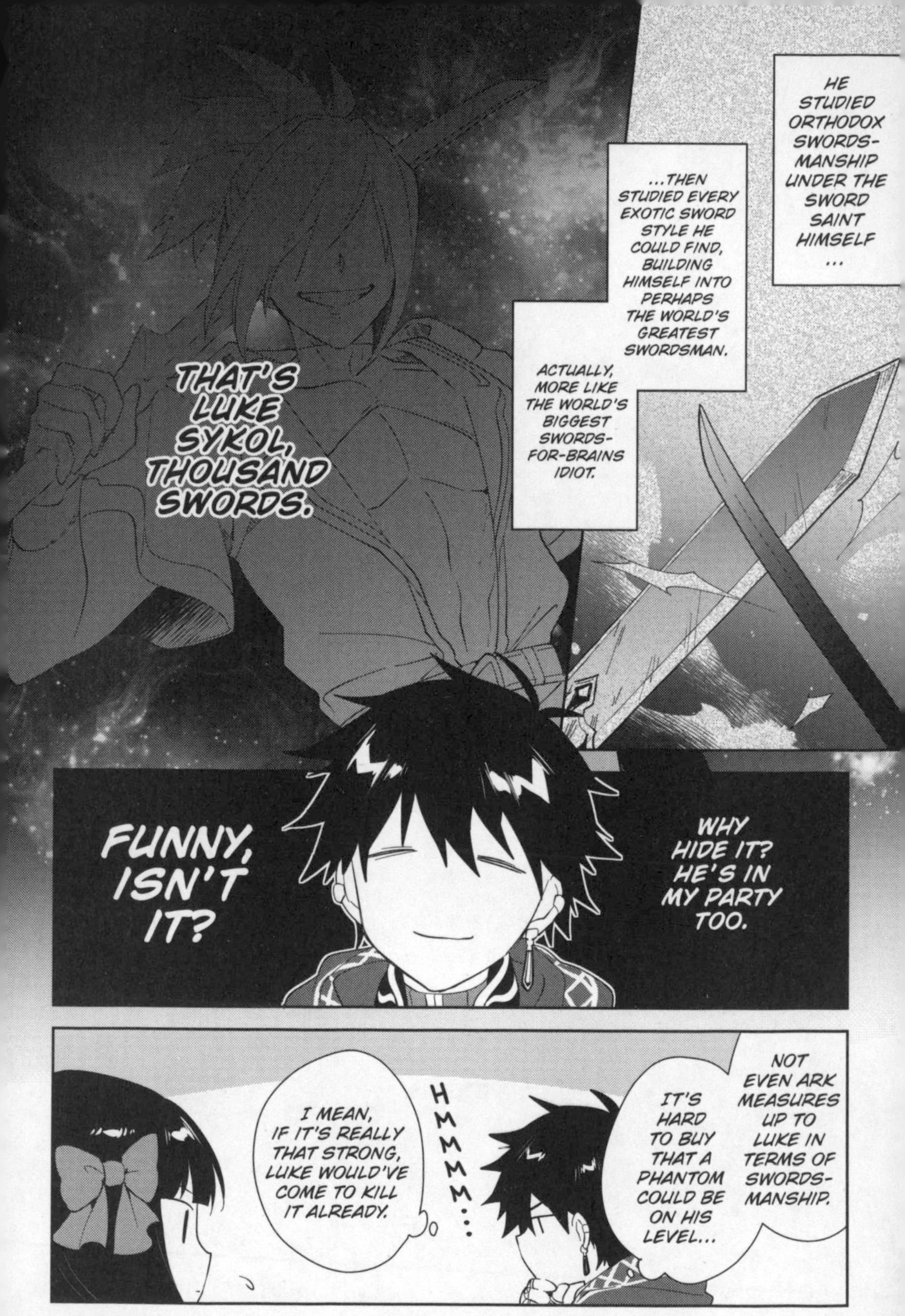
HE STUDIED ORTHODOX SWORDSMANSHIP UNDER THE SWORD SAINT HIMSELF...
...THEN STUDIED EVERY EXOTIC SWORD STYLE HE COULD FIND, BUILDING HIMSELF INTO PERHAPS THE WORLD'S GREATEST SWORDSMAN.
ACTUALLY, MORE LIKE THE WORLD'S BIGGEST SWORDS-FOR-BRAINS IDIOT.
THAT'S LUKE SYKOL, THOUSAND SWORDS.
WHY HIDE IT? HE'S IN MY PARTY TOO.
FUNNY, ISN'T IT?
NOT EVEN ARK MEASURES UP TO LUKE IN TERMS OF SWORDSMANSHIP.
IT'S HARD TO BUY THAT A PHANTOM COULD BE ON HIS LEVEL...
HMMMM...
I MEAN, IF IT'S REALLY THAT STRONG, LUKE WOULD'VE COME TO KILL IT ALREADY.

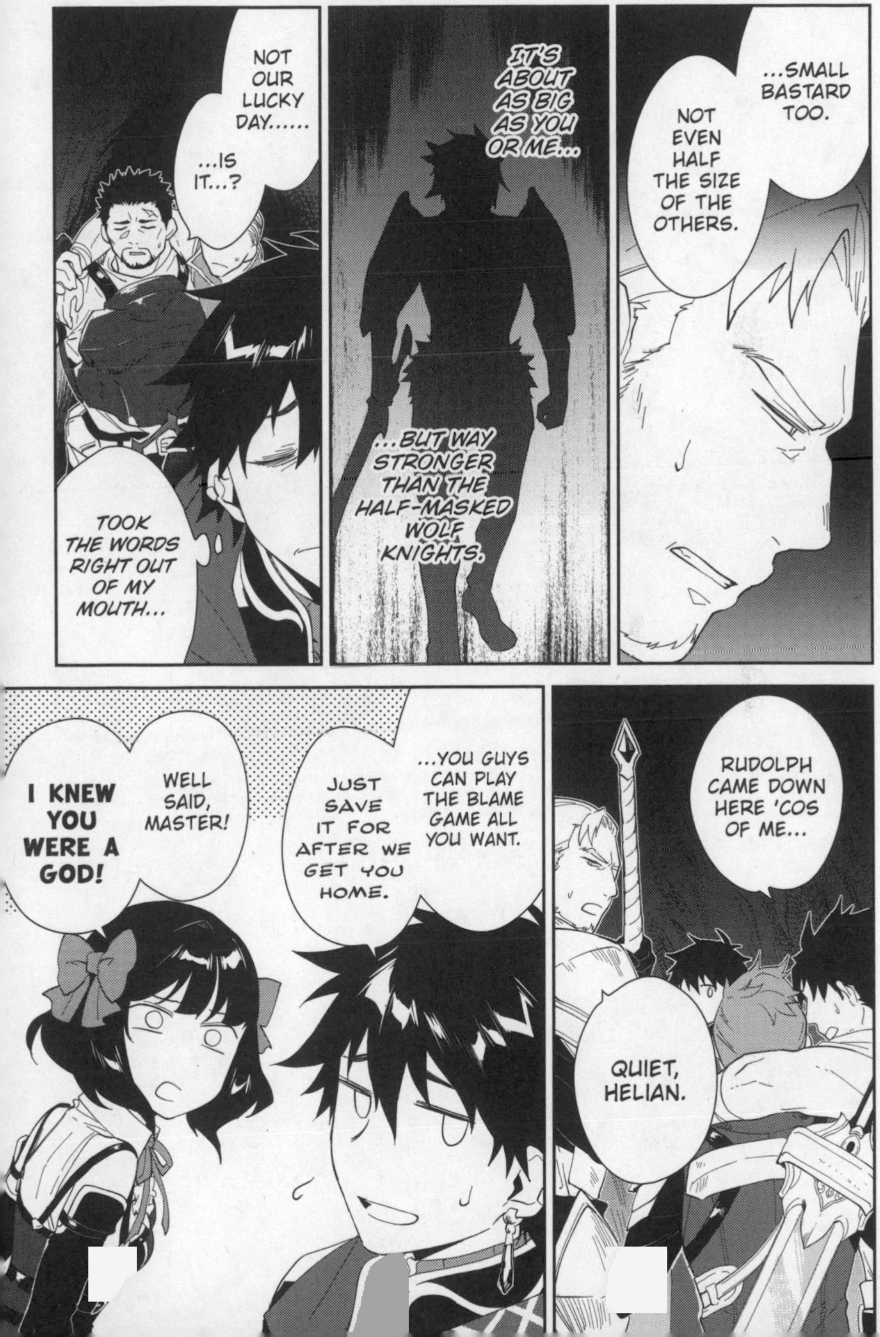
...SMALL BASTARD TOO.
NOT EVEN HALF THE SIZE OF THE OTHERS.
IT'S ABOUT AS BIG AS YOU OR ME...
...BUT WAY STRONGER THAN THE HALF-MASKED WOLF KNIGHTS.
NOT OUR LUCKY DAY......
...IS IT...?
TOOK THE WORDS RIGHT OUT OF MY MOUTH...
RUDOLPH CAME DOWN HERE 'COS OF ME...
QUIET, HELIAN.
...YOU GUYS CAN PLAY THE BLAME GAME ALL YOU WANT.
JUST SAVE IT FOR AFTER WE GET YOU HOME.
WELL SAID, MASTER!
I KNEW YOU WERE A GOD!

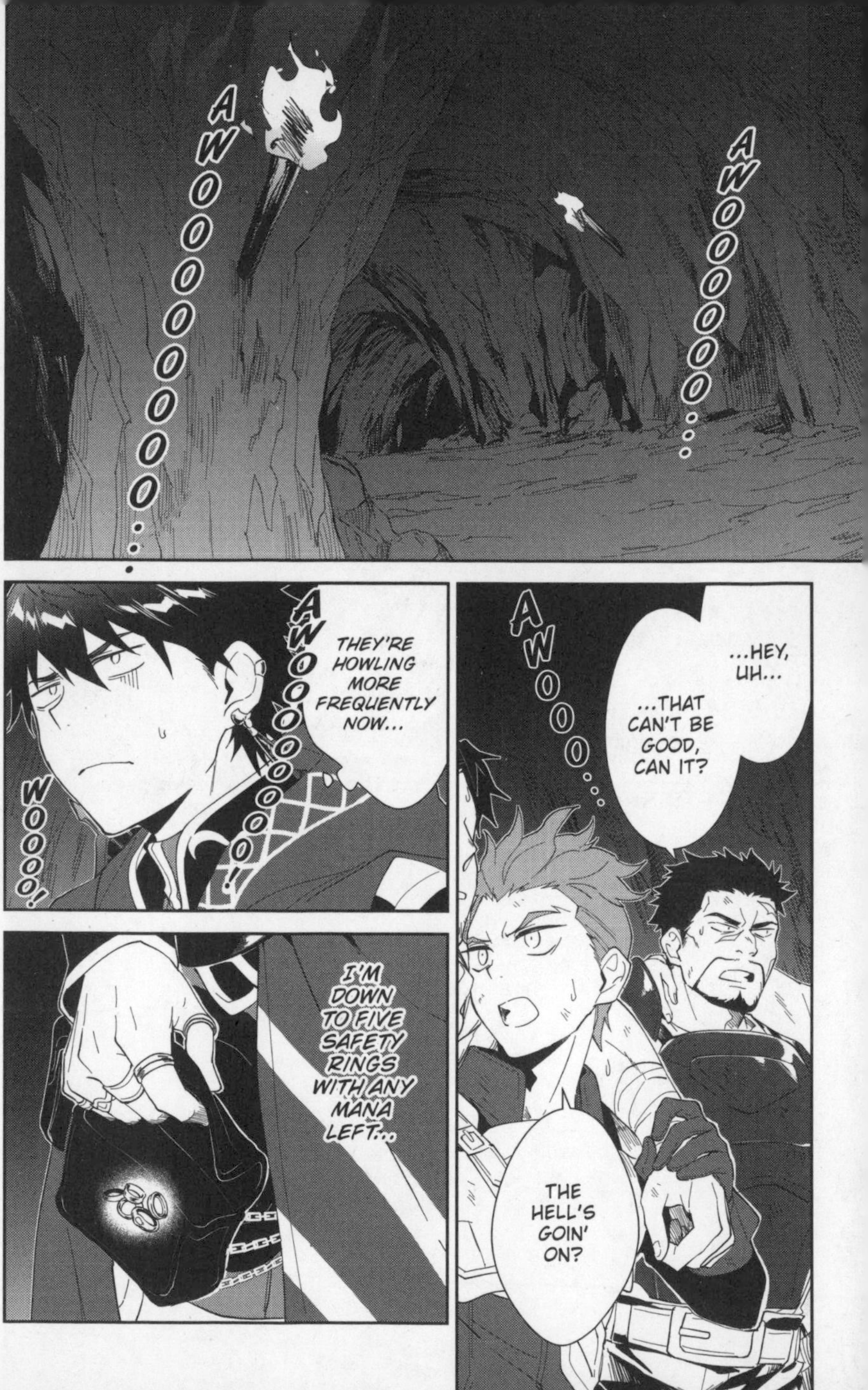
AWOOOOOOOOOO...
AWOOOOOOOOOOOOO...
AWOOOO...
...HEY, UH...
...THAT CAN'T BE GOOD, CAN IT?
THE HELL'S GOIN' ON?
AWOOOOOOOOOOOO!
THEY'RE HOWLING MORE FREQUENTLY NOW...
WOOOOO!
I'M DOWN TO FIVE SAFETY RINGS WITH ANY MANA LEFT...

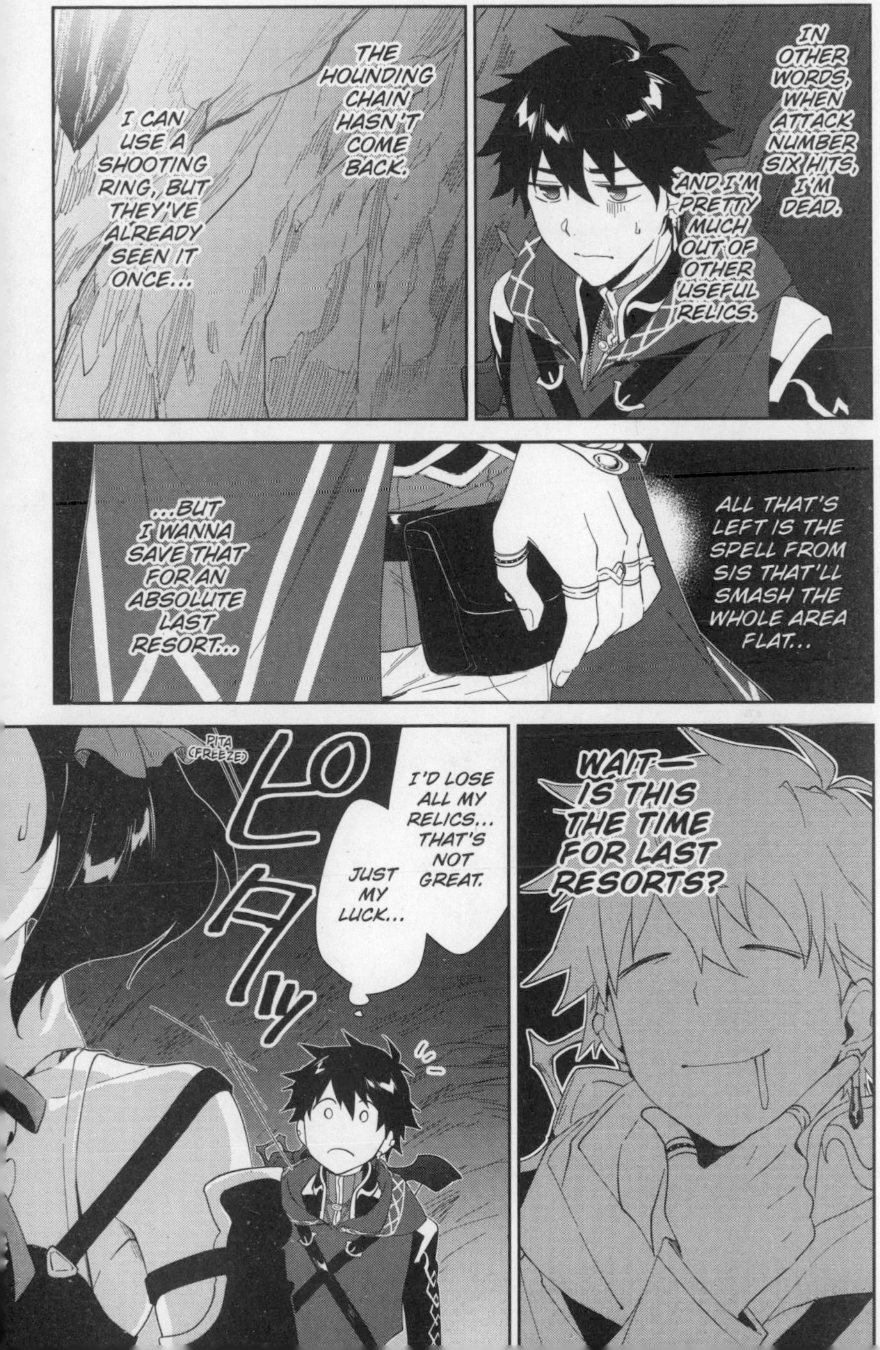
IN OTHER WORDS, WHEN ATTACK NUMBER SIX HITS, I'M DEAD.
AND I'M PRETTY MUCH OUT OF OTHER USEFUL RELICS.
THE HOUNDING CHAIN HASN'T COME BACK.
I CAN USE A SHOOTING RING, BUT THEY'VE ALREADY SEEN IT ONCE...
ALL THAT'S LEFT IS THE SPELL FROM SIS THAT'LL SMASH THE WHOLE AREA FLAT...
...BUT I WANNA SAVE THAT FOR AN ABSOLUTE LAST RESORT...
WAIT— IS THIS THE TIME FOR LAST RESORTS?
I'D LOSE ALL MY RELICS... THAT'S NOT GREAT.
JUST MY LUCK...
ピタッ
PITA (FREEZE)

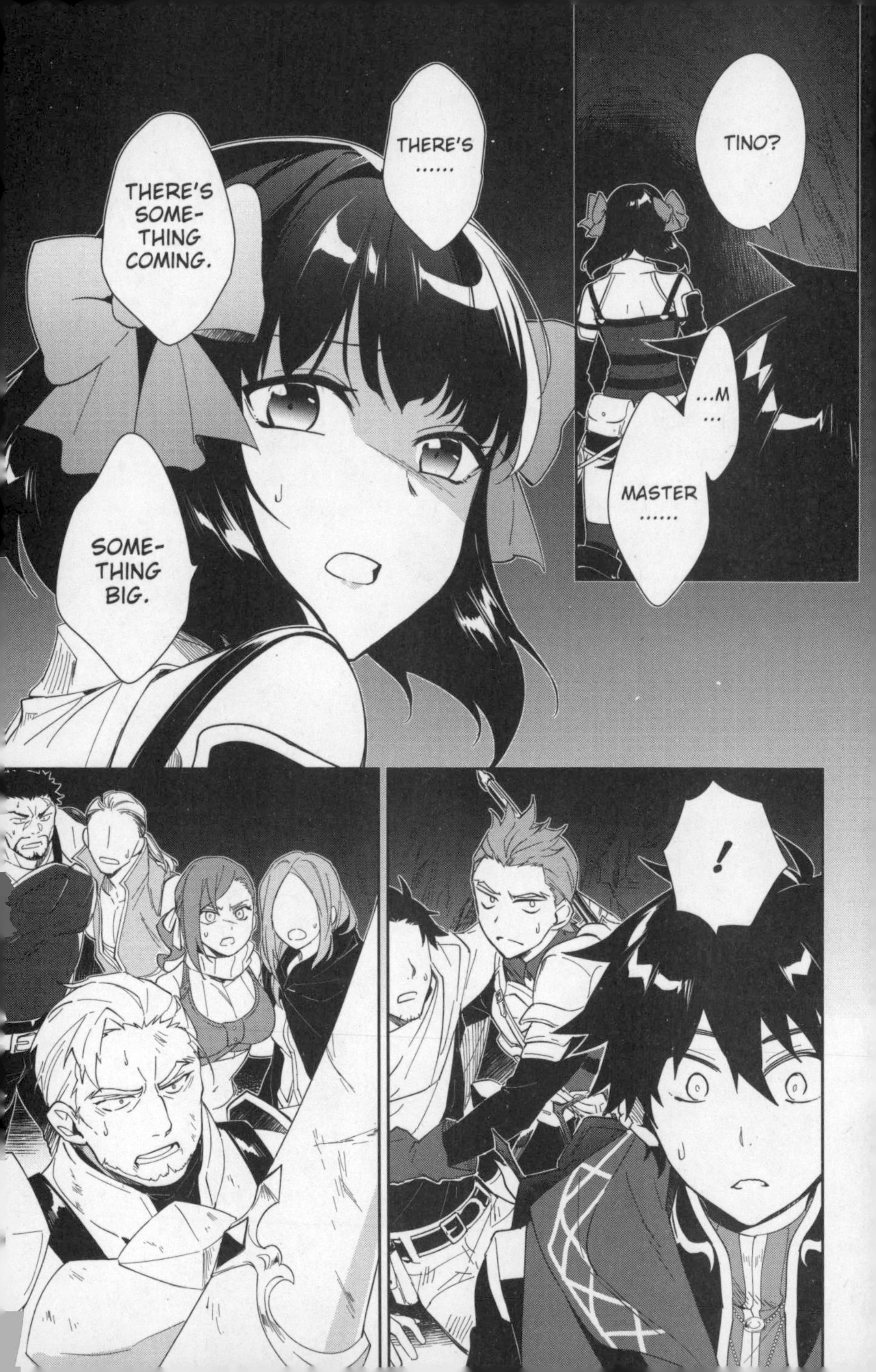
TINO?
...M ...
MASTER ......
THERE'S ......
THERE'S SOME-THING COMING.
SOME-THING BIG.
!

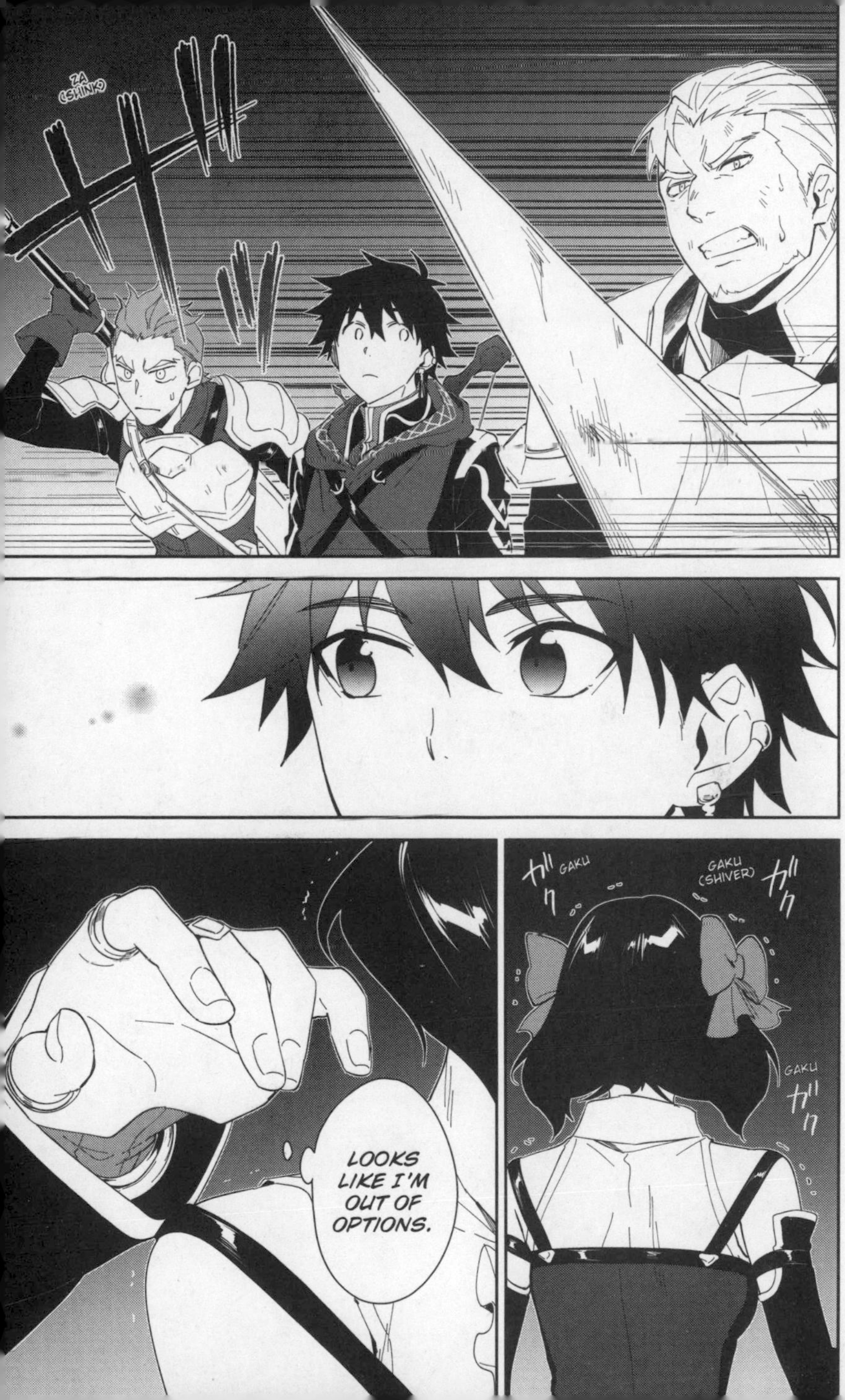
ZA
(SHINK)
ガク
GAKU
(SHIVER)
ガク
GAKU
ガク
GAKU
LOOKS LIKE I'M OUT OF OPTIONS.

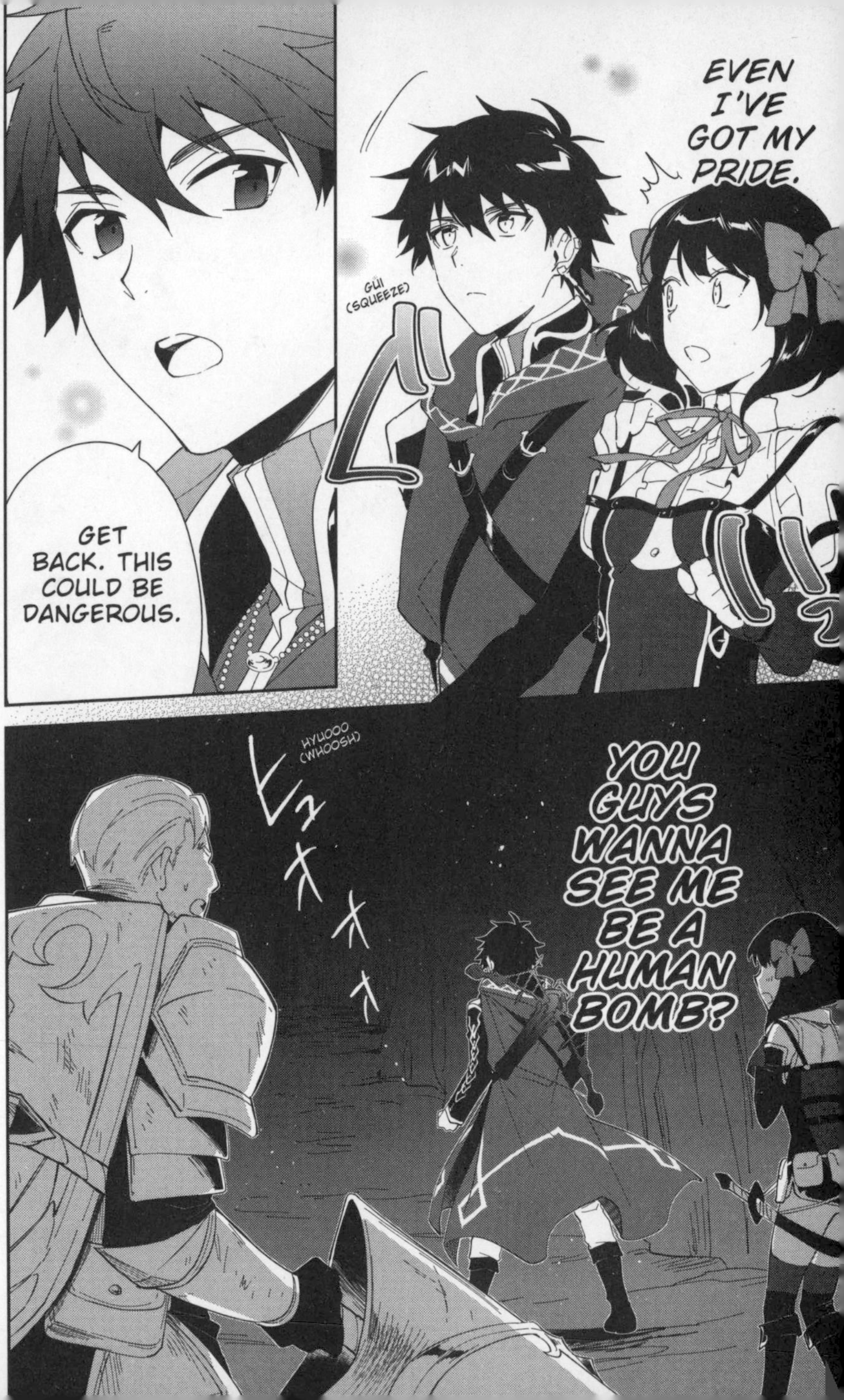
EVEN I'VE GOT MY PRIDE.
GÜI (SQUEEZE)
GET BACK. THIS COULD BE DANGEROUS.
HYUOOO (WHOOSH)
YOU GUYS WANNA SEE ME BE A HUMAN BOMB?

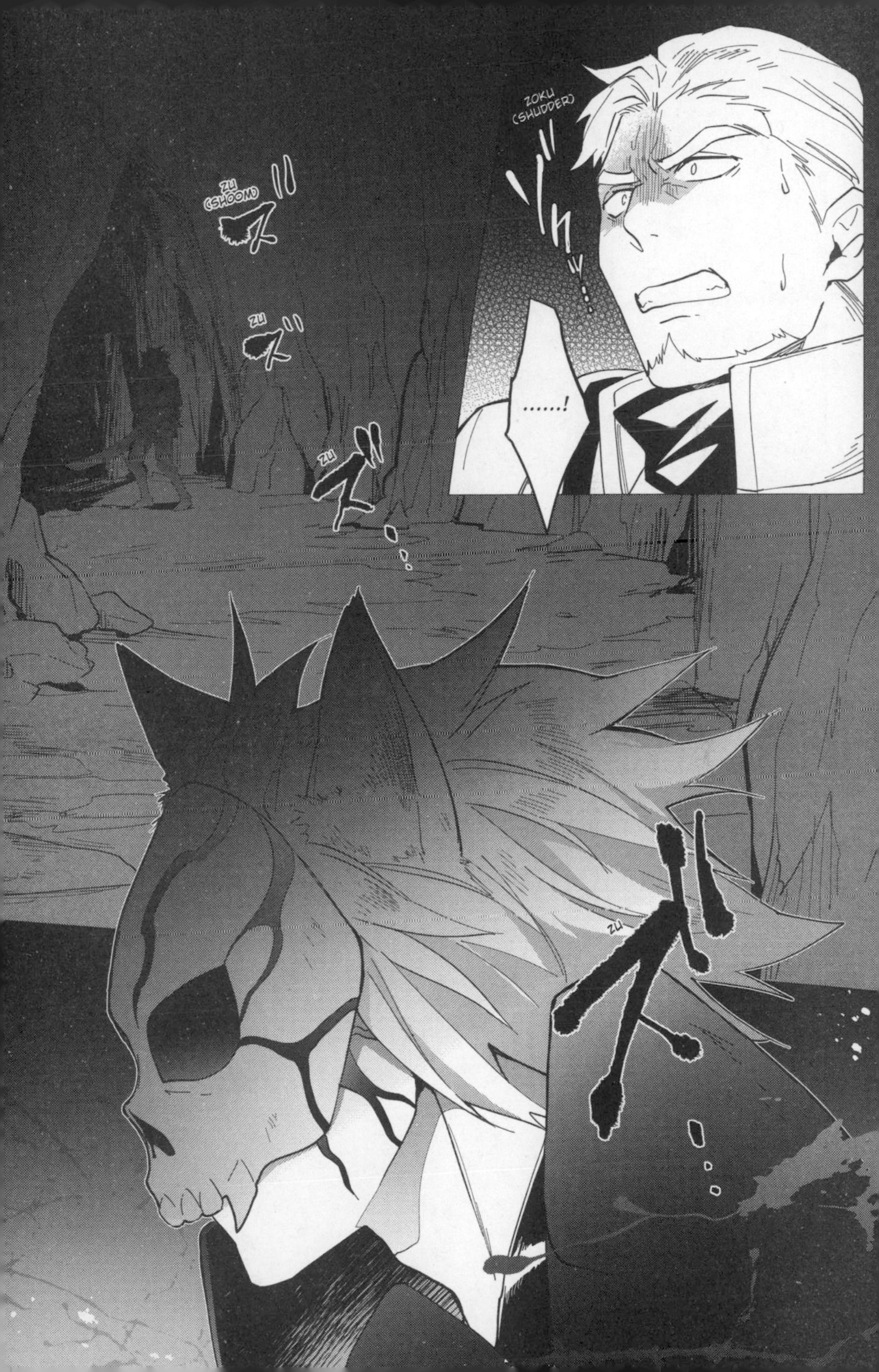
ZOKU (SHUDDER)
......!
ZU (SHOOM)
ZU
ZU
ZU

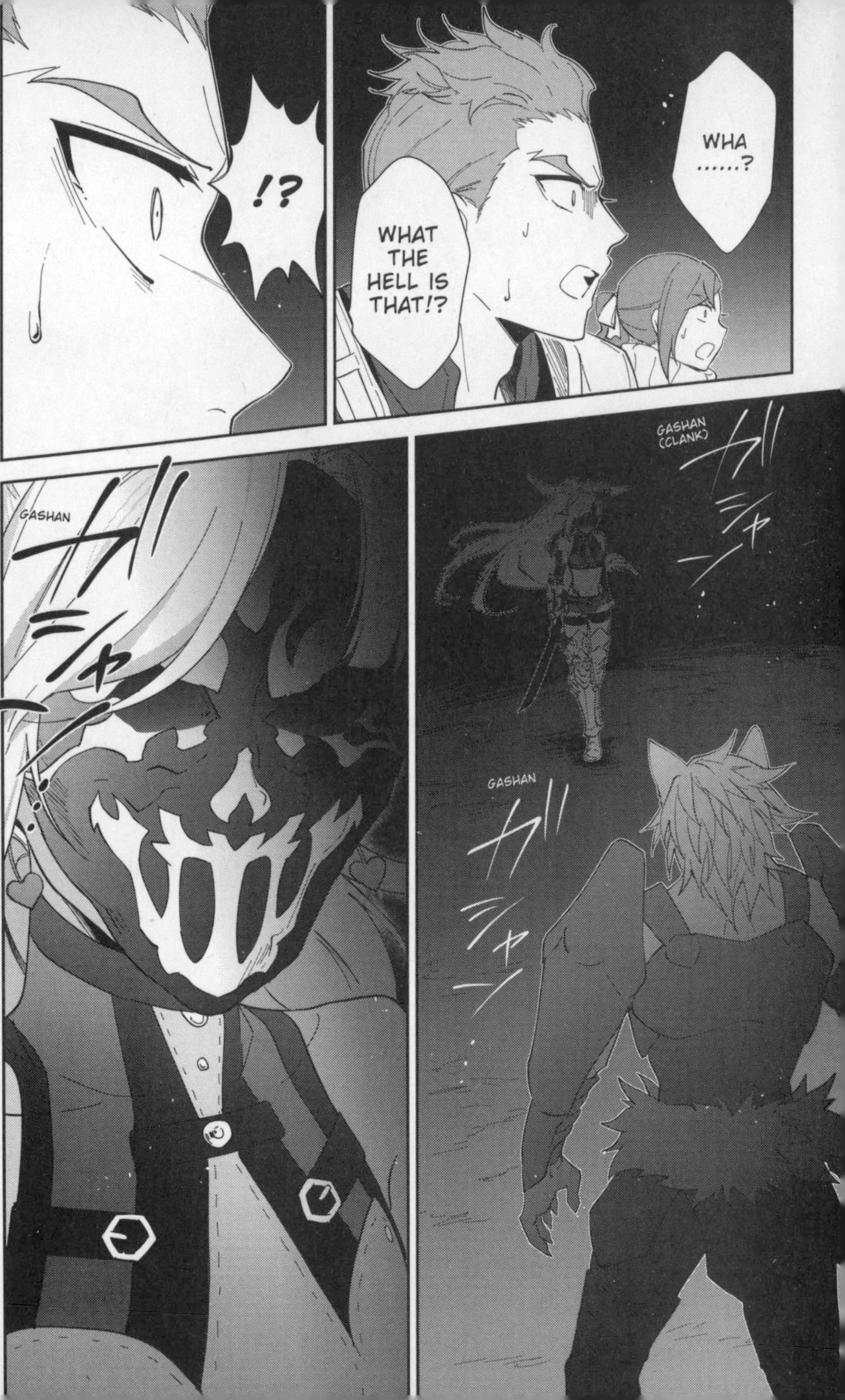
WHA ......?
WHAT THE HELL IS THAT!?
!?
GASHAN (CLANK)
GASHAN
GASHAN

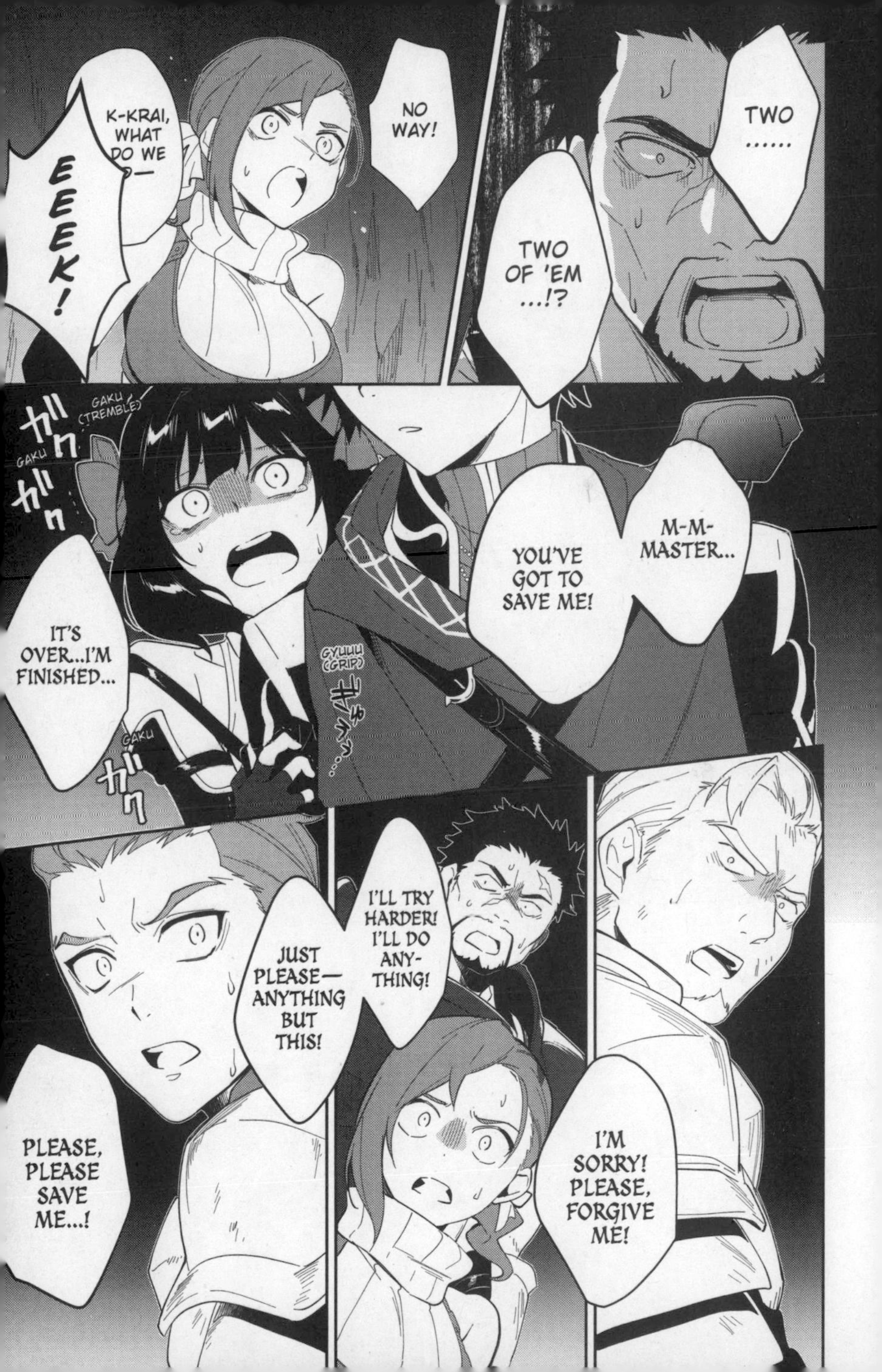
TWO......
TWO OF 'EM ...!?
NO WAY!
K-KRAI, WHAT DO WE D—
EEEEK!
M-M-MASTER...
YOU'VE GOT TO SAVE ME!
GAKU (TREMBLE)
GAKU
GYUUU (GRIP)
IT'S OVER...I'M FINISHED...
GAKU
I'M SORRY! PLEASE, FORGIVE ME!
I'LL TRY HARDER! I'LL DO ANY-THING!
JUST PLEASE—ANYTHING BUT THIS!
PLEASE, PLEASE SAVE ME...!

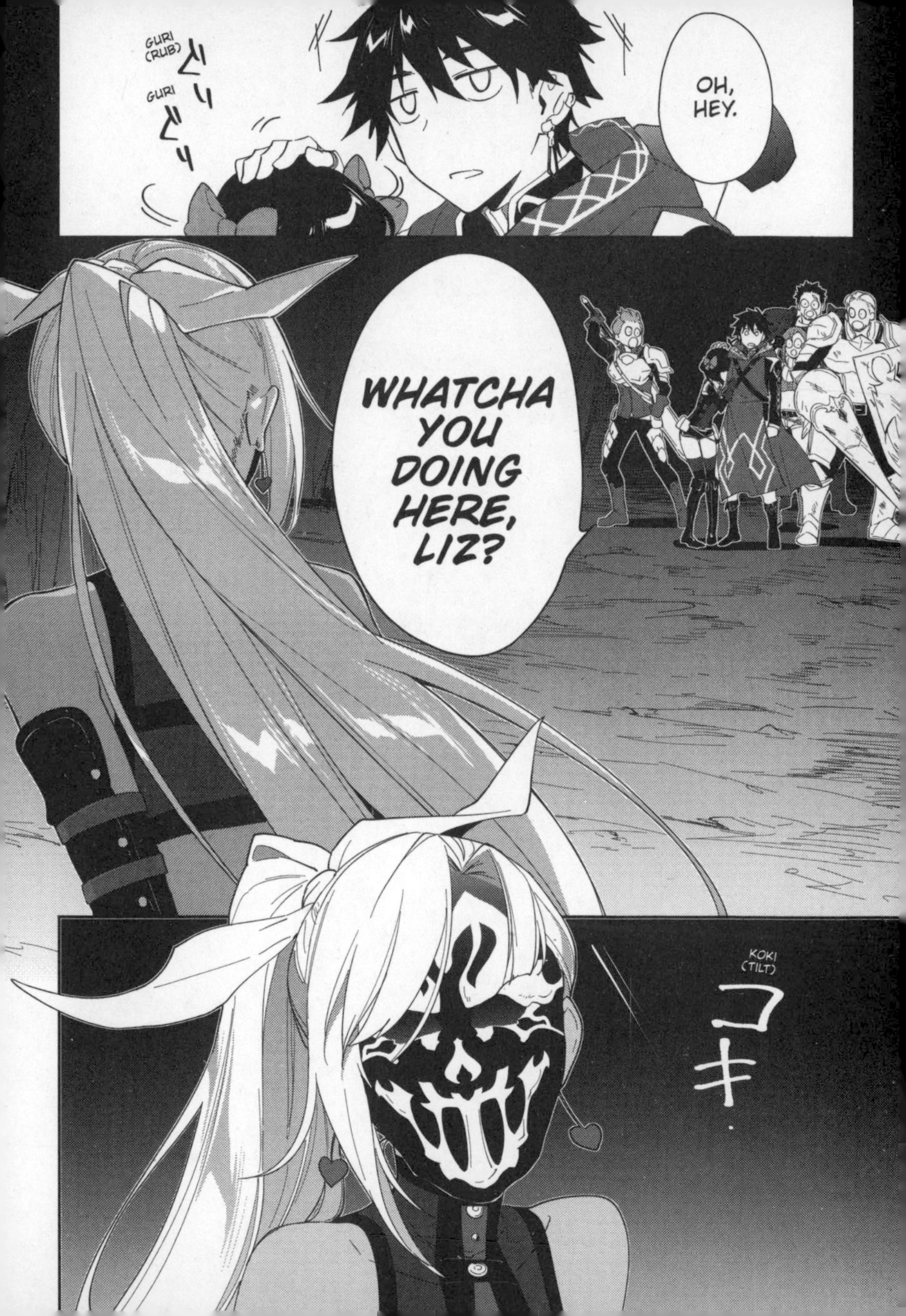
OH, HEY.
GURI (RUB)
ぐり
GURI
ぐり
WHATCHA YOU DOING HERE, LIZ?
KOKI (TILT)
コキ

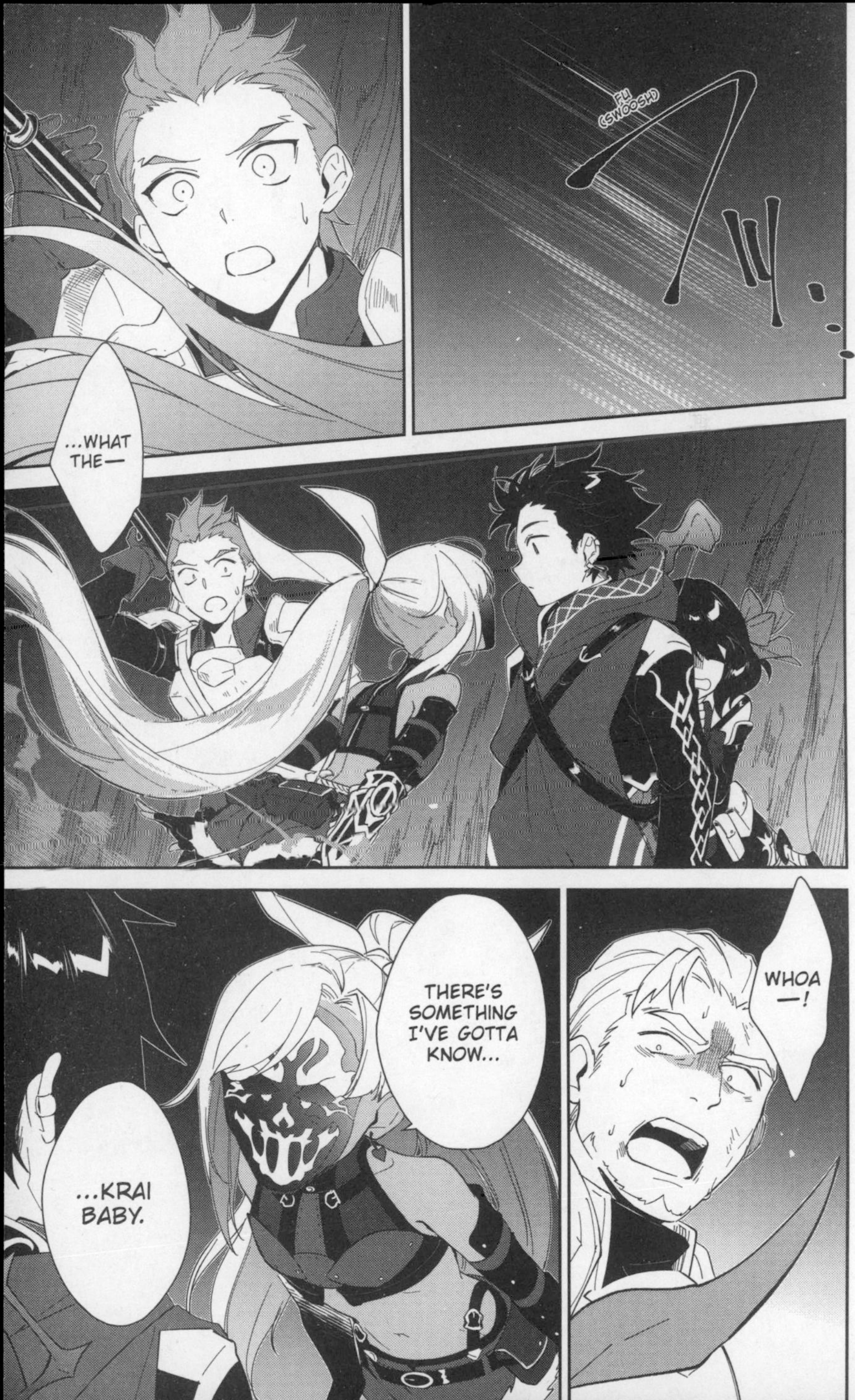
FU (SWOOSH)
...WHAT THE—
WHOA—!
THERE'S SOMETHING I'VE GOTTA KNOW...
...KRAI BABY.

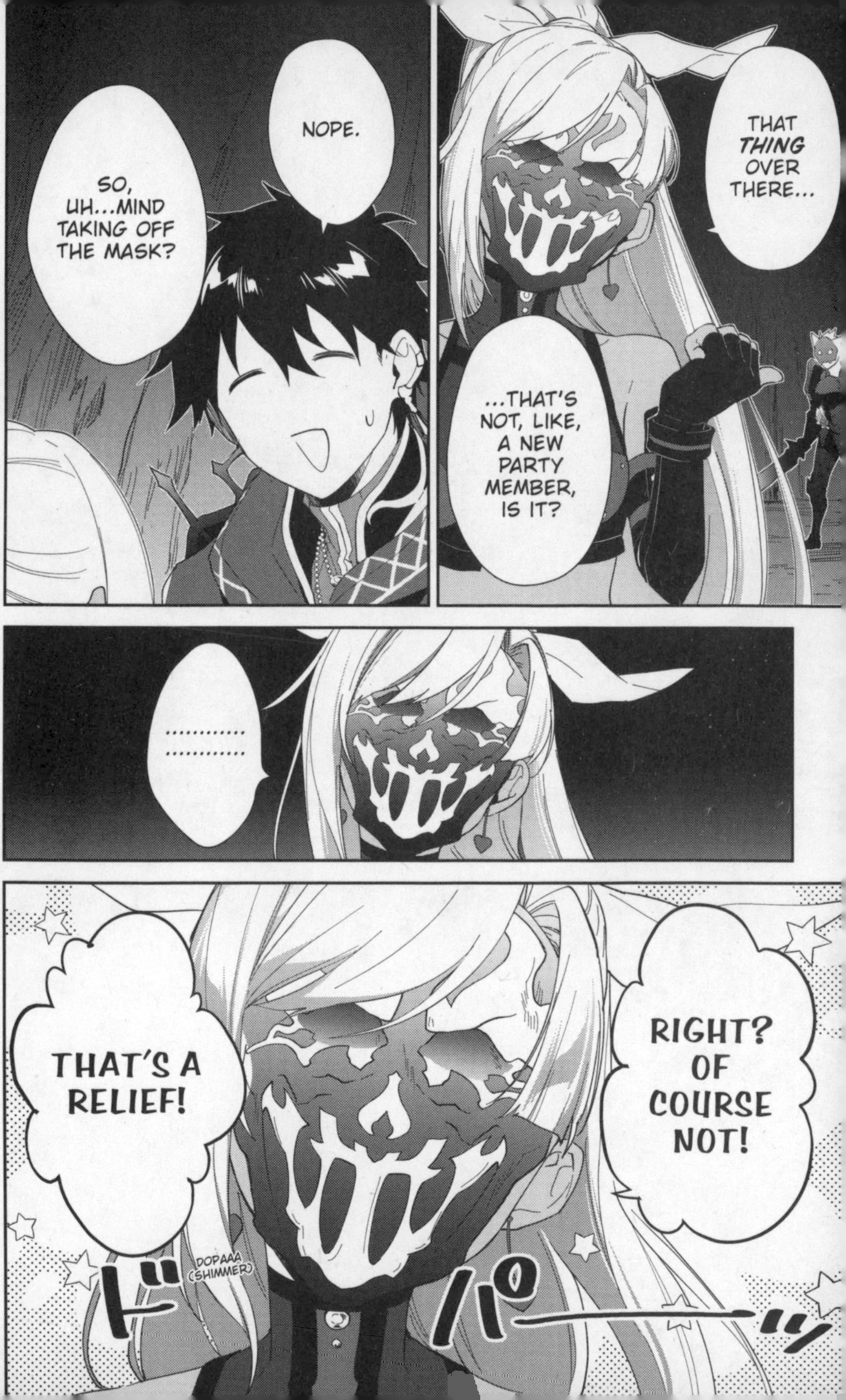
THAT *THING* OVER THERE...
...THAT'S NOT, LIKE, A NEW PARTY MEMBER, IS IT?
NOPE.
SO, UH...MIND TAKING OFF THE MASK?
....
....
RIGHT? OF COURSE NOT!
THAT'S A RELIEF!
DOPAAA (SHIMMER)

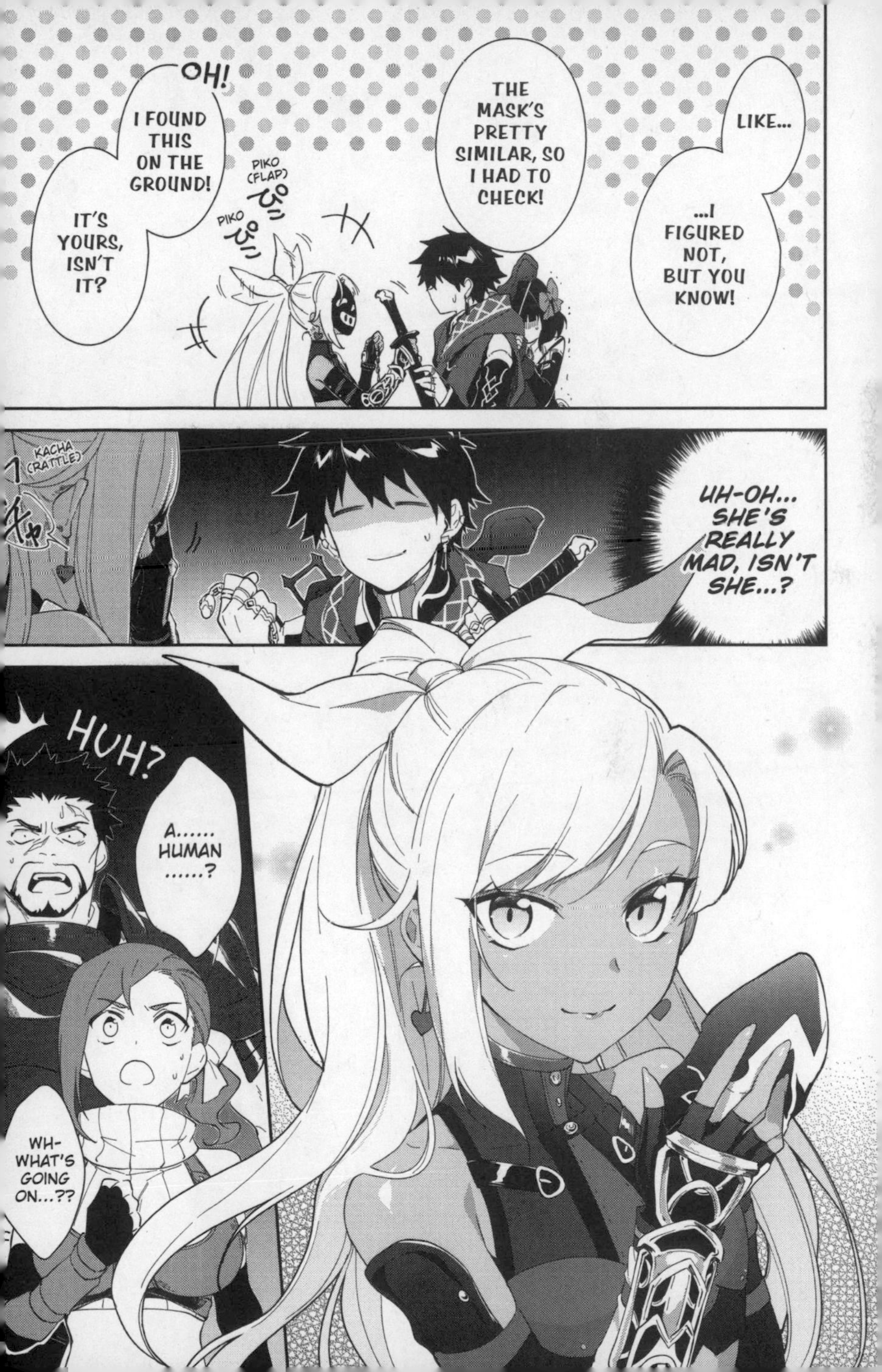

LIKE... ...I FIGURED NOT, BUT YOU KNOW!
THE MASK'S PRETTY SIMILAR, SO I HAD TO CHECK!
PIKO (FLAP)
PIKO
OH! I FOUND THIS ON THE GROUND! IT'S YOURS, ISN'T IT?
UH-OH... SHE'S REALLY MAD, ISN'T SHE...?
KACHA (RATTLE)
HUH?
A...... HUMAN ......?
WH- WHAT'S GOING ON...??

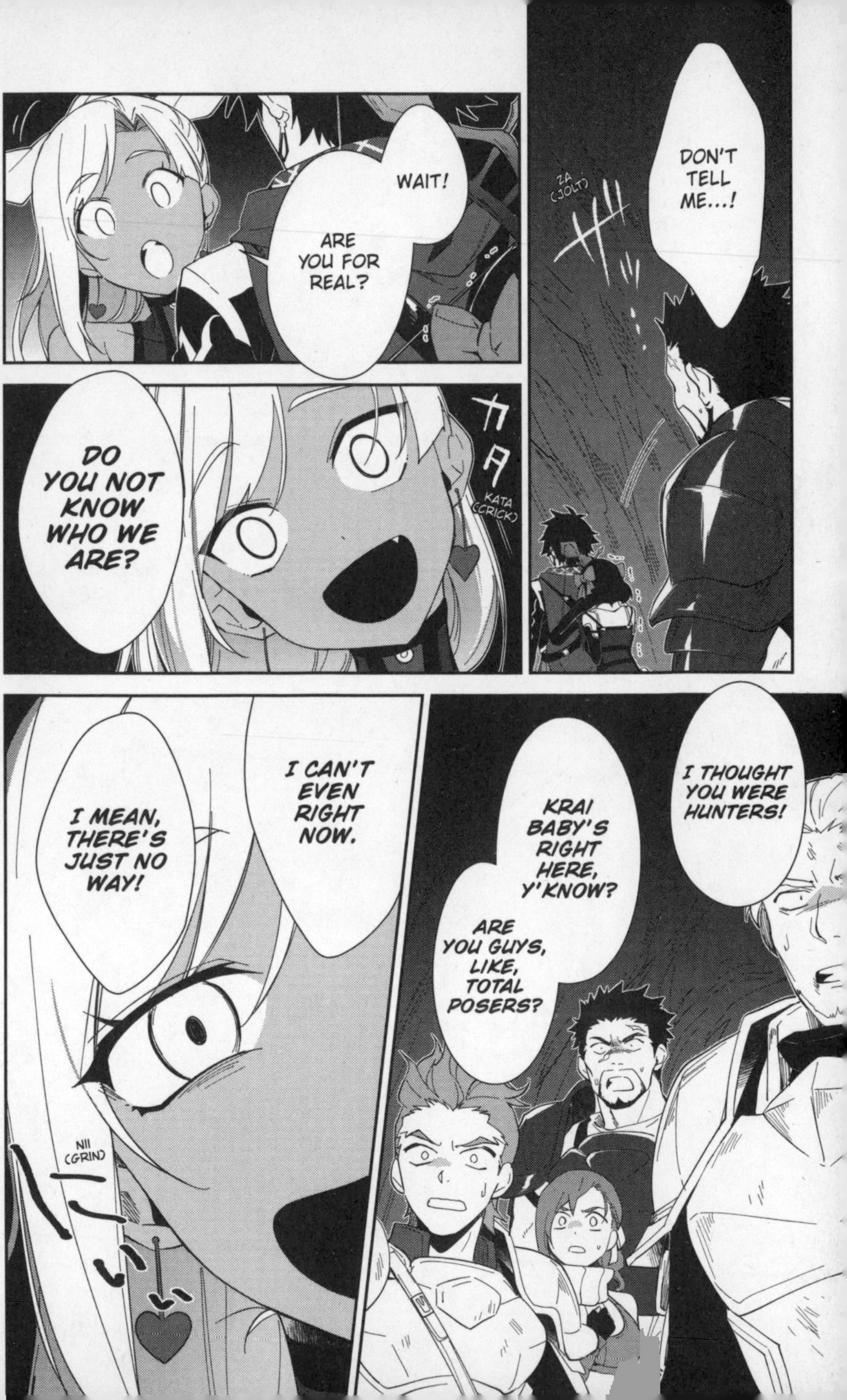
DON'T TELL ME...!
ZA (JOLT)
WAIT!
ARE YOU FOR REAL?
DO YOU NOT KNOW WHO WE ARE?
カタ
KATA (CRICK)
I THOUGHT YOU WERE HUNTERS!
KRAI BABY'S RIGHT HERE, Y'KNOW?
ARE YOU GUYS, LIKE, TOTAL POSERS?
I CAN'T EVEN RIGHT NOW.
I MEAN, THERE'S JUST NO WAY!
NII (GRIN)

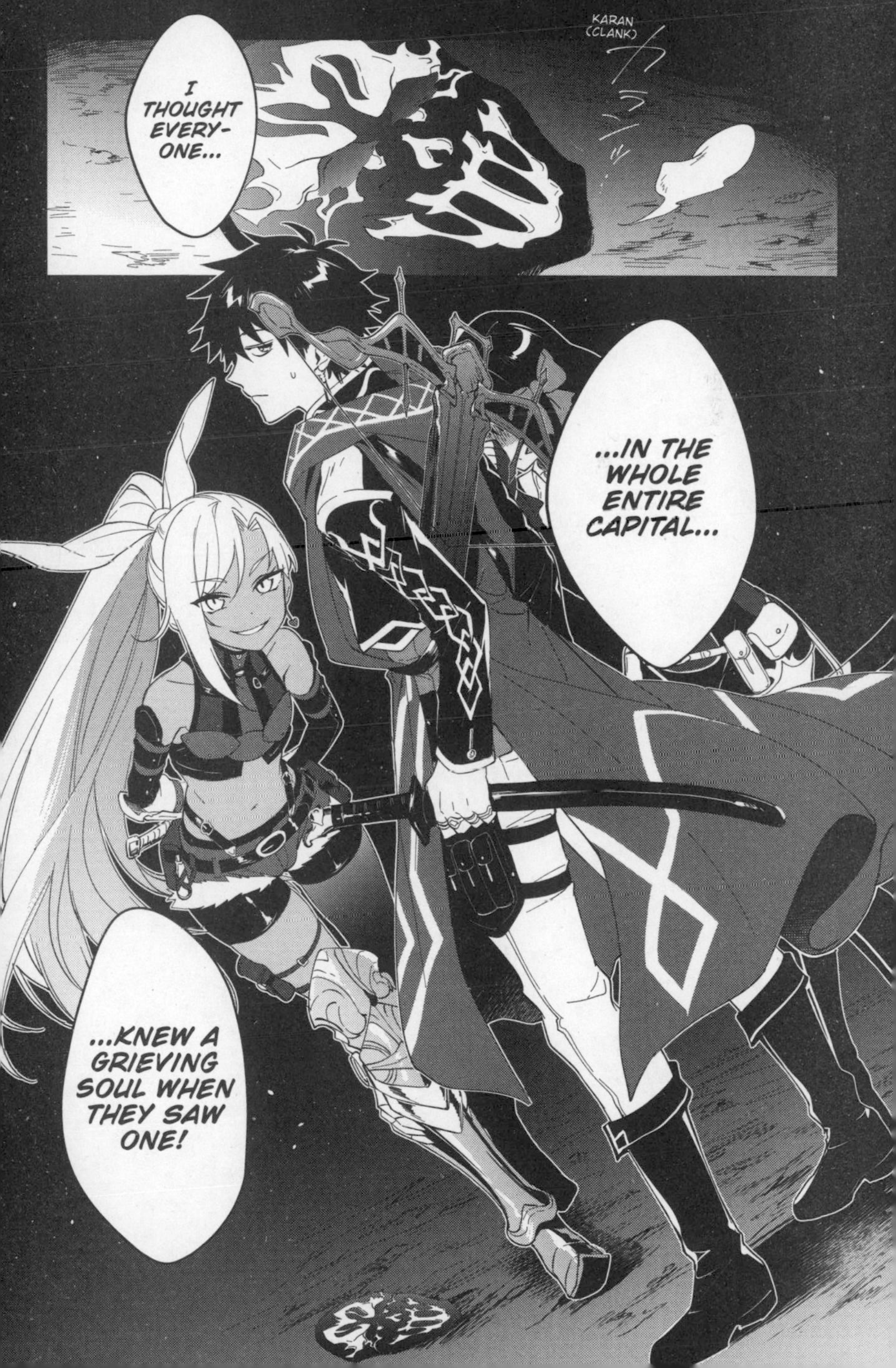
KARAN (CLANK)
I THOUGHT EVERY-ONE...
...IN THE WHOLE ENTIRE CAPITAL...
...KNEW A GRIEVING SOUL WHEN THEY SAW ONE!

LET THIS
Grieving Soul Retire

WOE IS THE WEAKLING WHO LEADS THE STRONGEST PARTY

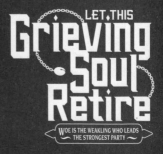

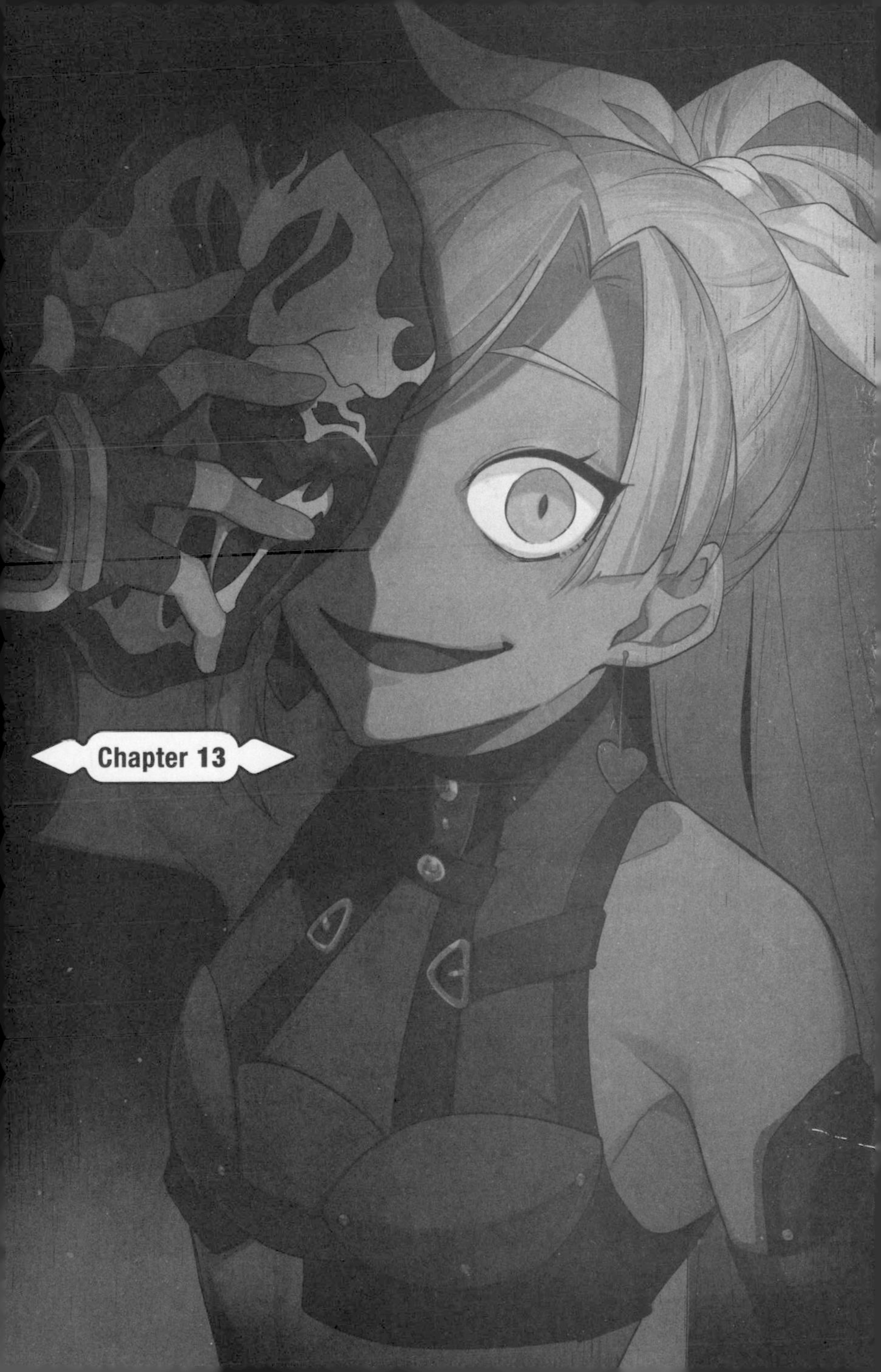
Chapter 13

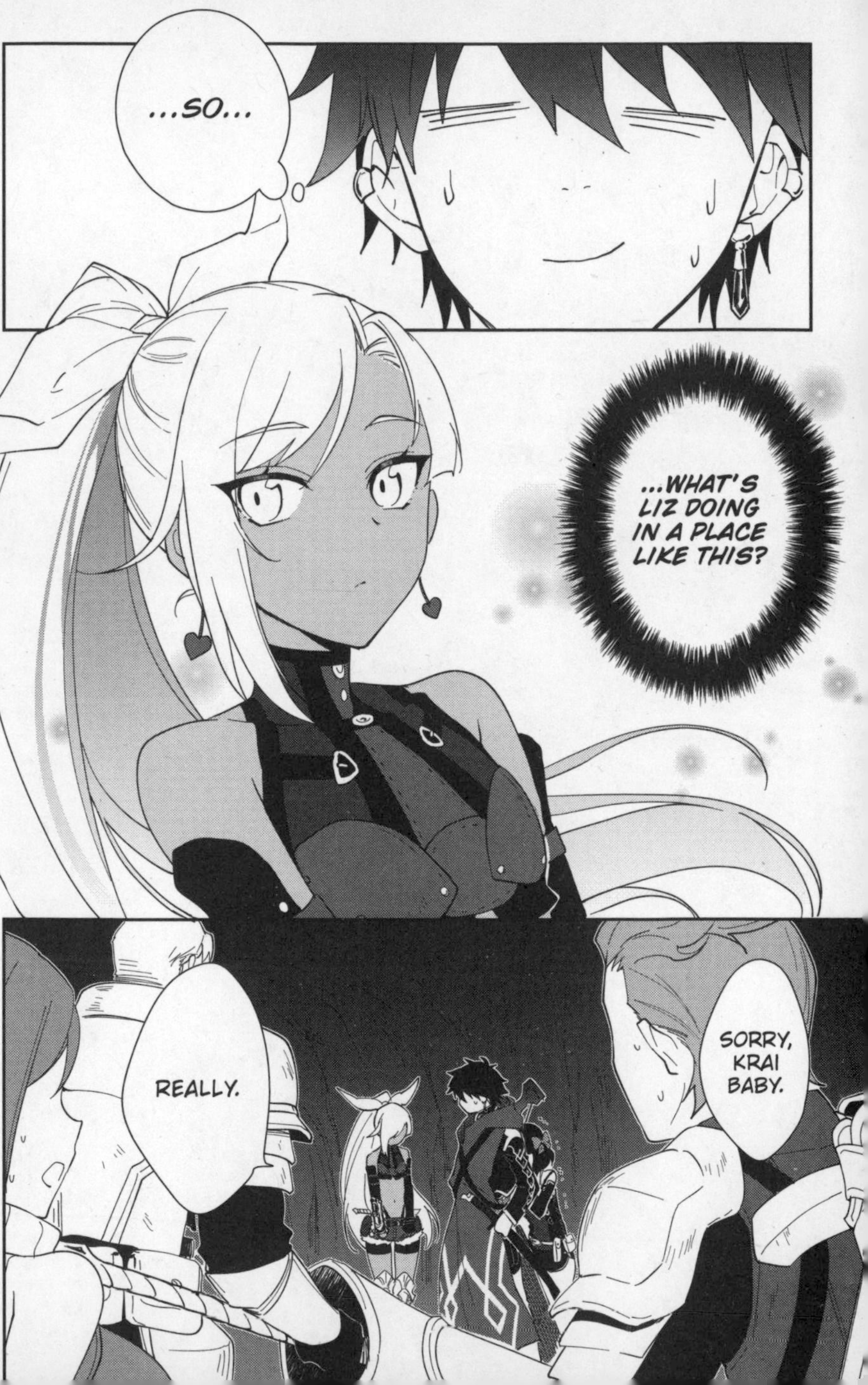
...SO...
...WHAT'S LIZ DOING IN A PLACE LIKE THIS?
SORRY, KRAI BABY.
REALLY.

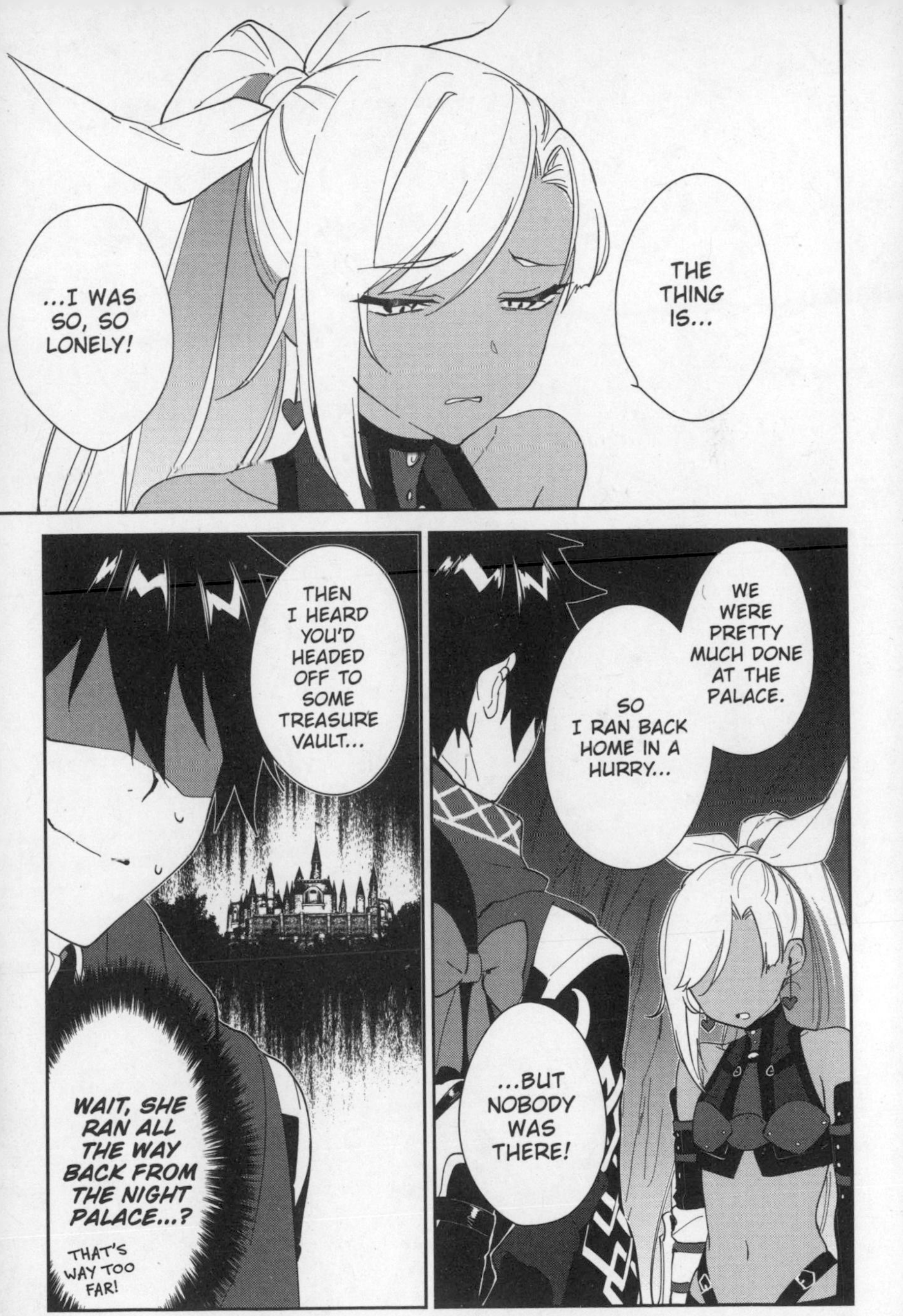
THE THING IS...
...I WAS SO, SO LONELY!
WE WERE PRETTY MUCH DONE AT THE PALACE.
SO I RAN BACK HOME IN A HURRY...
...BUT NOBODY WAS THERE!
THEN I HEARD YOU'D HEADED OFF TO SOME TREASURE VAULT...
WAIT, SHE RAN ALL THE WAY BACK FROM THE NIGHT PALACE...?
THAT'S WAY TOO FAR!

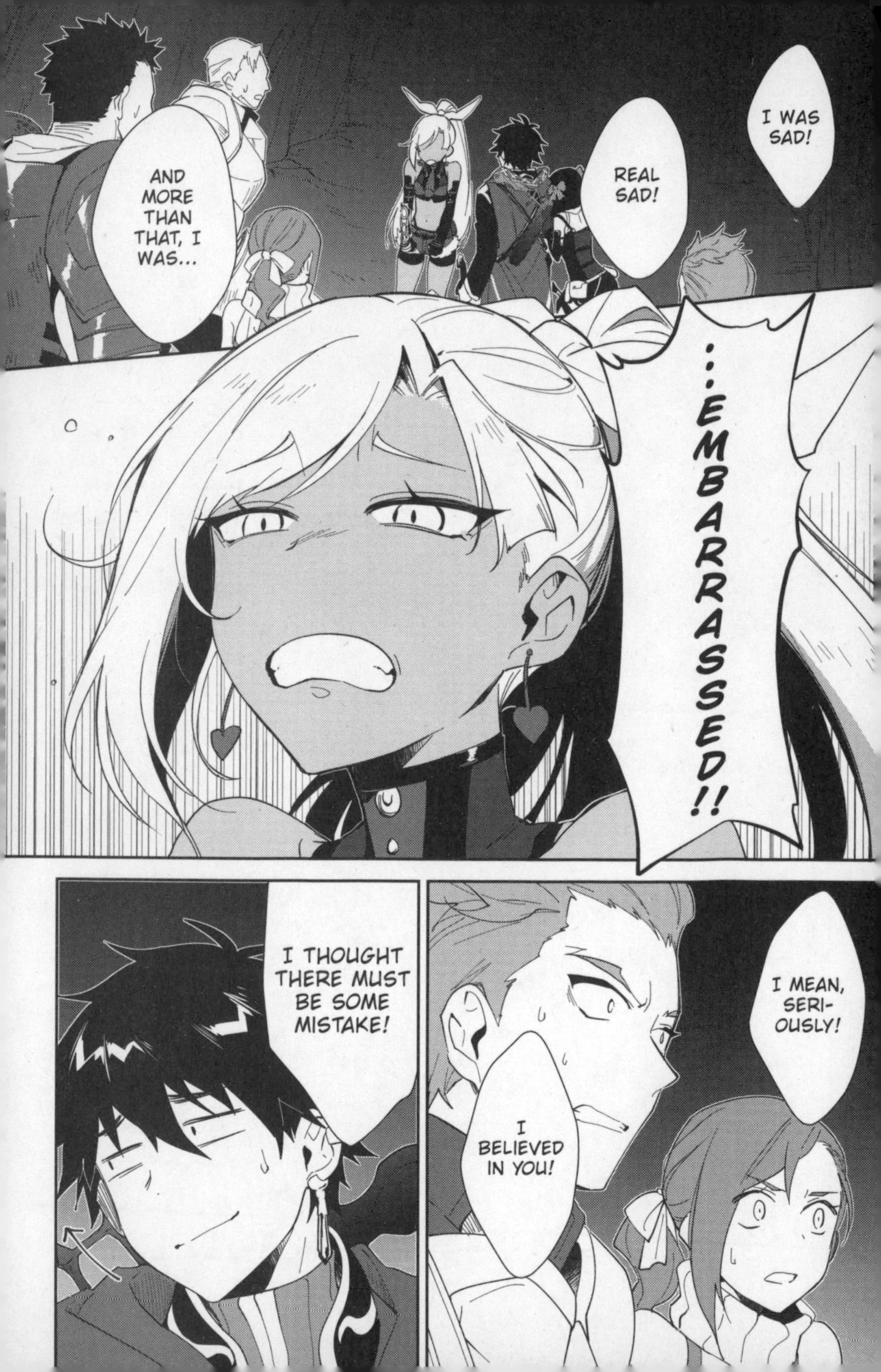
I WAS SAD!
REAL SAD!
AND MORE THAN THAT, I WAS...
...EMBARRASSED!!
I MEAN, SERIOUSLY!
I BELIEVED IN YOU!
I THOUGHT THERE MUST BE SOME MISTAKE!

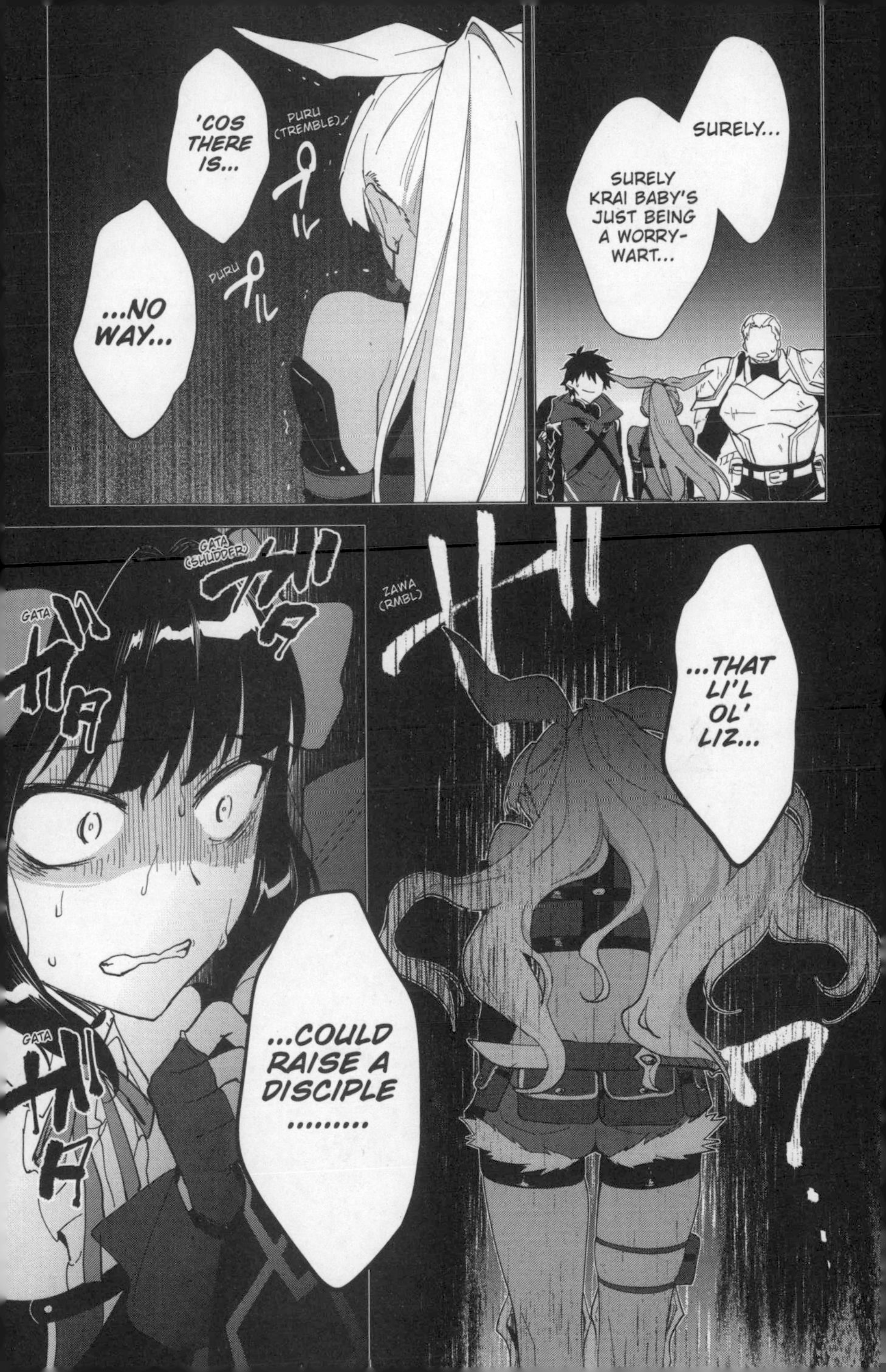
SURELY...
SURELY KRAI BABY'S JUST BEING A WORRY-WART...
PURU (TREMBLE)
'COS THERE IS...
PURU
...NO WAY...
ZAWA (RMBL)
...THAT LI'L OL' LIZ...
GATA (SHUDDER)
GATA
...COULD RAISE A DISCIPLE ....
GATA

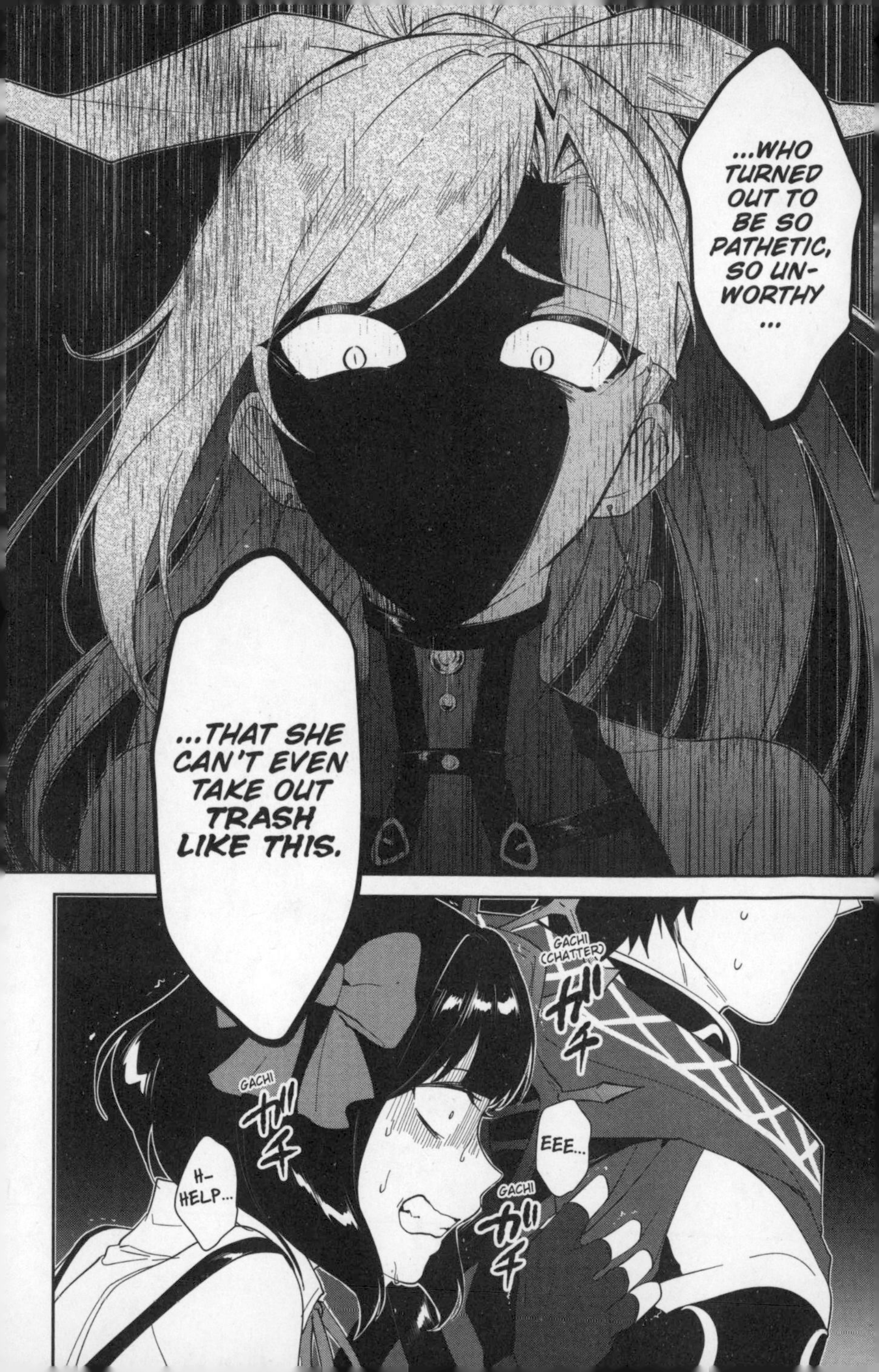
...WHO TURNED OUT TO BE SO PATHETIC, SO UN-WORTHY...
...THAT SHE CAN'T EVEN TAKE OUT TRASH LIKE THIS.
GACHI (CHATTER)
EEE...
GACHI
GACHI
H-HELP...

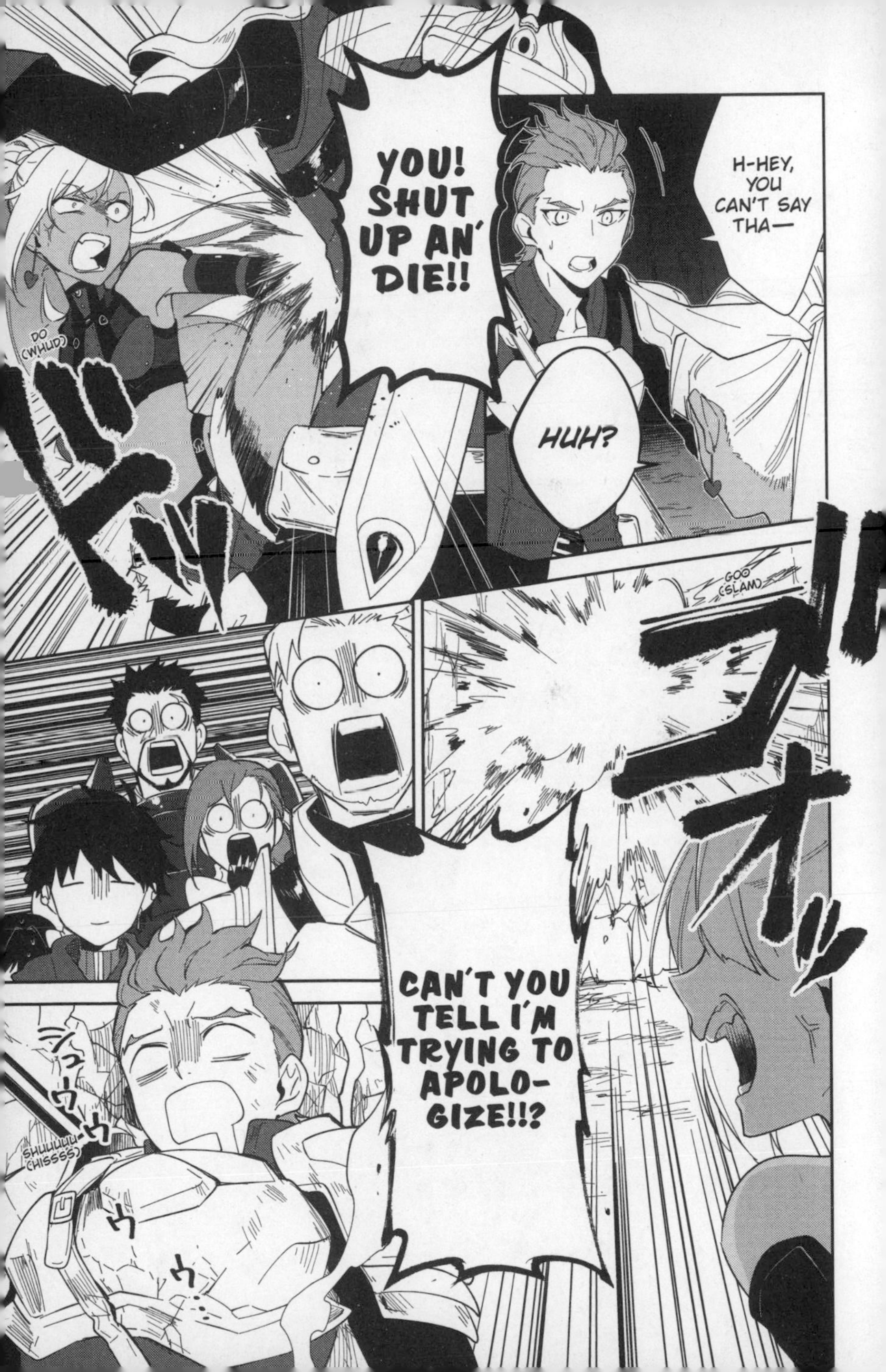
H-HEY, YOU CAN'T SAY THA—
YOU! SHUT UP AN' DIE!!
DO (WHUD)
HUH?
GOO (SLAM)
CAN'T YOU TELL I'M TRYING TO APOLO-GIZE!!?
SHUUUUU (HISSSS)

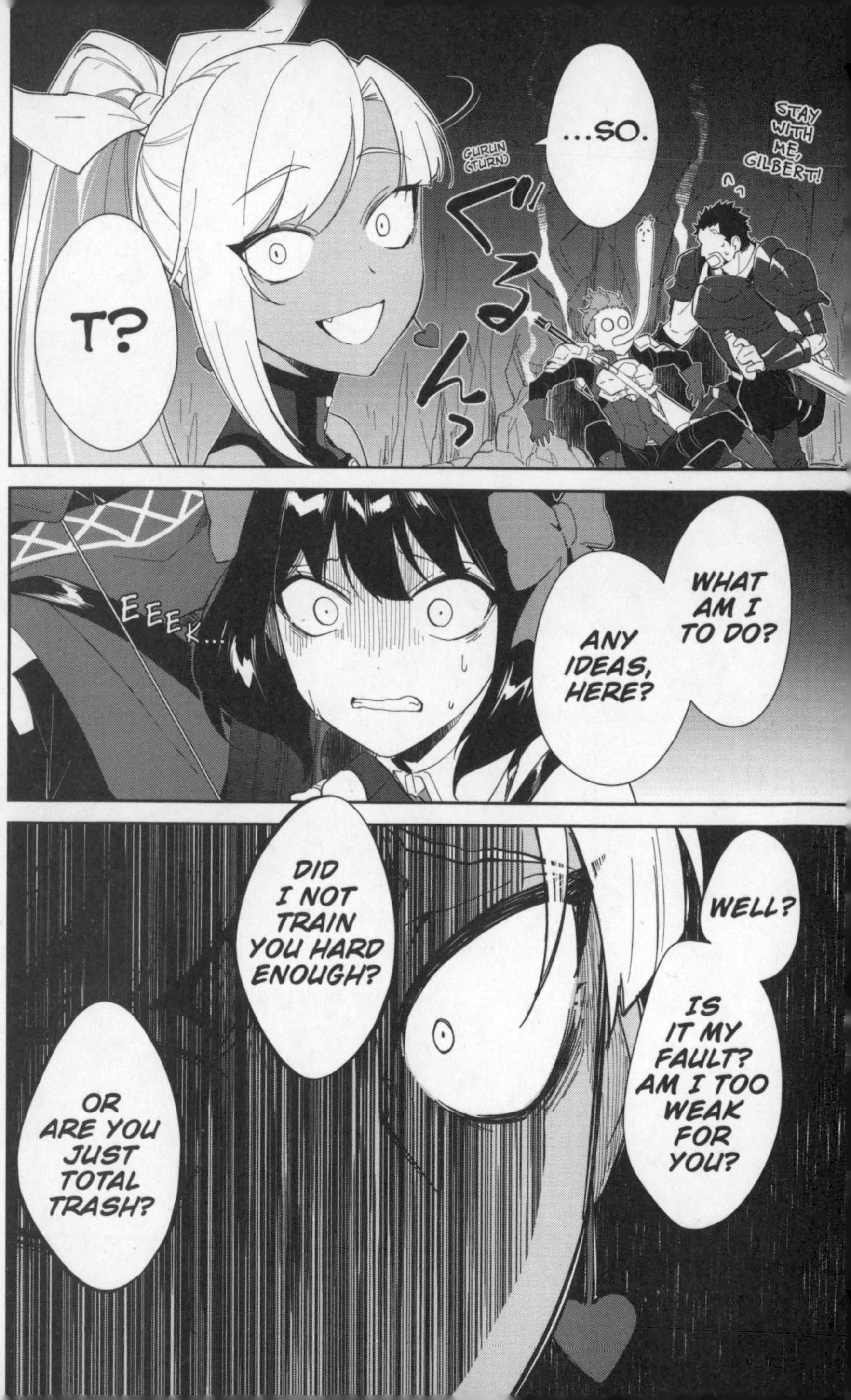
STAY WITH ME, GILBERT!
...SO.
GURUN (TURN)
T?
WHAT AM I TO DO?
ANY IDEAS, HERE?
EEEK...
WELL?
DID I NOT TRAIN YOU HARD ENOUGH?
IS IT MY FAULT? AM I TOO WEAK FOR YOU?
OR ARE YOU JUST TOTAL TRASH?

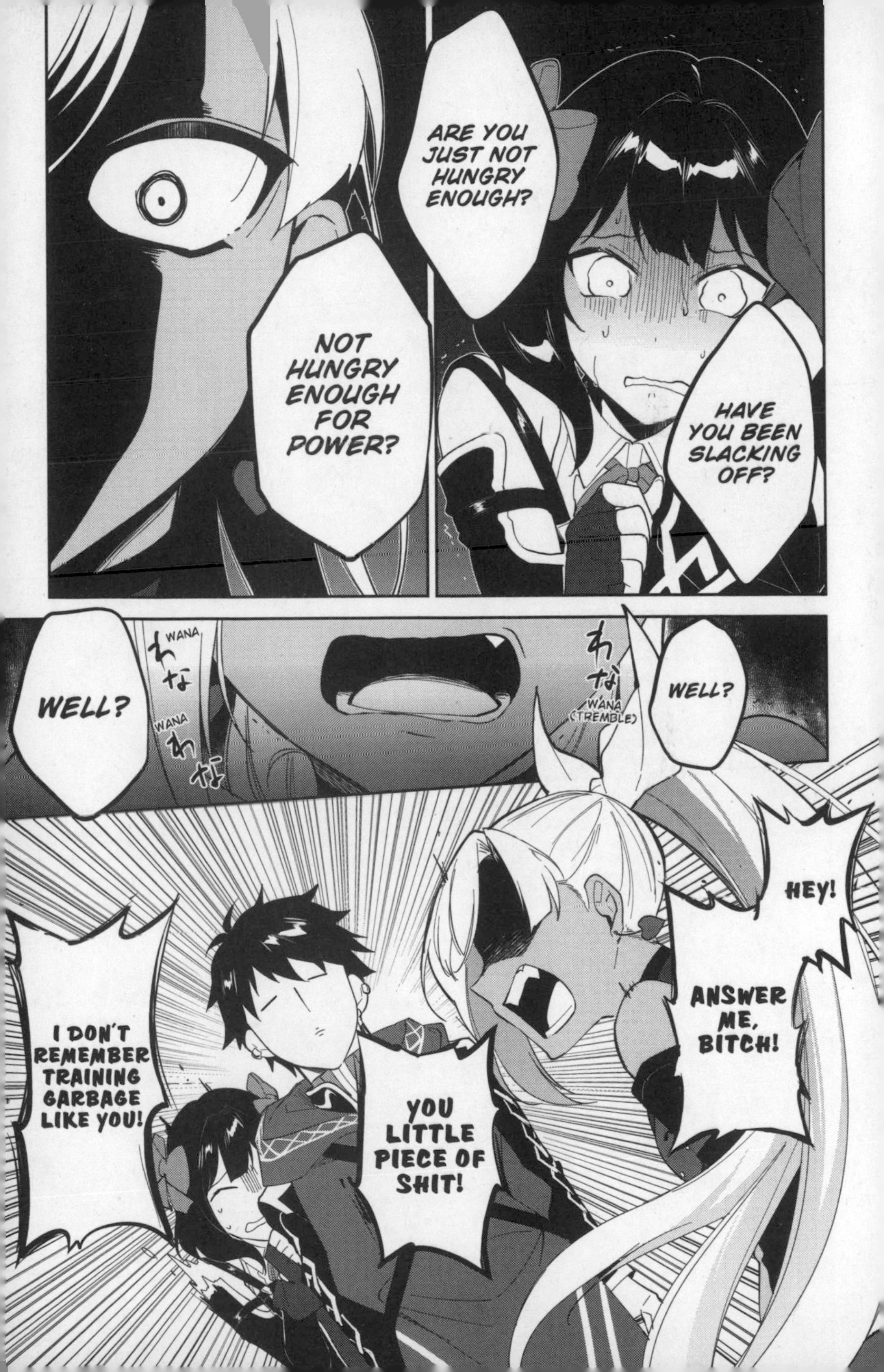

ARE YOU JUST NOT HUNGRY ENOUGH?
HAVE YOU BEEN SLACKING OFF?
NOT HUNGRY ENOUGH FOR POWER?
WELL?
わな
WANA (TREMBLE)
わな
WANA
わな
WANA
WELL?
HEY!
ANSWER ME, BITCH!
YOU LITTLE PIECE OF SHIT!
I DON'T REMEMBER TRAINING GARBAGE LIKE YOU!

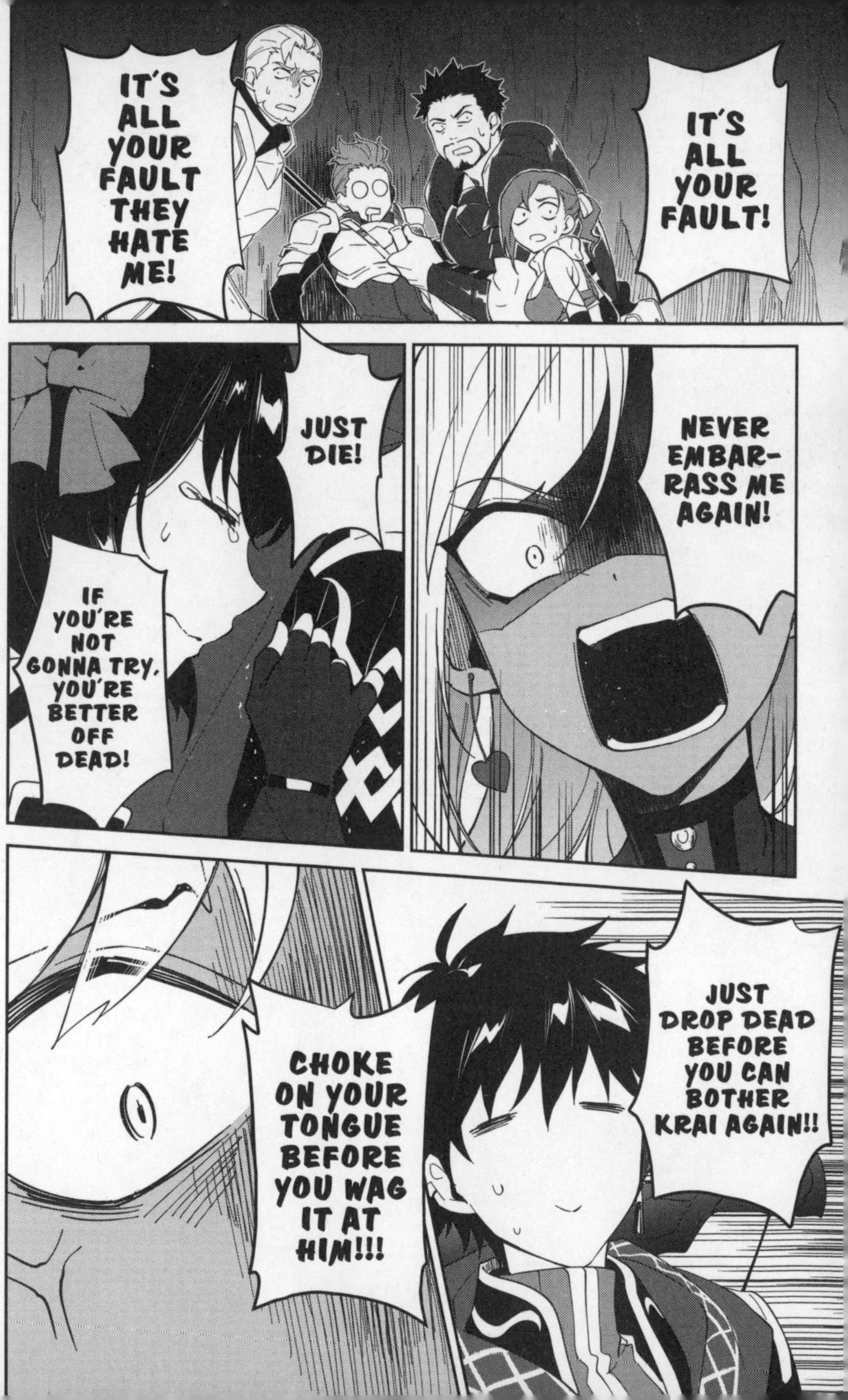
IT'S ALL YOUR FAULT!
IT'S ALL YOUR FAULT THEY HATE ME!
NEVER EMBARRASS ME AGAIN!
JUST DIE!
IF YOU'RE NOT GONNA TRY, YOU'RE BETTER OFF DEAD!
JUST DROP DEAD BEFORE YOU CAN BOTHER KRAI AGAIN!!
CHOKE ON YOUR TONGUE BEFORE YOU WAG IT AT HIM!!!

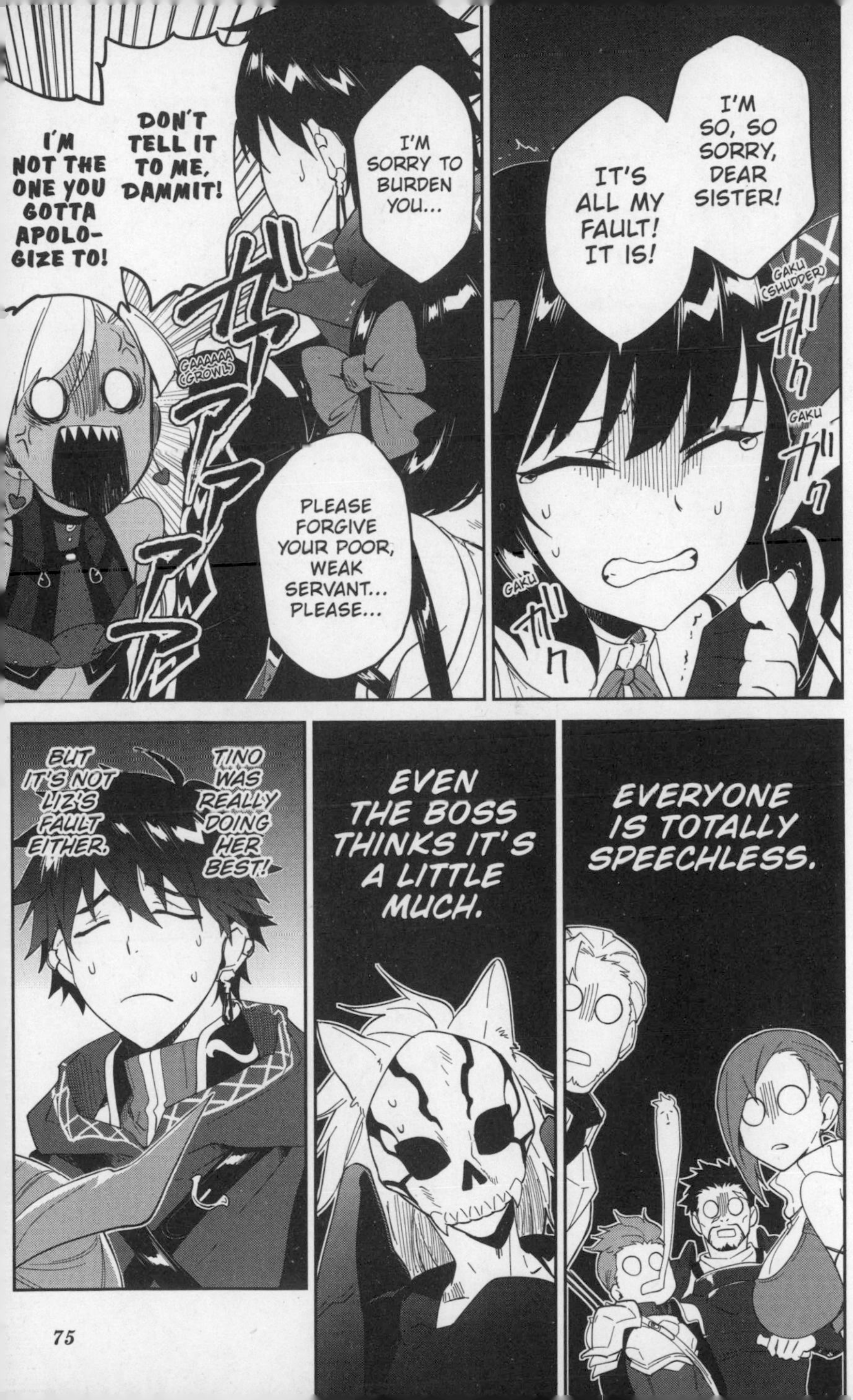
I'M SO, SO SORRY, DEAR SISTER!
IT'S ALL MY FAULT! IT IS!
GAKU (SHUDDER)
GAKU
GAKU
I'M SORRY TO BURDEN YOU...
DON'T TELL IT TO ME, DAMMIT!
I'M NOT THE ONE YOU GOTTA APOLO-GIZE TO!
GAAAAAA (GROWL)
PLEASE FORGIVE YOUR POOR, WEAK SERVANT... PLEASE...
EVERYONE IS TOTALLY SPEECHLESS.
EVEN THE BOSS THINKS IT'S A LITTLE MUCH.
TINO WAS REALLY DOING HER BEST!
BUT IT'S NOT LIZ'S FAULT EITHER.

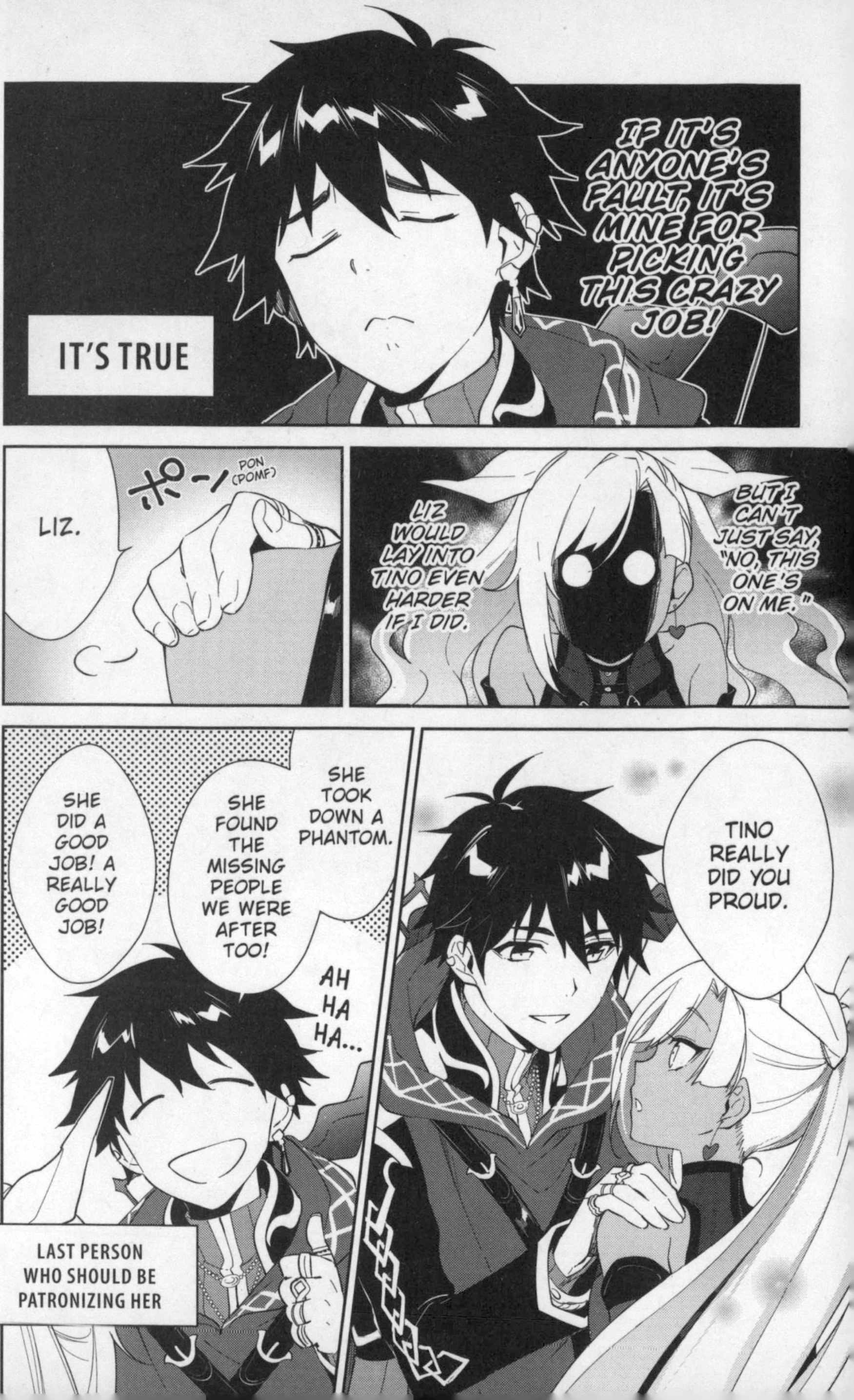
IF IT'S ANYONE'S FAULT, IT'S MINE FOR PICKING THIS CRAZY JOB!
IT'S TRUE
BUT I CAN'T JUST SAY, "NO, THIS ONE'S ON ME."
LIZ WOULD LAY INTO TINO EVEN HARDER IF I DID.
PON (POMF)
LIZ.
TINO REALLY DID YOU PROUD.
SHE TOOK DOWN A PHANTOM.
SHE FOUND THE MISSING PEOPLE WE WERE AFTER TOO!
SHE DID A GOOD JOB! A REALLY GOOD JOB!
AH HA HA...
LAST PERSON WHO SHOULD BE PATRONIZING HER

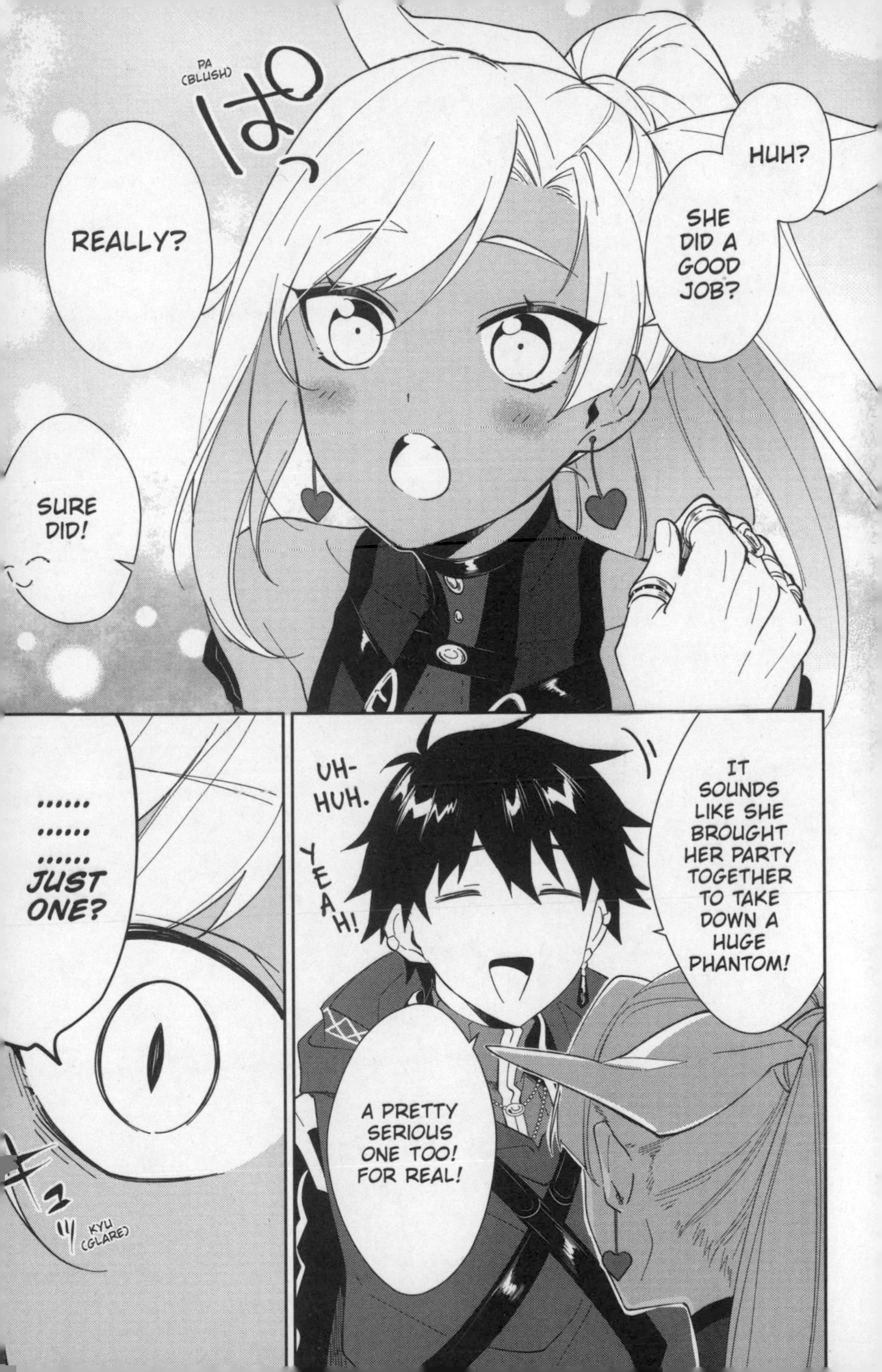
HUH?
SHE DID A GOOD JOB?
PA (BLUSH)
REALLY?
SURE DID!
IT SOUNDS LIKE SHE BROUGHT HER PARTY TOGETHER TO TAKE DOWN A HUGE PHANTOM!
UH-HUH.
YEAH!
A PRETTY SERIOUS ONE TOO! FOR REAL!
.... JUST ONE?
KYU (GLARE)

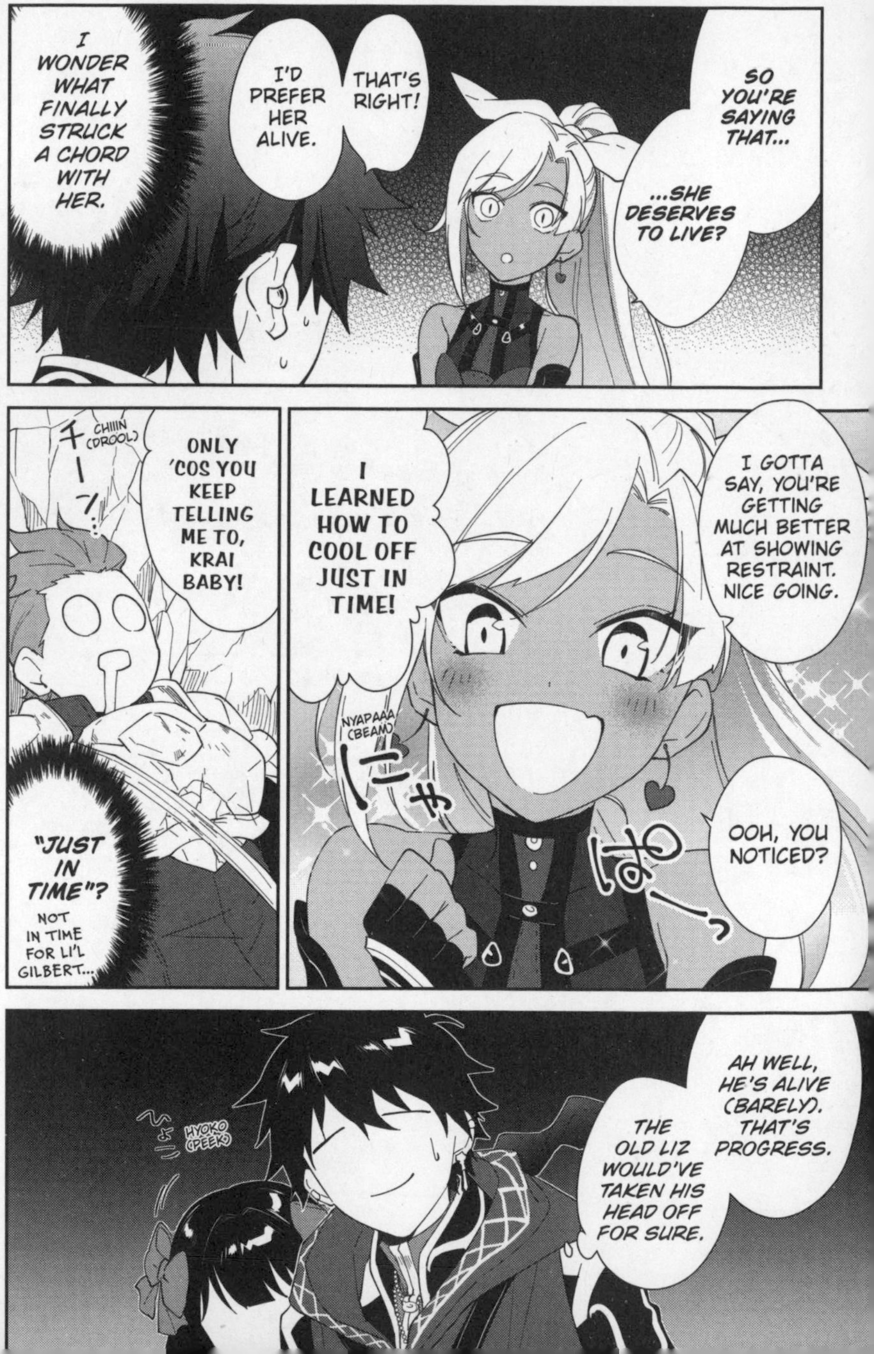

SO YOU'RE SAYING THAT...
...SHE DESERVES TO LIVE?
THAT'S RIGHT!
I'D PREFER HER ALIVE.
I WONDER WHAT FINALLY STRUCK A CHORD WITH HER.
I GOTTA SAY, YOU'RE GETTING MUCH BETTER AT SHOWING RESTRAINT. NICE GOING.
OOH, YOU NOTICED?
NYAPAAA (BEAM)
I LEARNED HOW TO COOL OFF JUST IN TIME!
ONLY 'COS YOU KEEP TELLING ME TO, KRAI BABY!
CHIIIN (DROOL)
"JUST IN TIME"? NOT IN TIME FOR LI'L GILBERT...
AH WELL, HE'S ALIVE (BARELY). THAT'S PROGRESS.
THE OLD LIZ WOULD'VE TAKEN HIS HEAD OFF FOR SURE.
HYOKO (PEEK)

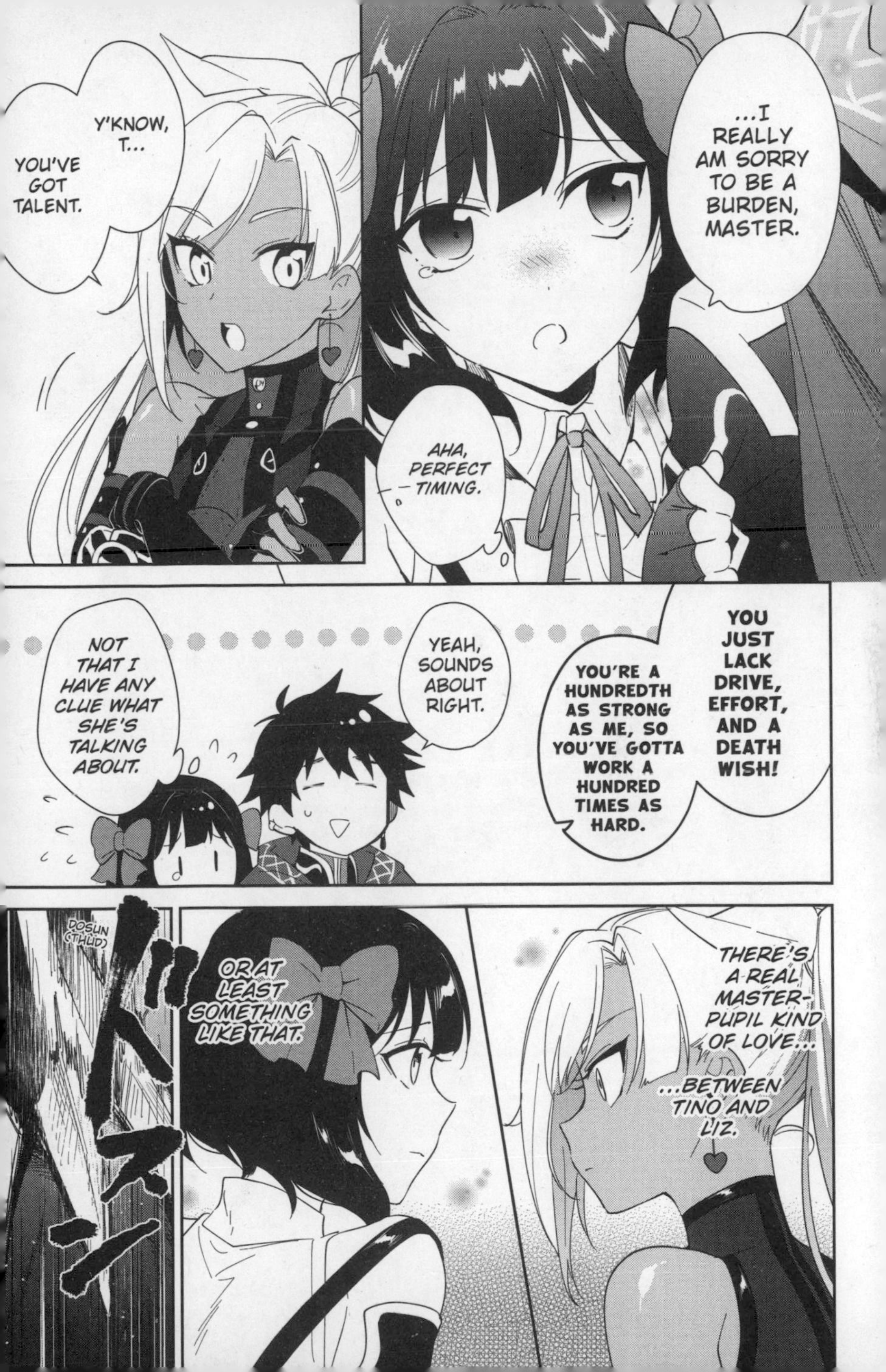
...I REALLY AM SORRY TO BE A BURDEN, MASTER.
AHA, PERFECT TIMING.
Y'KNOW, T...
YOU'VE GOT TALENT.
YOU JUST LACK DRIVE, EFFORT, AND A DEATH WISH!
YOU'RE A HUNDREDTH AS STRONG AS ME, SO YOU'VE GOTTA WORK A HUNDRED TIMES AS HARD.
YEAH, SOUNDS ABOUT RIGHT.
NOT THAT I HAVE ANY CLUE WHAT SHE'S TALKING ABOUT.
THERE'S A REAL MASTER-PUPIL KIND OF LOVE...
...BETWEEN TINO AND LIZ.
OR AT LEAST SOMETHING LIKE THAT.
DOSUN (THUD)

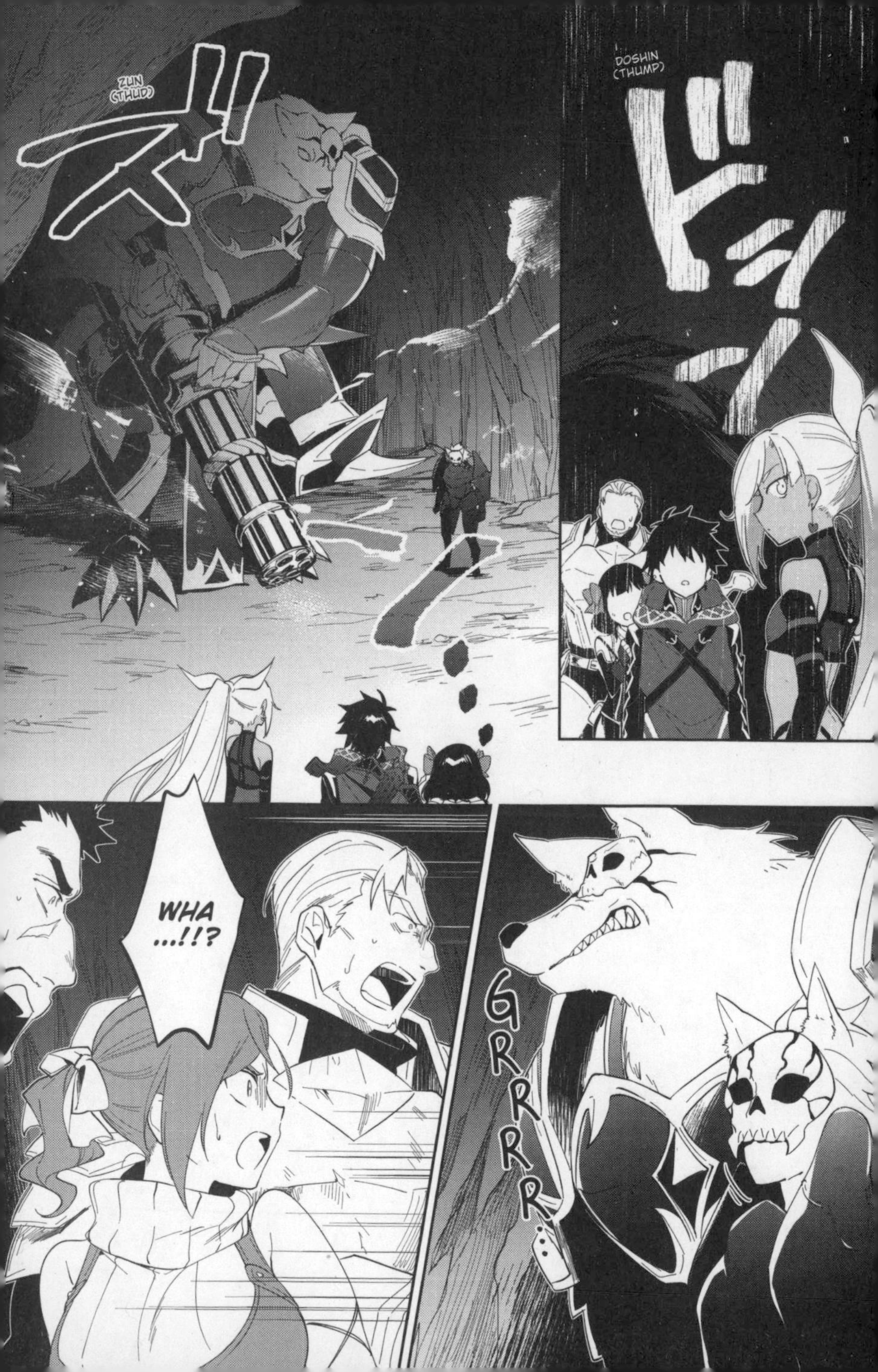
DOSHIN (THUMP)
ZUN (THUD)
GRRRR...
WHA ...!!?

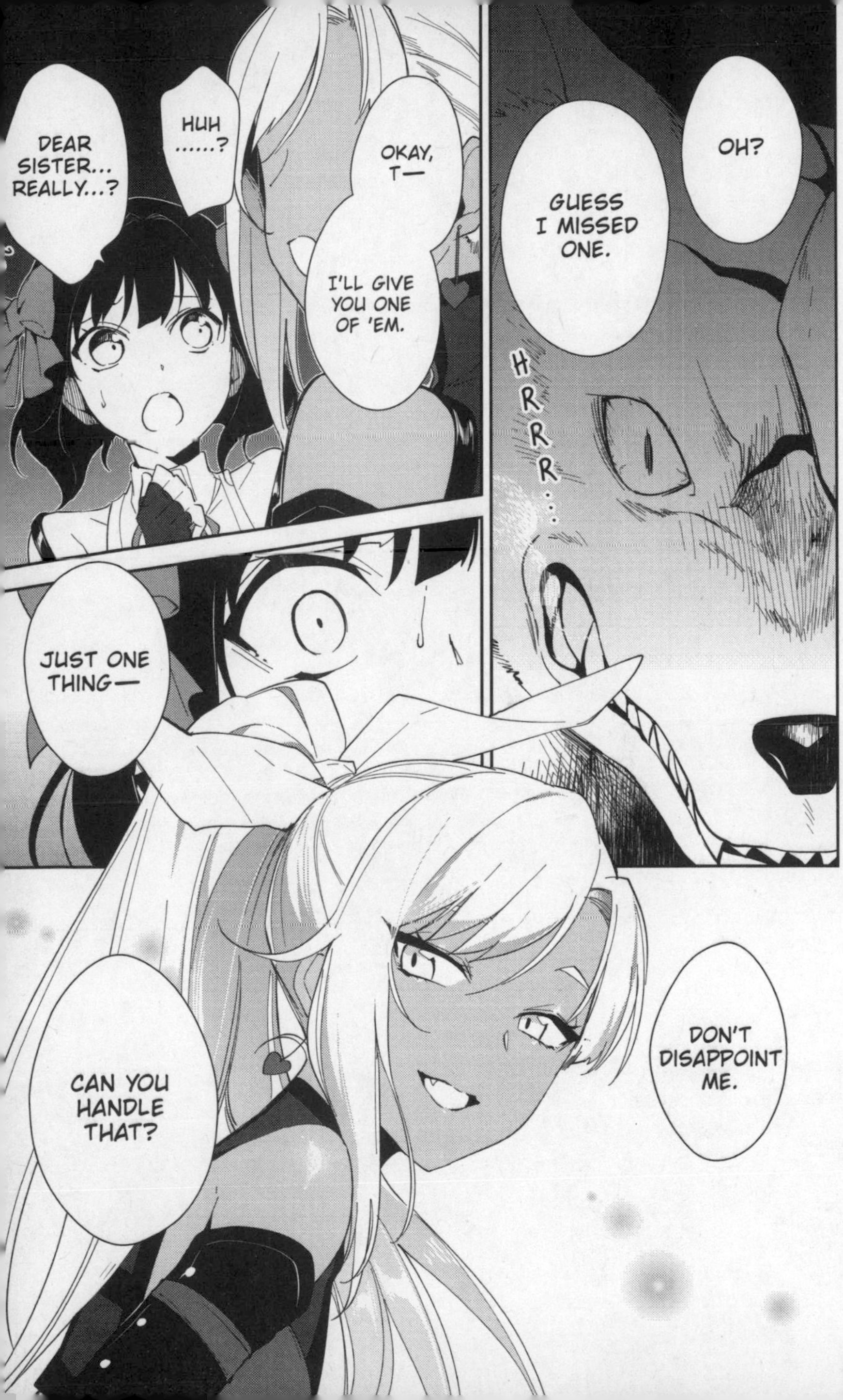
OH?
GUESS I MISSED ONE.
HRRR...
OKAY, T—
I'LL GIVE YOU ONE OF 'EM.
HUH......?
DEAR SISTER... REALLY...?
JUST ONE THING—
DON'T DISAPPOINT ME.
CAN YOU HANDLE THAT?

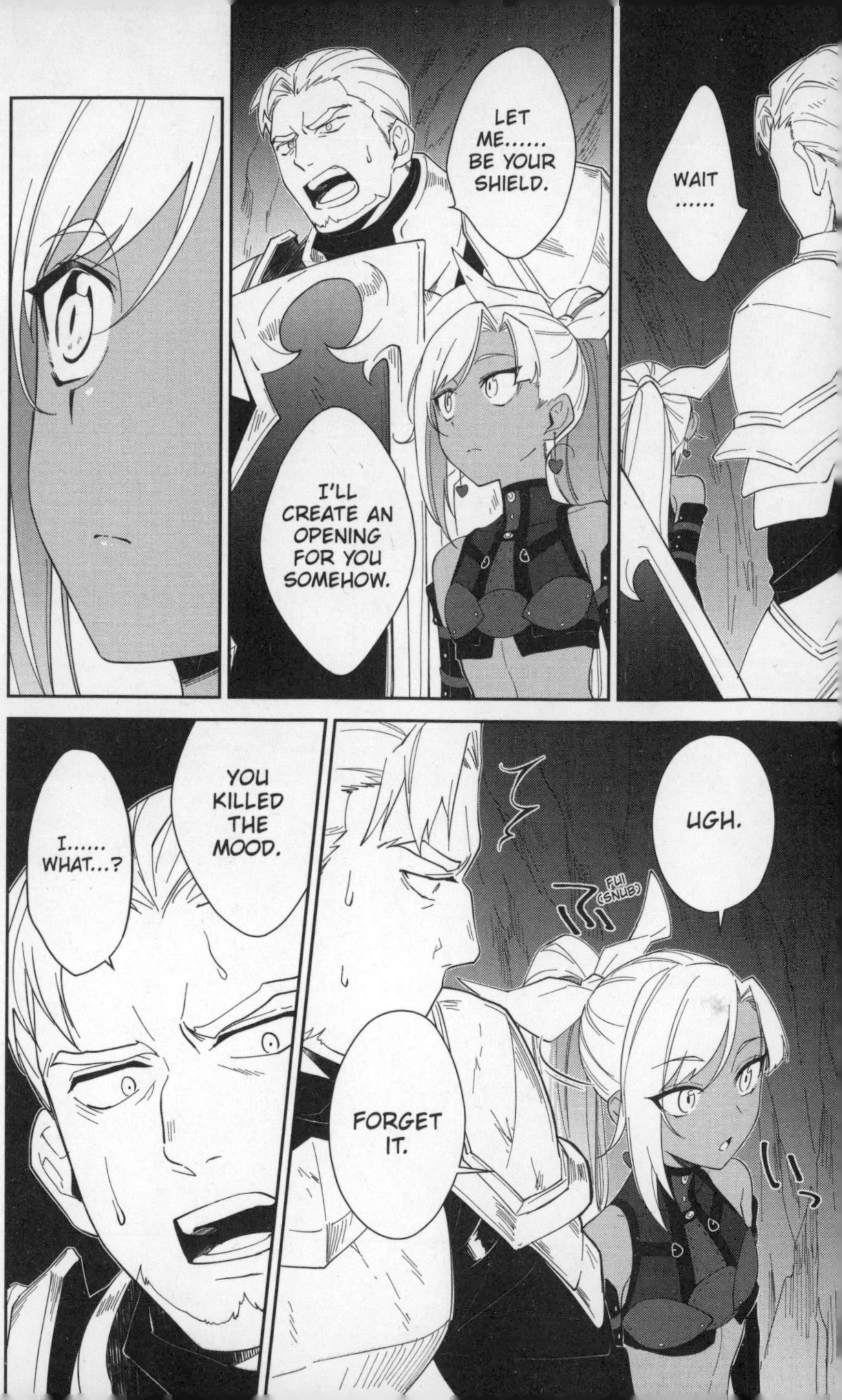
WAIT ......
LET ME...... BE YOUR SHIELD.
I'LL CREATE AN OPENING FOR YOU SOMEHOW.
UGH.
FUI (SNUB)
FORGET IT.
YOU KILLED THE MOOD.
I...... WHAT...?

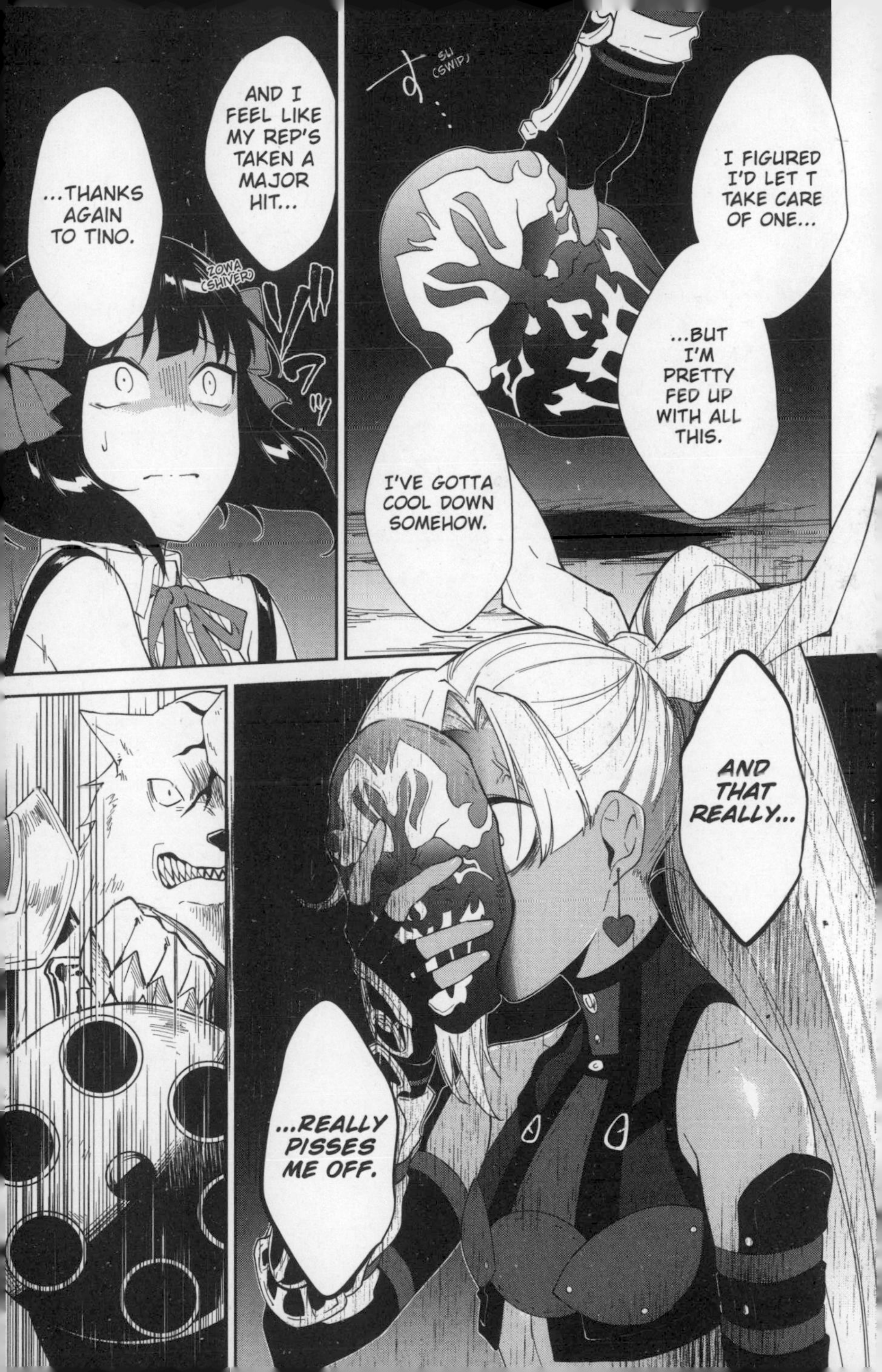
SU
(SWIP)
I FIGURED I'D LET T TAKE CARE OF ONE...
...BUT I'M PRETTY FED UP WITH ALL THIS.
I'VE GOTTA COOL DOWN SOMEHOW.
AND I FEEL LIKE MY REP'S TAKEN A MAJOR HIT...
...THANKS AGAIN TO TINO.
ZOWA
(SHIVER)
AND THAT REALLY...
...REALLY PISSES ME OFF.

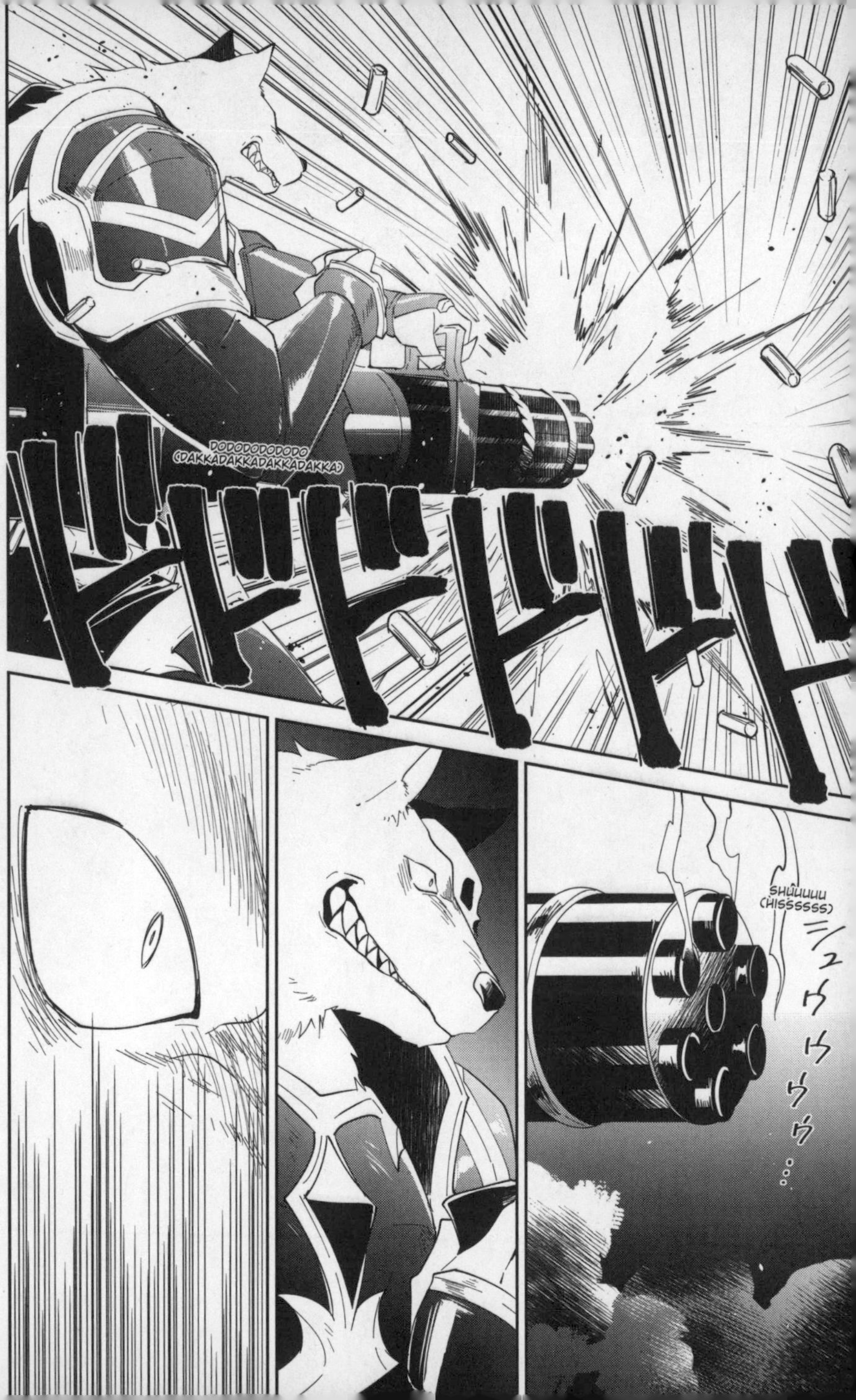
DODODODODODO
(DAKKADAKKADAKKADAKKA)
ドドドドドドドドドドド
SHUUUUU
(HISSSSSS)
シュウウウウ…

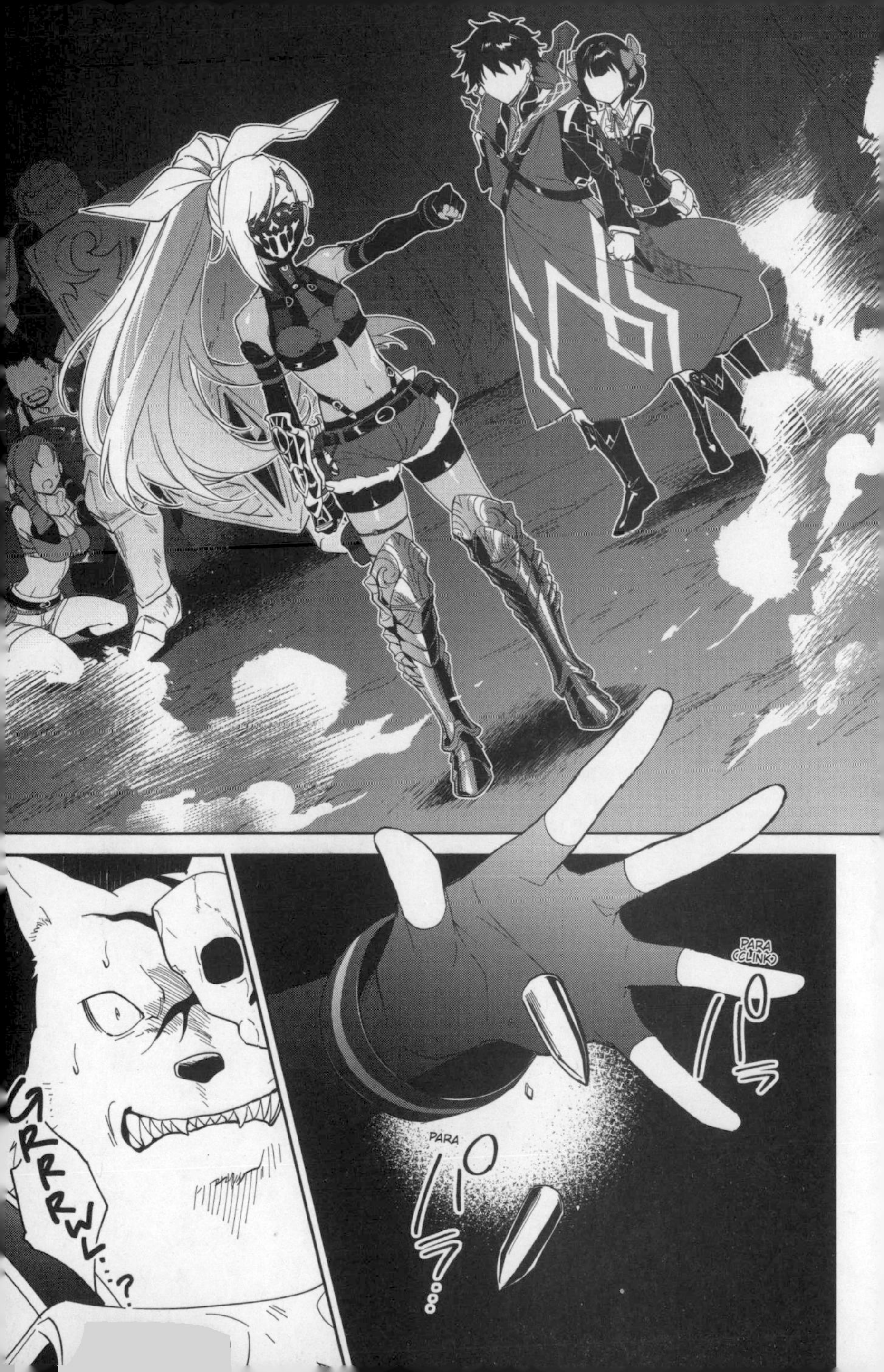
PARA
(CLINK)
PARA
GRRRWL...?

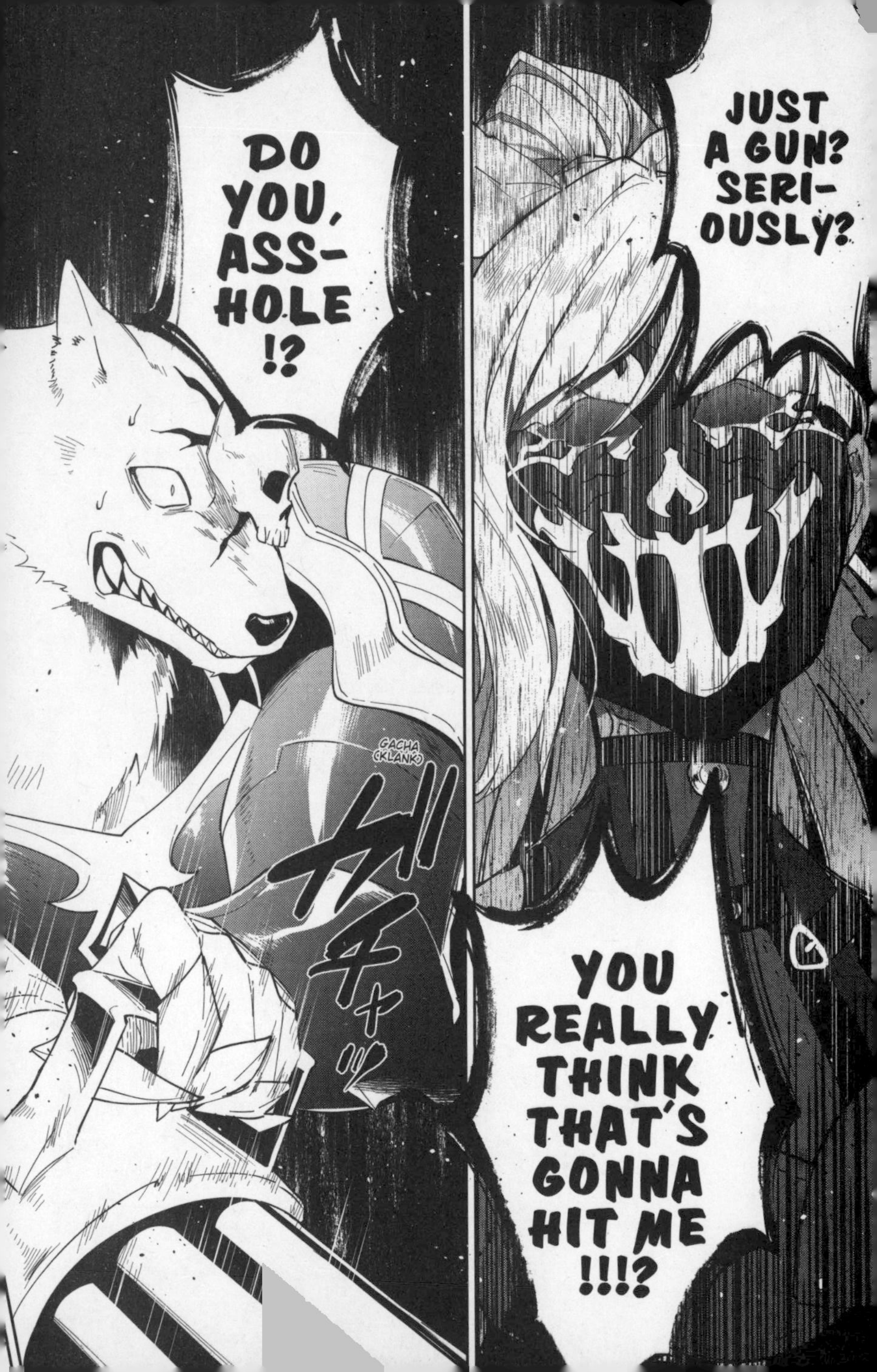
JUST A GUN? SERI-OUSLY?
YOU REALLY THINK THAT'S GONNA HIT ME !!!?
DO YOU, ASS-HOLE !?
GACHA (KLANK)

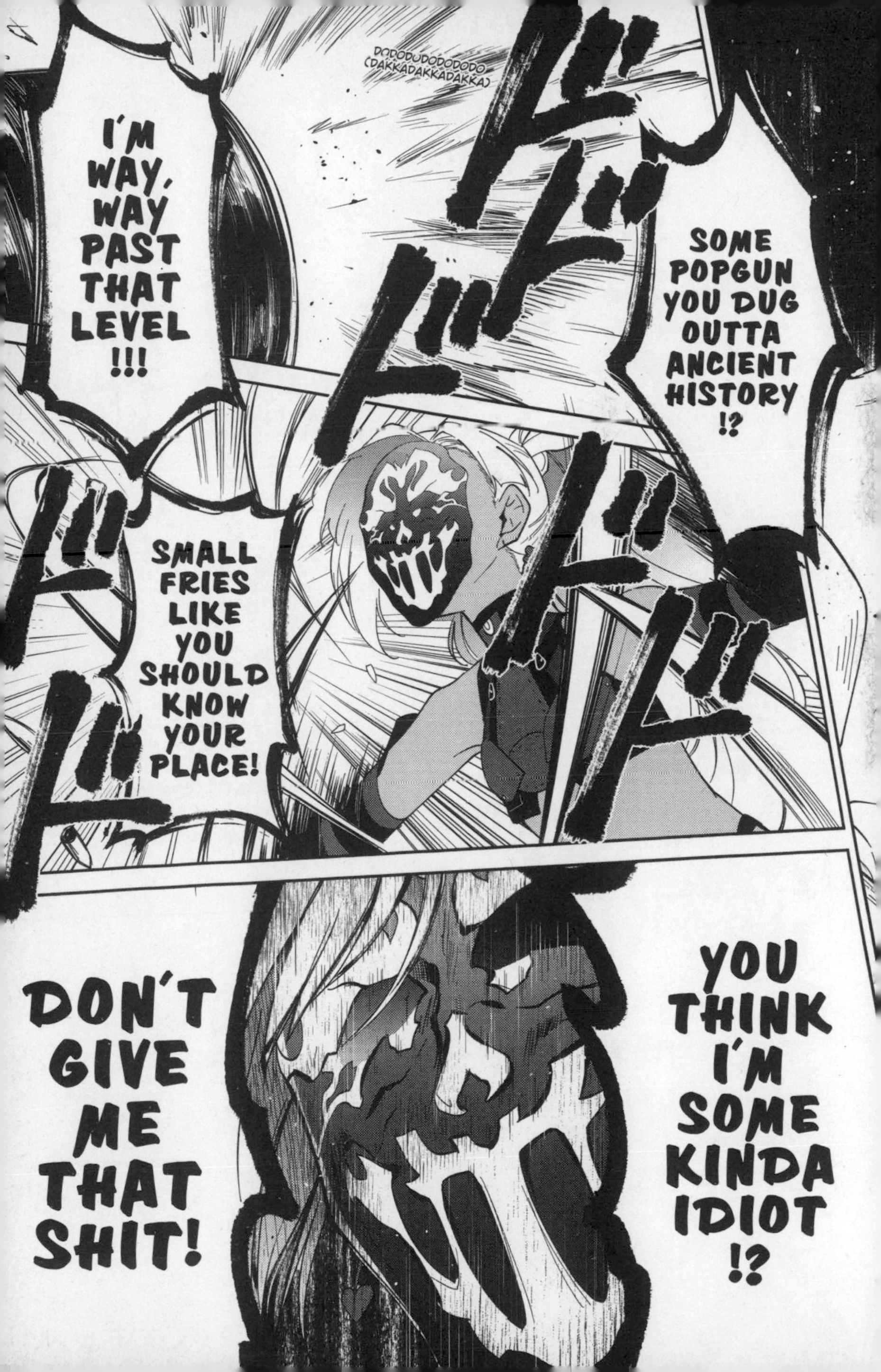
DODODUDODODODO
(DAKKADAKKADAKKA)
SOME POPGUN YOU DUG OUTTA ANCIENT HISTORY !?
I'M WAY, WAY PAST THAT LEVEL !!!
SMALL FRIES LIKE YOU SHOULD KNOW YOUR PLACE!
YOU THINK I'M SOME KINDA IDIOT !?
DON'T GIVE ME THAT SHIT!

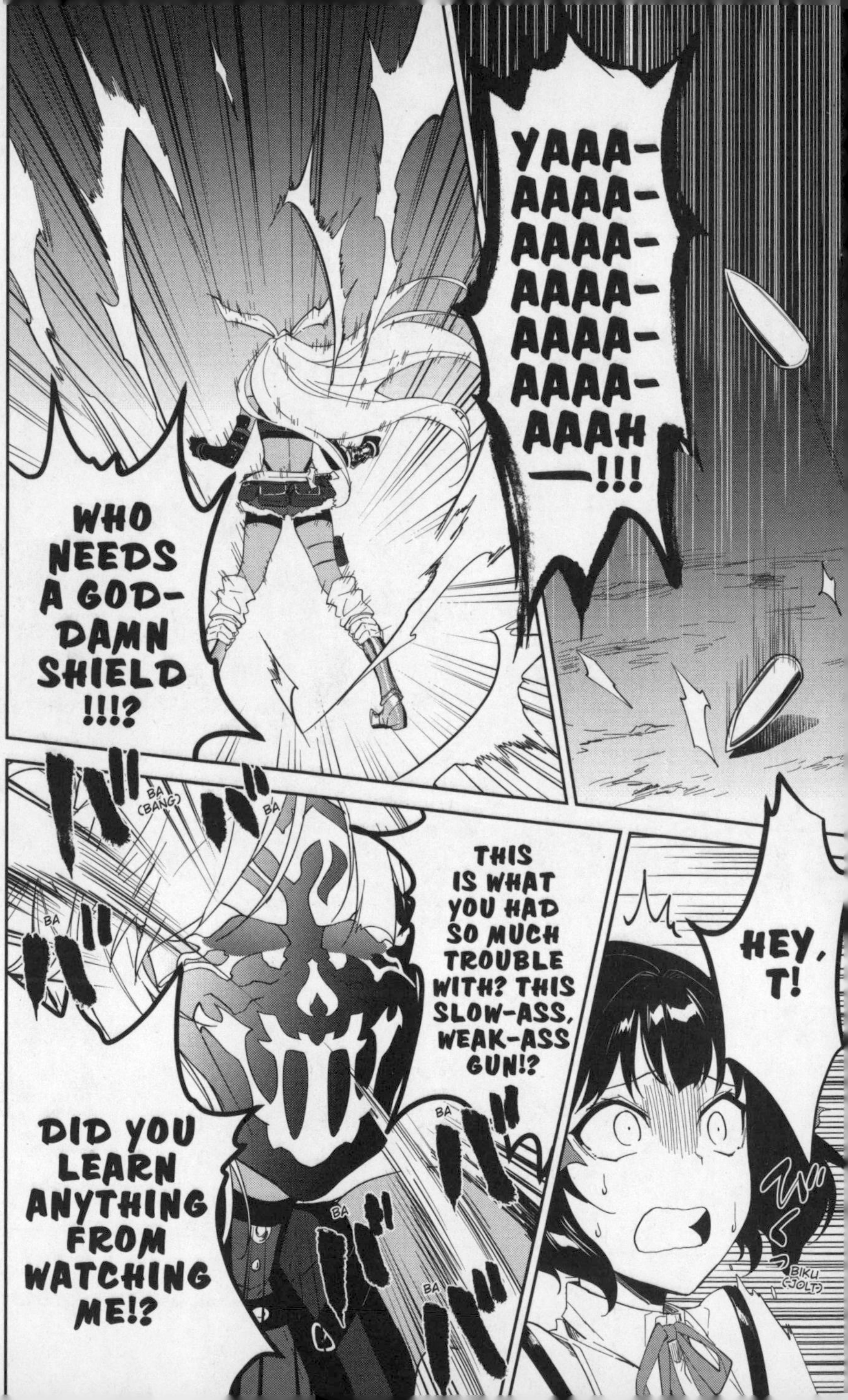
YAAA-AAAA-AAAA-AAAA-AAAA-AAAA-AAAH—!!!
WHO NEEDS A GOD-DAMN SHIELD!!!?
HEY, T!
BIKU (JOLT)
BA (BANG)
BA
BA
THIS IS WHAT YOU HAD SO MUCH TROUBLE WITH? THIS SLOW-ASS, WEAK-ASS GUN!?
BA
BA
BA
DID YOU LEARN ANYTHING FROM WATCHING ME!?

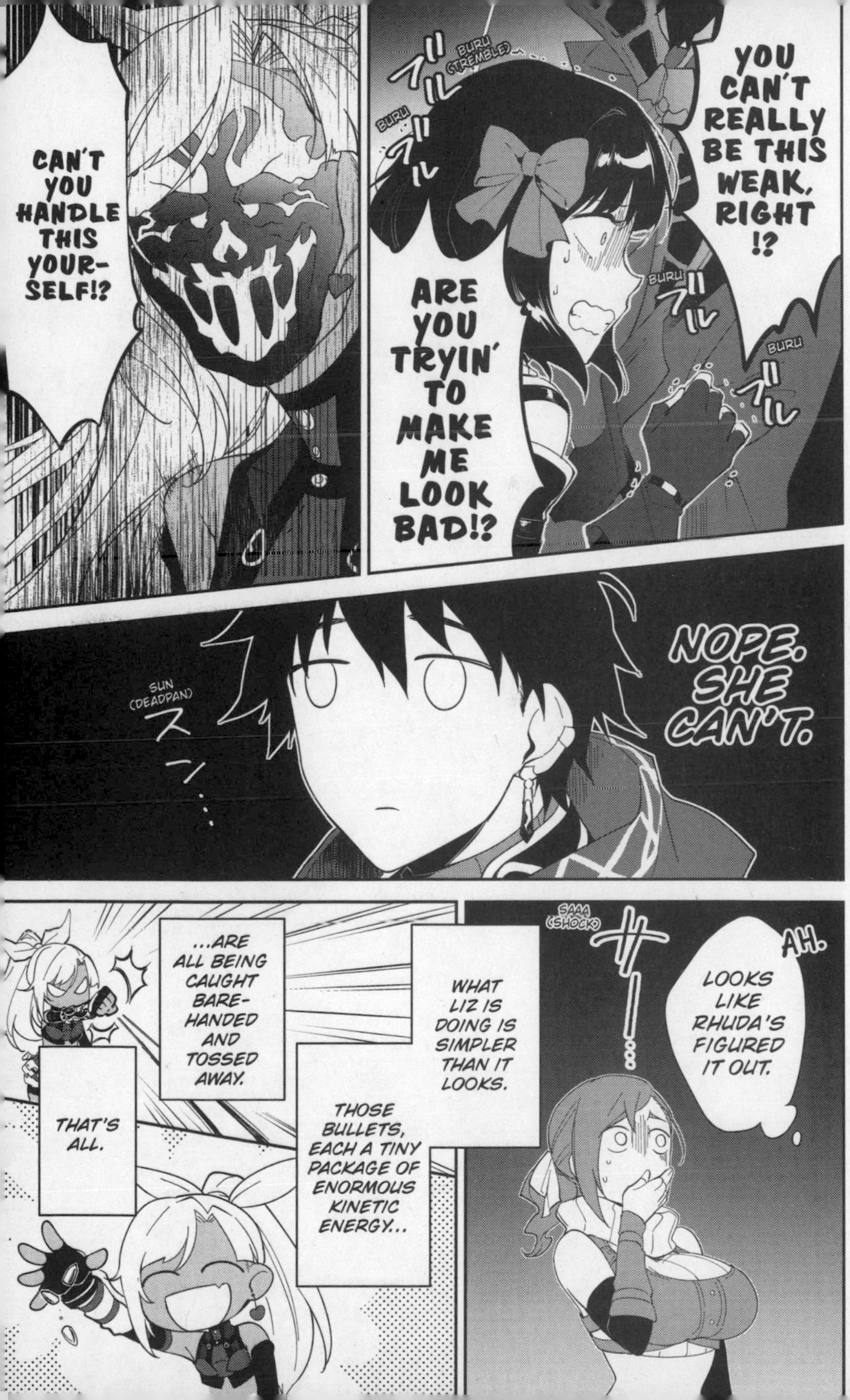
BURU (TREMBLE)
BURU
YOU CAN'T REALLY BE THIS WEAK, RIGHT!?
BURU
BURU
ARE YOU TRYIN' TO MAKE ME LOOK BAD!?
CAN'T YOU HANDLE THIS YOURSELF!?
NOPE. SHE CAN'T.
SUN (DEADPAN)
SAAA (SHOCK)
AH.
LOOKS LIKE RHUDA'S FIGURED IT OUT.
WHAT LIZ IS DOING IS SIMPLER THAN IT LOOKS.
THOSE BULLETS, EACH A TINY PACKAGE OF ENORMOUS KINETIC ENERGY...
...ARE ALL BEING CAUGHT BARE-HANDED AND TOSSED AWAY.
THAT'S ALL.

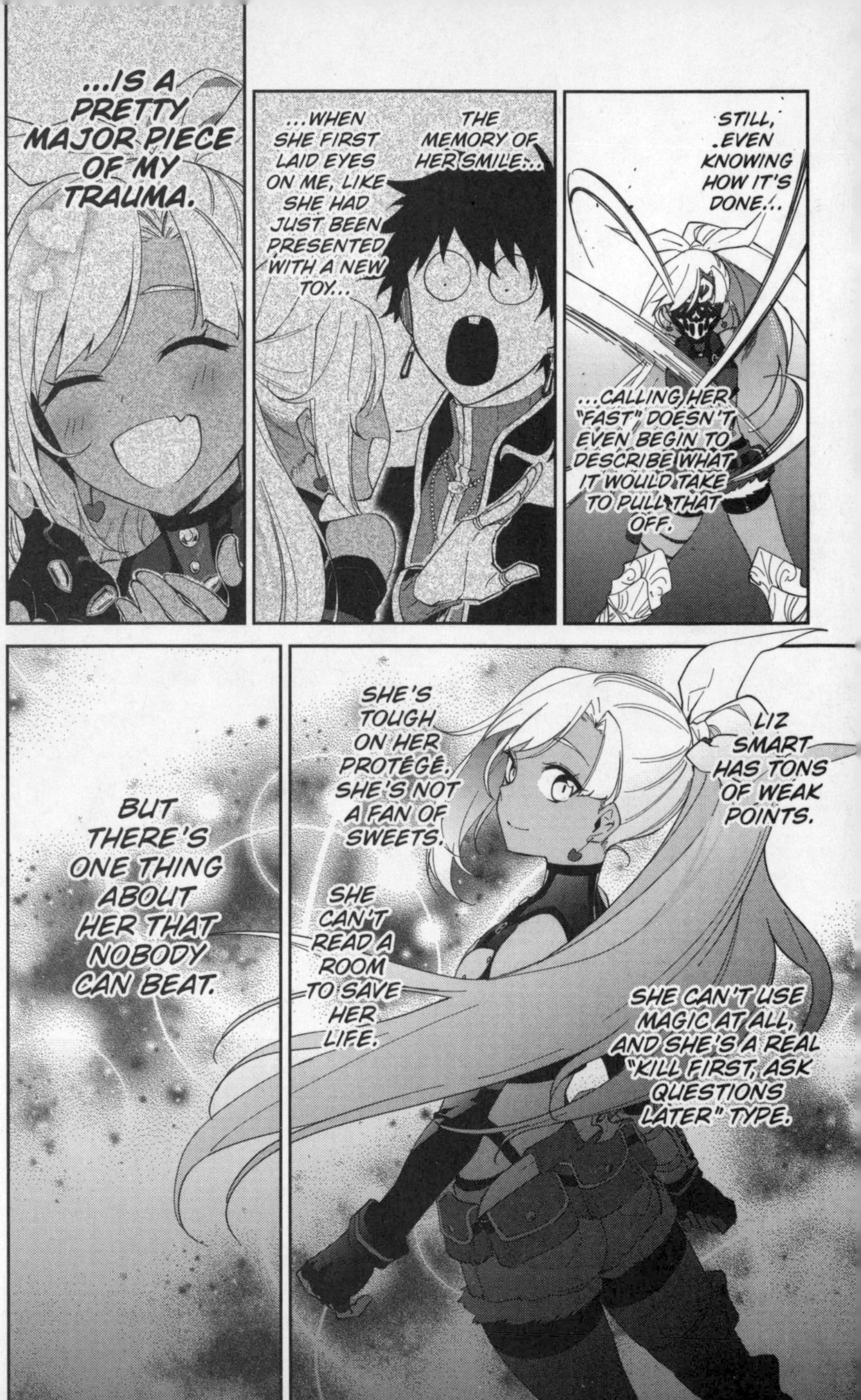
STILL, EVEN KNOWING HOW IT'S DONE...
...CALLING HER "FAST" DOESN'T EVEN BEGIN TO DESCRIBE WHAT IT WOULD TAKE TO PULL THAT OFF.
THE MEMORY OF HER SMILE...
...WHEN SHE FIRST LAID EYES ON ME, LIKE SHE HAD JUST BEEN PRESENTED WITH A NEW TOY...
...IS A PRETTY MAJOR PIECE OF MY TRAUMA.
LIZ SMART HAS TONS OF WEAK POINTS.
SHE'S TOUGH ON HER PROTEGE. SHE'S NOT A FAN OF SWEETS.
SHE CAN'T READ A ROOM TO SAVE HER LIFE.
SHE CAN'T USE MAGIC AT ALL, AND SHE'S A REAL "KILL FIRST, ASK QUESTIONS LATER" TYPE.
BUT THERE'S ONE THING ABOUT HER THAT NOBODY CAN BEAT.

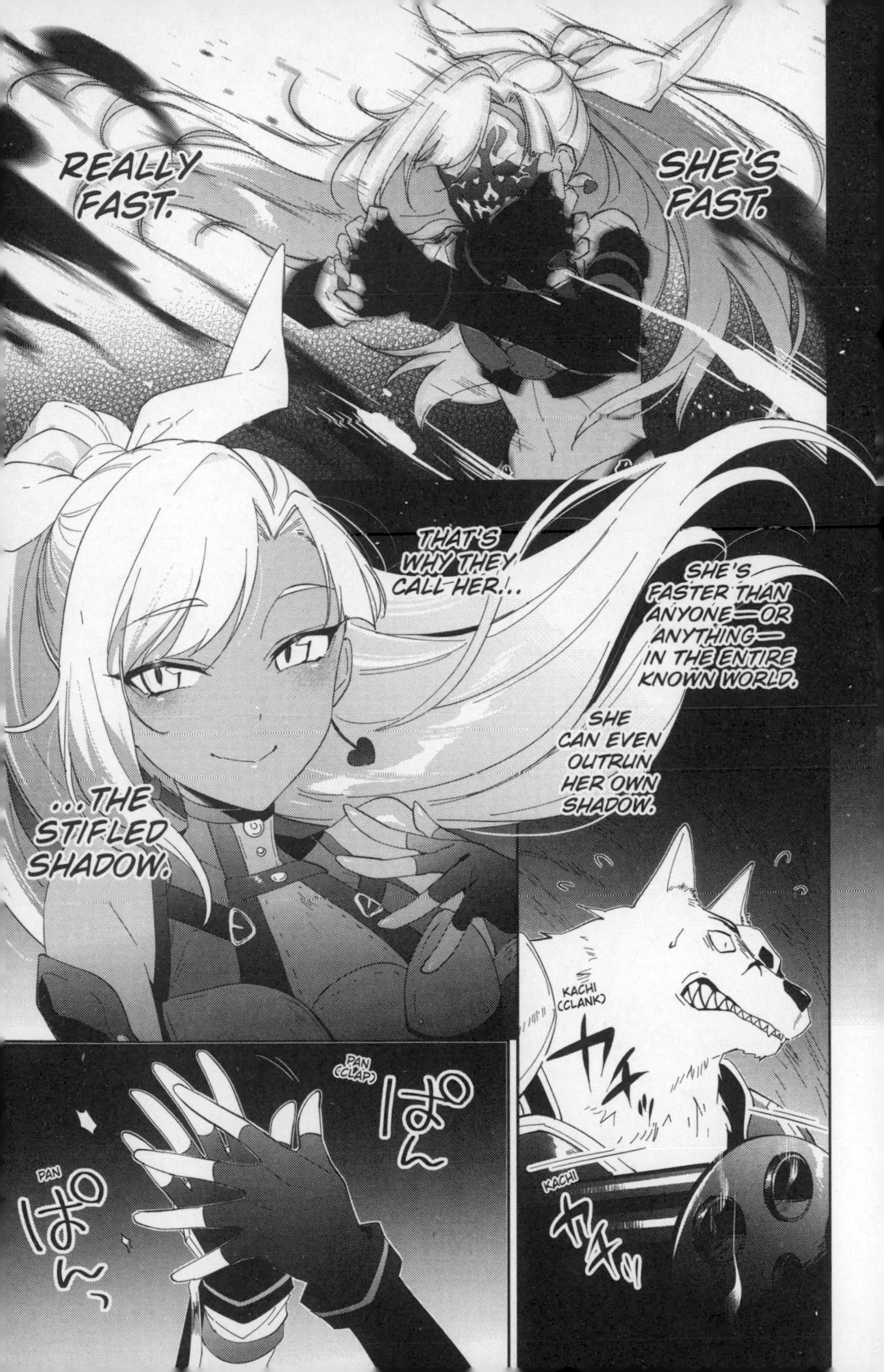
SHE'S FAST.
REALLY FAST.
SHE'S FASTER THAN ANYONE—OR ANYTHING—IN THE ENTIRE KNOWN WORLD.
SHE CAN EVEN OUTRUN HER OWN SHADOW.
THAT'S WHY THEY CALL HER...
...THE STIFLED SHADOW.
KACHI (CLANK)
カチ
KACHI
カチ
PAN (CLAP)
ぱん
PAN
ぱん

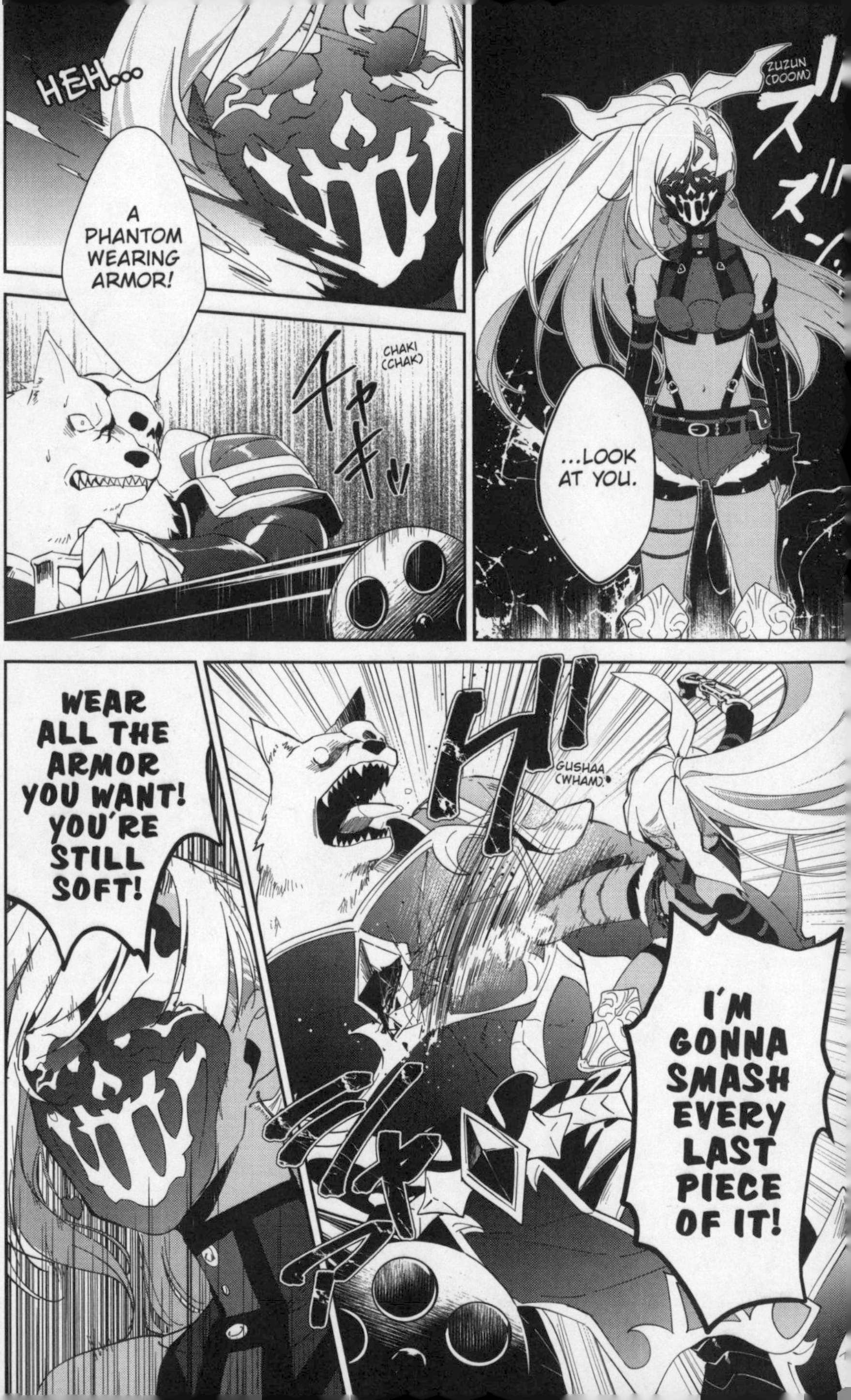
ZUZUN (DOOM)
...LOOK AT YOU.
HEH...
A PHANTOM WEARING ARMOR!
CHAKI (CHAK)
GUSHAA (WHAM)
I'M GONNA SMASH EVERY LAST PIECE OF IT!
WEAR ALL THE ARMOR YOU WANT! YOU'RE STILL SOFT!

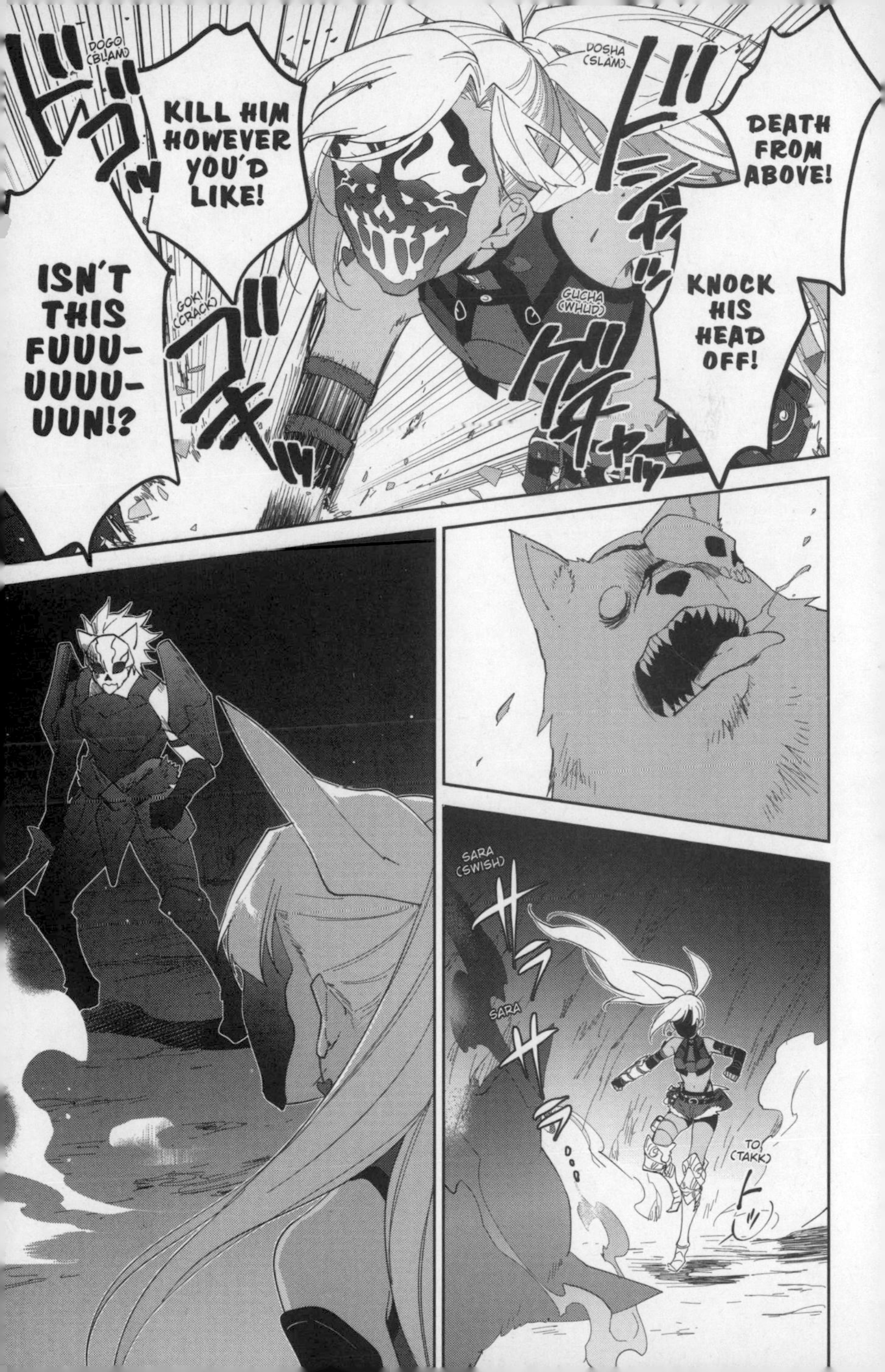
DOSHA (SLAM)
DEATH FROM ABOVE!
KNOCK HIS HEAD OFF!
GUCHA (WHUD)
DOGO (BLAM)
KILL HIM HOWEVER YOU'D LIKE!
GOKI (CRACK)
ISN'T THIS FUUU-UUUU-UUN!?
SARA (SWISH)
SARA
TO (TAKK)

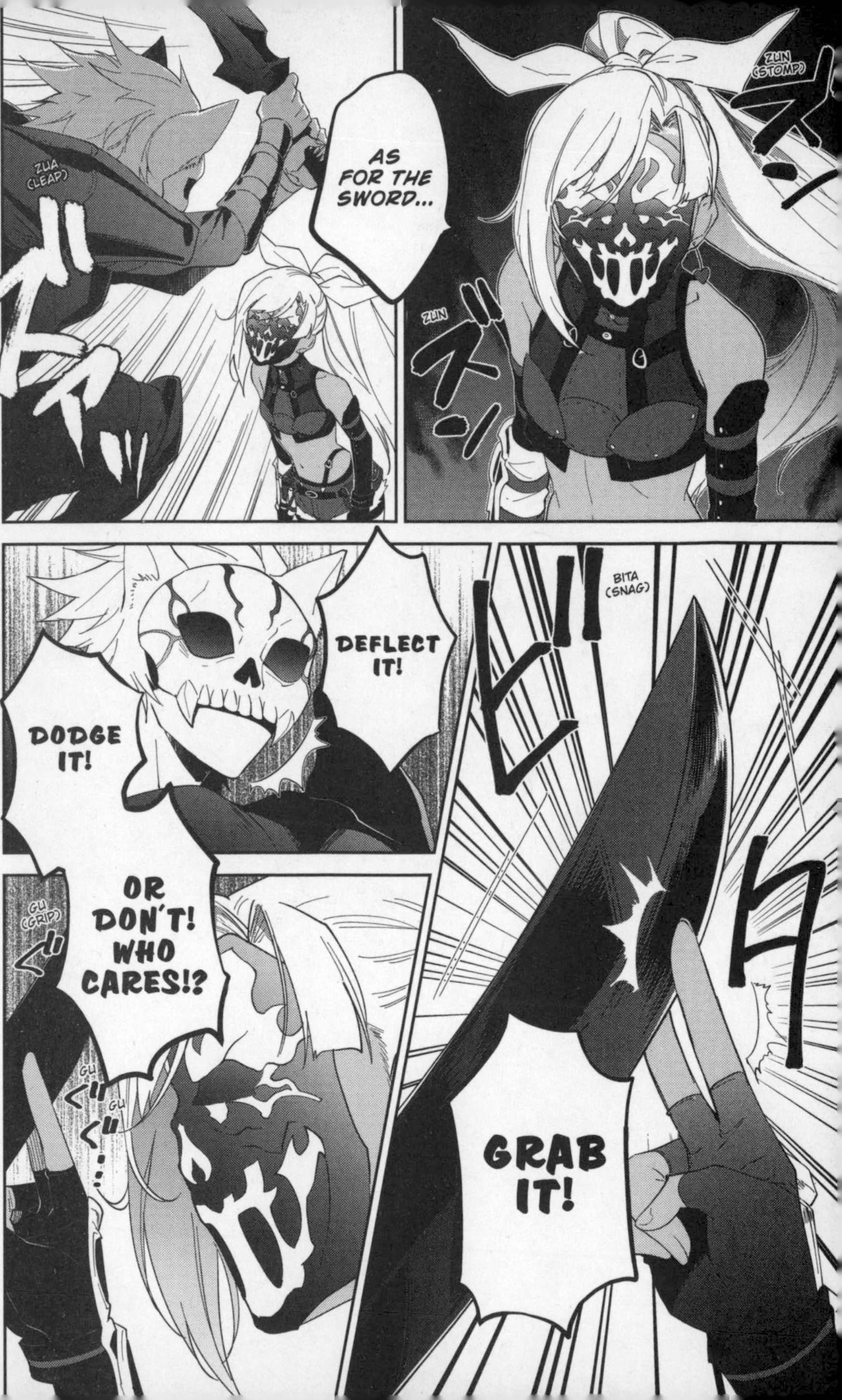
ZUN (STOMP)
ZUN
AS FOR THE SWORD...
ZUA (LEAP)
BITA (SNAG)
GRAB IT!
DEFLECT IT!
DODGE IT!
OR DON'T! WHO CARES!?
GU (GRIP)
GU
GU

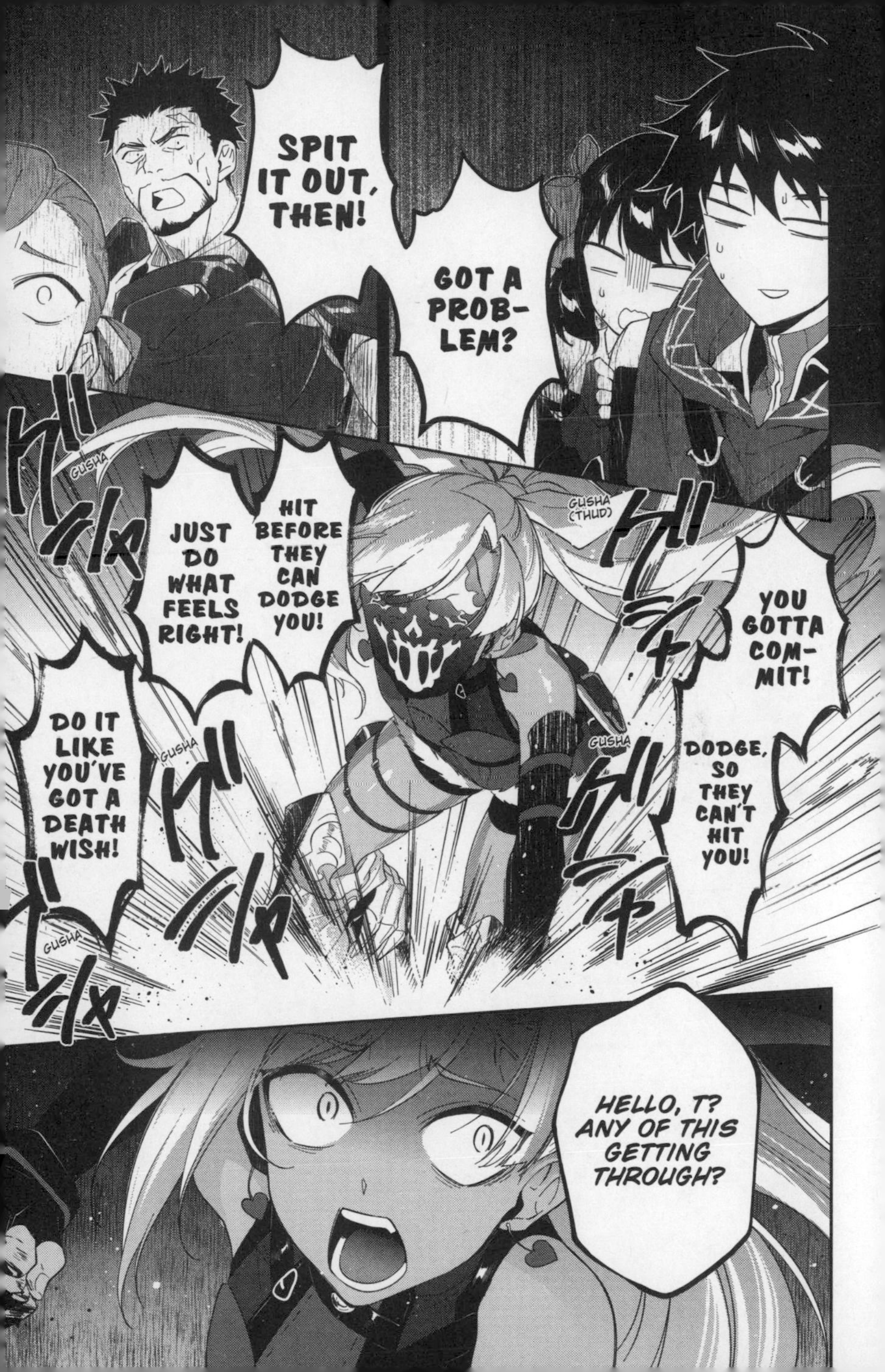
GOT A PROB-LEM?
SPIT IT OUT, THEN!
GUSHA (THUD)
YOU GOTTA COM-MIT!
HIT BEFORE THEY CAN DODGE YOU!
JUST DO WHAT FEELS RIGHT!
GUSHA
GUSHA
DODGE, SO THEY CAN'T HIT YOU!
GUSHA
DO IT LIKE YOU'VE GOT A DEATH WISH!
GUSHA
HELLO, T? ANY OF THIS GETTING THROUGH?

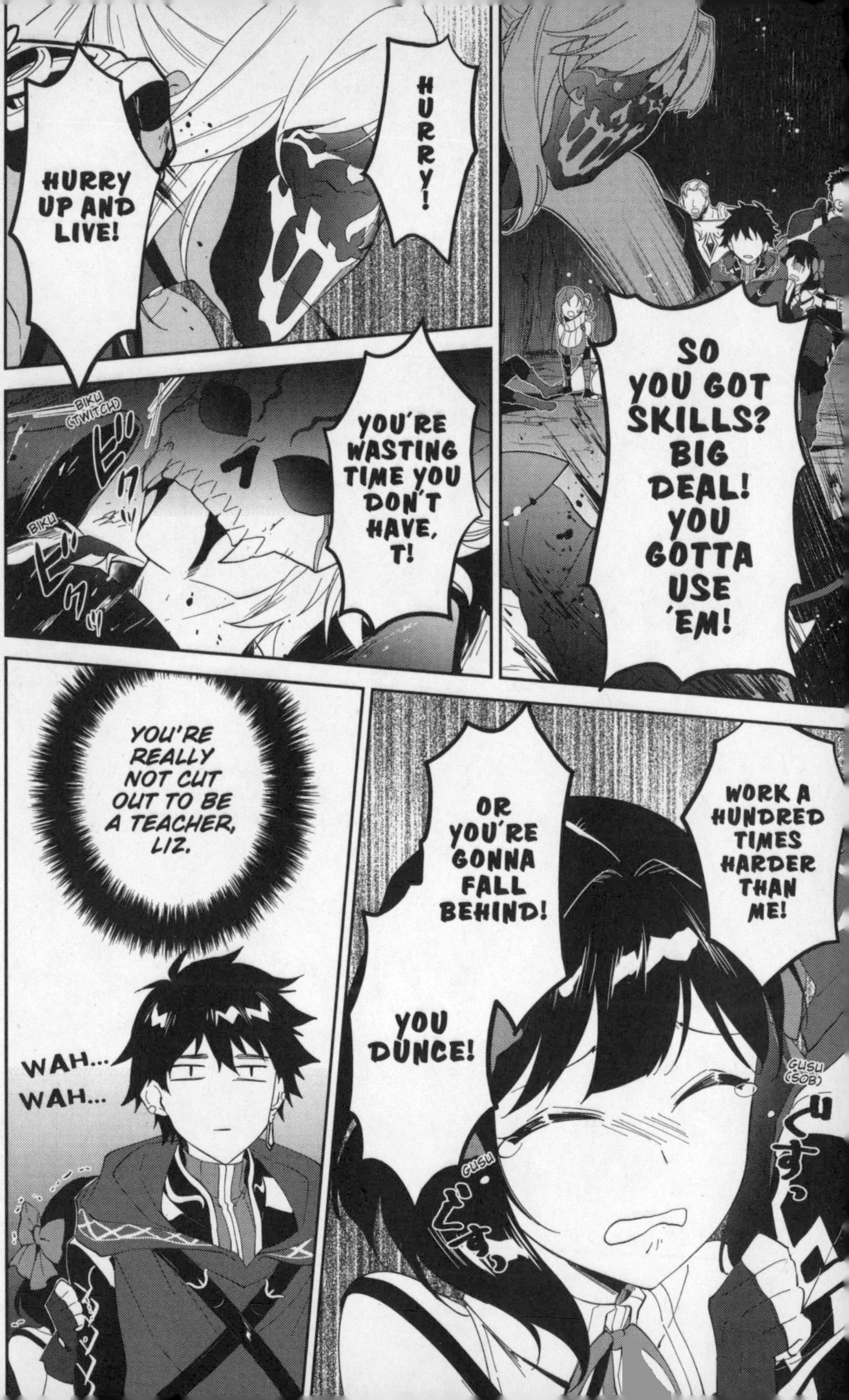
SO YOU GOT SKILLS? BIG DEAL! YOU GOTTA USE 'EM!
HURRY!
HURRY UP AND LIVE!
YOU'RE WASTING TIME YOU DON'T HAVE, T!
BIKU (TWITCH)
BIKU
WORK A HUNDRED TIMES HARDER THAN ME!
OR YOU'RE GONNA FALL BEHIND!
GUSU (SOB)
YOU DUNCE!
GUSU
YOU'RE REALLY NOT CUT OUT TO BE A TEACHER, LIZ.
WAH... WAH...

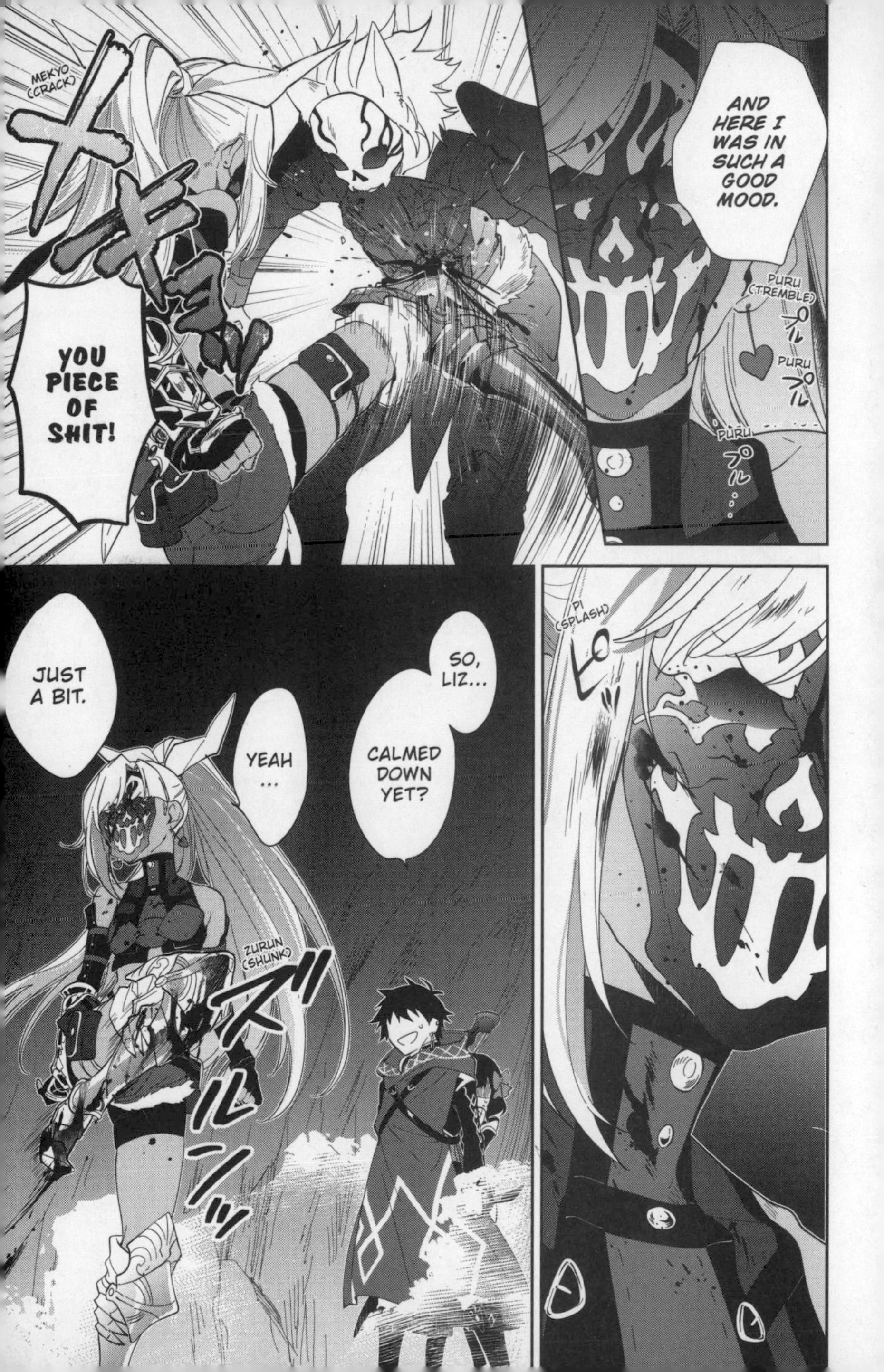
AND HERE I WAS IN SUCH A GOOD MOOD.
PURU (TREMBLE)
PURU
PURU
MEKYO (CRACK)
YOU PIECE OF SHIT!
PI (SPLASH)
SO, LIZ... CALMED DOWN YET?
YEAH ...
JUST A BIT.
ZURUN (SHUNK)

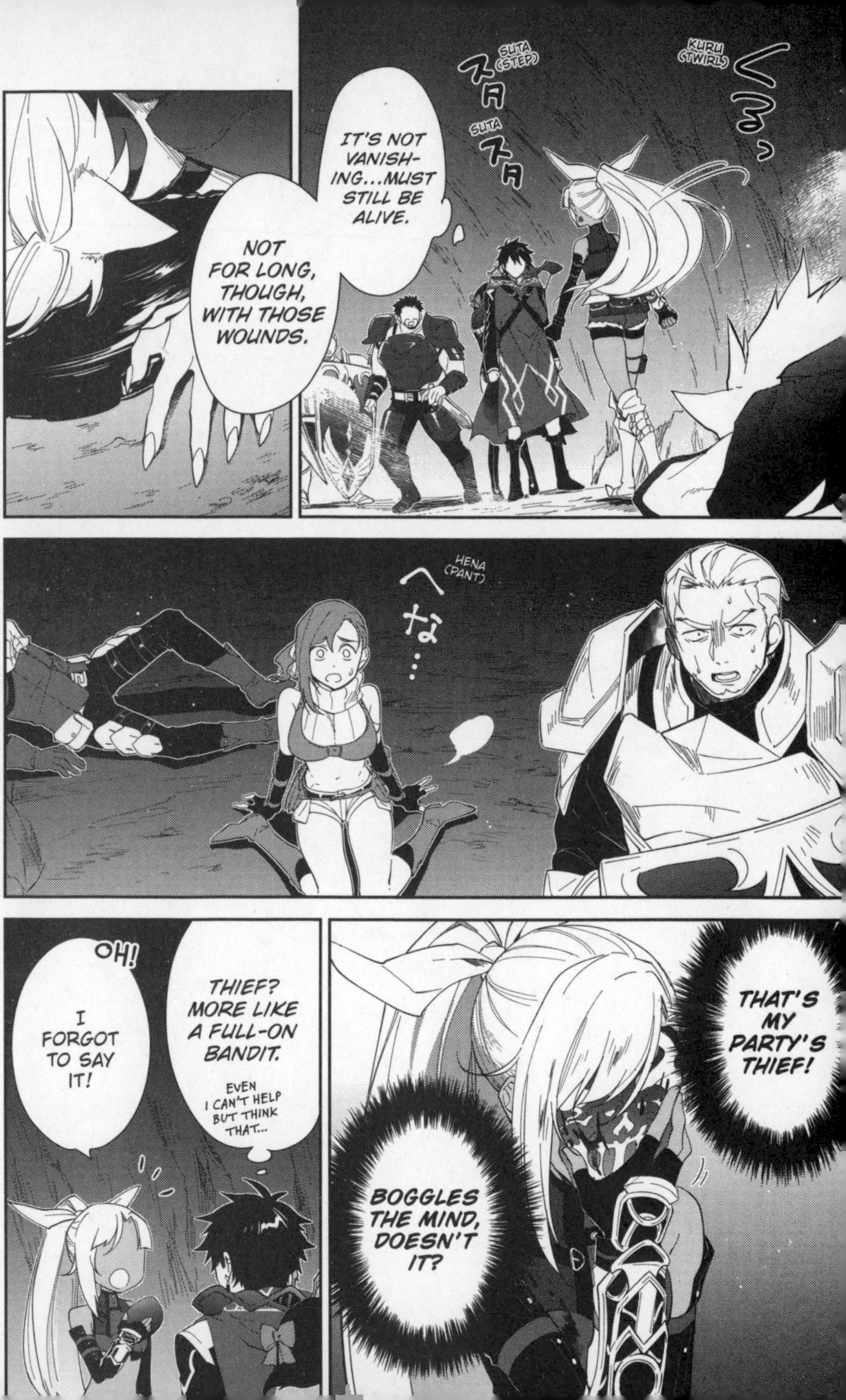
KURU (TWIRL)
くるっ
SUTA (STEP)
スタ
SUTA
スタ
IT'S NOT VANISHING...MUST STILL BE ALIVE.
NOT FOR LONG, THOUGH, WITH THOSE WOUNDS.
HENA (PANT)
へな…
THAT'S MY PARTY'S THIEF!
BOGGLES THE MIND, DOESN'T IT?
THIEF? MORE LIKE A FULL-ON BANDIT.
EVEN I CAN'T HELP BUT THINK THAT...
OH!
I FORGOT TO SAY IT!

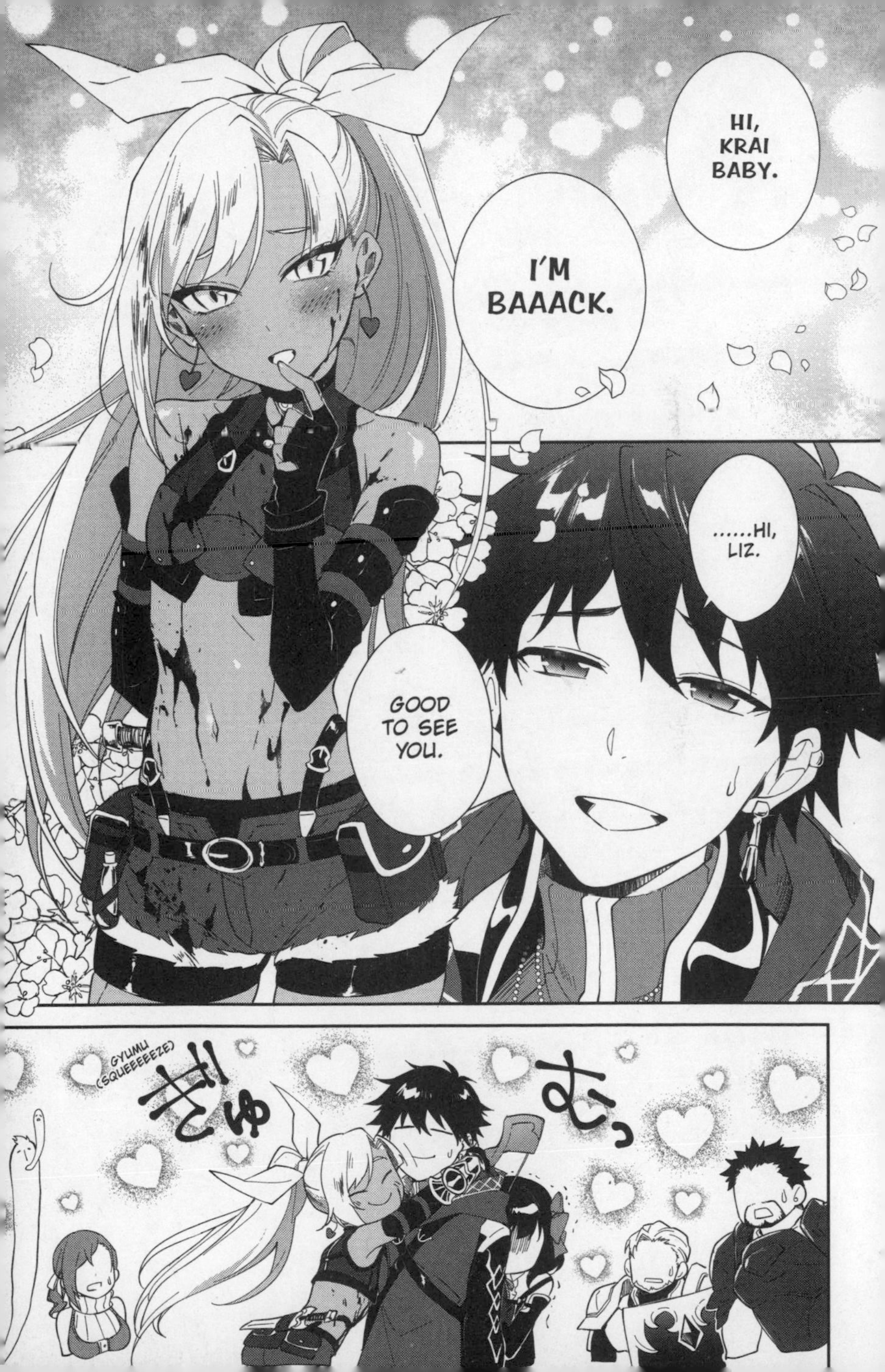
HI, KRAI BABY.
I'M BAAACK.
......HI, LIZ.
GOOD TO SEE YOU.
GYUMU (SQUEEEEEZE)

LET THIS
Grieving Soul Retire
WOE IS THE WEAKLING WHO LEADS THE STRONGEST PARTY

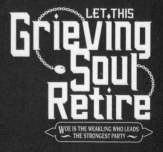

Chapter 14

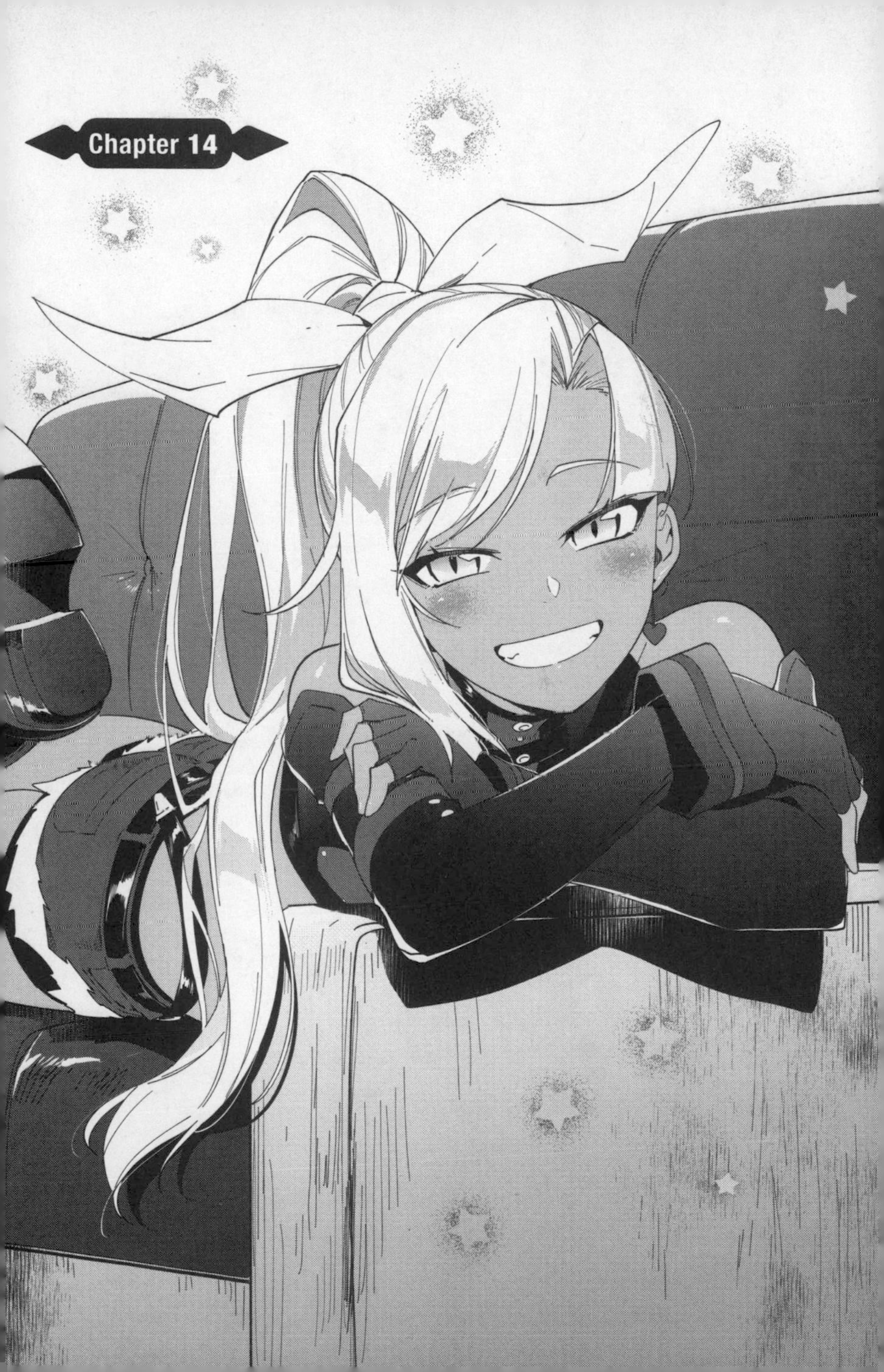

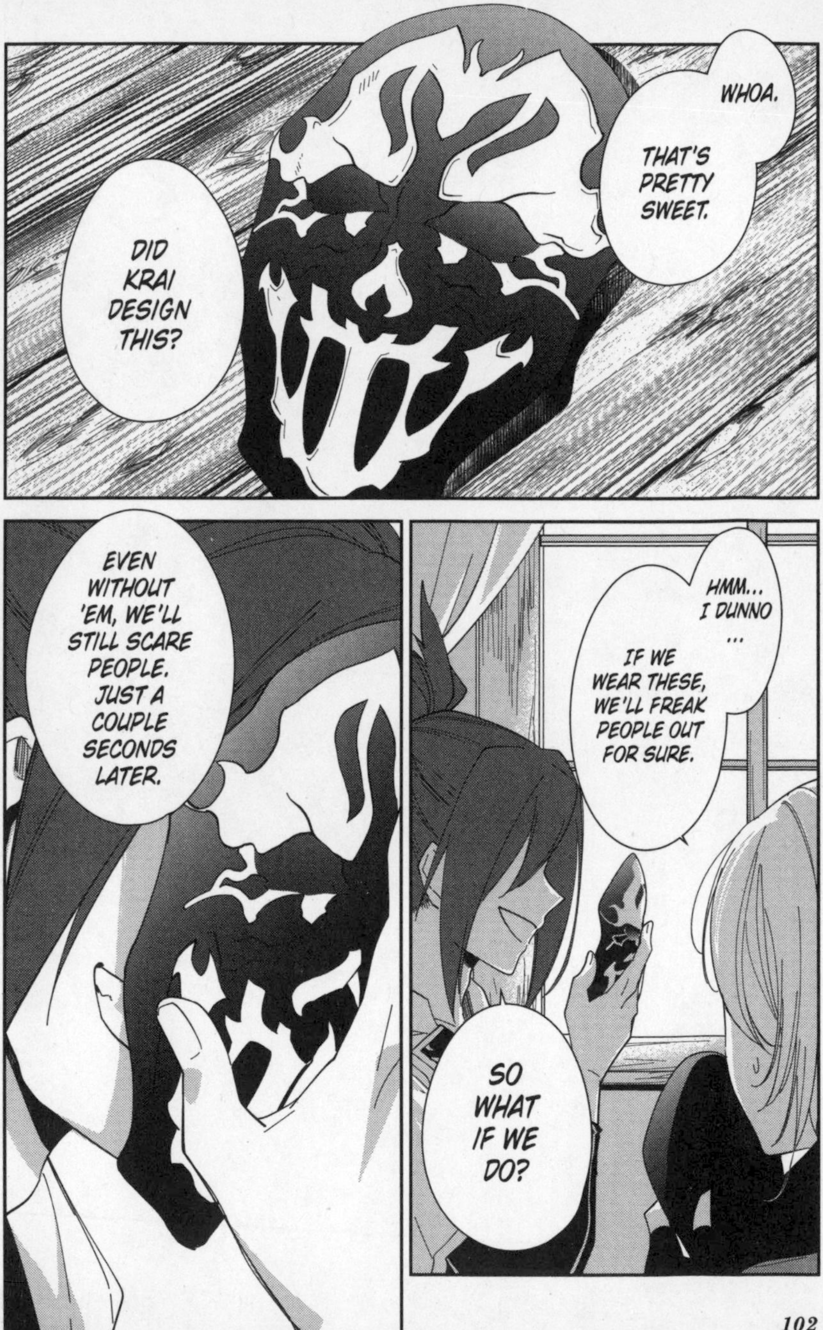
WHOA.
THAT'S PRETTY SWEET.
DID KRAI DESIGN THIS?
HMM... I DUNNO ...
IF WE WEAR THESE, WE'LL FREAK PEOPLE OUT FOR SURE.
SO WHAT IF WE DO?
EVEN WITHOUT 'EM, WE'LL STILL SCARE PEOPLE. JUST A COUPLE SECONDS LATER.

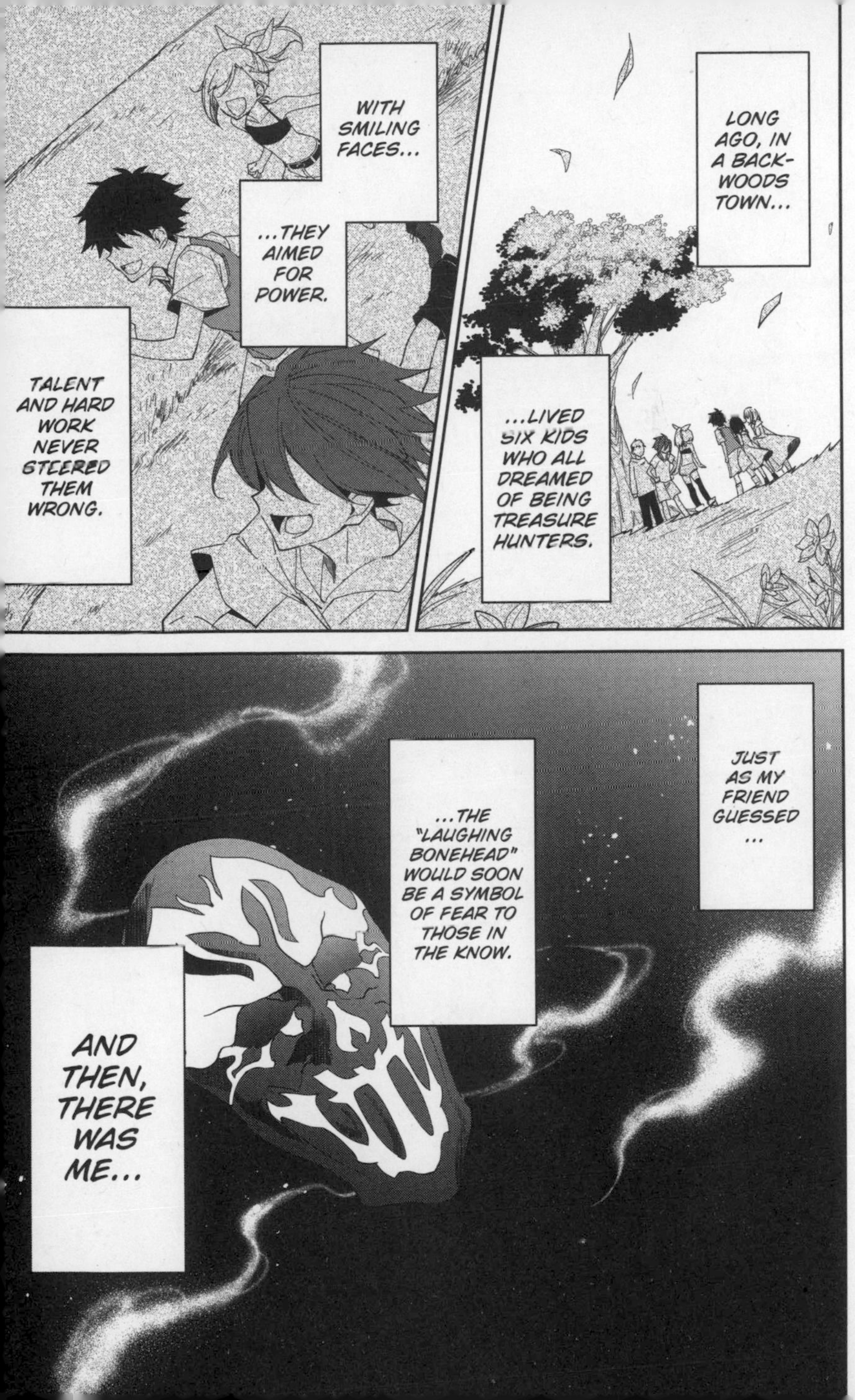
LONG AGO, IN A BACK-WOODS TOWN...
...LIVED SIX KIDS WHO ALL DREAMED OF BEING TREASURE HUNTERS.
WITH SMILING FACES...
...THEY AIMED FOR POWER.
TALENT AND HARD WORK NEVER STEERED THEM WRONG.
JUST AS MY FRIEND GUESSED...
...THE "LAUGHING BONEHEAD" WOULD SOON BE A SYMBOL OF FEAR TO THOSE IN THE KNOW.
AND THEN, THERE WAS ME...

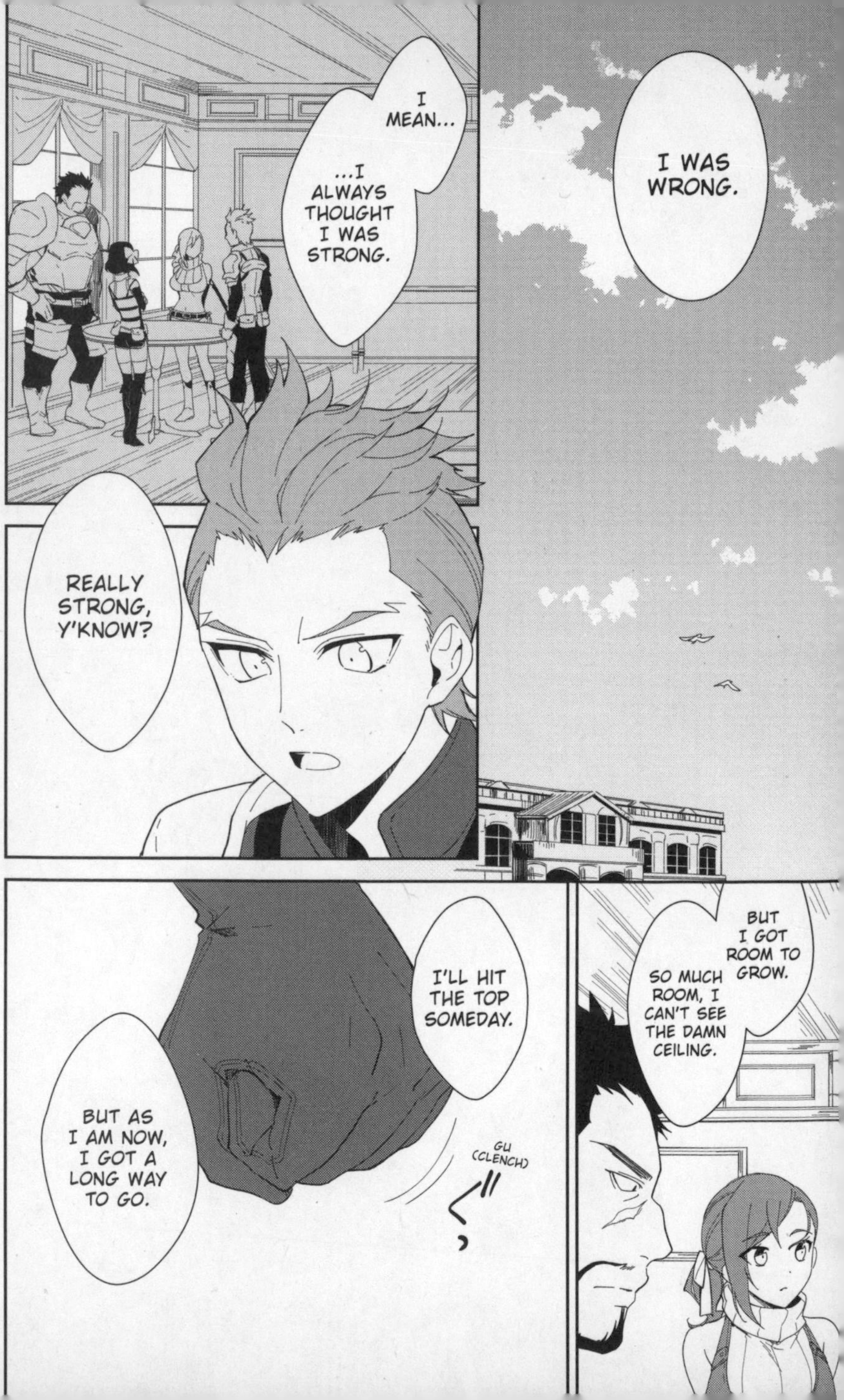
I WAS WRONG.
I MEAN...
...I ALWAYS THOUGHT I WAS STRONG.
REALLY STRONG, Y'KNOW?
BUT I GOT ROOM TO GROW.
SO MUCH ROOM, I CAN'T SEE THE DAMN CEILING.
I'LL HIT THE TOP SOMEDAY.
BUT AS I AM NOW, I GOT A LONG WAY TO GO.
GU (CLENCH)

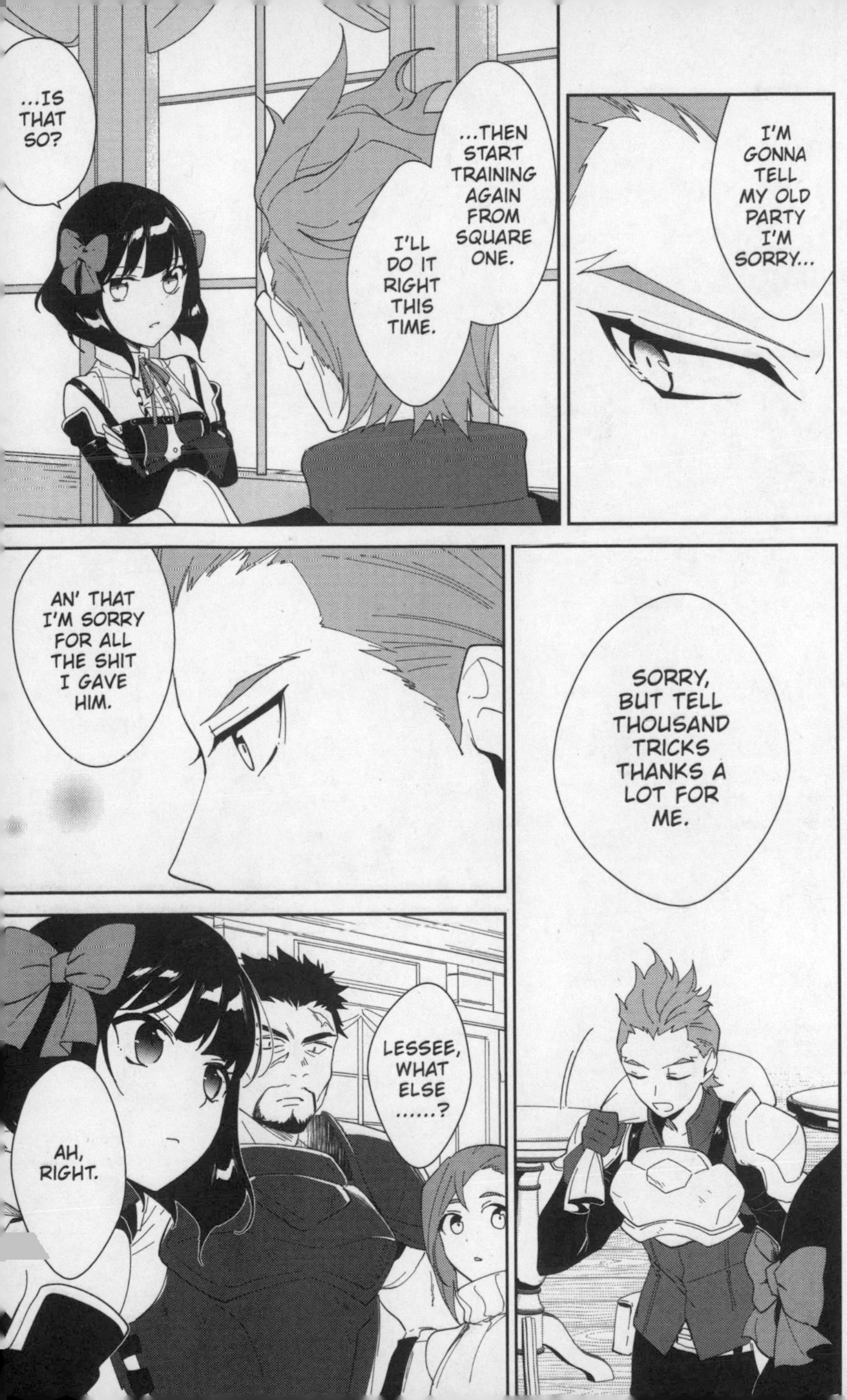
I'M GONNA TELL MY OLD PARTY I'M SORRY...
...THEN START TRAINING AGAIN FROM SQUARE ONE.
I'LL DO IT RIGHT THIS TIME.
...IS THAT SO?
SORRY, BUT TELL THOUSAND TRICKS THANKS A LOT FOR ME.
AN' THAT I'M SORRY FOR ALL THE SHIT I GAVE HIM.
LESSEE, WHAT ELSE ......?
AH, RIGHT.

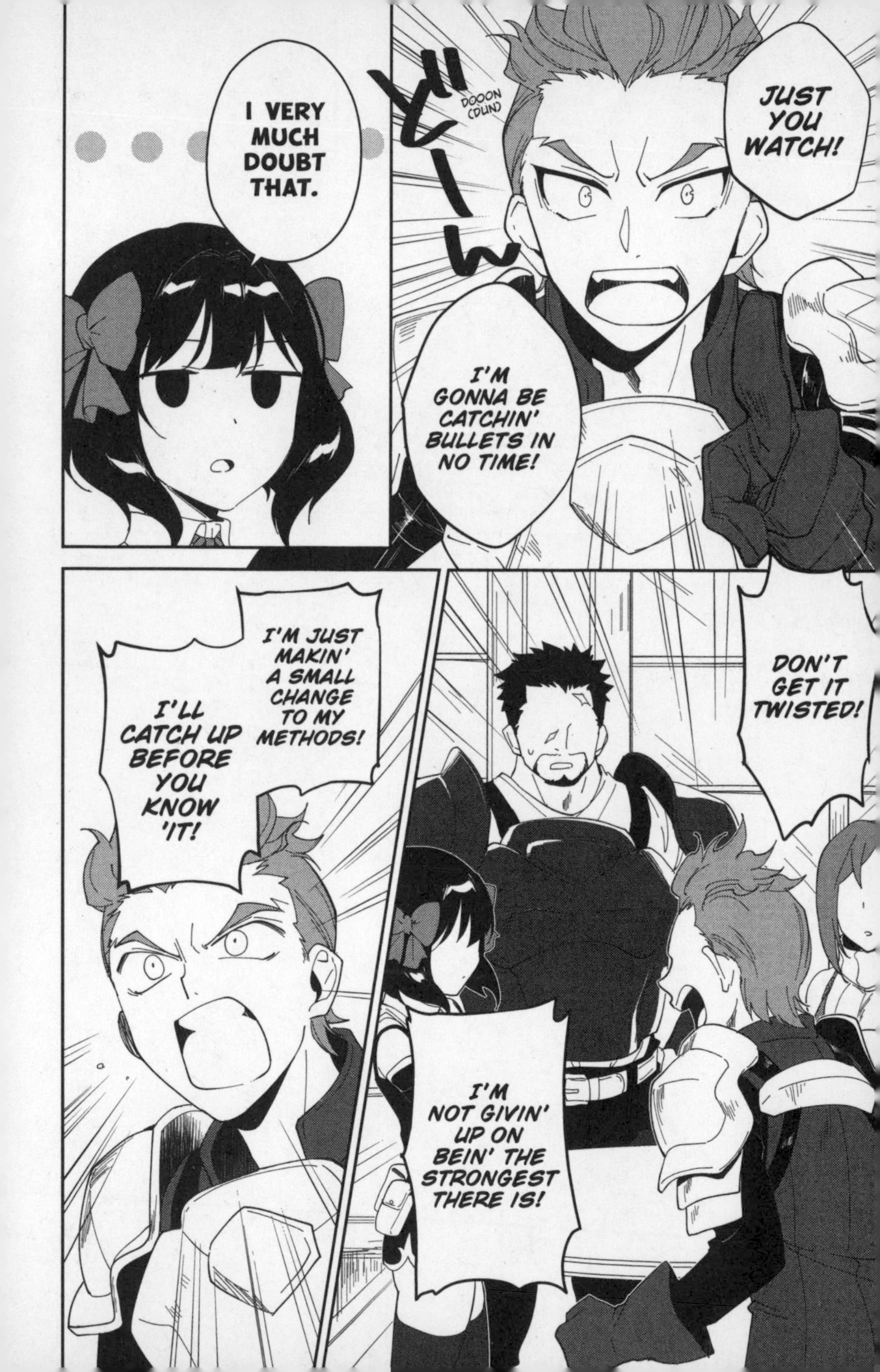
JUST YOU WATCH!
DOOON (DUN)
I'M GONNA BE CATCHIN' BULLETS IN NO TIME!
I VERY MUCH DOUBT THAT.
DON'T GET IT TWISTED!
I'M NOT GIVIN' UP ON BEIN' THE STRONGEST THERE IS!
I'M JUST MAKIN' A SMALL CHANGE TO MY METHODS!
I'LL CATCH UP BEFORE YOU KNOW 'IT!

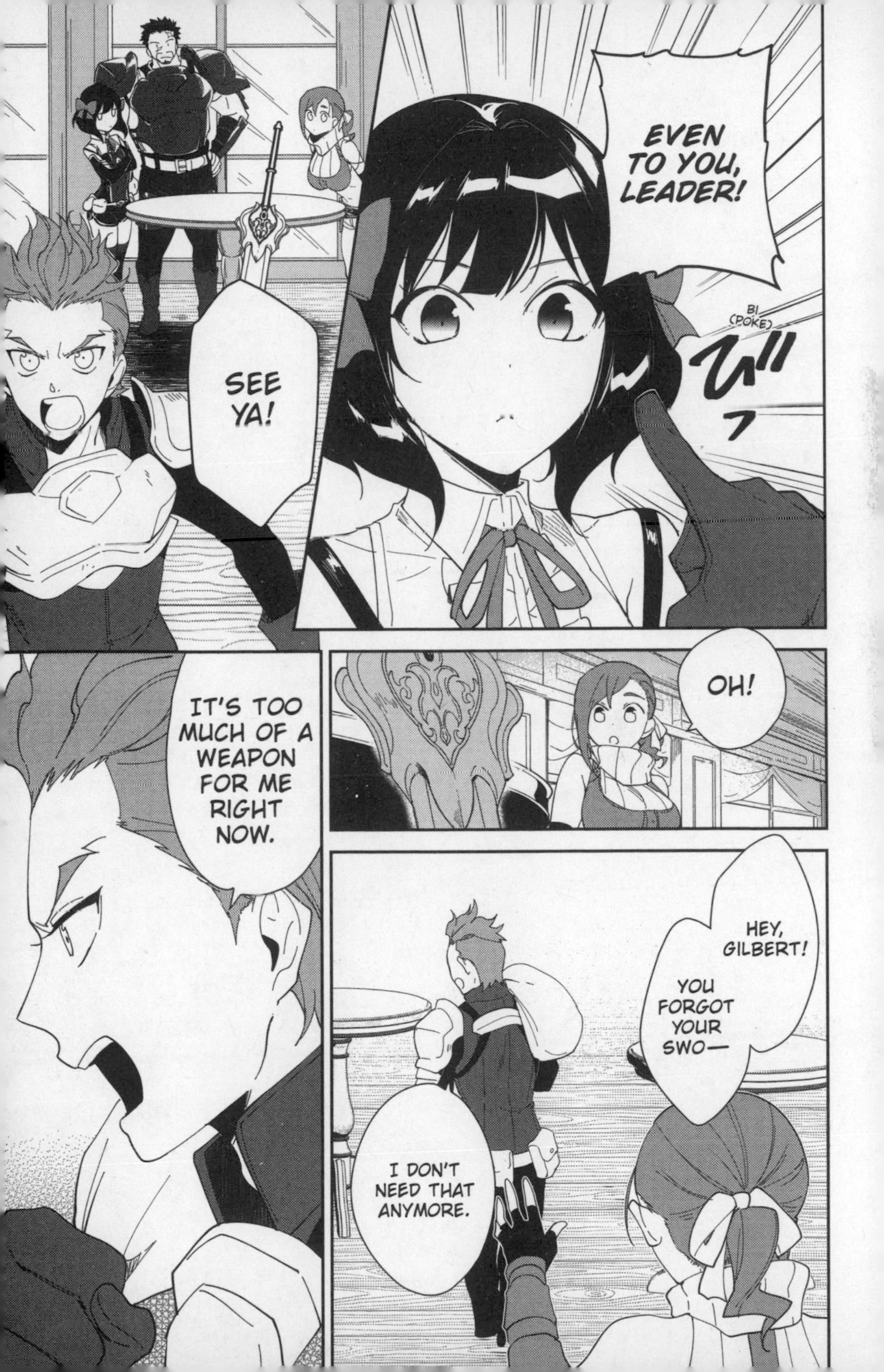
EVEN TO YOU, LEADER!
BI (POKE)
びッ
SEE YA!
OH!
HEY, GILBERT!
YOU FORGOT YOUR SWO—
I DON'T NEED THAT ANYMORE.
IT'S TOO MUCH OF A WEAPON FOR ME RIGHT NOW.

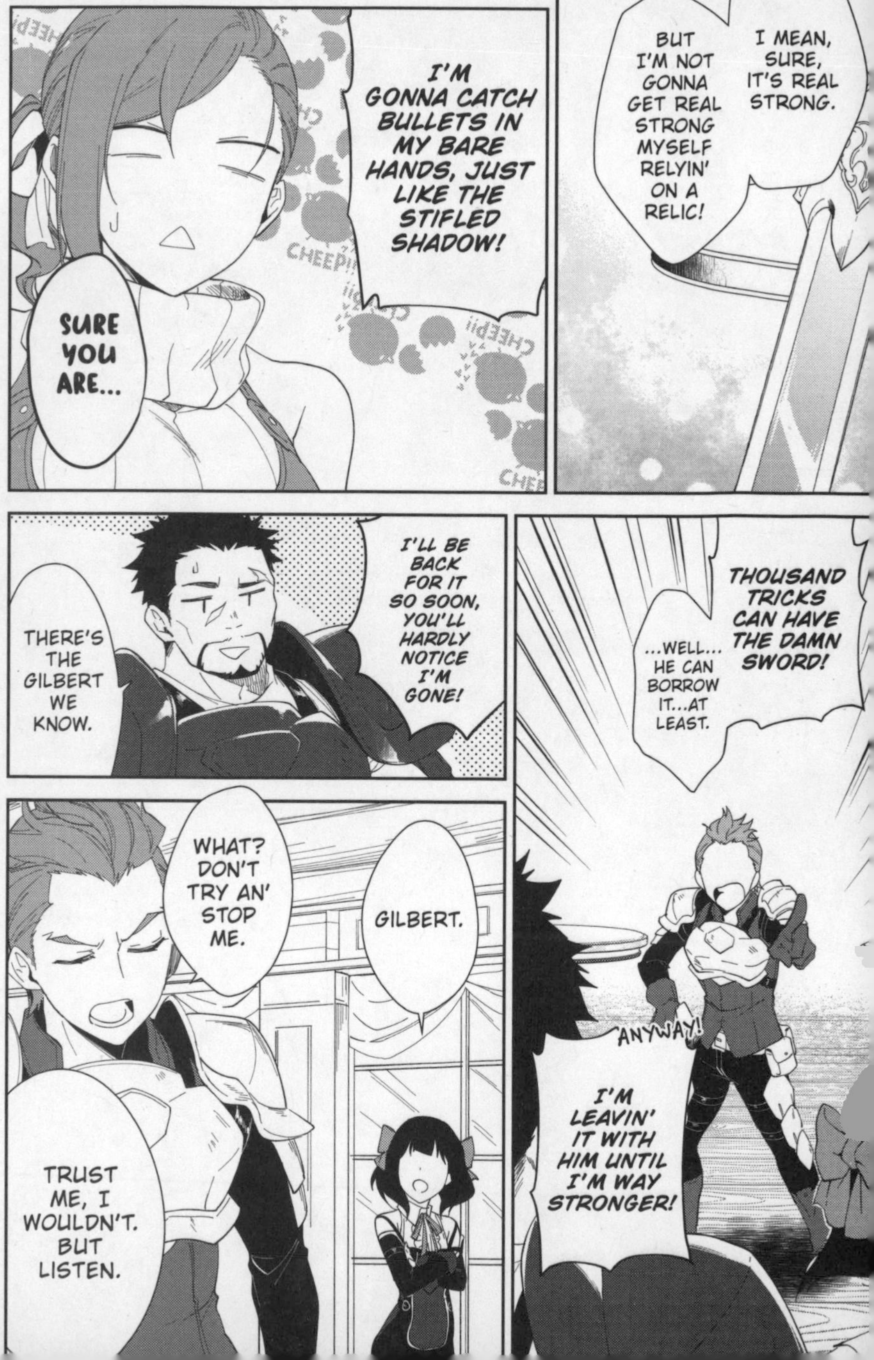

I MEAN, SURE, IT'S REAL STRONG.
BUT I'M NOT GONNA GET REAL STRONG MYSELF RELYIN' ON A RELIC!
I'M GONNA CATCH BULLETS IN MY BARE HANDS, JUST LIKE THE STIFLED SHADOW!
CHEEP!!
SURE YOU ARE...
THOUSAND TRICKS CAN HAVE THE DAMN SWORD!
...WELL... HE CAN BORROW IT...AT LEAST.
I'LL BE BACK FOR IT SO SOON, YOU'LL HARDLY NOTICE I'M GONE!
THERE'S THE GILBERT WE KNOW.
ANYWAY!
I'M LEAVIN' IT WITH HIM UNTIL I'M WAY STRONGER!
GILBERT.
WHAT? DON'T TRY AN' STOP ME.
TRUST ME, I WOULDN'T. BUT LISTEN.

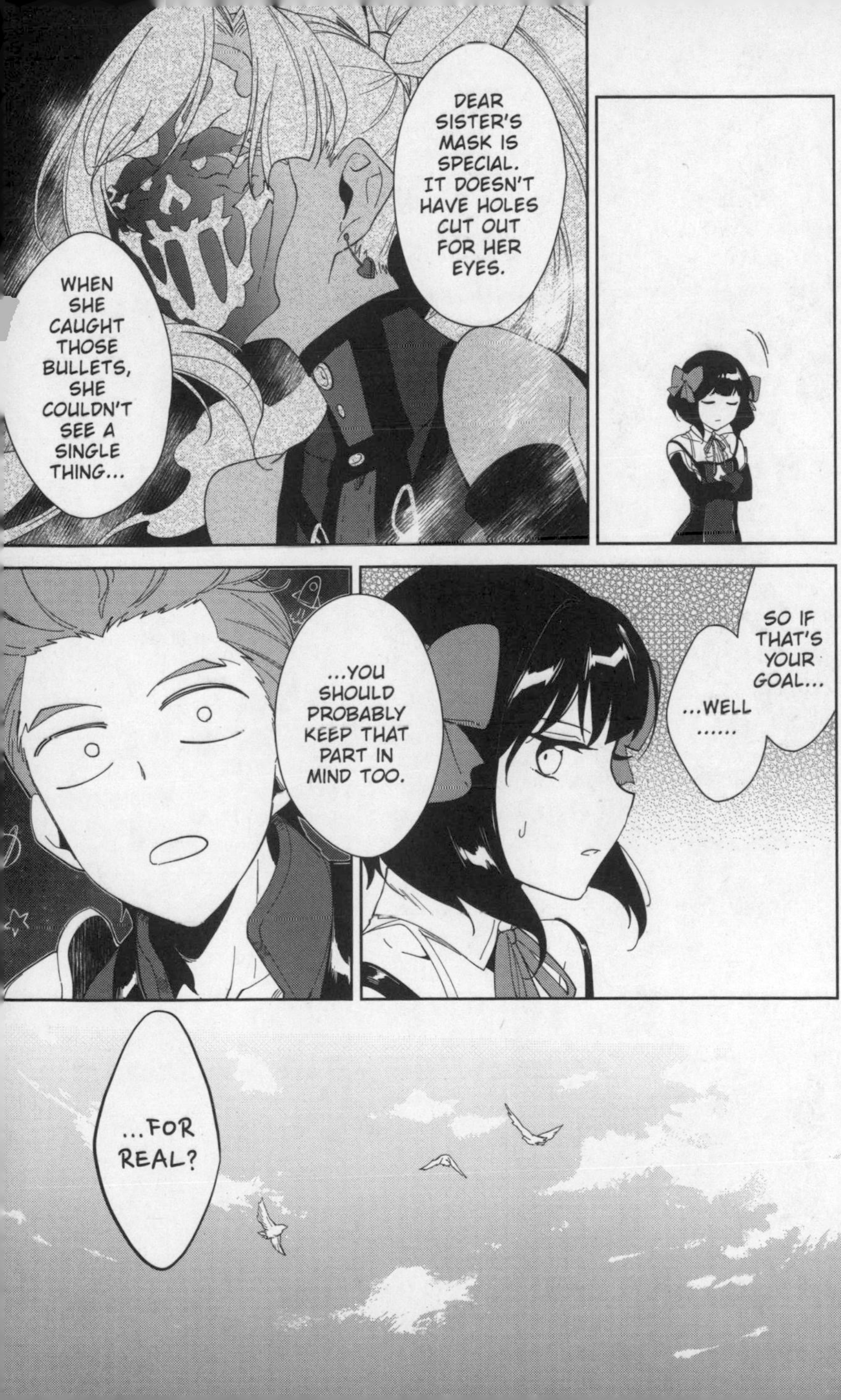
DEAR SISTER'S MASK IS SPECIAL. IT DOESN'T HAVE HOLES CUT OUT FOR HER EYES.
WHEN SHE CAUGHT THOSE BULLETS, SHE COULDN'T SEE A SINGLE THING...
SO IF THAT'S YOUR GOAL...
...WELL ......
...YOU SHOULD PROBABLY KEEP THAT PART IN MIND TOO.
...FOR REAL?

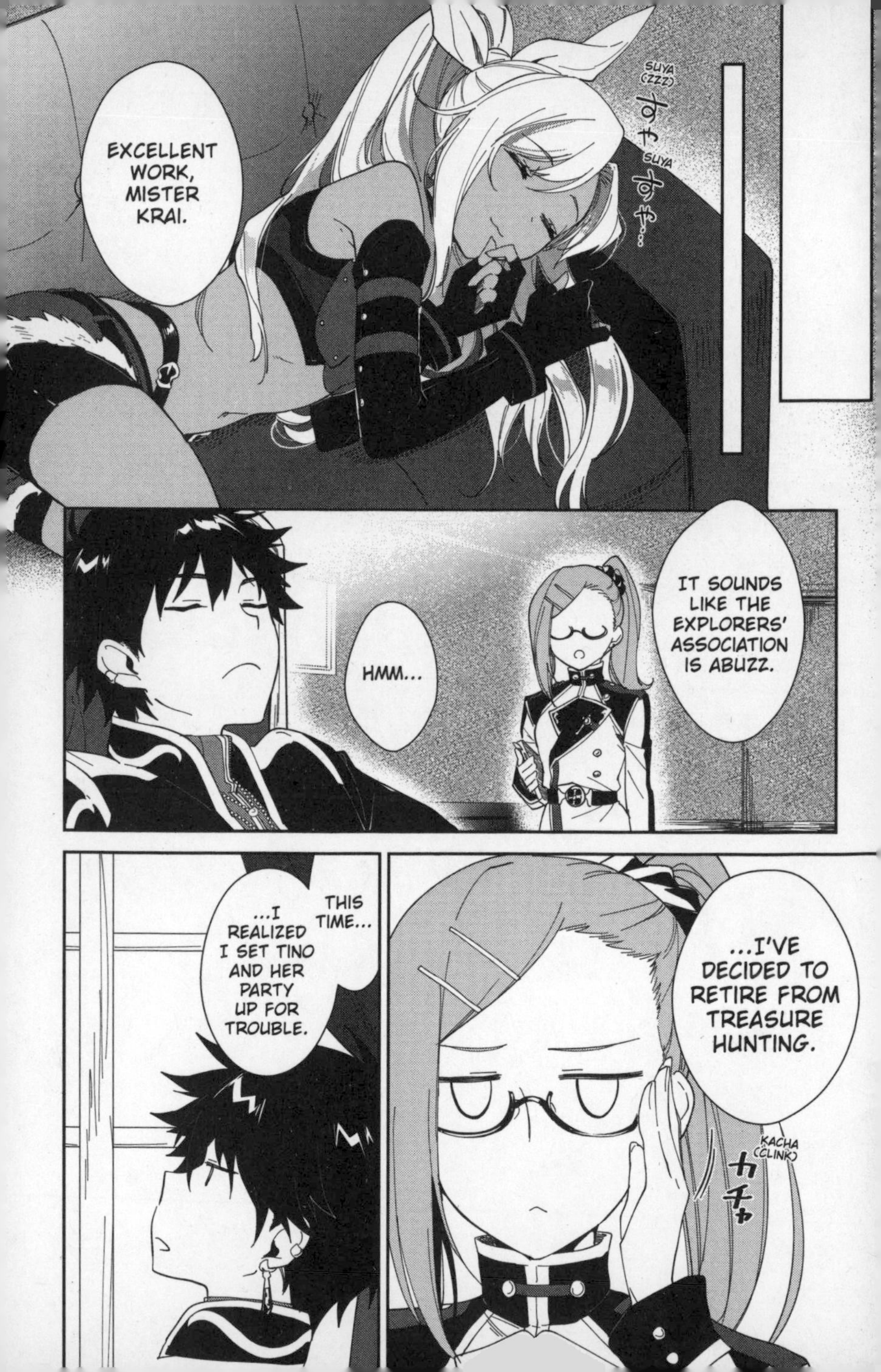

SUYA (ZZZ)
すや
SUYA
すや…
EXCELLENT WORK, MISTER KRAI.
IT SOUNDS LIKE THE EXPLORERS' ASSOCIATION IS ABUZZ.
HMM...
...I'VE DECIDED TO RETIRE FROM TREASURE HUNTING.
KACHA (CLINK)
カチャ
THIS TIME...
...I REALIZED I SET TINO AND HER PARTY UP FOR TROUBLE.

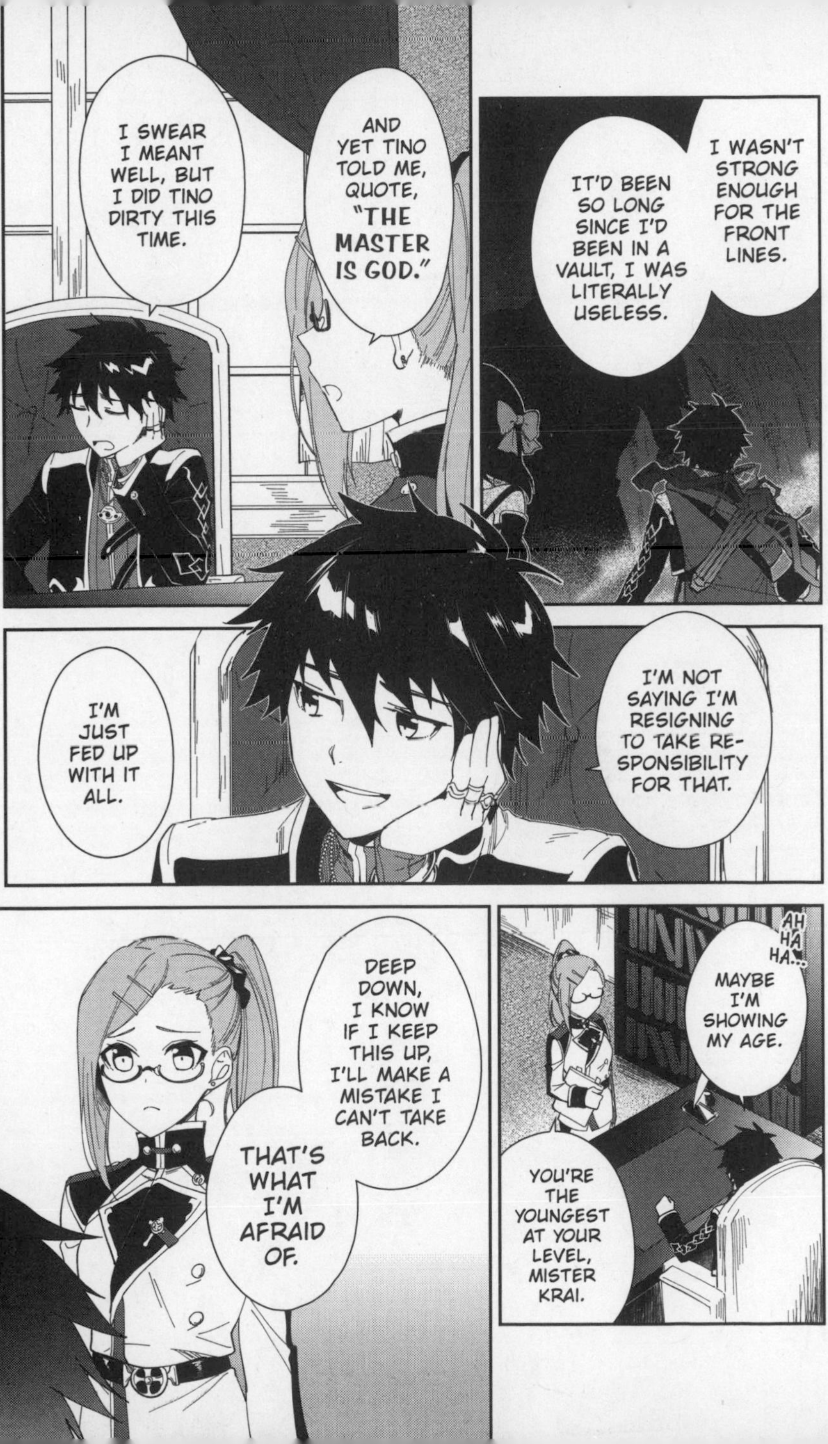
I WASN'T STRONG ENOUGH FOR THE FRONT LINES.
IT'D BEEN SO LONG SINCE I'D BEEN IN A VAULT, I WAS LITERALLY USELESS.
AND YET TINO TOLD ME, QUOTE, **"THE MASTER IS GOD."**
I SWEAR I MEANT WELL, BUT I DID TINO DIRTY THIS TIME.
I'M NOT SAYING I'M RESIGNING TO TAKE RE-SPONSIBILITY FOR THAT.
I'M JUST FED UP WITH IT ALL.
AH HA HA...
MAYBE I'M SHOWING MY AGE.
YOU'RE THE YOUNGEST AT YOUR LEVEL, MISTER KRAI.
DEEP DOWN, I KNOW IF I KEEP THIS UP, I'LL MAKE A MISTAKE I CAN'T TAKE BACK.
THAT'S WHAT I'M AFRAID OF.

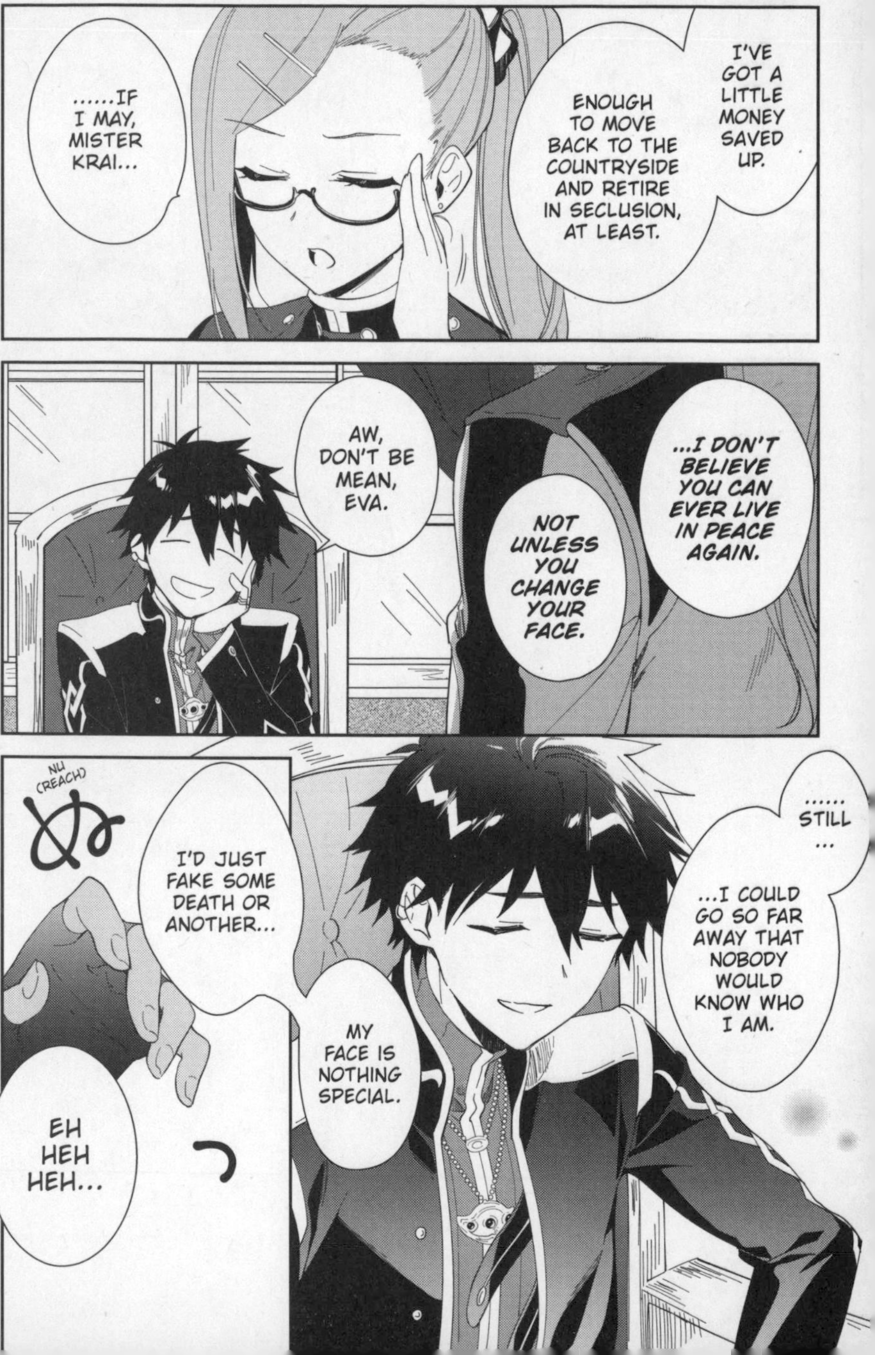
I'VE GOT A LITTLE MONEY SAVED UP.
ENOUGH TO MOVE BACK TO THE COUNTRYSIDE AND RETIRE IN SECLUSION, AT LEAST.
......IF I MAY, MISTER KRAI...
...I DON'T BELIEVE YOU CAN EVER LIVE IN PEACE AGAIN.
NOT UNLESS YOU CHANGE YOUR FACE.
AW, DON'T BE MEAN, EVA.
...... STILL ...
...I COULD GO SO FAR AWAY THAT NOBODY WOULD KNOW WHO I AM.
I'D JUST FAKE SOME DEATH OR ANOTHER...
MY FACE IS NOTHING SPECIAL.
NU (REACH)
ぬ
EH HEH HEH...
つ

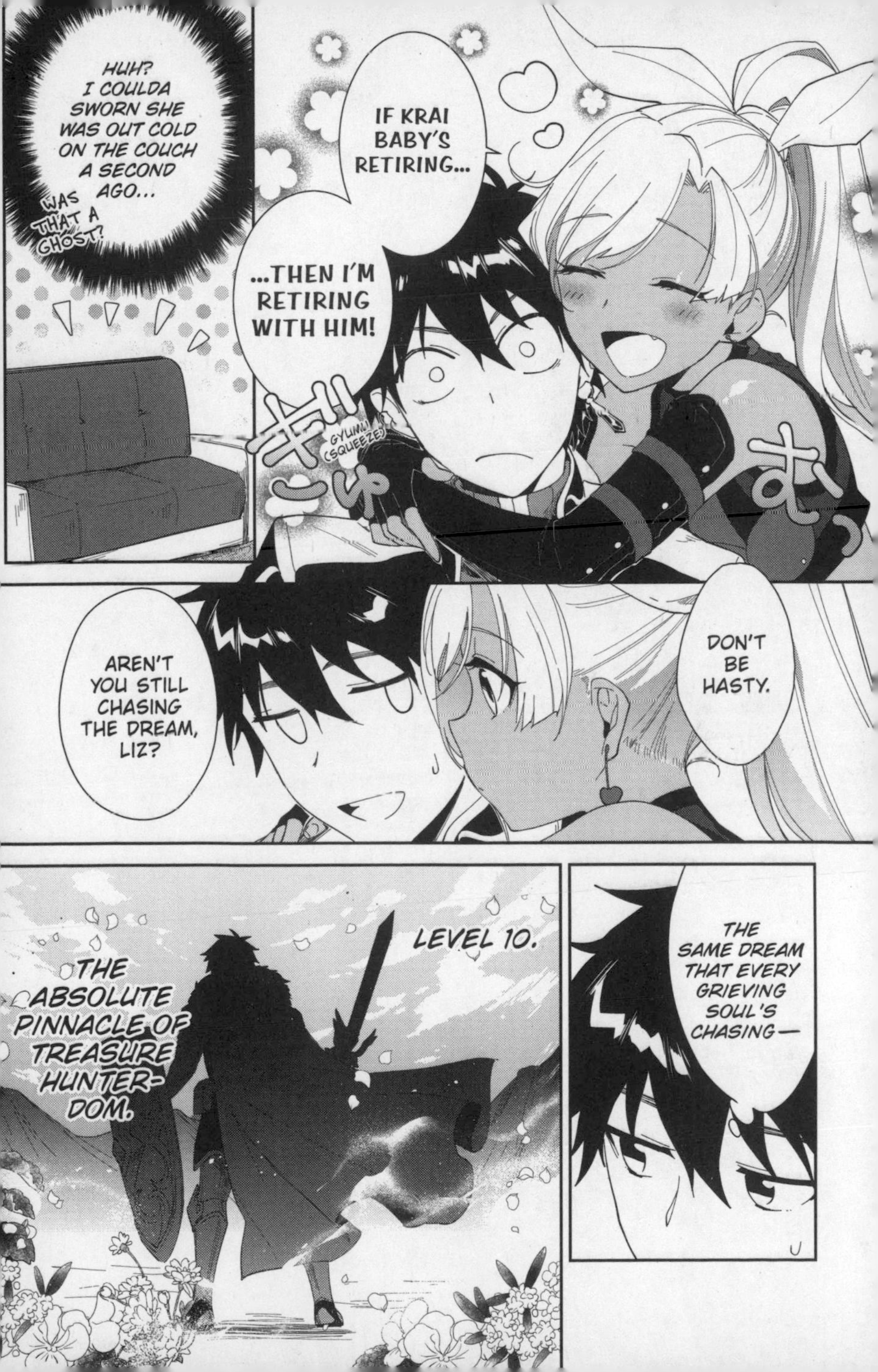
IF KRAI BABY'S RETIRING...
...THEN I'M RETIRING WITH HIM!
GYUMU (SQUEEZE)
HUH? I COULDA SWORN SHE WAS OUT COLD ON THE COUCH A SECOND AGO...
WAS THAT A GHOST?
DON'T BE HASTY.
AREN'T YOU STILL CHASING THE DREAM, LIZ?
THE SAME DREAM THAT EVERY GRIEVING SOUL'S CHASING—
LEVEL 10.
THE ABSOLUTE PINNACLE OF TREASURE HUNTER-DOM.

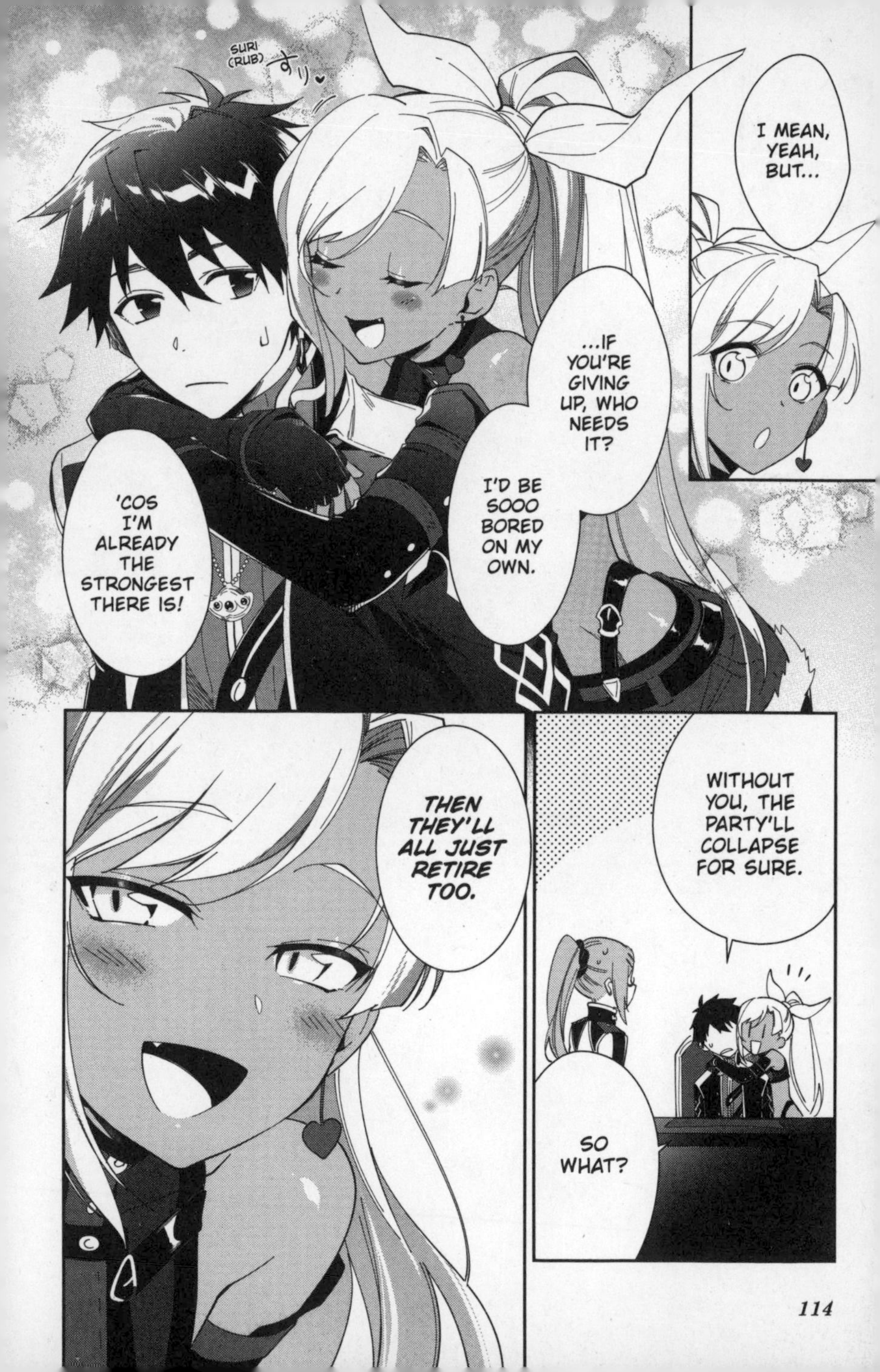
I MEAN, YEAH, BUT...
SURI (RUB)
...IF YOU'RE GIVING UP, WHO NEEDS IT?
I'D BE SOOO BORED ON MY OWN.
'COS I'M ALREADY THE STRONGEST THERE IS!
WITHOUT YOU, THE PARTY'LL COLLAPSE FOR SURE.
SO WHAT?
THEN THEY'LL ALL JUST RETIRE TOO.

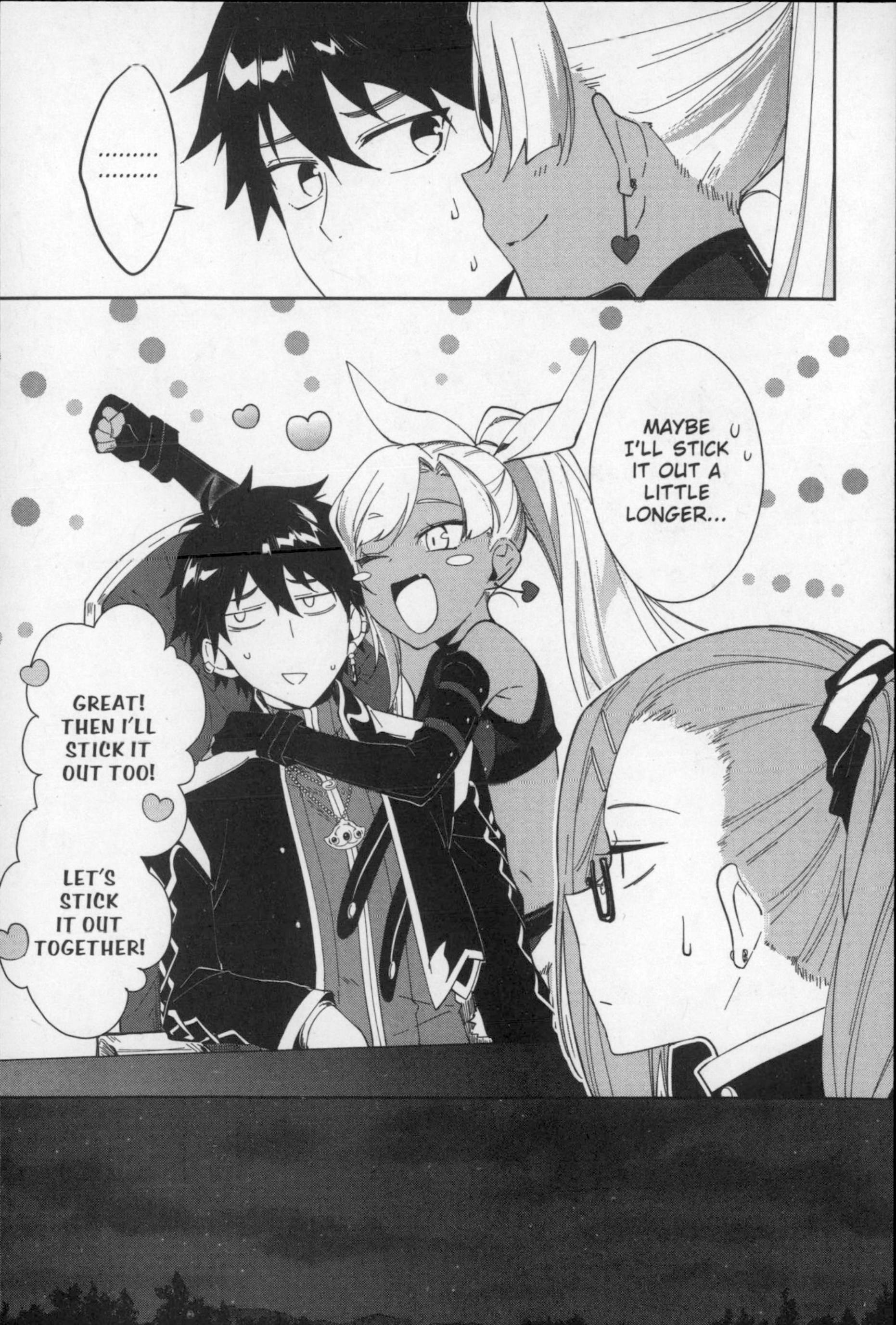
....
....
MAYBE I'LL STICK IT OUT A LITTLE LONGER...
GREAT! THEN I'LL STICK IT OUT TOO!
LET'S STICK IT OUT TOGETHER!

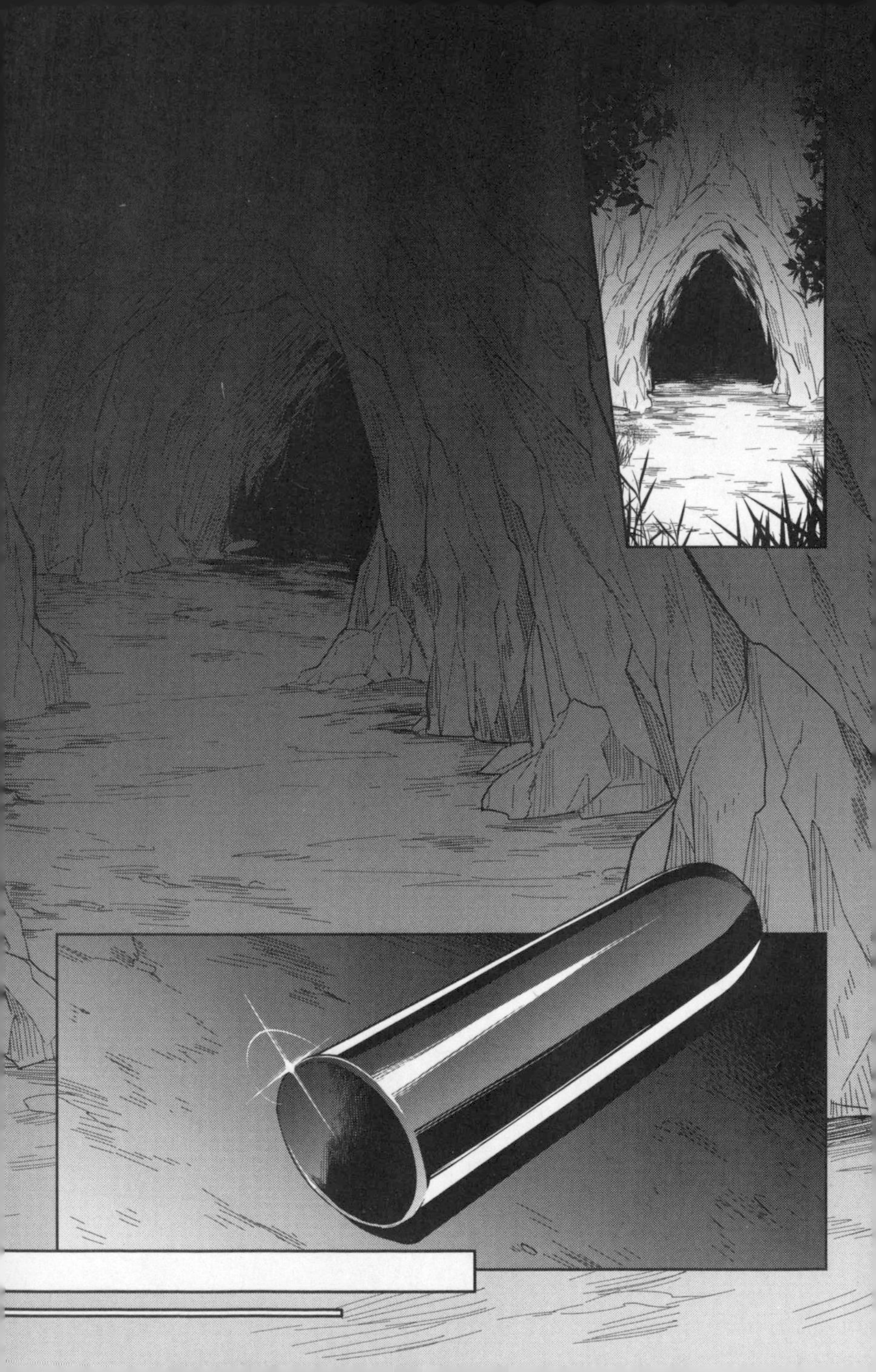

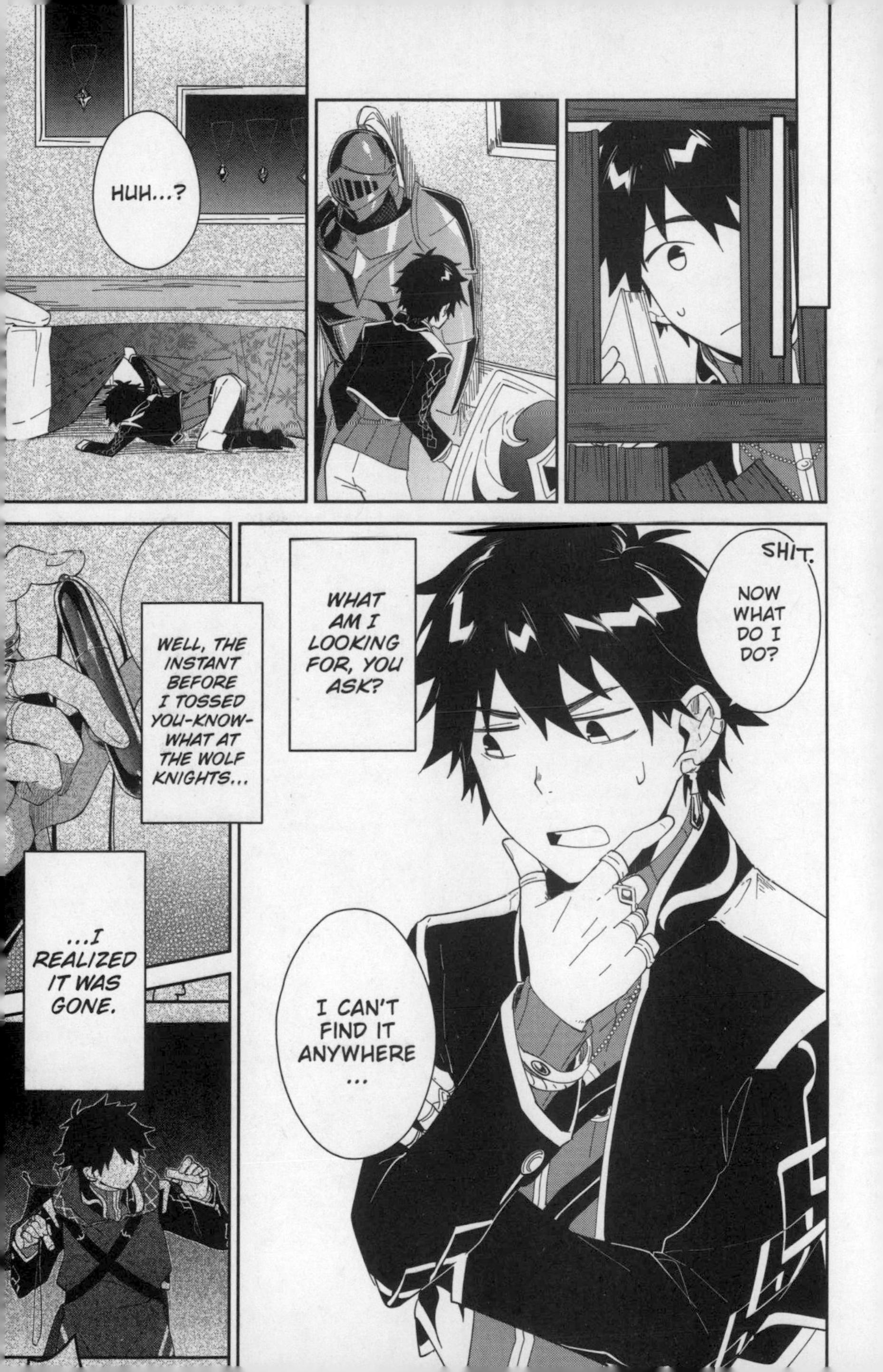
HUH...?
SHIT.
NOW WHAT DO I DO?
WHAT AM I LOOKING FOR, YOU ASK?
I CAN'T FIND IT ANYWHERE...
WELL, THE INSTANT BEFORE I TOSSED YOU-KNOW-WHAT AT THE WOLF KNIGHTS...
...I REALIZED IT WAS GONE.

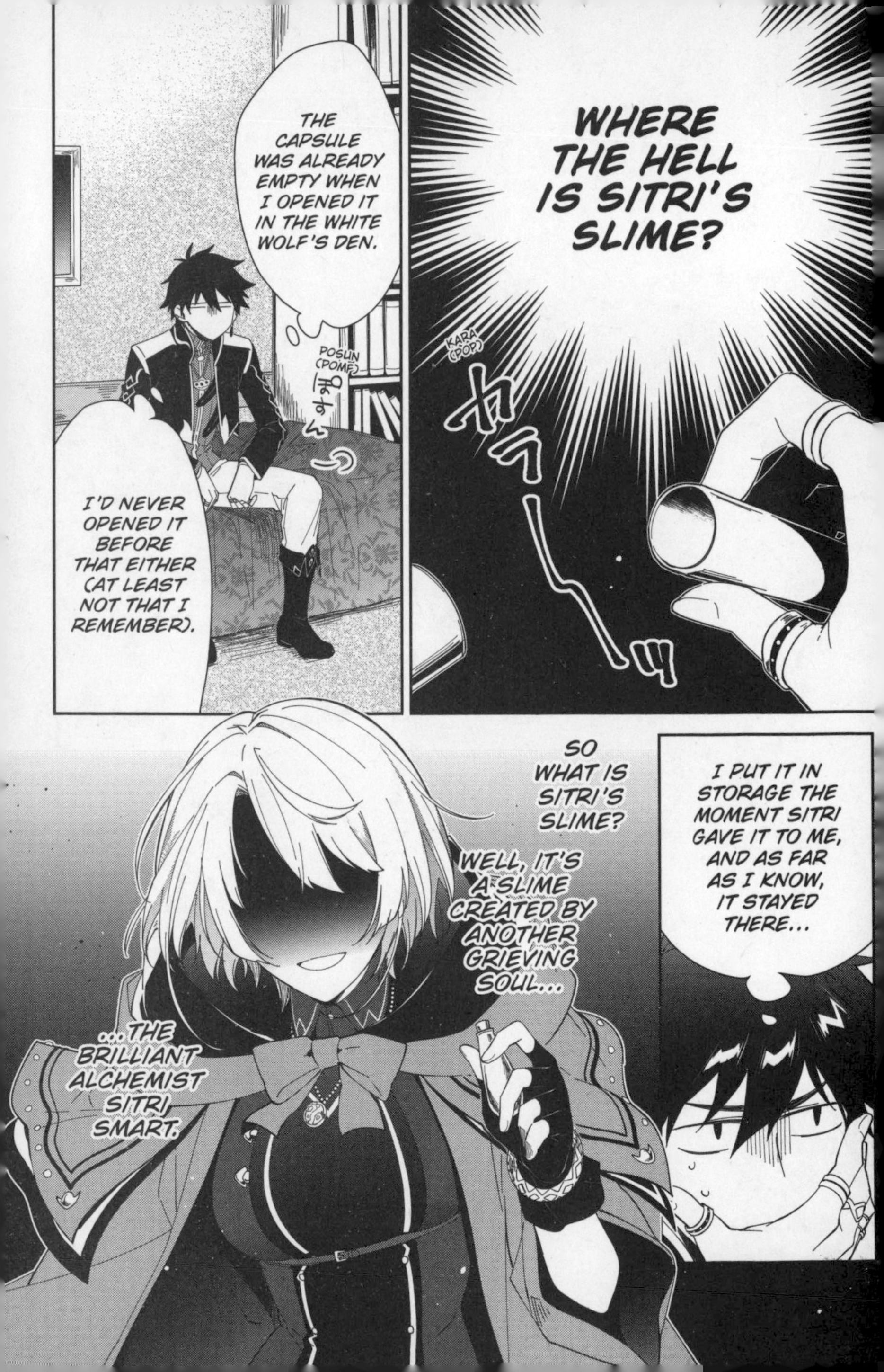
WHERE THE HELL IS SITRI'S SLIME?
KARA (POP)
カラーッ
THE CAPSULE WAS ALREADY EMPTY WHEN I OPENED IT IN THE WHITE WOLF'S DEN.
POSLIN (POMF)
ぽすん
I'D NEVER OPENED IT BEFORE THAT EITHER (AT LEAST NOT THAT I REMEMBER).
I PUT IT IN STORAGE THE MOMENT SITRI GAVE IT TO ME, AND AS FAR AS I KNOW, IT STAYED THERE...
SO WHAT IS SITRI'S SLIME?
WELL, IT'S A SLIME CREATED BY ANOTHER GRIEVING SOUL...
...THE BRILLIANT ALCHEMIST SITRI SMART.

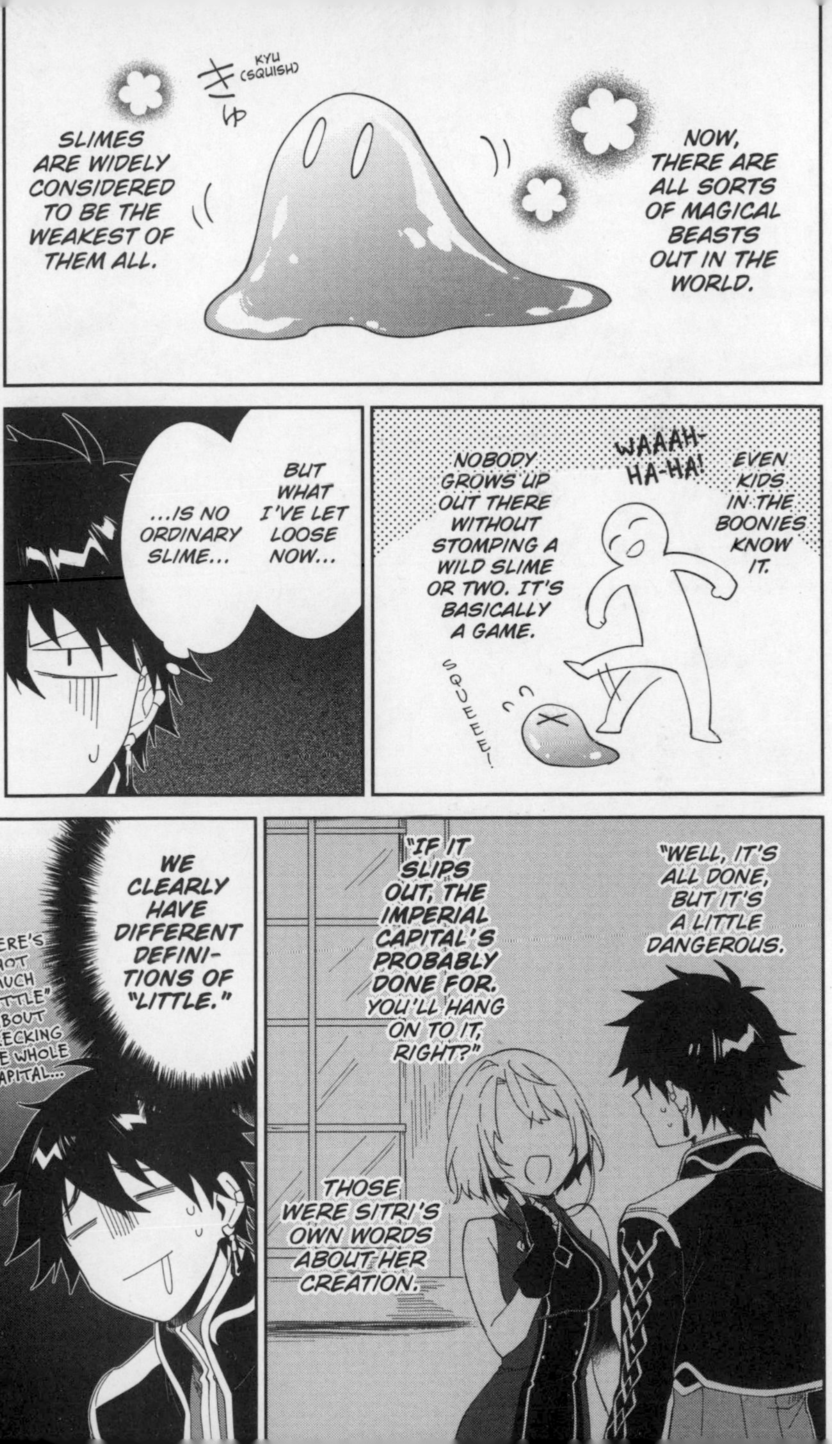
NOW, THERE ARE ALL SORTS OF MAGICAL BEASTS OUT IN THE WORLD.
KYU (SQUISH)
SLIMES ARE WIDELY CONSIDERED TO BE THE WEAKEST OF THEM ALL.
EVEN KIDS IN THE BOONIES KNOW IT.
WAAAH-HA-HA!
NOBODY GROWS UP OUT THERE WITHOUT STOMPING A WILD SLIME OR TWO. IT'S BASICALLY A GAME.
SQUEEEE!
BUT WHAT I'VE LET LOOSE NOW...
...IS NO ORDINARY SLIME...
"WELL, IT'S ALL DONE, BUT IT'S A LITTLE DANGEROUS.
"IF IT SLIPS OUT, THE IMPERIAL CAPITAL'S PROBABLY DONE FOR. YOU'LL HANG ON TO IT, RIGHT?"
THOSE WERE SITRI'S OWN WORDS ABOUT HER CREATION.
WE CLEARLY HAVE DIFFERENT DEFINITIONS OF "LITTLE."
THERE'S NOT MUCH "LITTLE" ABOUT WRECKING THE WHOLE CAPITAL...

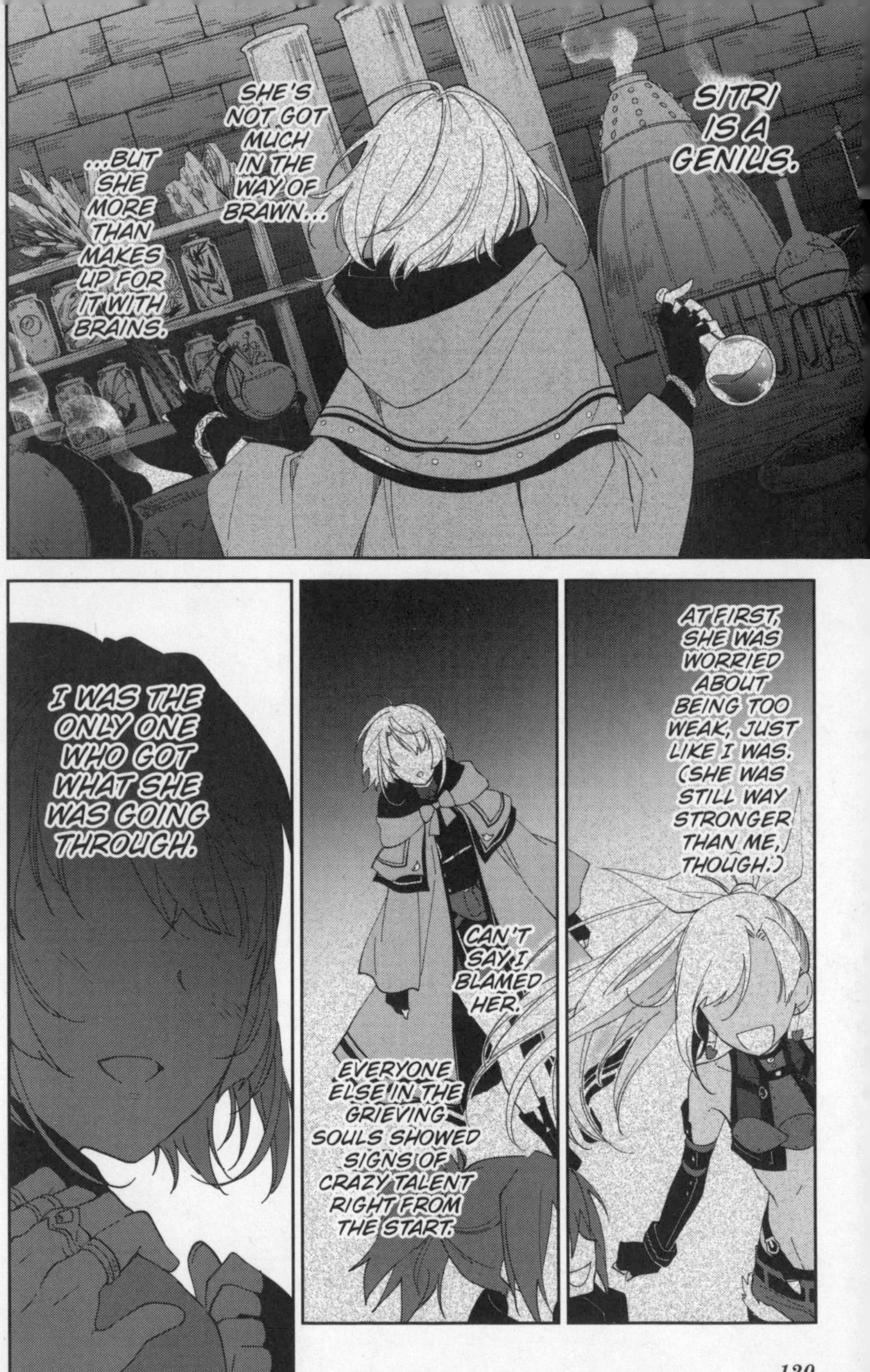
SITRI IS A GENIUS.
SHE'S NOT GOT MUCH IN THE WAY OF BRAWN...
...BUT SHE MORE THAN MAKES UP FOR IT WITH BRAINS.
AT FIRST, SHE WAS WORRIED ABOUT BEING TOO WEAK, JUST LIKE I WAS. (SHE WAS STILL WAY STRONGER THAN ME, THOUGH.)
CAN'T SAY I BLAMED HER.
EVERYONE ELSE IN THE GRIEVING SOULS SHOWED SIGNS OF CRAZY TALENT RIGHT FROM THE START.
I WAS THE ONLY ONE WHO GOT WHAT SHE WAS GOING THROUGH.

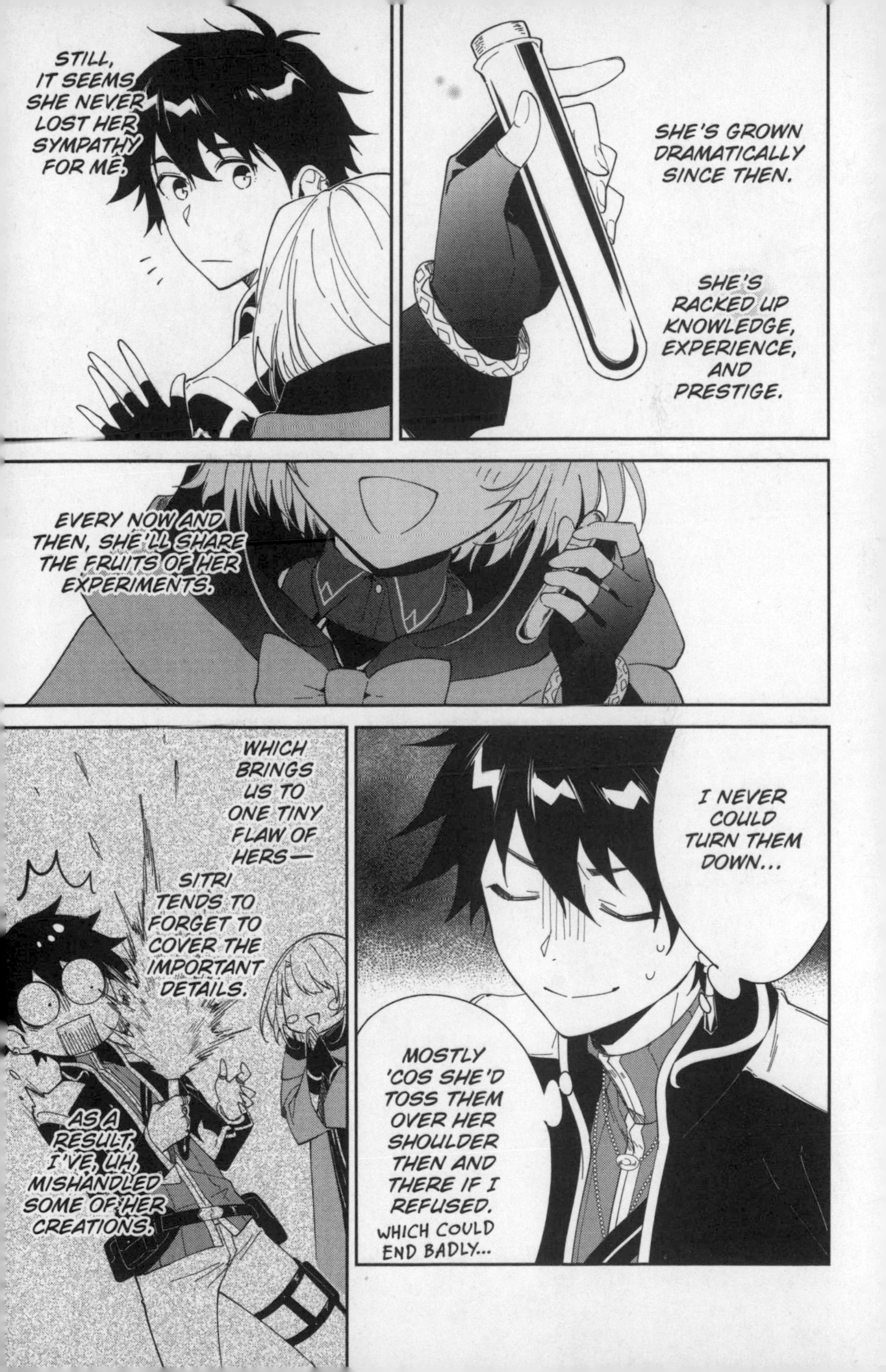
SHE'S GROWN DRAMATICALLY SINCE THEN.
SHE'S RACKED UP KNOWLEDGE, EXPERIENCE, AND PRESTIGE.
STILL, IT SEEMS SHE NEVER LOST HER SYMPATHY FOR ME.
EVERY NOW AND THEN, SHE'LL SHARE THE FRUITS OF HER EXPERIMENTS.
I NEVER COULD TURN THEM DOWN...
MOSTLY 'COS SHE'D TOSS THEM OVER HER SHOULDER THEN AND THERE IF I REFUSED.
WHICH COULD END BADLY...
WHICH BRINGS US TO ONE TINY FLAW OF HERS—
SITRI TENDS TO FORGET TO COVER THE IMPORTANT DETAILS.
AS A RESULT, I'VE, UH, MISHANDLED SOME OF HER CREATIONS.

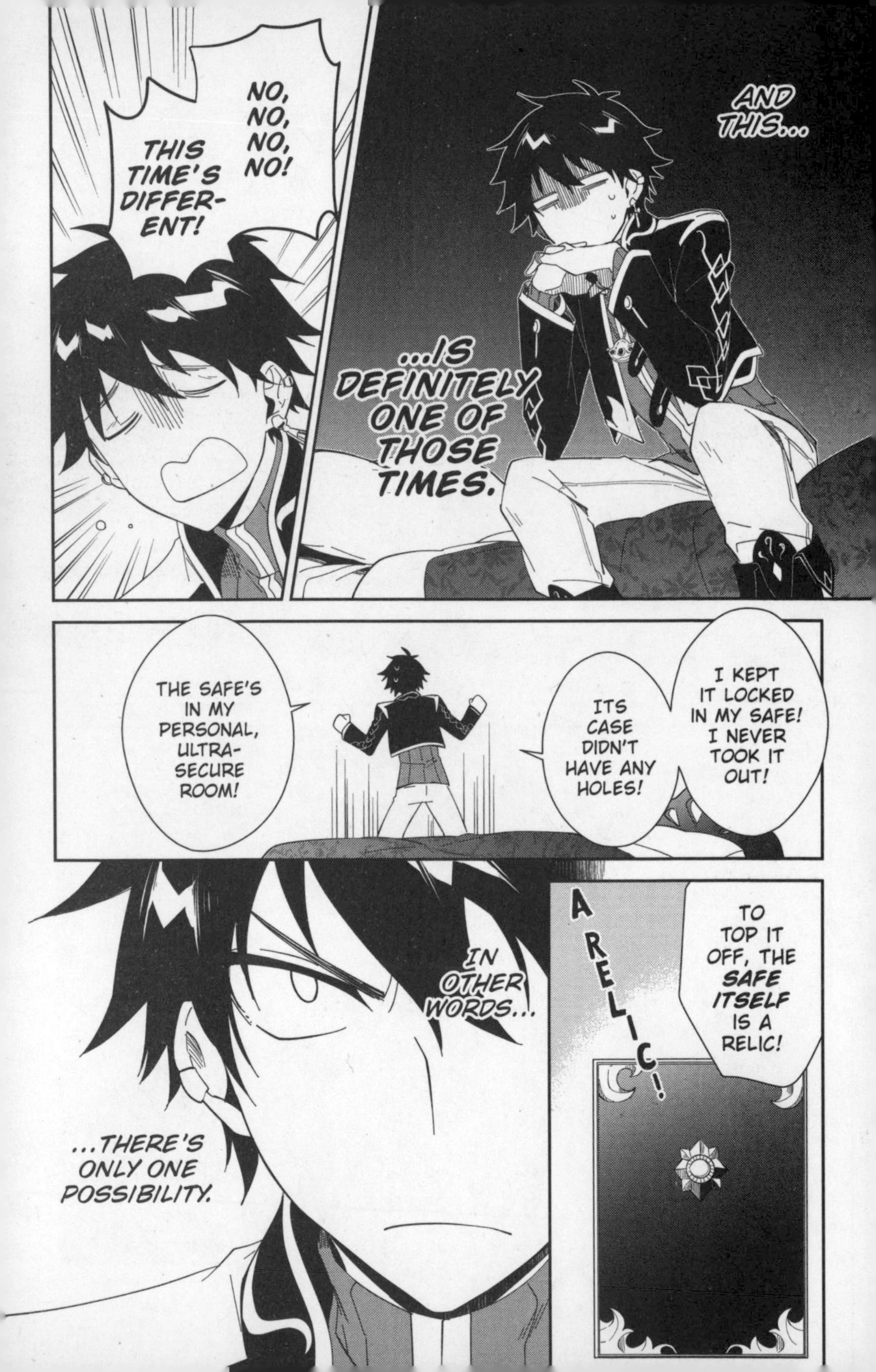
AND THIS...
...IS DEFINITELY ONE OF THOSE TIMES.
NO, NO, NO, NO!
THIS TIME'S DIFFERENT!
I KEPT IT LOCKED IN MY SAFE! I NEVER TOOK IT OUT!
ITS CASE DIDN'T HAVE ANY HOLES!
THE SAFE'S IN MY PERSONAL, ULTRA-SECURE ROOM!
TO TOP IT OFF, THE SAFE ITSELF IS A RELIC!
A RELIC!
IN OTHER WORDS...
...THERE'S ONLY ONE POSSIBILITY.

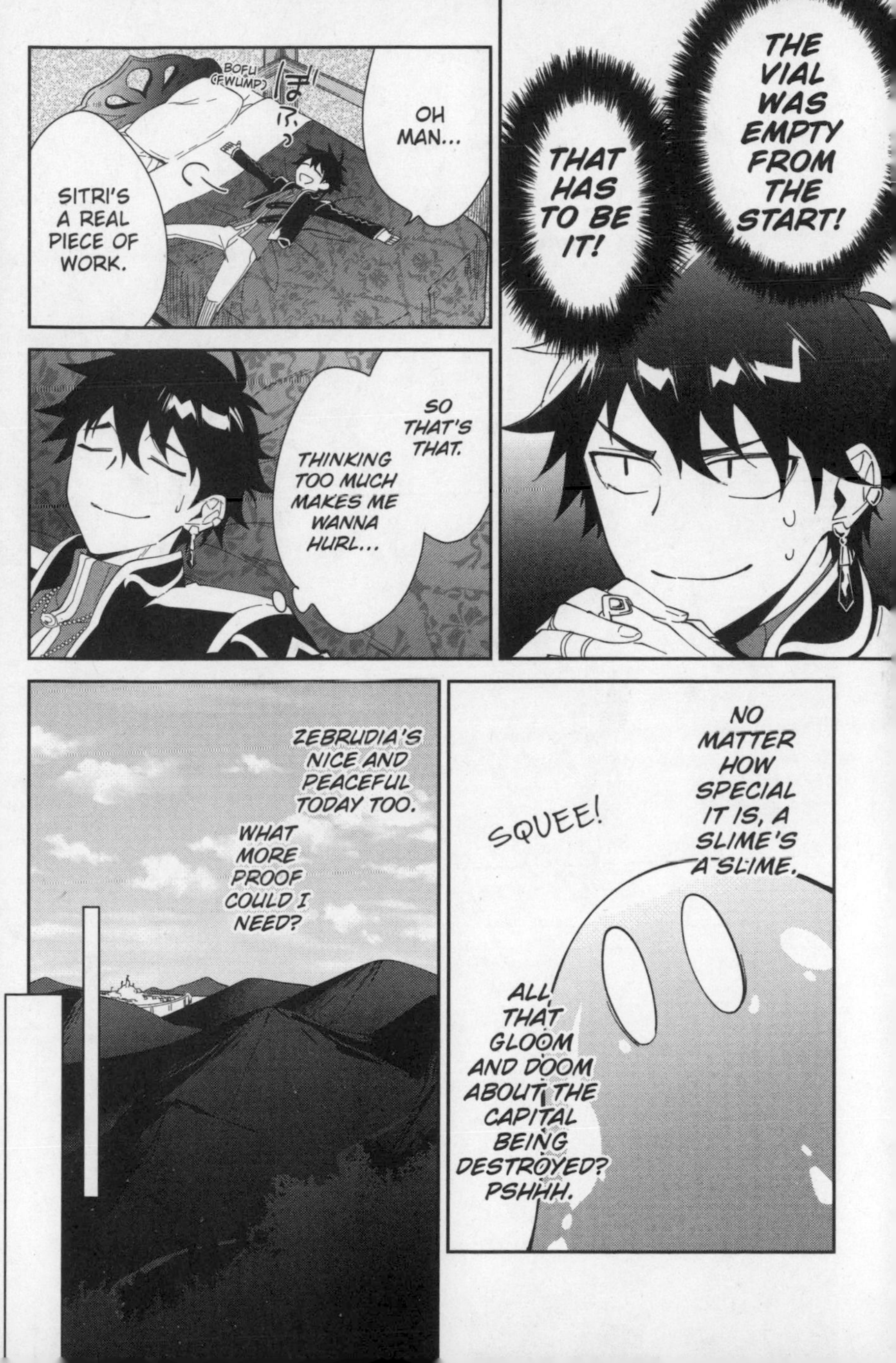
THE VIAL WAS EMPTY FROM THE START!
THAT HAS TO BE IT!
BOFU (FWUMP)
ぼふっ
OH MAN...
SITRI'S A REAL PIECE OF WORK.
SO THAT'S THAT.
THINKING TOO MUCH MAKES ME WANNA HURL...
NO MATTER HOW SPECIAL IT IS, A SLIME'S A SLIME.
SQUEE!
ALL THAT GLOOM AND DOOM ABOUT THE CAPITAL BEING DESTROYED? PSHHH.
ZEBRUDIA'S NICE AND PEACEFUL TODAY TOO.
WHAT MORE PROOF COULD I NEED?

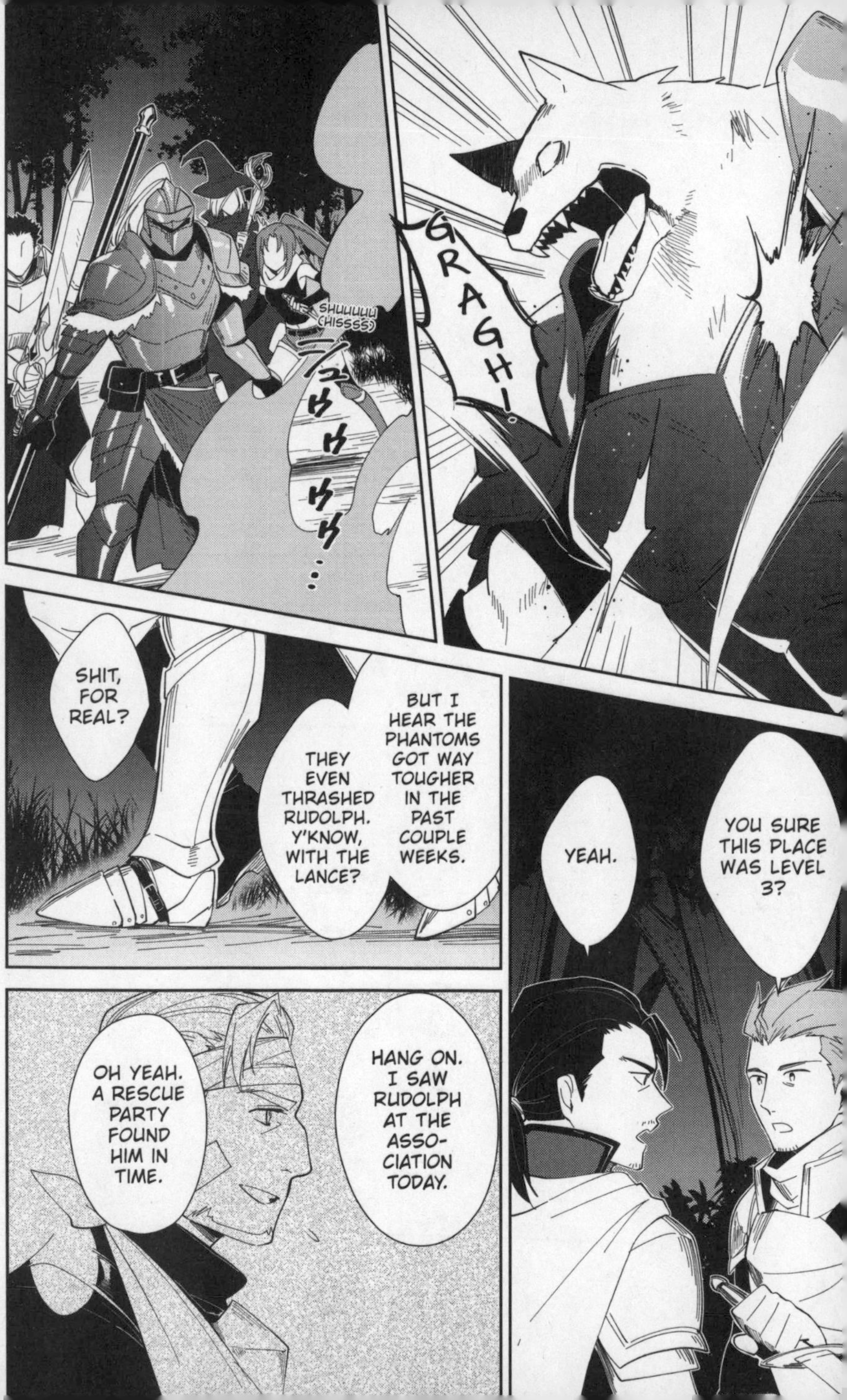
GRAGH!
SHUUUUU (HISSSS)
YOU SURE THIS PLACE WAS LEVEL 3?
YEAH.
BUT I HEAR THE PHANTOMS GOT WAY TOUGHER IN THE PAST COUPLE WEEKS.
THEY EVEN THRASHED RUDOLPH. Y'KNOW, WITH THE LANCE?
SHIT, FOR REAL?
HANG ON. I SAW RUDOLPH AT THE ASSO-CIATION TODAY.
OH YEAH. A RESCUE PARTY FOUND HIM IN TIME.

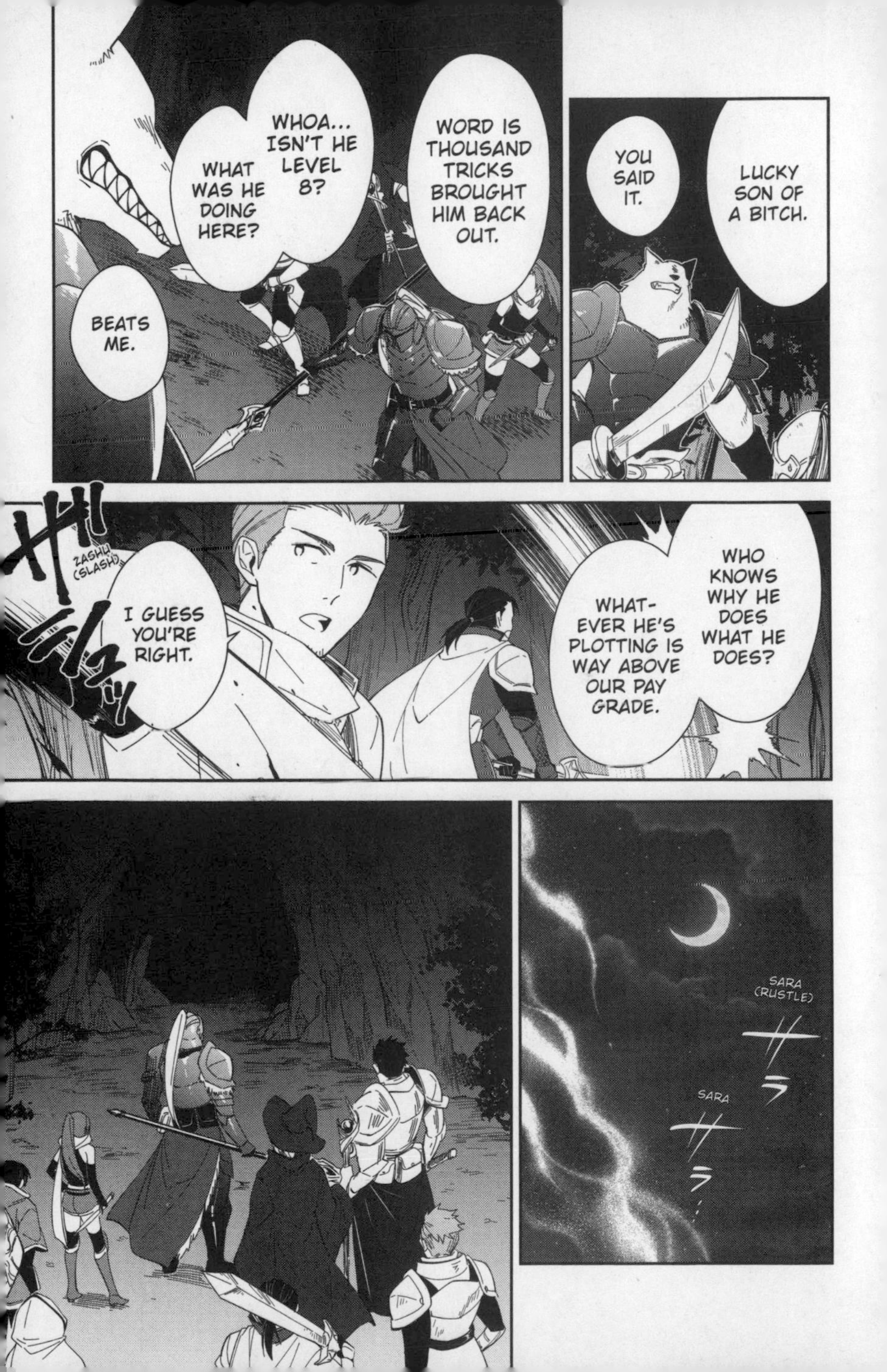
LUCKY SON OF A BITCH.
YOU SAID IT.
WORD IS THOUSAND TRICKS BROUGHT HIM BACK OUT.
WHOA... ISN'T HE LEVEL 8?
WHAT WAS HE DOING HERE?
BEATS ME.
WHO KNOWS WHY HE DOES WHAT HE DOES?
WHAT-EVER HE'S PLOTTING IS WAY ABOVE OUR PAY GRADE.
ZASHU (SLASH)
I GUESS YOU'RE RIGHT.
SARA (RUSTLE)
SARA

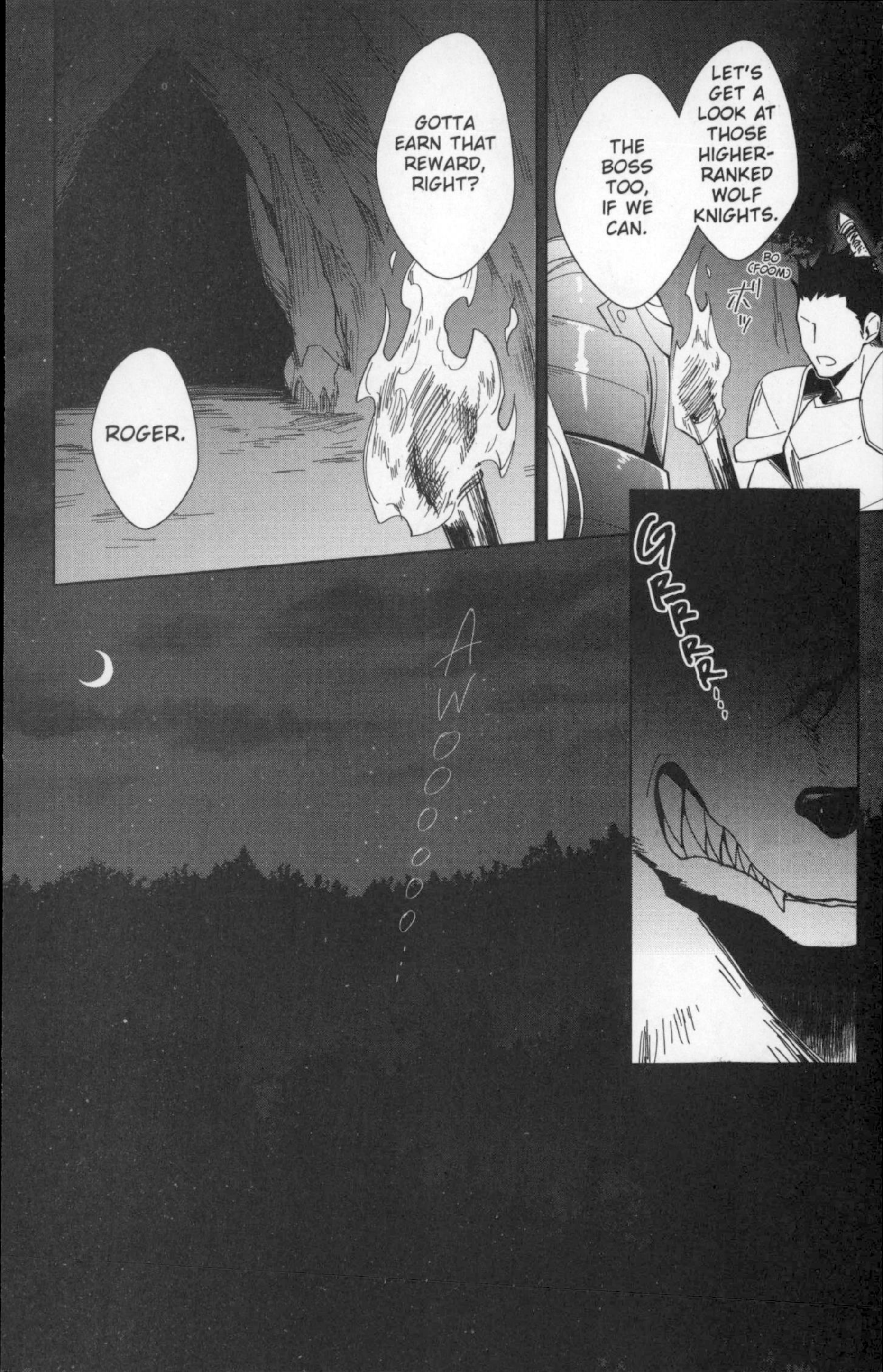

LET'S GET A LOOK AT THOSE HIGHER-RANKED WOLF KNIGHTS.
THE BOSS TOO, IF WE CAN.
BO (FOOM)
ボッ
GOTTA EARN THAT REWARD, RIGHT?
ROGER.
GRRRR...
AWOOOOOOO...

Chapter 15

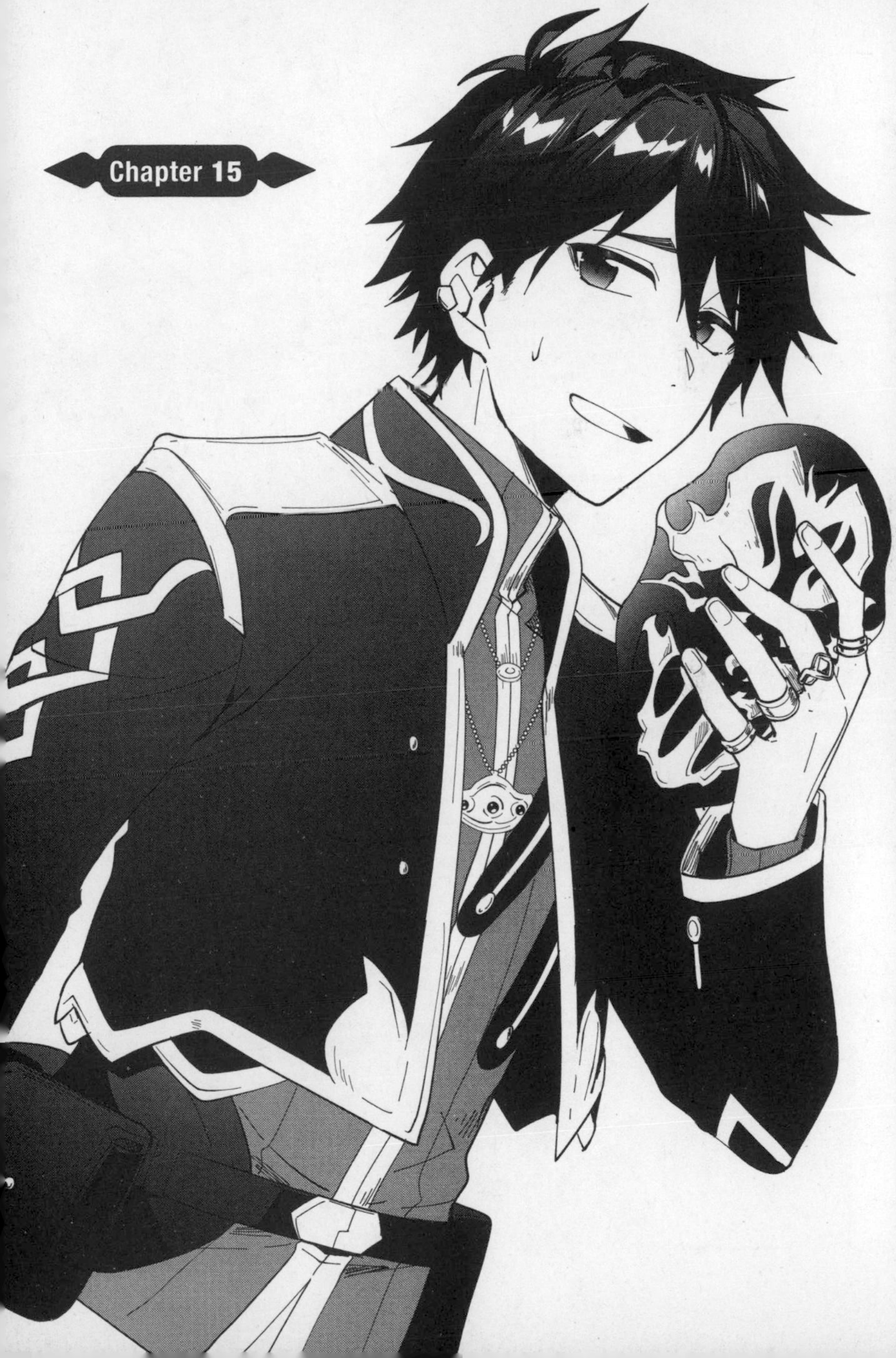

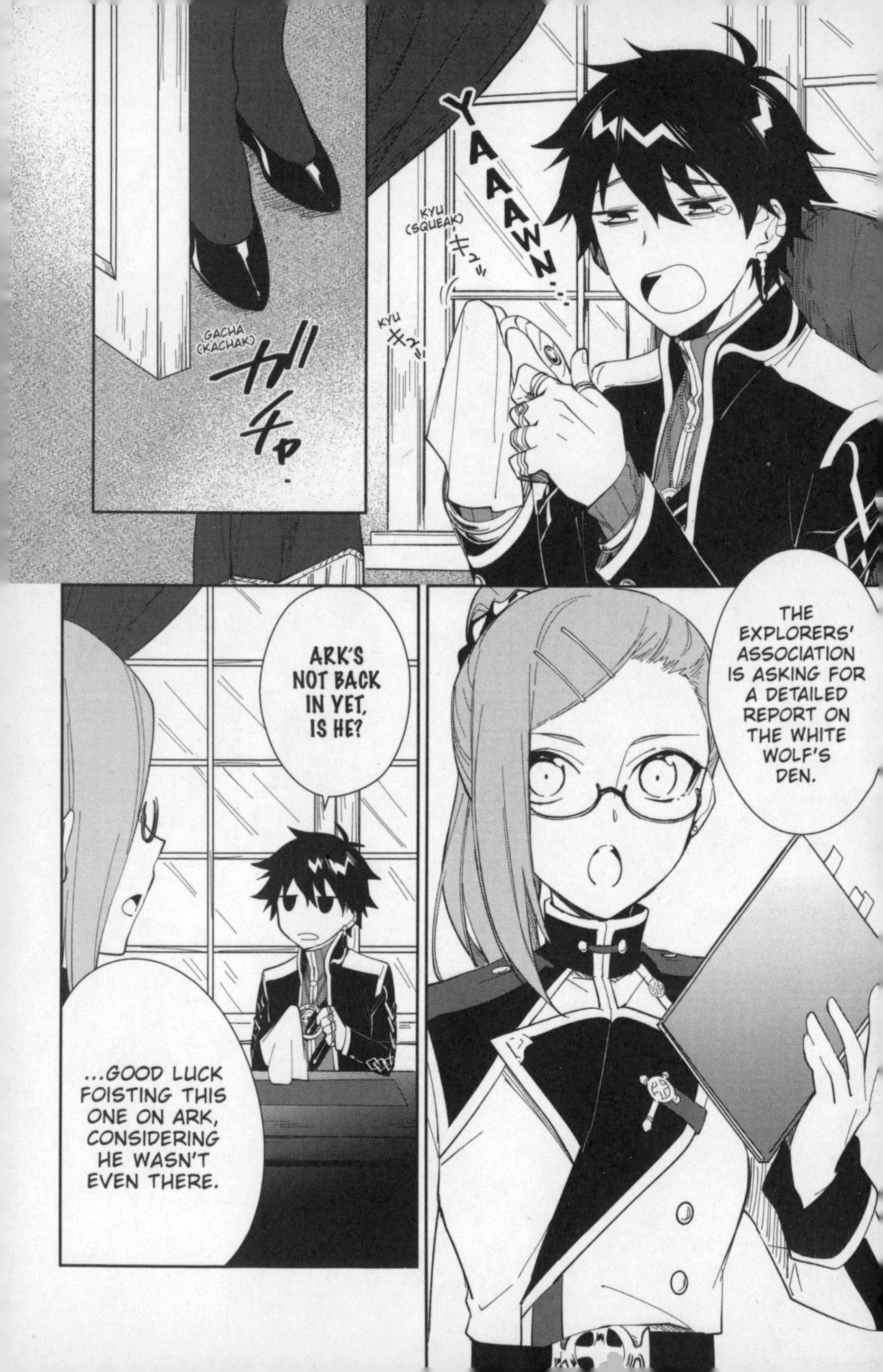
YAAAWN...
KYU (SQUEAK)
キュッ
KYU
キュ
GACHA (KACHAK)
ガチャ
THE EXPLORERS' ASSOCIATION IS ASKING FOR A DETAILED REPORT ON THE WHITE WOLF'S DEN.
ARK'S NOT BACK IN YET, IS HE?
...GOOD LUCK FOISTING THIS ONE ON ARK, CONSIDERING HE WASN'T EVEN THERE.

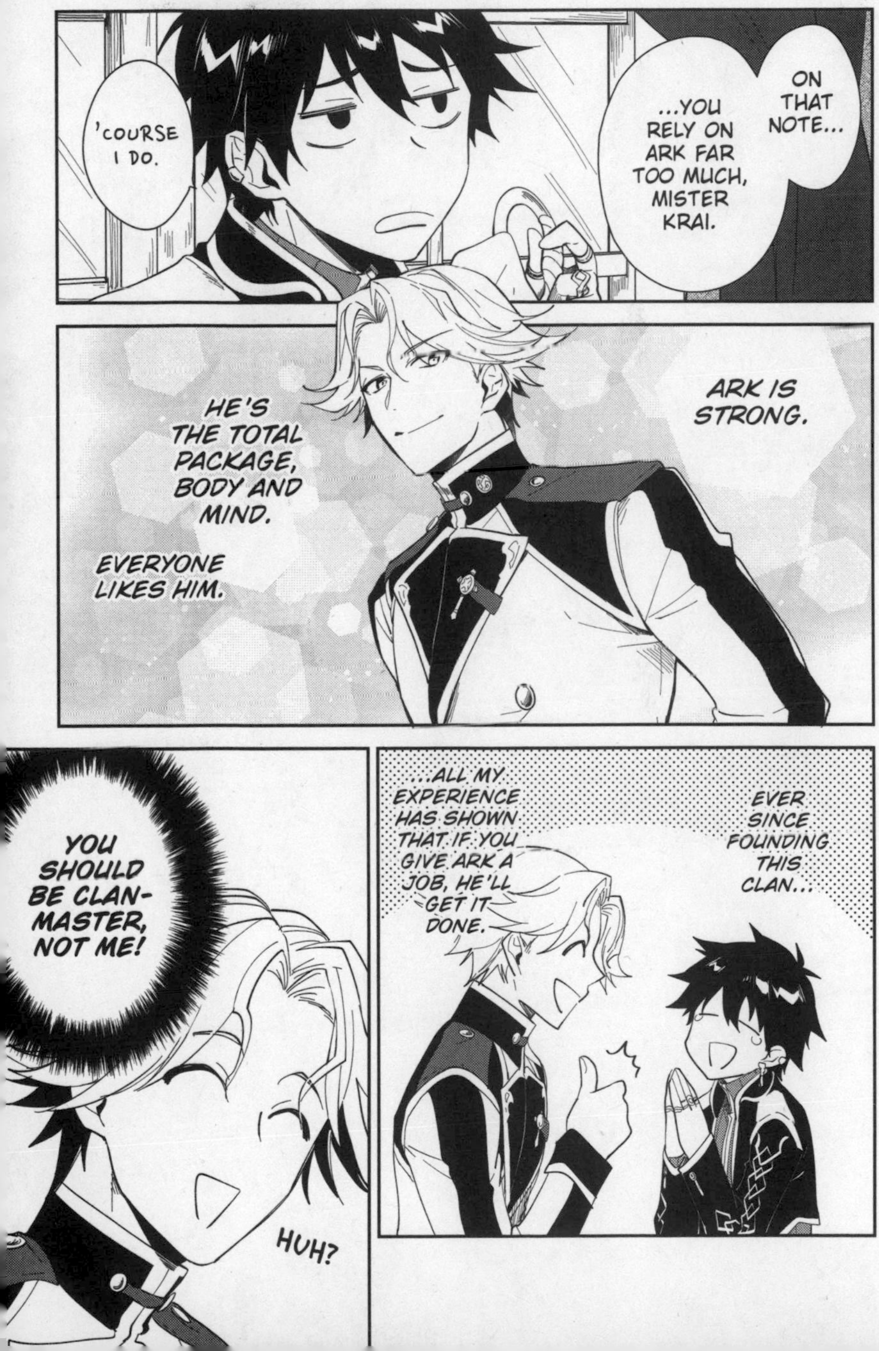
ON THAT NOTE...
...YOU RELY ON ARK FAR TOO MUCH, MISTER KRAI.
'COURSE I DO.
ARK IS STRONG.
HE'S THE TOTAL PACKAGE, BODY AND MIND.
EVERYONE LIKES HIM.
EVER SINCE FOUNDING THIS CLAN...
...ALL MY EXPERIENCE HAS SHOWN THAT IF YOU GIVE ARK A JOB, HE'LL GET IT DONE.
YOU SHOULD BE CLAN-MASTER, NOT ME!
HUH?

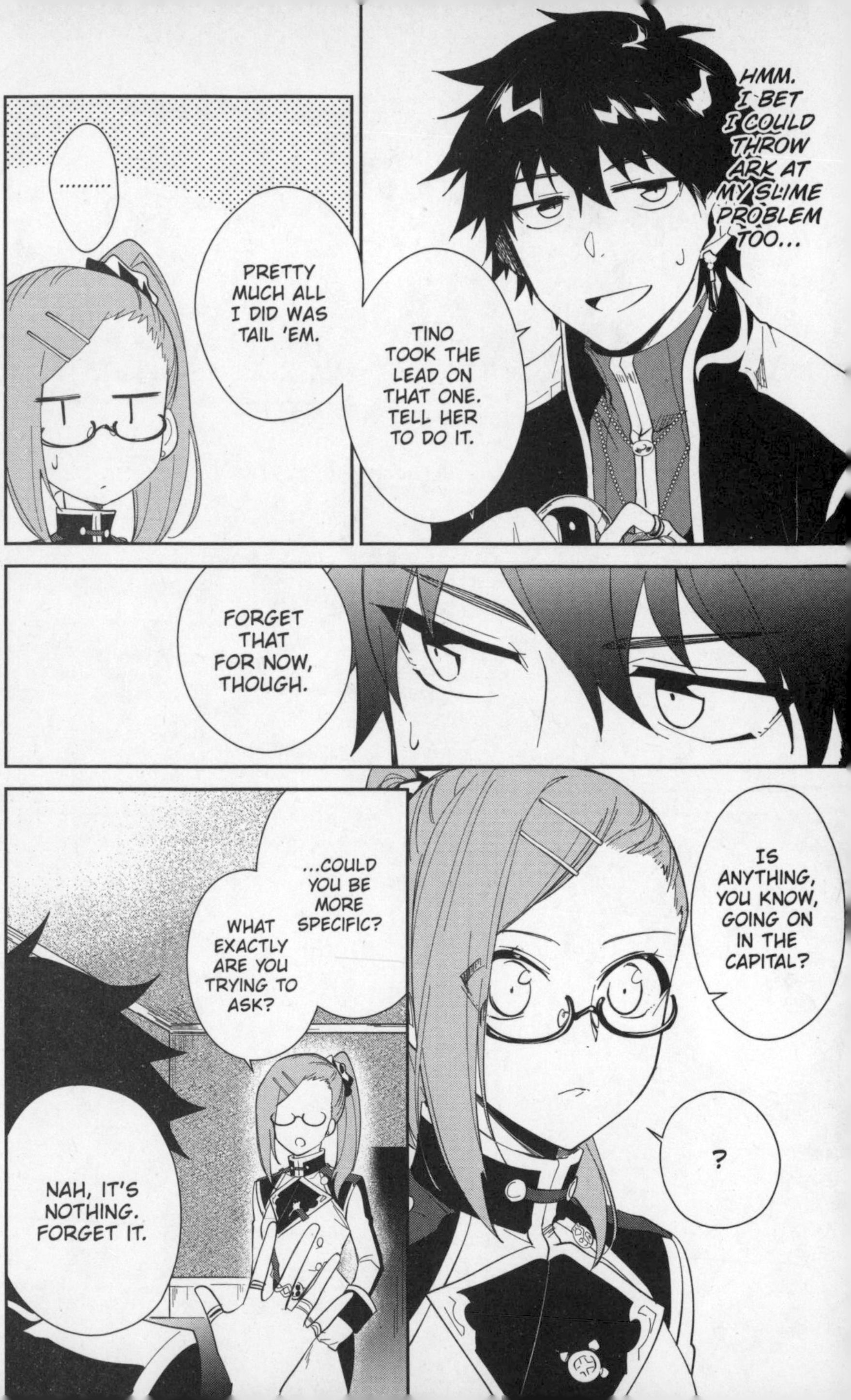

HMM. I BET I COULD THROW ARK AT MY SLIME PROBLEM TOO...
PRETTY MUCH ALL I DID WAS TAIL 'EM.
TINO TOOK THE LEAD ON THAT ONE. TELL HER TO DO IT.
....
FORGET THAT FOR NOW, THOUGH.
IS ANYTHING, YOU KNOW, GOING ON IN THE CAPITAL?
?
...COULD YOU BE MORE SPECIFIC?
WHAT EXACTLY ARE YOU TRYING TO ASK?
NAH, IT'S NOTHING. FORGET IT.

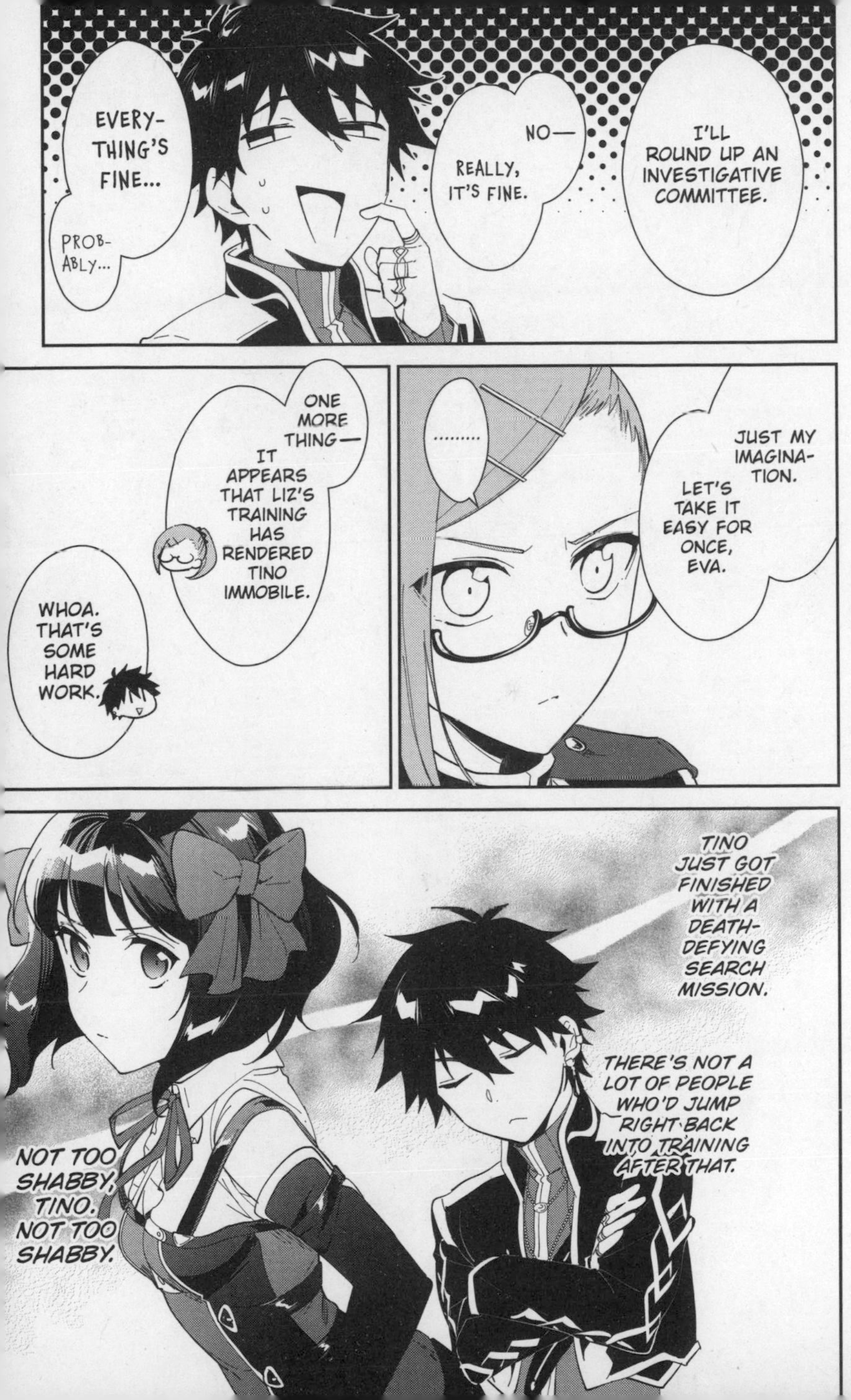
I'LL ROUND UP AN INVESTIGATIVE COMMITTEE.
NO— REALLY, IT'S FINE.
EVERY-THING'S FINE... PROB-ABLY...
JUST MY IMAGINATION.
LET'S TAKE IT EASY FOR ONCE, EVA.
....
ONE MORE THING— IT APPEARS THAT LIZ'S TRAINING HAS RENDERED TINO IMMOBILE.
WHOA. THAT'S SOME HARD WORK.
TINO JUST GOT FINISHED WITH A DEATH-DEFYING SEARCH MISSION.
THERE'S NOT A LOT OF PEOPLE WHO'D JUMP RIGHT BACK INTO TRAINING AFTER THAT.
NOT TOO SHABBY, TINO. NOT TOO SHABBY.

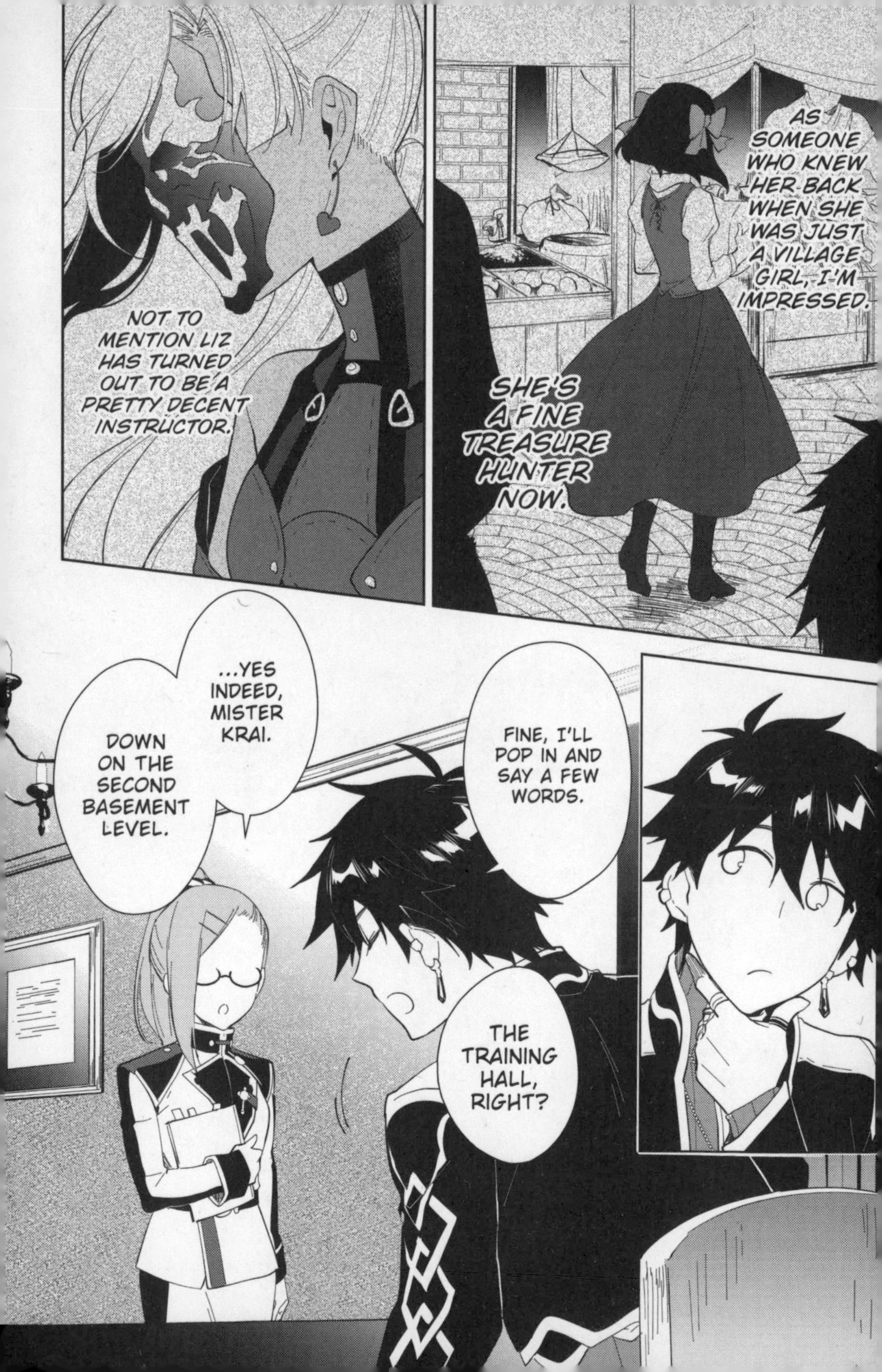
AS SOMEONE WHO KNEW HER BACK WHEN SHE WAS JUST A VILLAGE GIRL, I'M IMPRESSED.
SHE'S A FINE TREASURE HUNTER NOW.
NOT TO MENTION LIZ HAS TURNED OUT TO BE A PRETTY DECENT INSTRUCTOR.
FINE, I'LL POP IN AND SAY A FEW WORDS.
THE TRAINING HALL, RIGHT?
...YES INDEED, MISTER KRAI.
DOWN ON THE SECOND BASEMENT LEVEL.

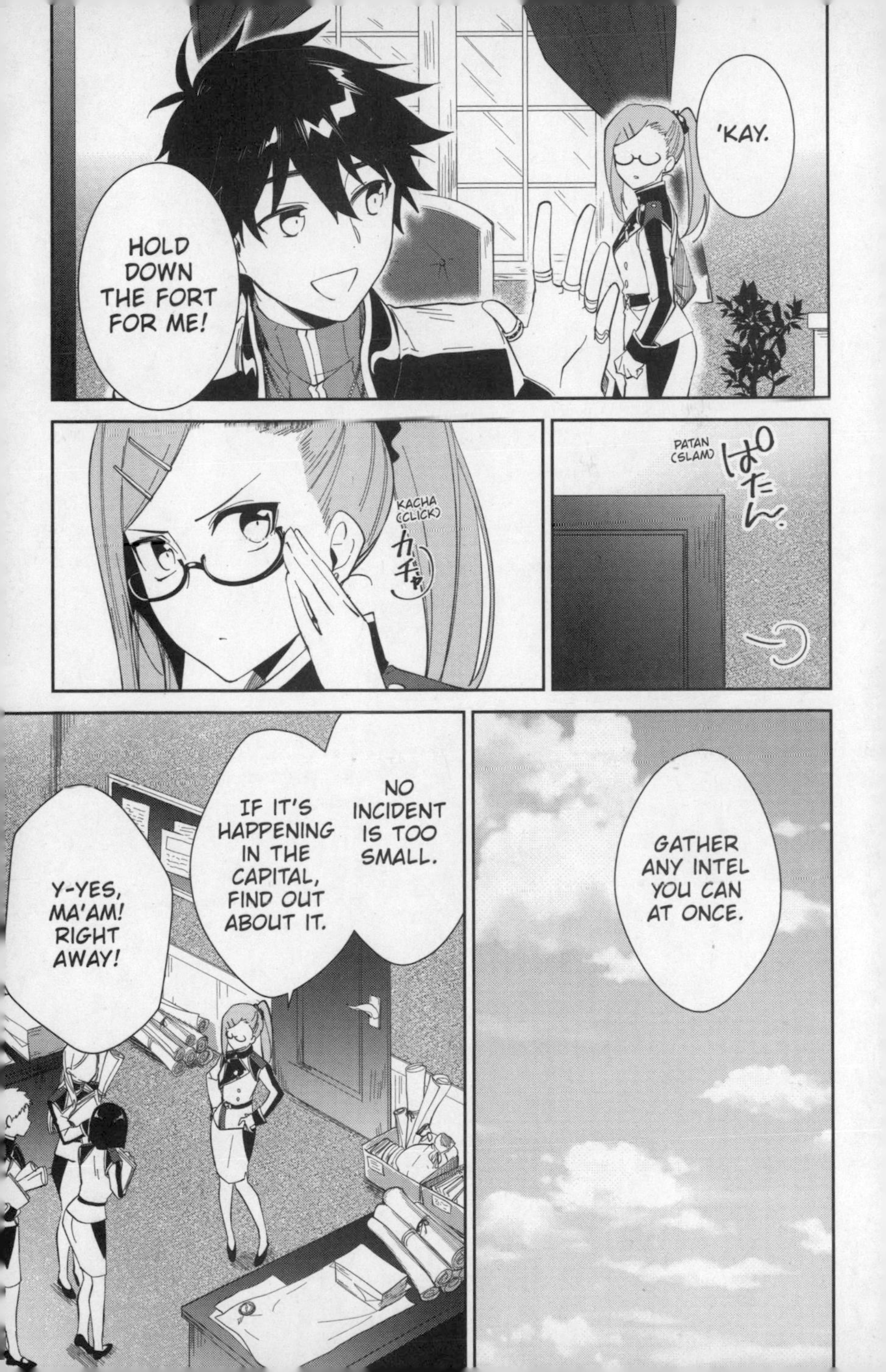
'KAY.
HOLD DOWN THE FORT FOR ME!
PATAN (SLAM)
ぱたん.
KACHA (CLICK)
カチャ
GATHER ANY INTEL YOU CAN AT ONCE.
NO INCIDENT IS TOO SMALL.
IF IT'S HAPPENING IN THE CAPITAL, FIND OUT ABOUT IT.
Y-YES, MA'AM! RIGHT AWAY!

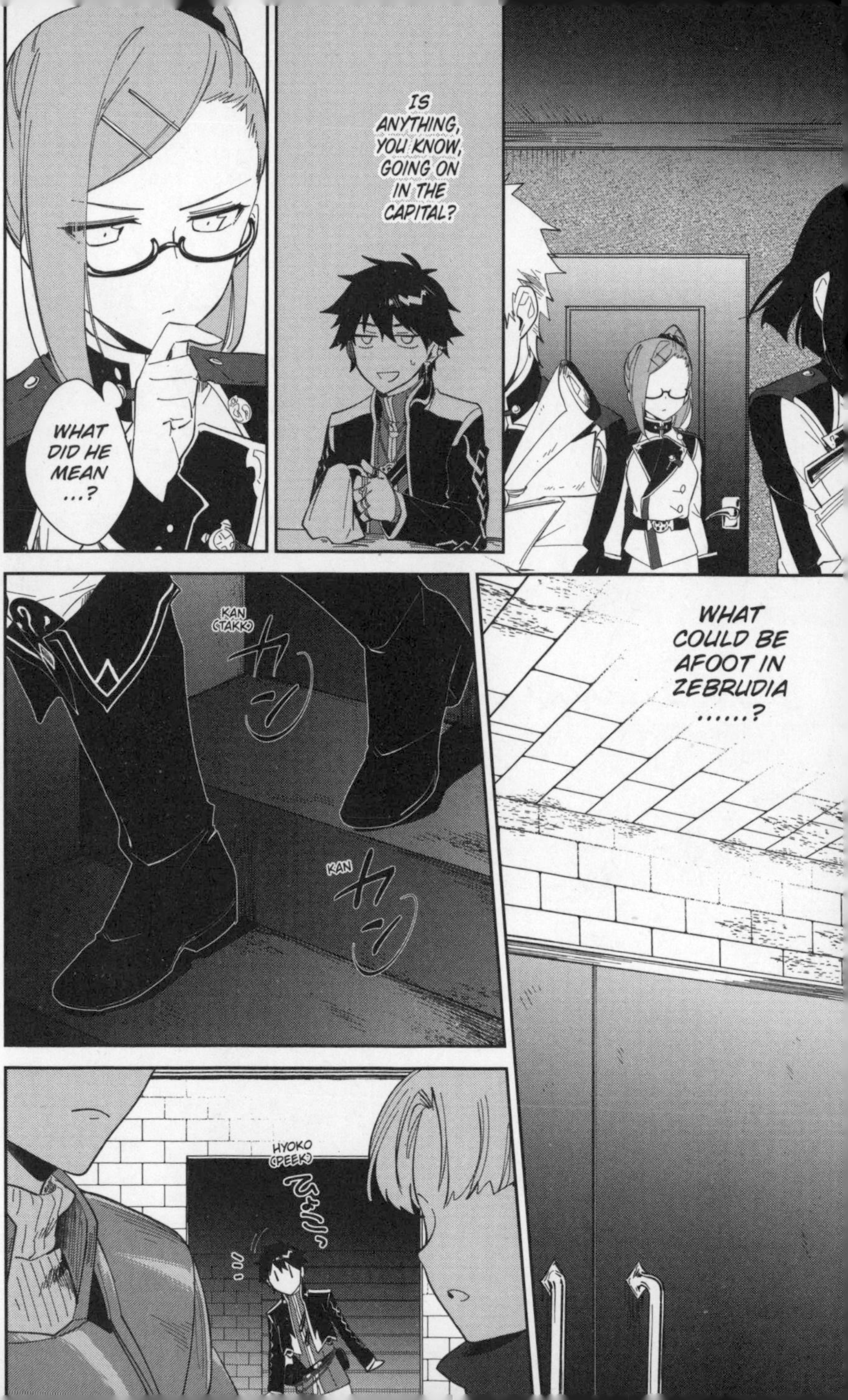
IS ANYTHING, YOU KNOW, GOING ON IN THE CAPITAL?
WHAT DID HE MEAN ...?
WHAT COULD BE AFOOT IN ZEBRUDIA ......?
KAN (TAKK)
KAN
HYOKO (PEEK)

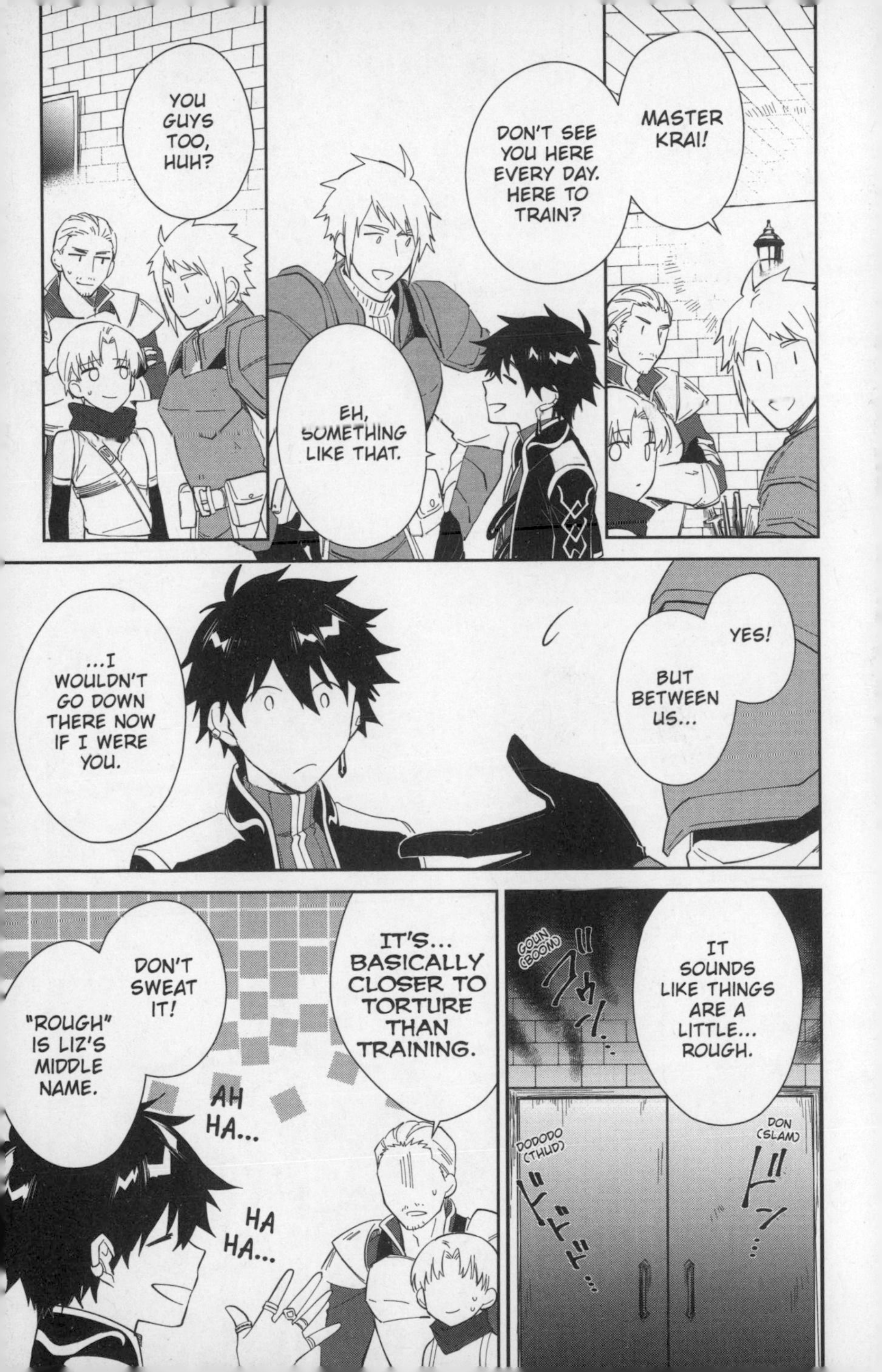
MASTER KRAI!
DON'T SEE YOU HERE EVERY DAY. HERE TO TRAIN?
EH, SOMETHING LIKE THAT.
YOU GUYS TOO, HUH?
YES!
BUT BETWEEN US...
...I WOULDN'T GO DOWN THERE NOW IF I WERE YOU.
GOUN (BOOM)
IT SOUNDS LIKE THINGS ARE A LITTLE... ROUGH.
DON (SLAM)
DODODO (THUD)
IT'S... BASICALLY CLOSER TO TORTURE THAN TRAINING.
DON'T SWEAT IT!
"ROUGH" IS LIZ'S MIDDLE NAME.
AH HA...
HA HA...

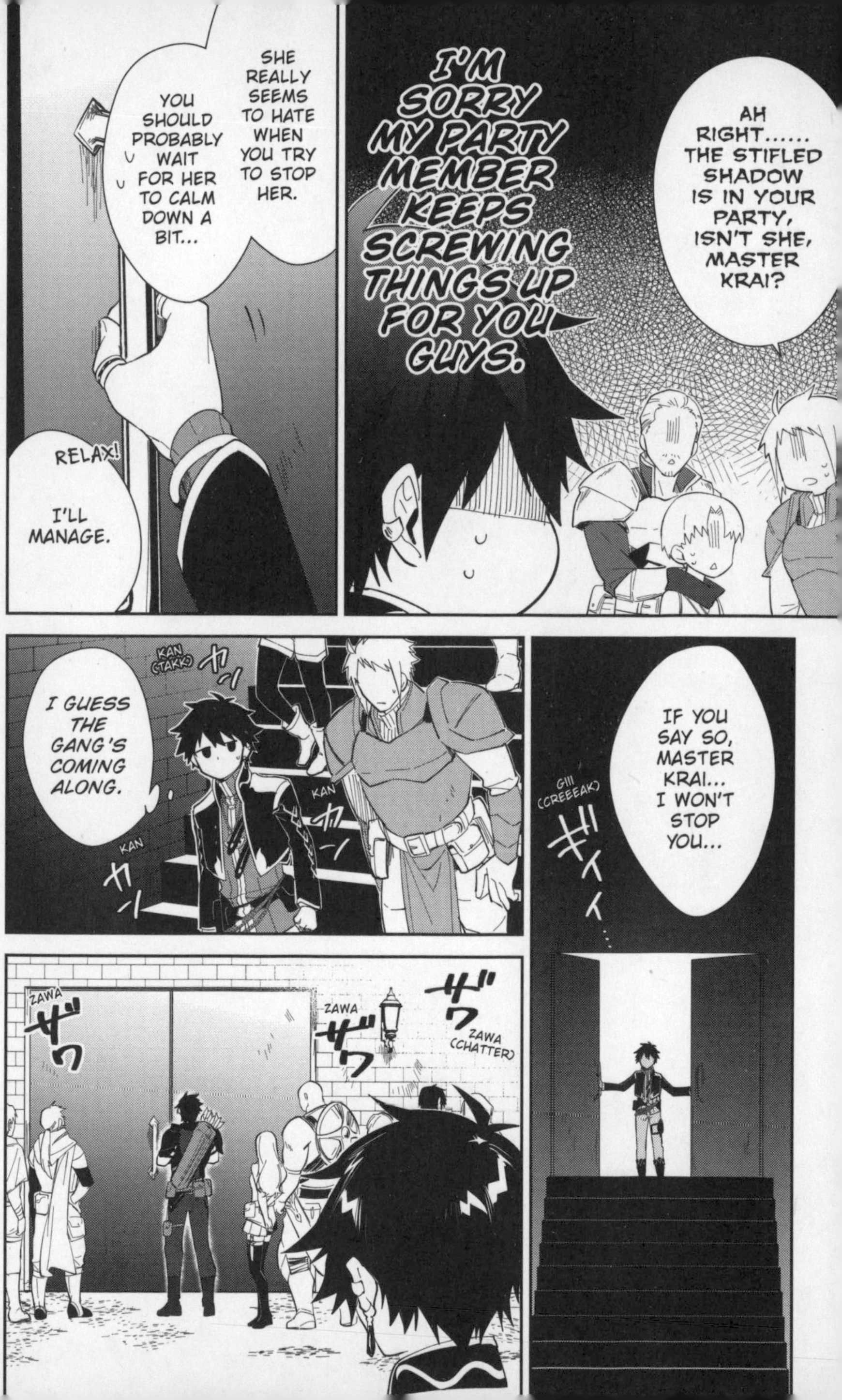
AH RIGHT...... THE STIFLED SHADOW IS IN YOUR PARTY, ISN'T SHE, MASTER KRAI?
I'M SORRY MY PARTY MEMBER KEEPS SCREWING THINGS UP FOR YOU GUYS.
SHE REALLY SEEMS TO HATE WHEN YOU TRY TO STOP HER.
YOU SHOULD PROBABLY WAIT FOR HER TO CALM DOWN A BIT...
RELAX!
I'LL MANAGE.
IF YOU SAY SO, MASTER KRAI... I WON'T STOP YOU...
GIII (CREEEAK)
ギイィ...
KAN (TAKK)
カン
I GUESS THE GANG'S COMING ALONG.
KAN
カン
KAN
カン
ZAWA
ザワ
ZAWA
ザワ
ZAWA (CHATTER)
ザワ

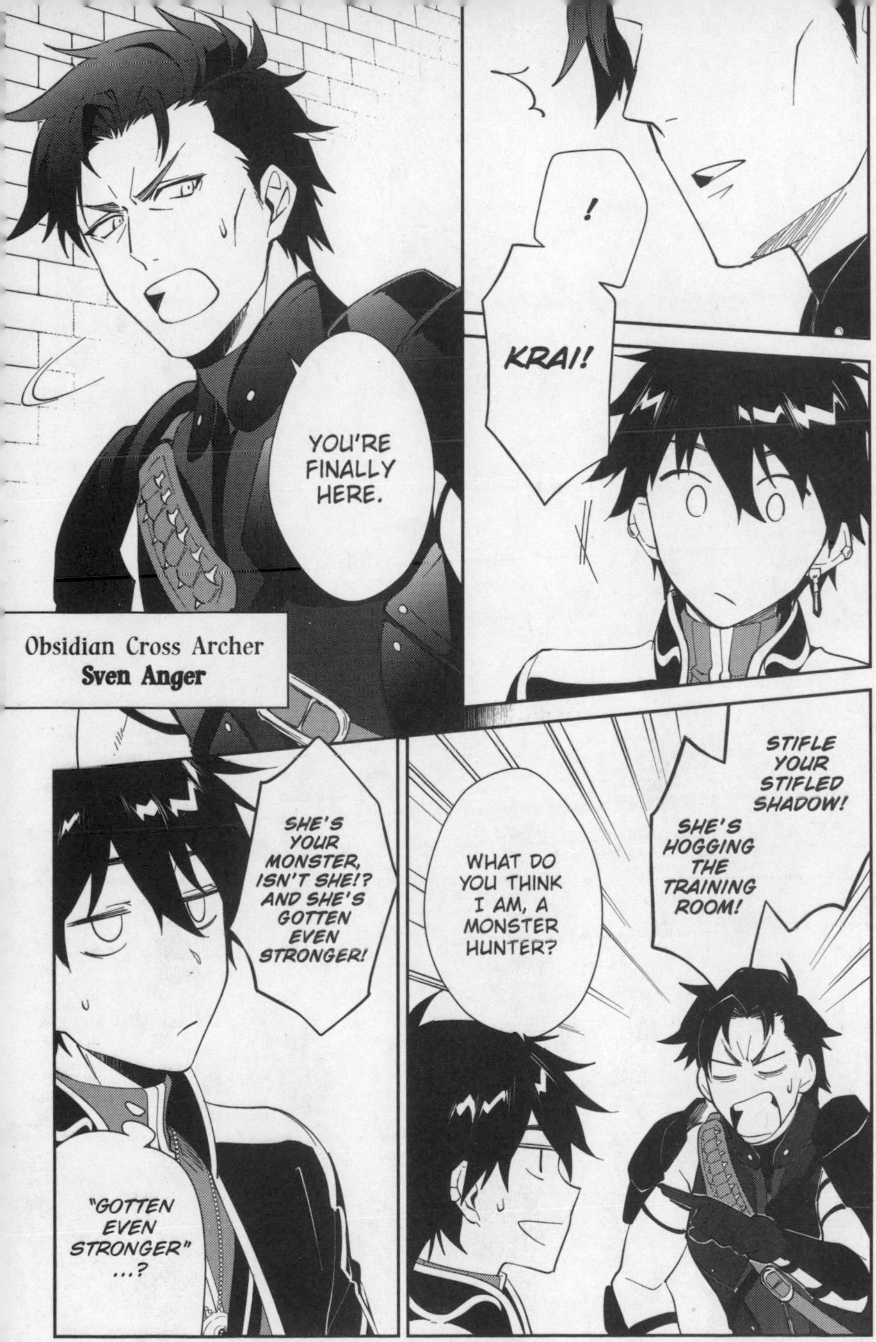
!
KRAI!
YOU'RE FINALLY HERE.
Obsidian Cross Archer
Sven Anger
STIFLE YOUR STIFLED SHADOW!
SHE'S HOGGING THE TRAINING ROOM!
WHAT DO YOU THINK I AM, A MONSTER HUNTER?
SHE'S YOUR MONSTER, ISN'T SHE!? AND SHE'S GOTTEN EVEN STRONGER!
"GOTTEN EVEN STRONGER" ...?

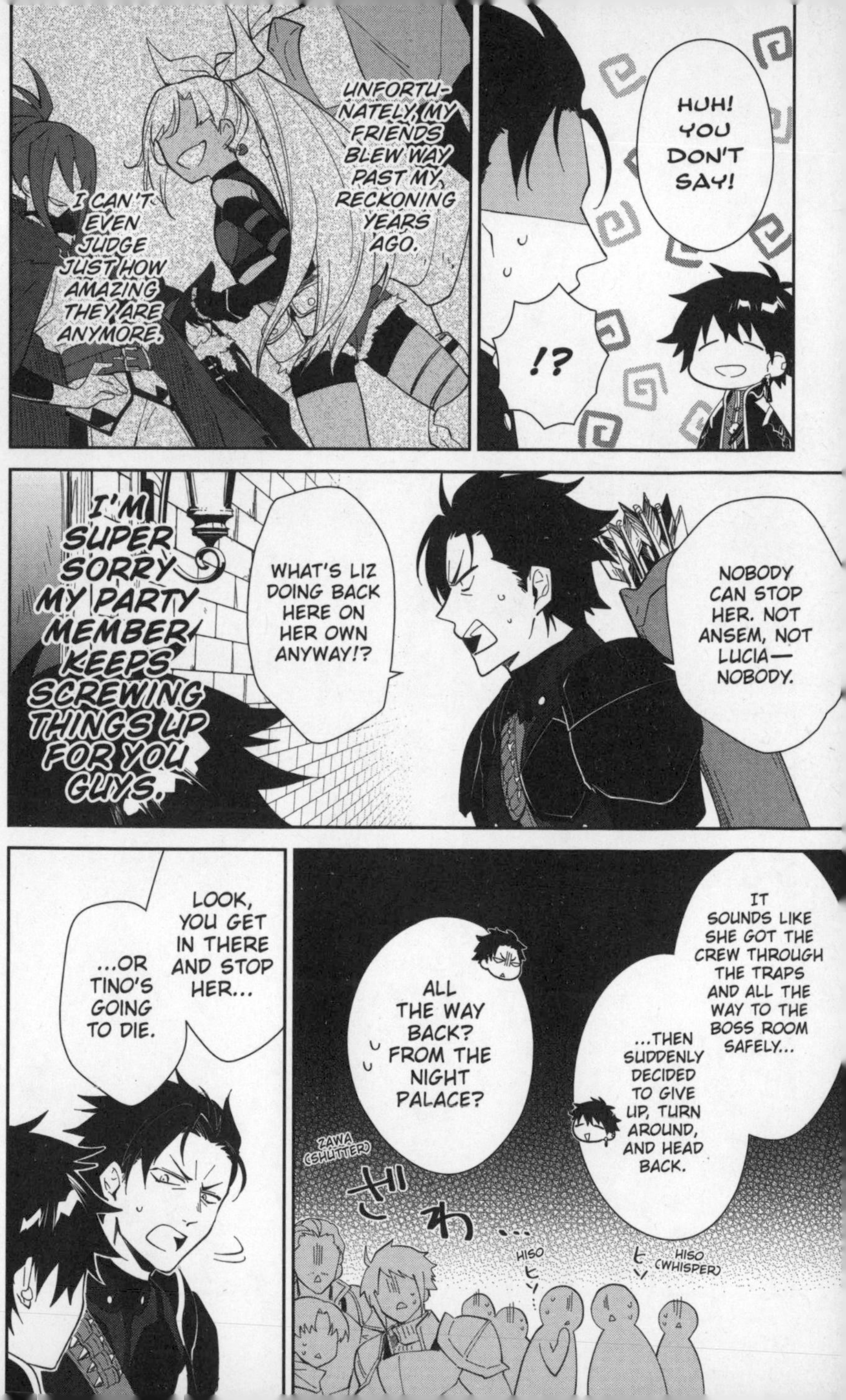
HUH! YOU DON'T SAY!
!?
UNFORTUNATELY, MY FRIENDS BLEW WAY PAST MY RECKONING YEARS AGO.
I CAN'T EVEN JUDGE JUST HOW AMAZING THEY ARE ANYMORE.
NOBODY CAN STOP HER. NOT ANSEM, NOT LUCIA—NOBODY.
WHAT'S LIZ DOING BACK HERE ON HER OWN ANYWAY!?
I'M SUPER SORRY MY PARTY MEMBER KEEPS SCREWING THINGS UP FOR YOU GUYS.
IT SOUNDS LIKE SHE GOT THE CREW THROUGH THE TRAPS AND ALL THE WAY TO THE BOSS ROOM SAFELY...
...THEN SUDDENLY DECIDED TO GIVE UP, TURN AROUND, AND HEAD BACK.
ALL THE WAY BACK? FROM THE NIGHT PALACE?
HISO (WHISPER)
ヒソ
HISO
ヒソ
ZAWA (SHUTTER)
ざわ…
LOOK, YOU GET IN THERE AND STOP HER...
...OR TINO'S GOING TO DIE.

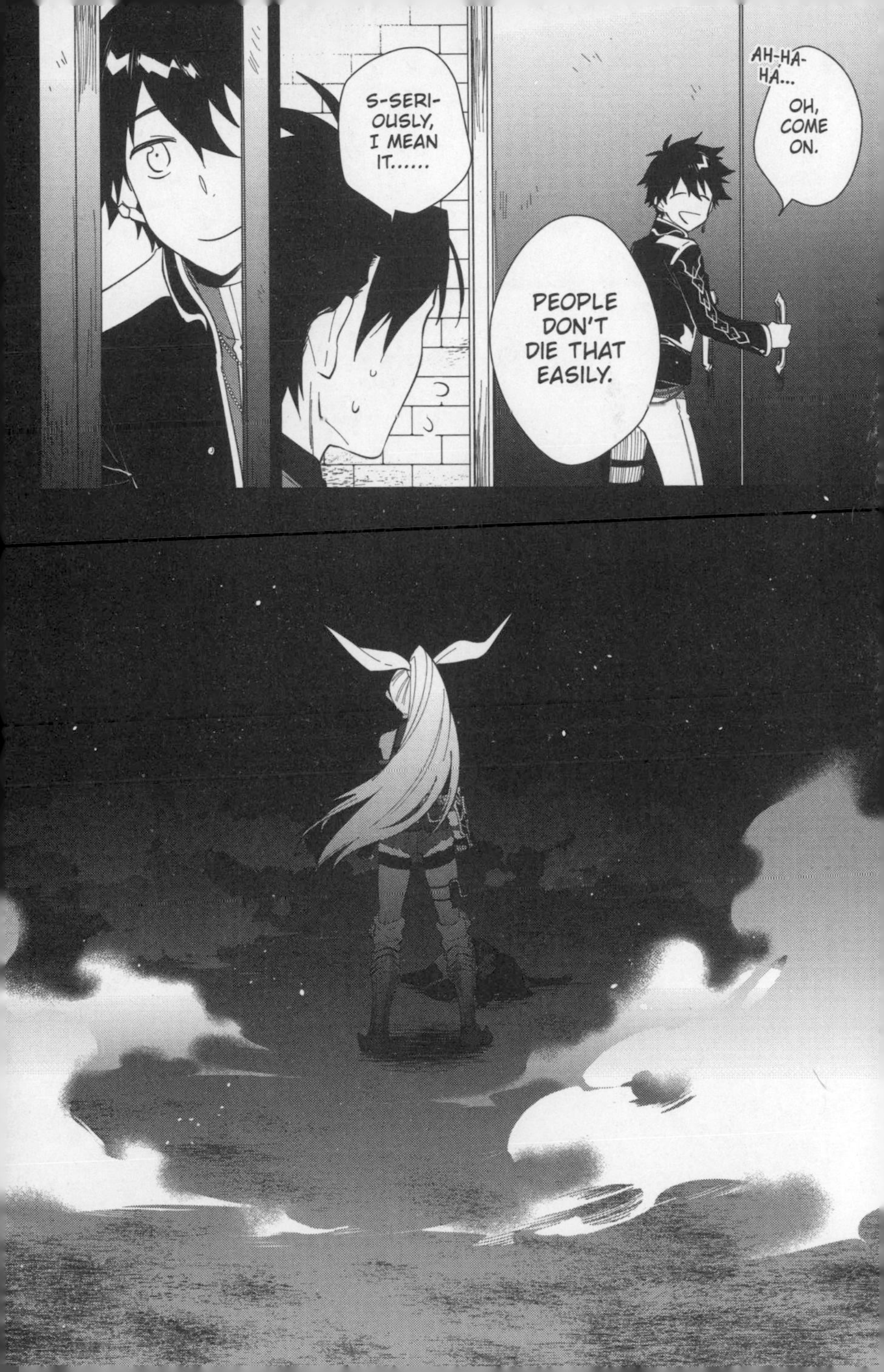
AH-HA-HA...
OH, COME ON.
PEOPLE DON'T DIE THAT EASILY.
S-SERIOUSLY, I MEAN IT......

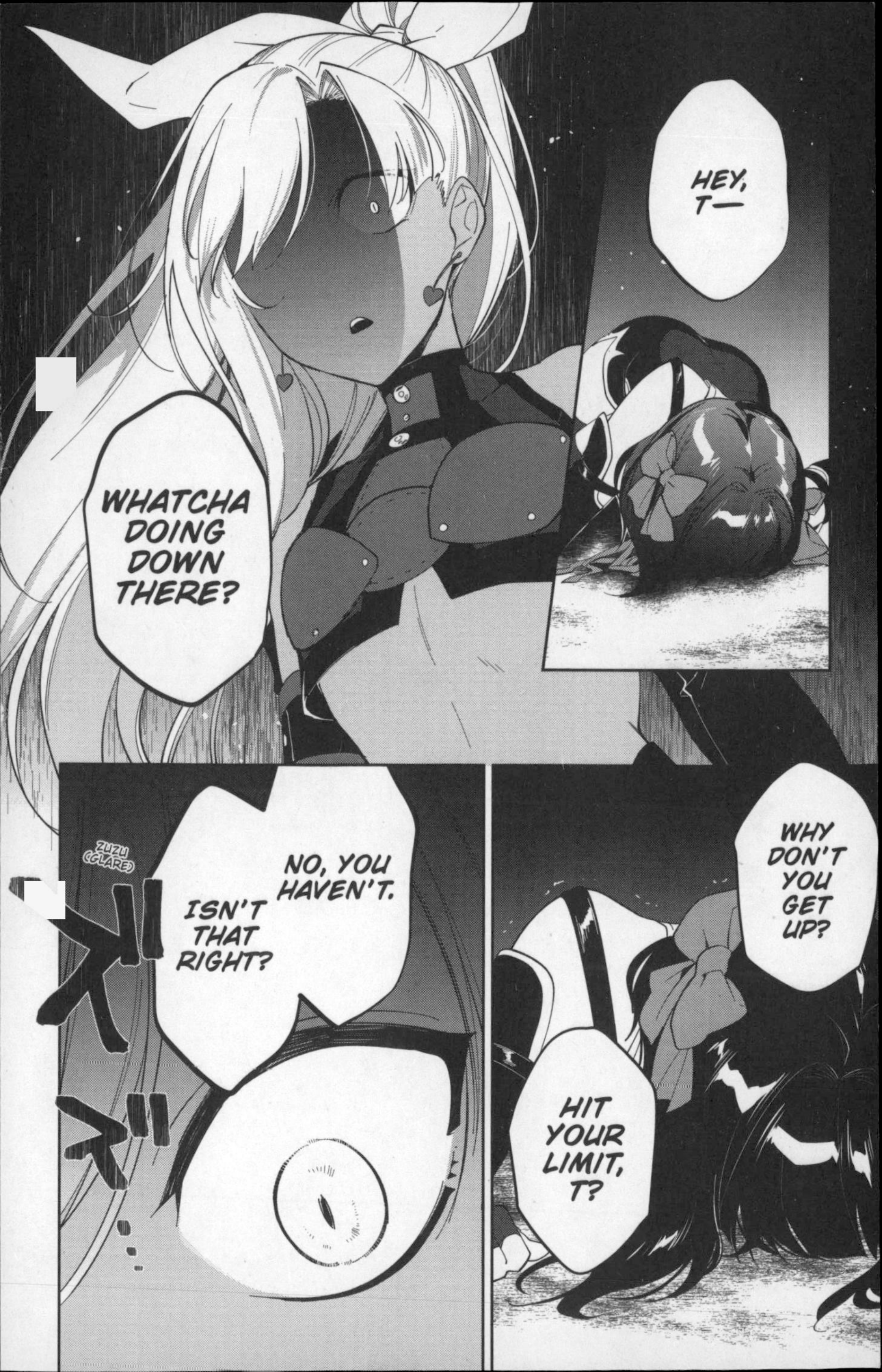
HEY, T—
WHATCHA DOING DOWN THERE?
WHY DON'T YOU GET UP?
HIT YOUR LIMIT, T?
NO, YOU HAVEN'T.
ISN'T THAT RIGHT?
ZUZU (GLARE)

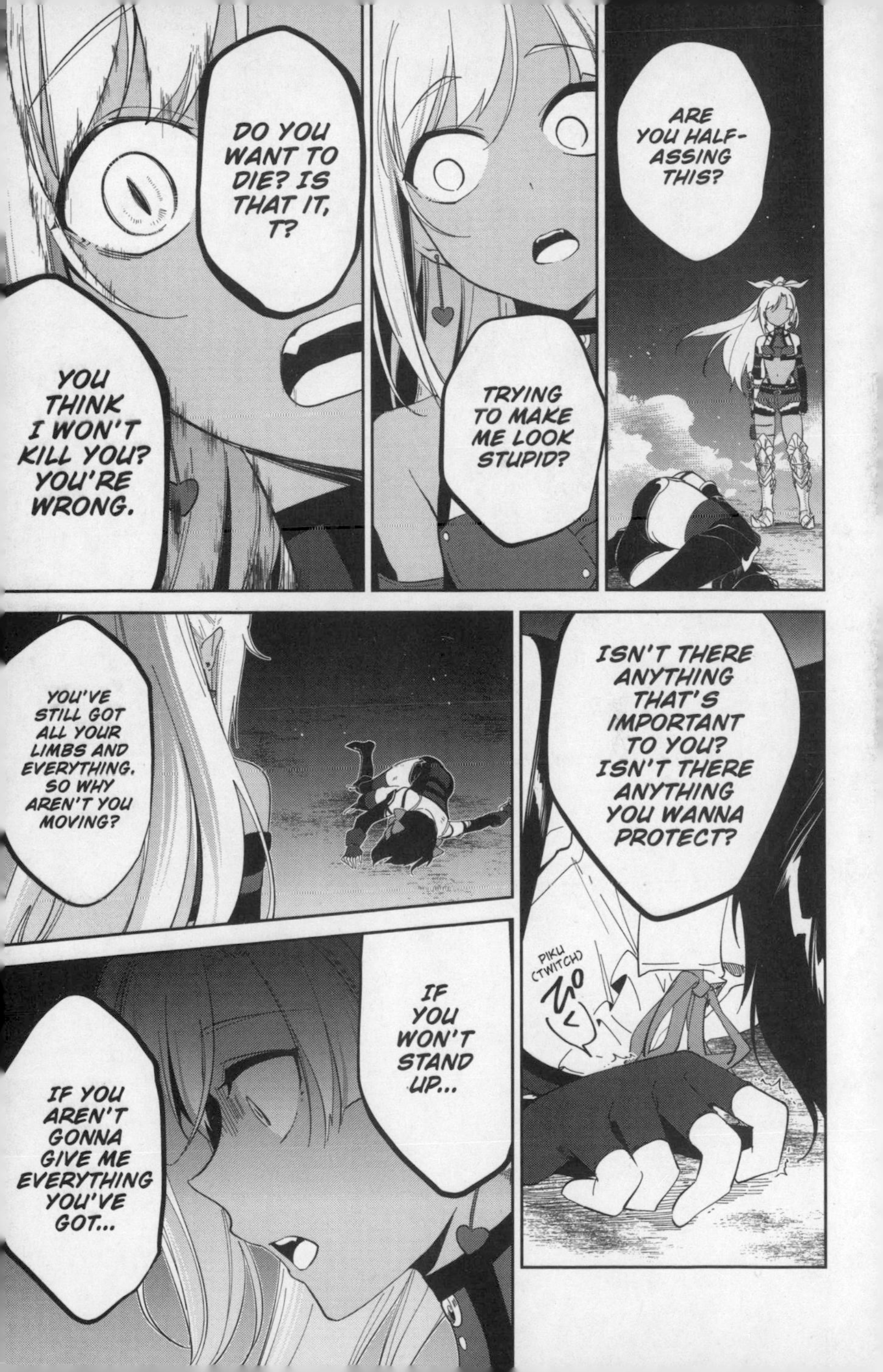
ARE YOU HALF-ASSING THIS?
TRYING TO MAKE ME LOOK STUPID?
DO YOU WANT TO DIE? IS THAT IT, T?
YOU THINK I WON'T KILL YOU? YOU'RE WRONG.
ISN'T THERE ANYTHING THAT'S IMPORTANT TO YOU? ISN'T THERE ANYTHING YOU WANNA PROTECT?
PIKU (TWITCH)
YOU'VE STILL GOT ALL YOUR LIMBS AND EVERYTHING. SO WHY AREN'T YOU MOVING?
IF YOU WON'T STAND UP...
IF YOU AREN'T GONNA GIVE ME EVERYTHING YOU'VE GOT...

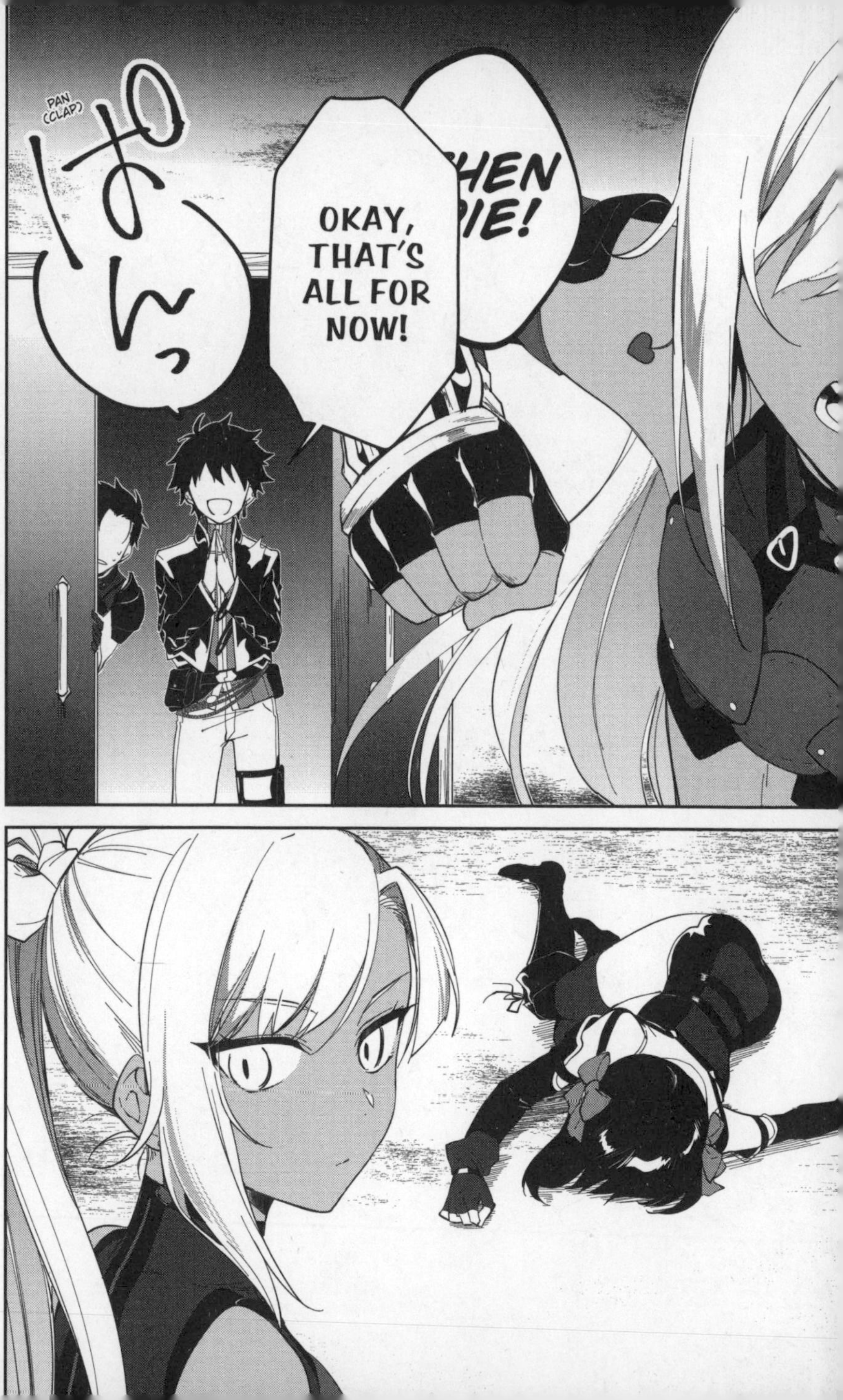
OKAY, THAT'S ALL FOR NOW!
PAN (CLAP)

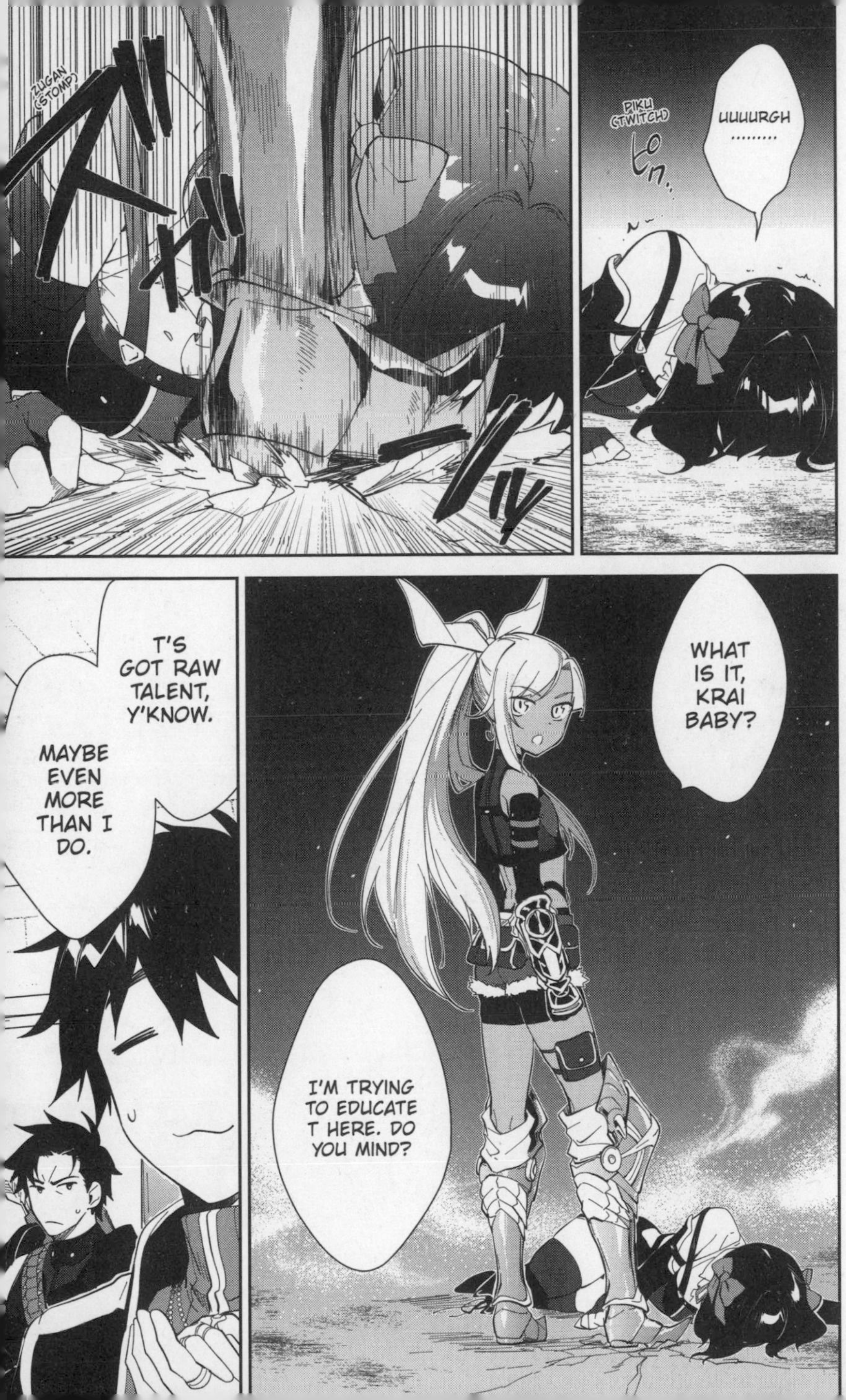
PIKU (TWITCH)
UUUURGH ....
ZUGAN (STOMP)
WHAT IS IT, KRAI BABY?
I'M TRYING TO EDUCATE T HERE. DO YOU MIND?
T'S GOT RAW TALENT, Y'KNOW.
MAYBE EVEN MORE THAN I DO.

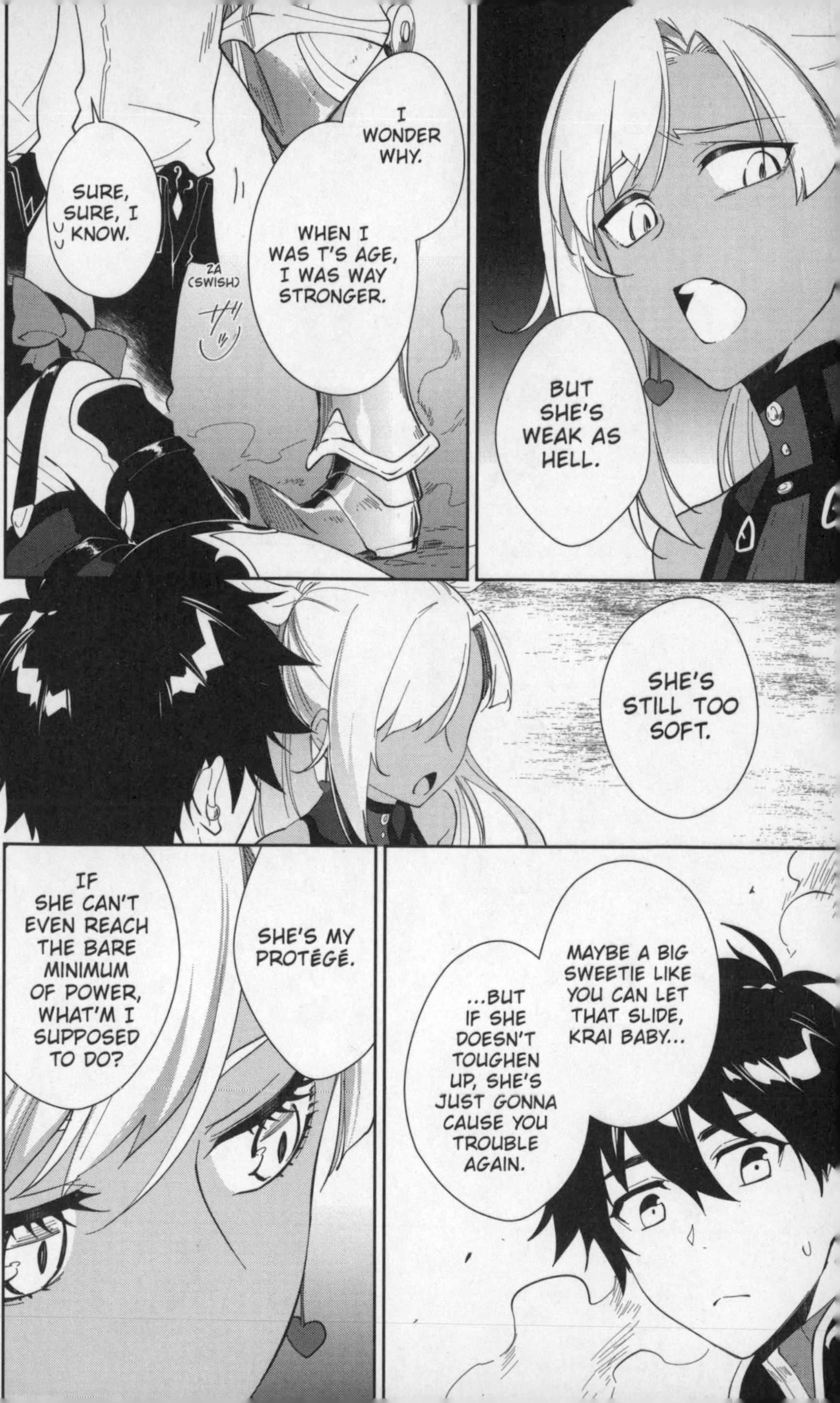
BUT SHE'S WEAK AS HELL.
I WONDER WHY.
WHEN I WAS T'S AGE, I WAS WAY STRONGER.
SURE, SURE, I KNOW.
ZA (SWISH)
SHE'S STILL TOO SOFT.
MAYBE A BIG SWEETIE LIKE YOU CAN LET THAT SLIDE, KRAI BABY...
...BUT IF SHE DOESN'T TOUGHEN UP, SHE'S JUST GONNA CAUSE YOU TROUBLE AGAIN.
SHE'S MY PROTÉGÉ.
IF SHE CAN'T EVEN REACH THE BARE MINIMUM OF POWER, WHAT'M I SUPPOSED TO DO?

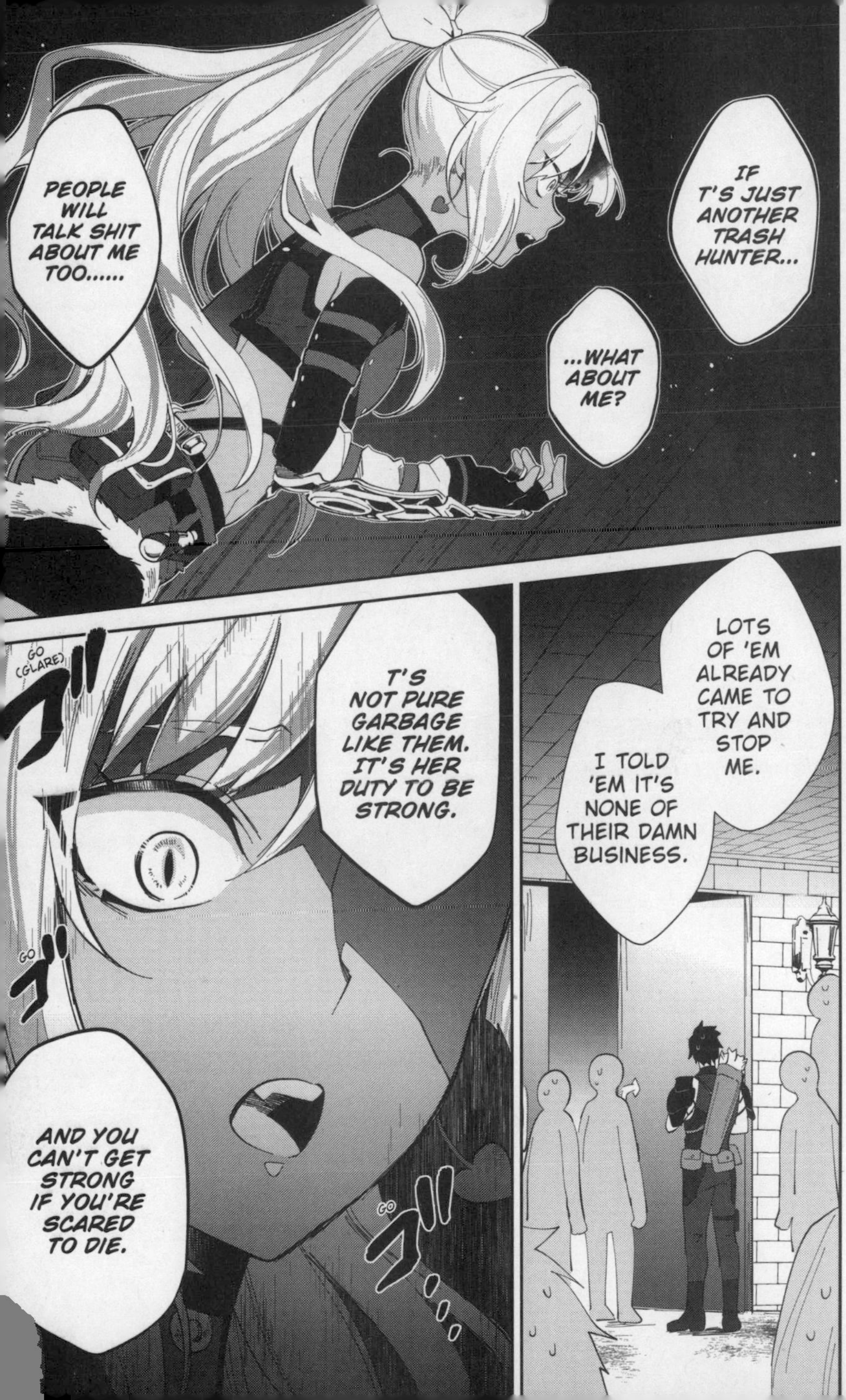
IF T'S JUST ANOTHER TRASH HUNTER...
...WHAT ABOUT ME?
PEOPLE WILL TALK SHIT ABOUT ME TOO......
LOTS OF 'EM ALREADY CAME TO TRY AND STOP ME.
I TOLD 'EM IT'S NONE OF THEIR DAMN BUSINESS.
T'S NOT PURE GARBAGE LIKE THEM. IT'S HER DUTY TO BE STRONG.
GO (GLARE)
GO
AND YOU CAN'T GET STRONG IF YOU'RE SCARED TO DIE.
GO

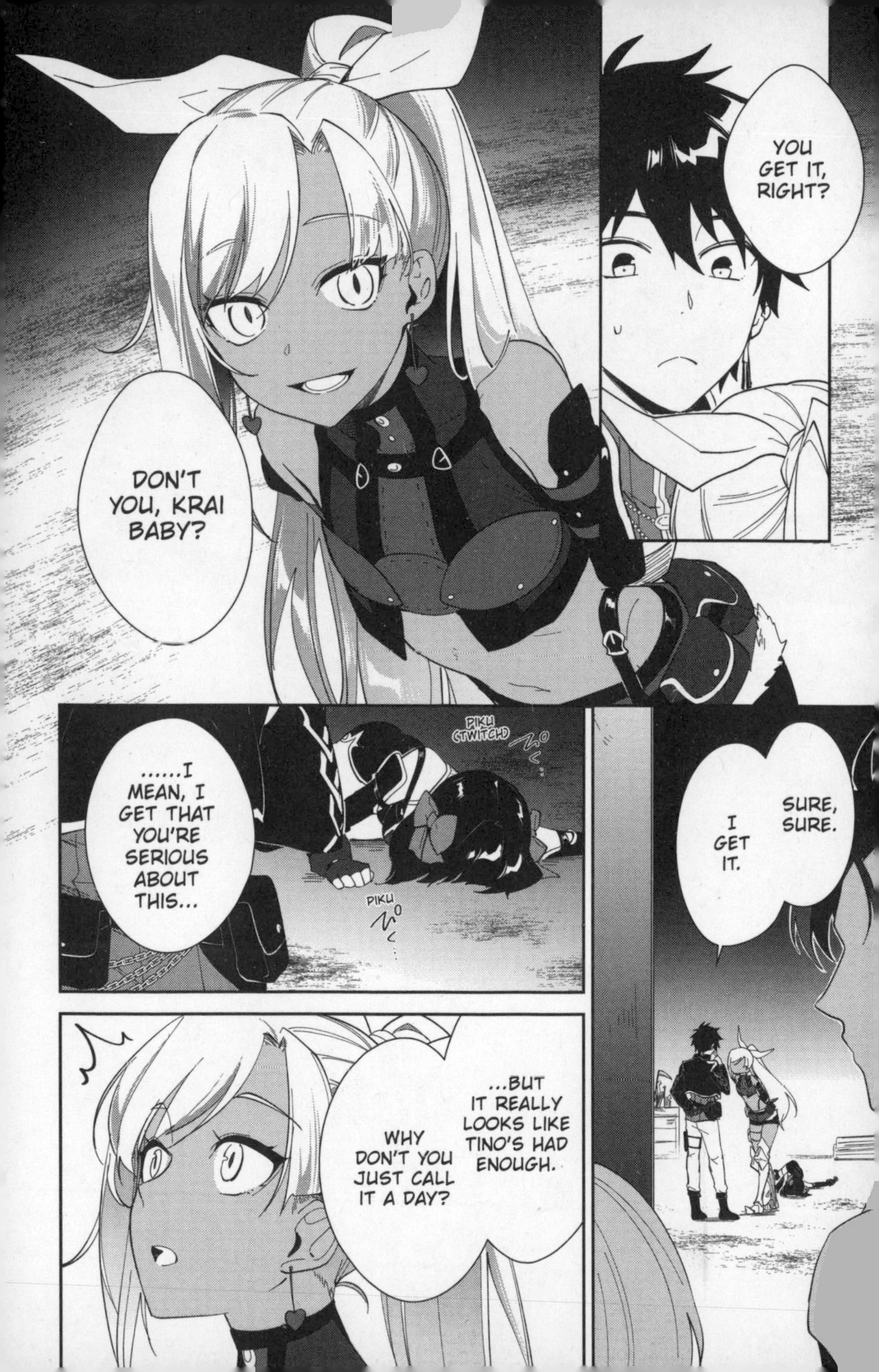
YOU GET IT, RIGHT?
DON'T YOU, KRAI BABY?
SURE, SURE.
I GET IT.
PIKU (TWITCH)
......I MEAN, I GET THAT YOU'RE SERIOUS ABOUT THIS...
PIKU
...BUT IT REALLY LOOKS LIKE TINO'S HAD ENOUGH.
WHY DON'T YOU JUST CALL IT A DAY?

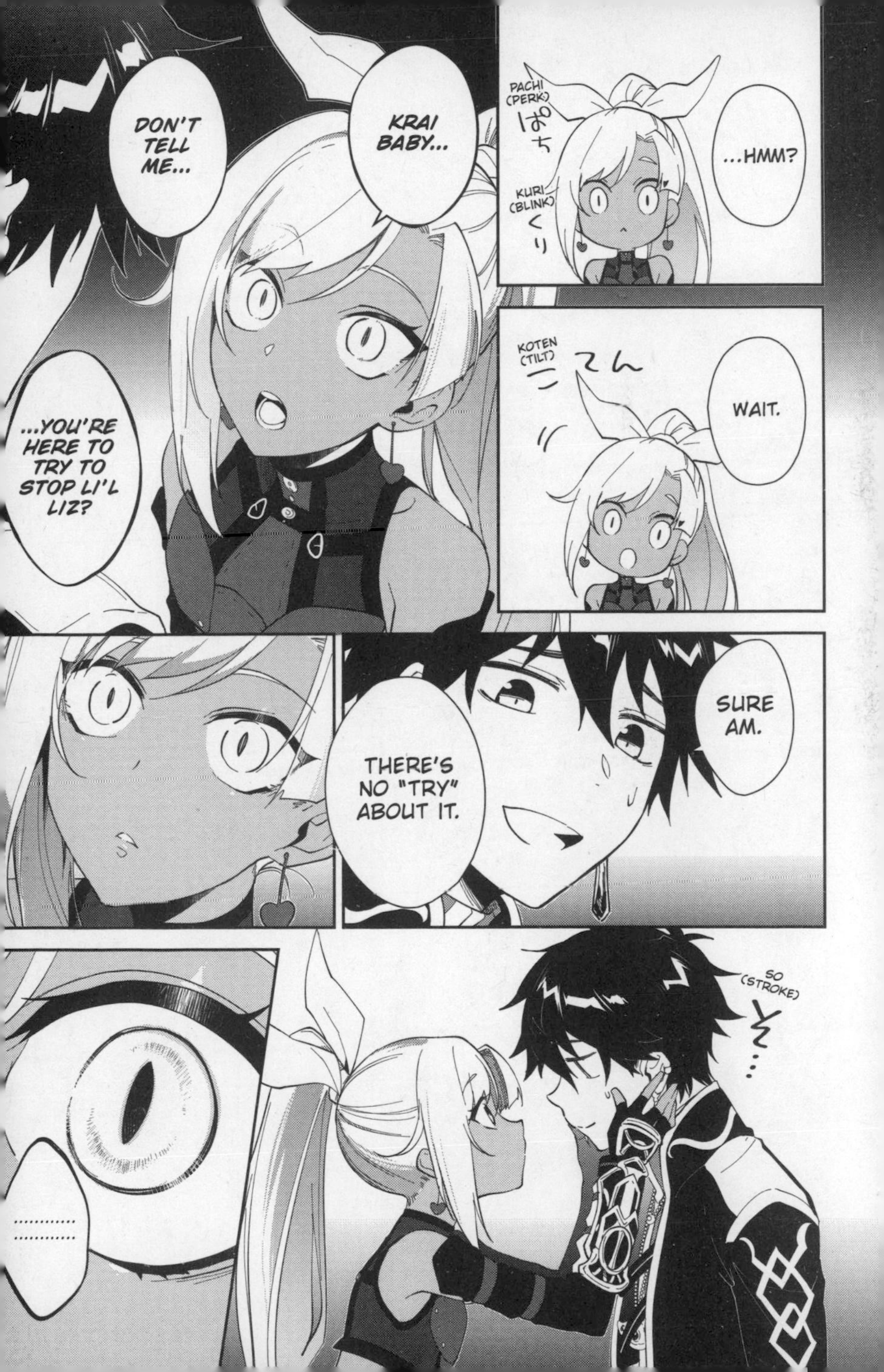
PACHI (PERK)
ぱち
KURI (BLINK)
くり
...HMM?
KOTEN (TILT)
こてん
WAIT.
KRAI BABY...
DON'T TELL ME...
...YOU'RE HERE TO TRY TO STOP LI'L LIZ?
SURE AM.
THERE'S NO "TRY" ABOUT IT.
SO (STROKE)
そ...
....
....

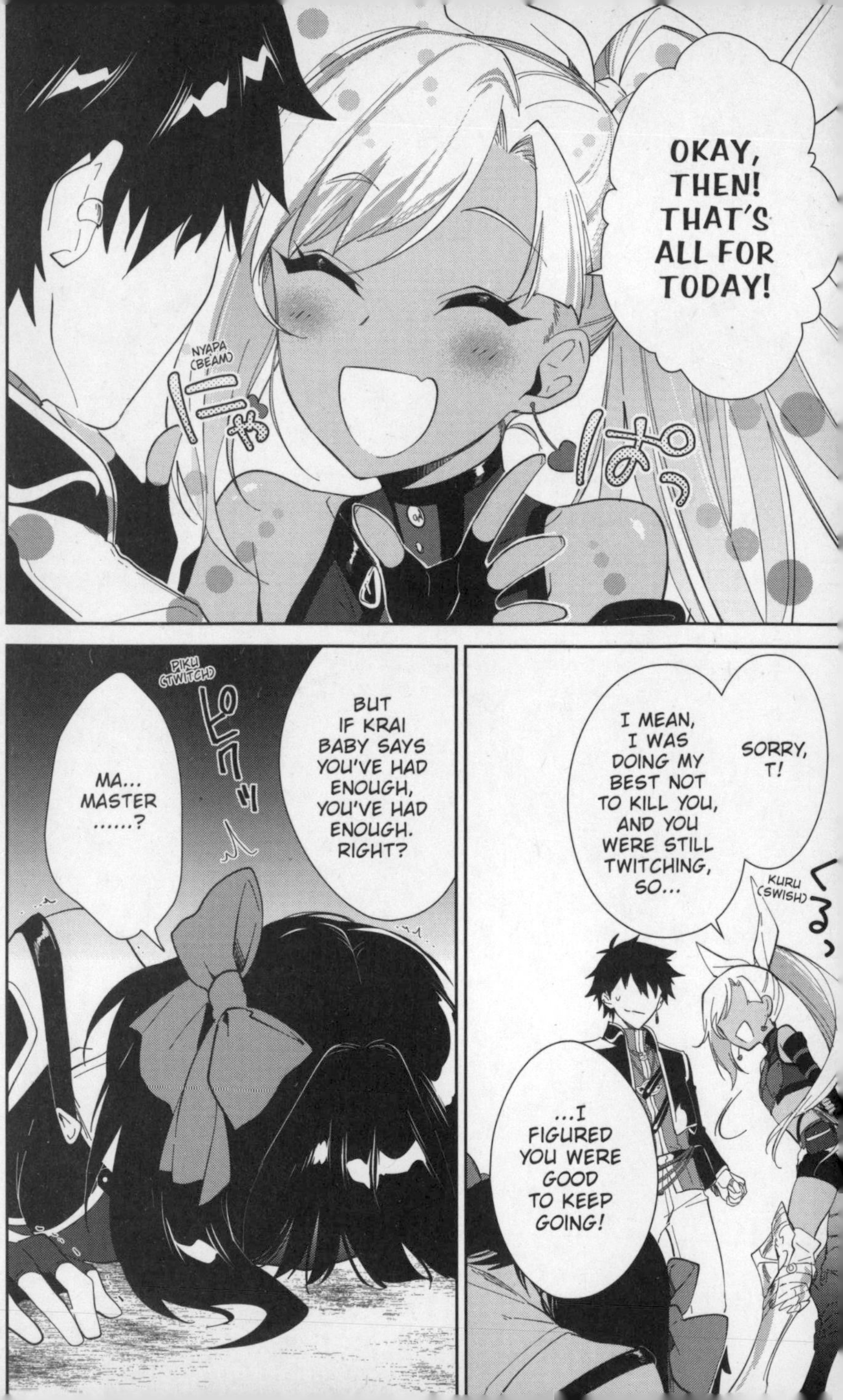
OKAY, THEN! THAT'S ALL FOR TODAY!
NYAPA (BEAM)
SORRY, T!
KURU (SWISH)
I MEAN, I WAS DOING MY BEST NOT TO KILL YOU, AND YOU WERE STILL TWITCHING, SO...
...I FIGURED YOU WERE GOOD TO KEEP GOING!
BUT IF KRAI BABY SAYS YOU'VE HAD ENOUGH, YOU'VE HAD ENOUGH. RIGHT?
PIKU (TWITCH)
MA... MASTER ......?

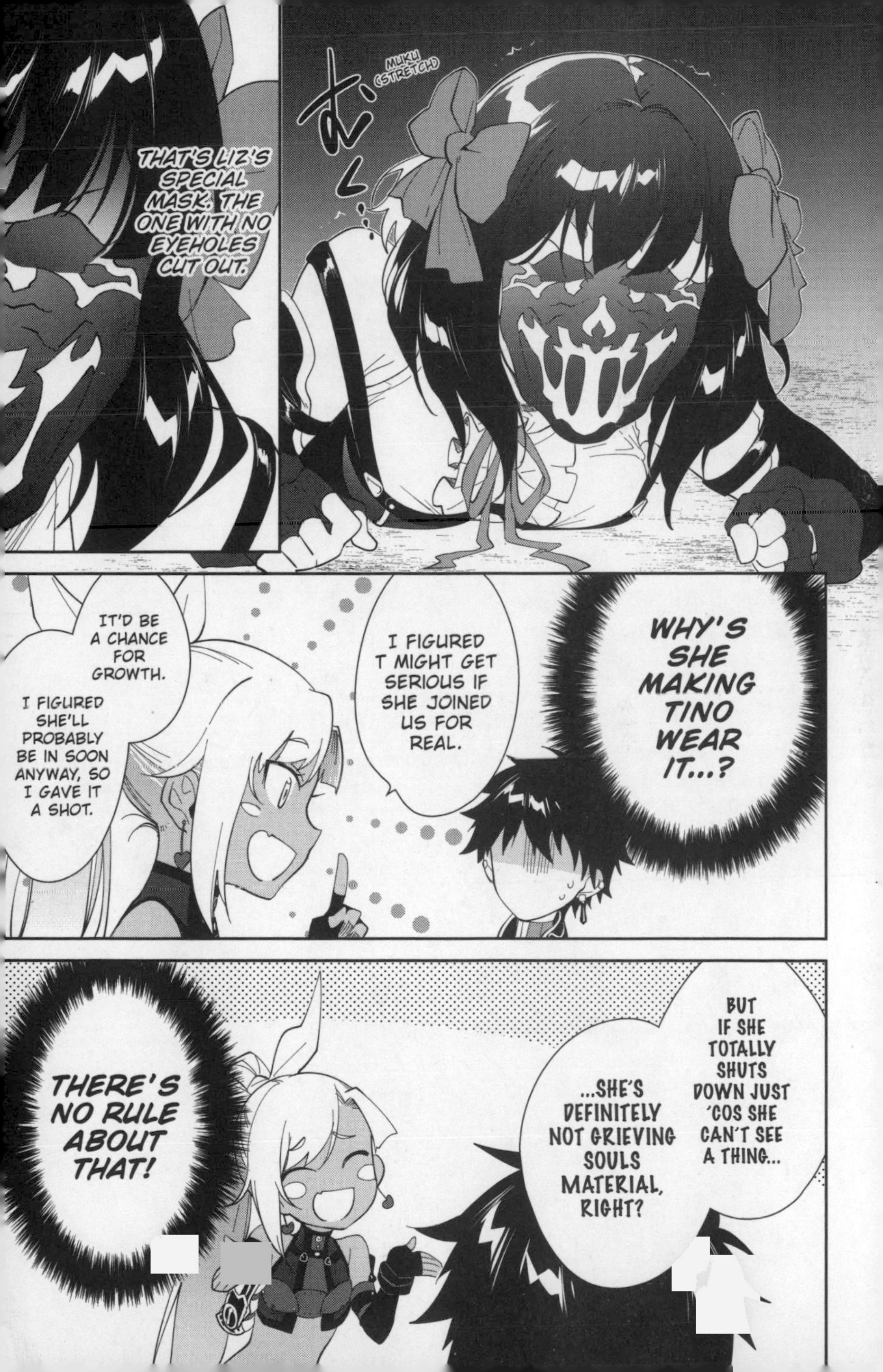
MUKU (STRETCH)
THAT'S LIZ'S SPECIAL MASK. THE ONE WITH NO EYEHOLES CUT OUT.
WHY'S SHE MAKING TINO WEAR IT...?
I FIGURED T MIGHT GET SERIOUS IF SHE JOINED US FOR REAL.
IT'D BE A CHANCE FOR GROWTH.
I FIGURED SHE'LL PROBABLY BE IN SOON ANYWAY, SO I GAVE IT A SHOT.
BUT IF SHE TOTALLY SHUTS DOWN JUST 'COS SHE CAN'T SEE A THING...
...SHE'S DEFINITELY NOT GRIEVING SOULS MATERIAL, RIGHT?
THERE'S NO RULE ABOUT THAT!

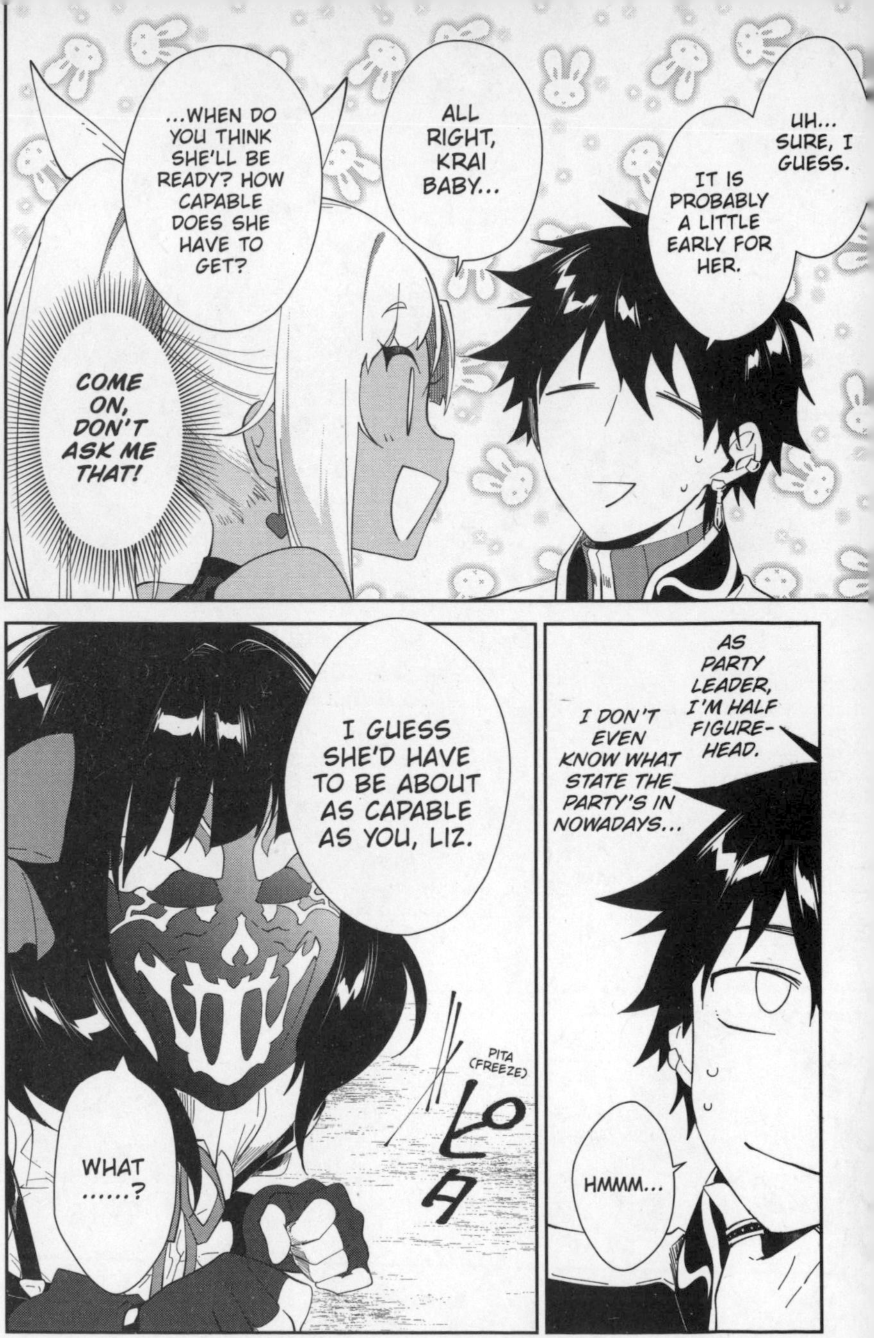
UH... SURE, I GUESS.
IT IS PROBABLY A LITTLE EARLY FOR HER.
ALL RIGHT, KRAI BABY...
...WHEN DO YOU THINK SHE'LL BE READY? HOW CAPABLE DOES SHE HAVE TO GET?
COME ON, DON'T ASK ME THAT!
AS PARTY LEADER, I'M HALF FIGURE-HEAD.
I DON'T EVEN KNOW WHAT STATE THE PARTY'S IN NOWADAYS...
HMMM...
I GUESS SHE'D HAVE TO BE ABOUT AS CAPABLE AS YOU, LIZ.
PITA (FREEZE)
WHAT ......?

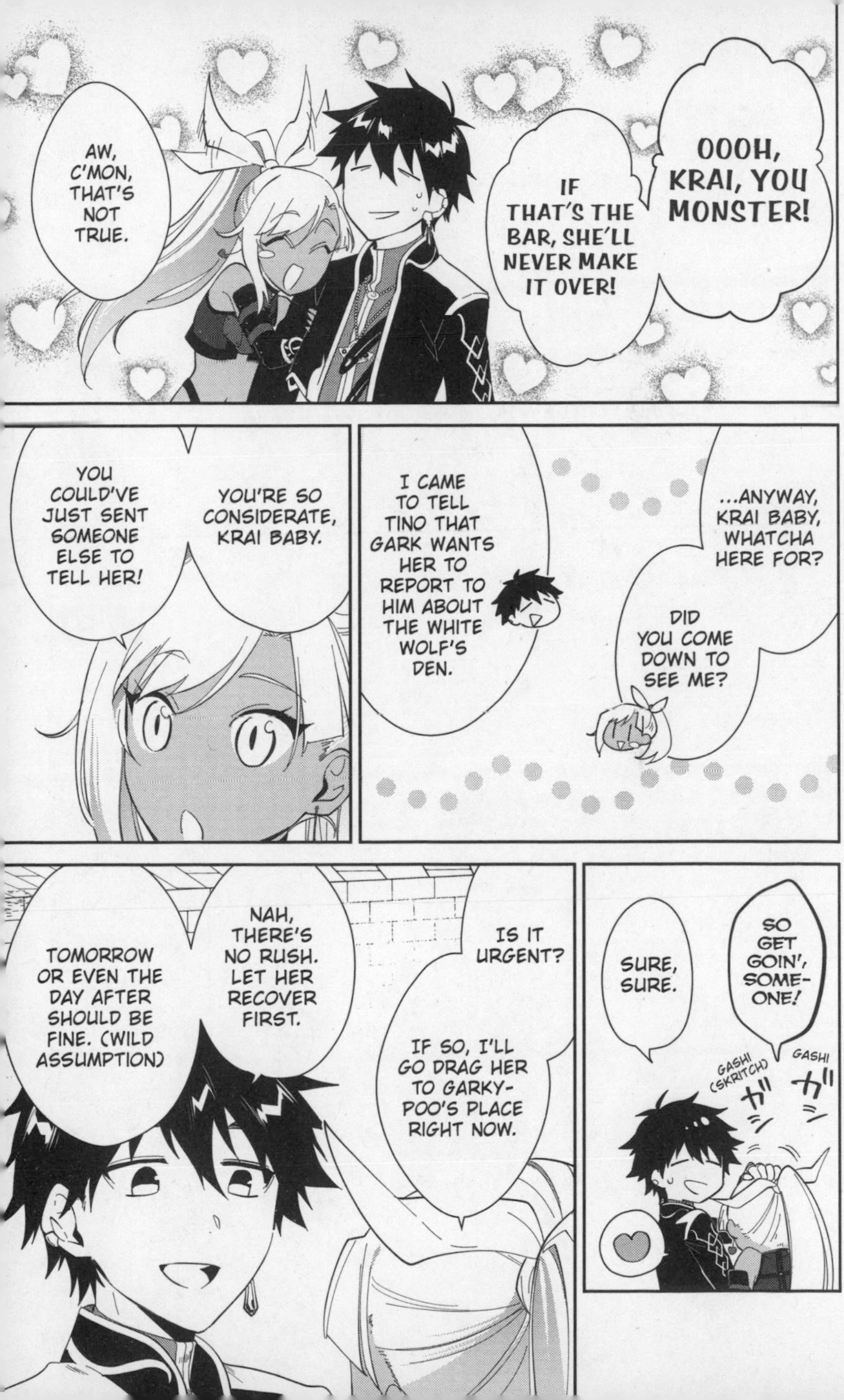
OOOH, KRAI, YOU MONSTER!
IF THAT'S THE BAR, SHE'LL NEVER MAKE IT OVER!
AW, C'MON, THAT'S NOT TRUE.
...ANYWAY, KRAI BABY, WHATCHA HERE FOR?
DID YOU COME DOWN TO SEE ME?
I CAME TO TELL TINO THAT GARK WANTS HER TO REPORT TO HIM ABOUT THE WHITE WOLF'S DEN.
YOU'RE SO CONSIDERATE, KRAI BABY.
YOU COULD'VE JUST SENT SOMEONE ELSE TO TELL HER!
SO GET GOIN', SOMEONE!
SURE, SURE.
GASHI
ガ
GASHI (SKRITCH)
ガ
IS IT URGENT?
IF SO, I'LL GO DRAG HER TO GARKY-POO'S PLACE RIGHT NOW.
NAH, THERE'S NO RUSH. LET HER RECOVER FIRST.
TOMORROW OR EVEN THE DAY AFTER SHOULD BE FINE. (WILD ASSUMPTION)

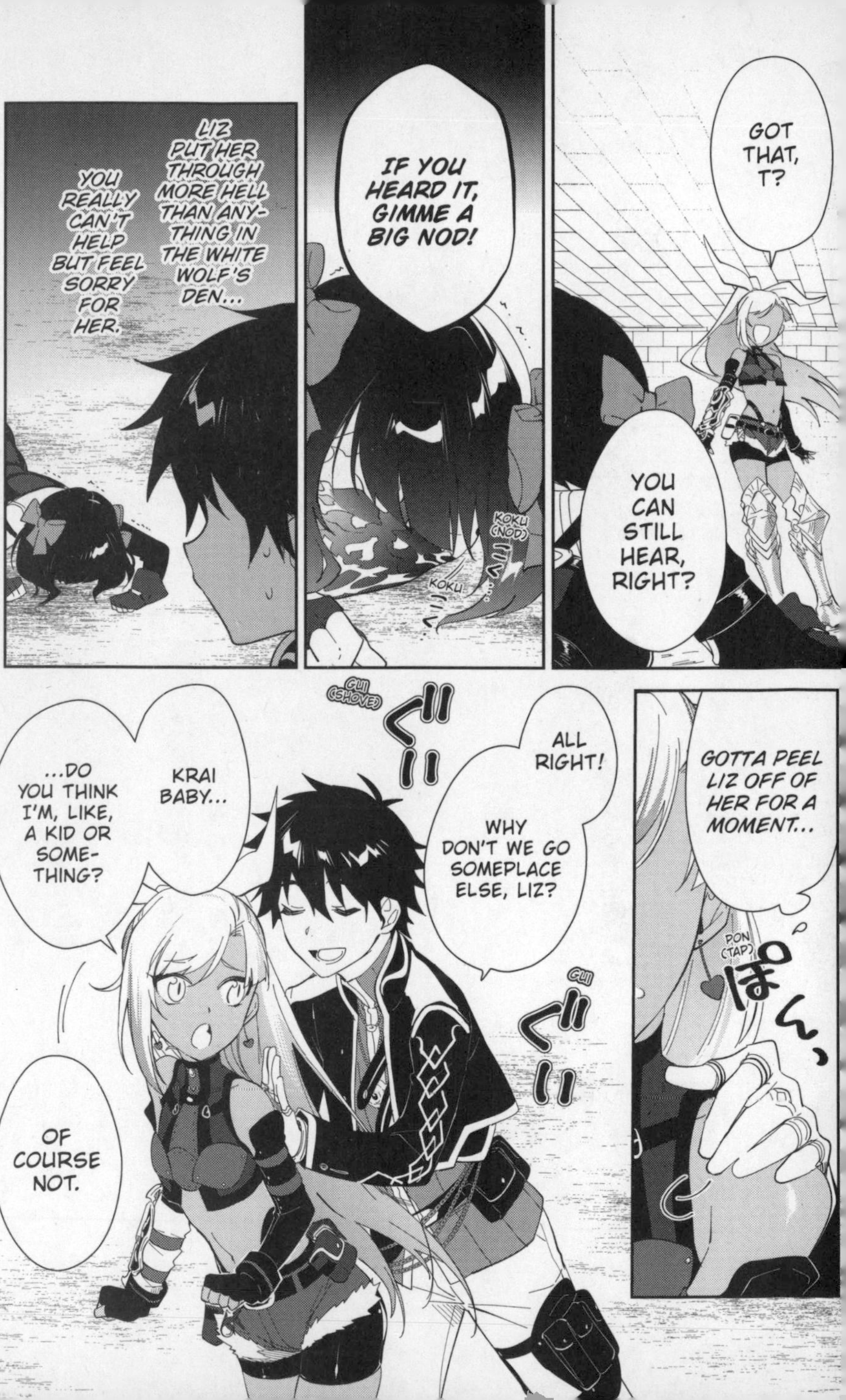
GOT THAT, T?
YOU CAN STILL HEAR, RIGHT?
IF YOU HEARD IT, GIMME A BIG NOD!
KOKU (NOD)
KOKU
LIZ PUT HER THROUGH MORE HELL THAN ANY-THING IN THE WHITE WOLF'S DEN...
YOU REALLY CAN'T HELP BUT FEEL SORRY FOR HER.
GOTTA PEEL LIZ OFF OF HER FOR A MOMENT...
PON (TAP)
GUI (SHOVE)
ALL RIGHT!
WHY DON'T WE GO SOMEPLACE ELSE, LIZ?
GUI
KRAI BABY...
...DO YOU THINK I'M, LIKE, A KID OR SOME-THING?
OF COURSE NOT.

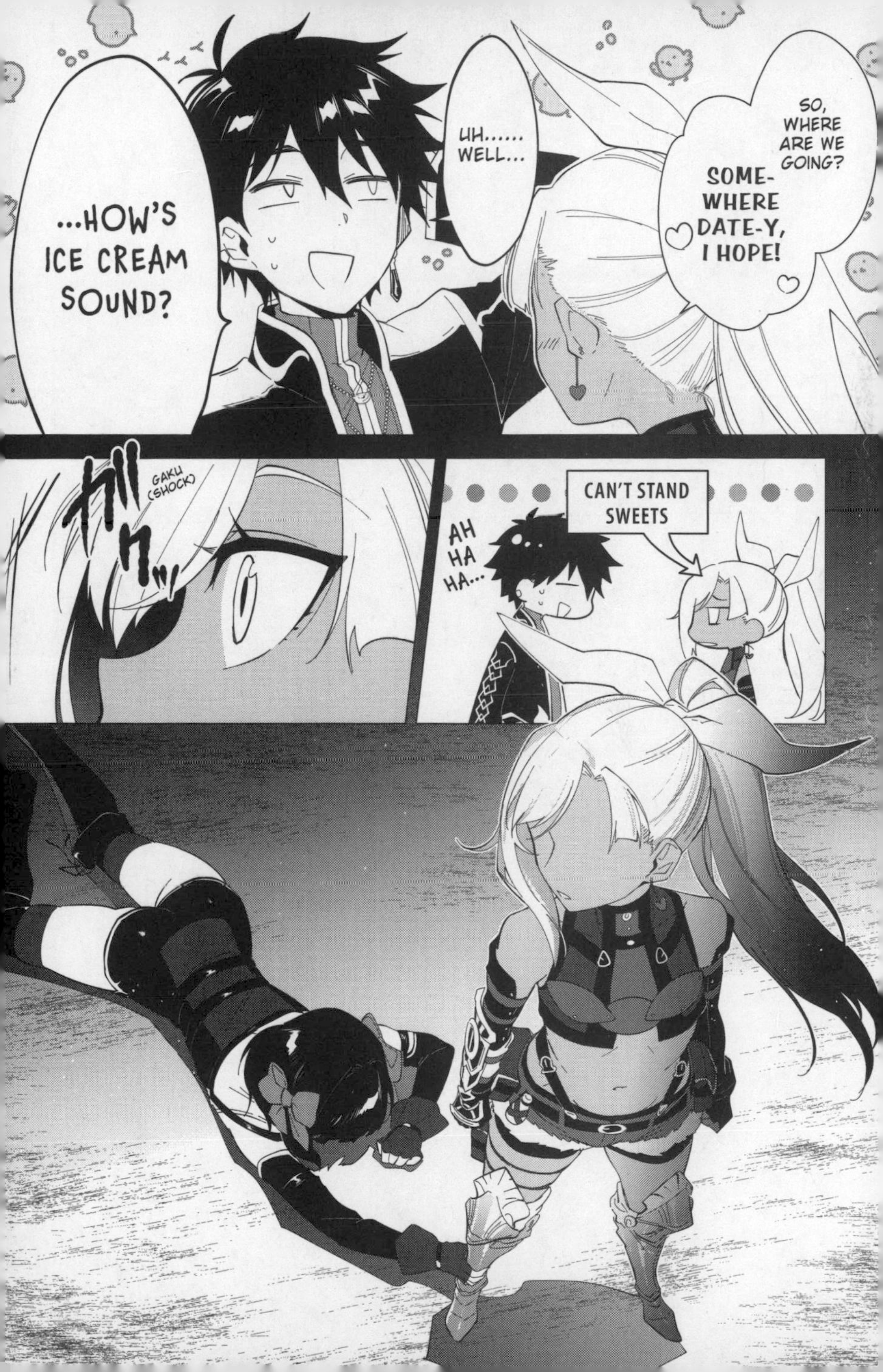
SO, WHERE ARE WE GOING?
SOME-WHERE DATE-Y, I HOPE!
UH...... WELL...
...HOW'S ICE CREAM SOUND?
CAN'T STAND SWEETS
AH HA HA...
GAKU (SHOCK)

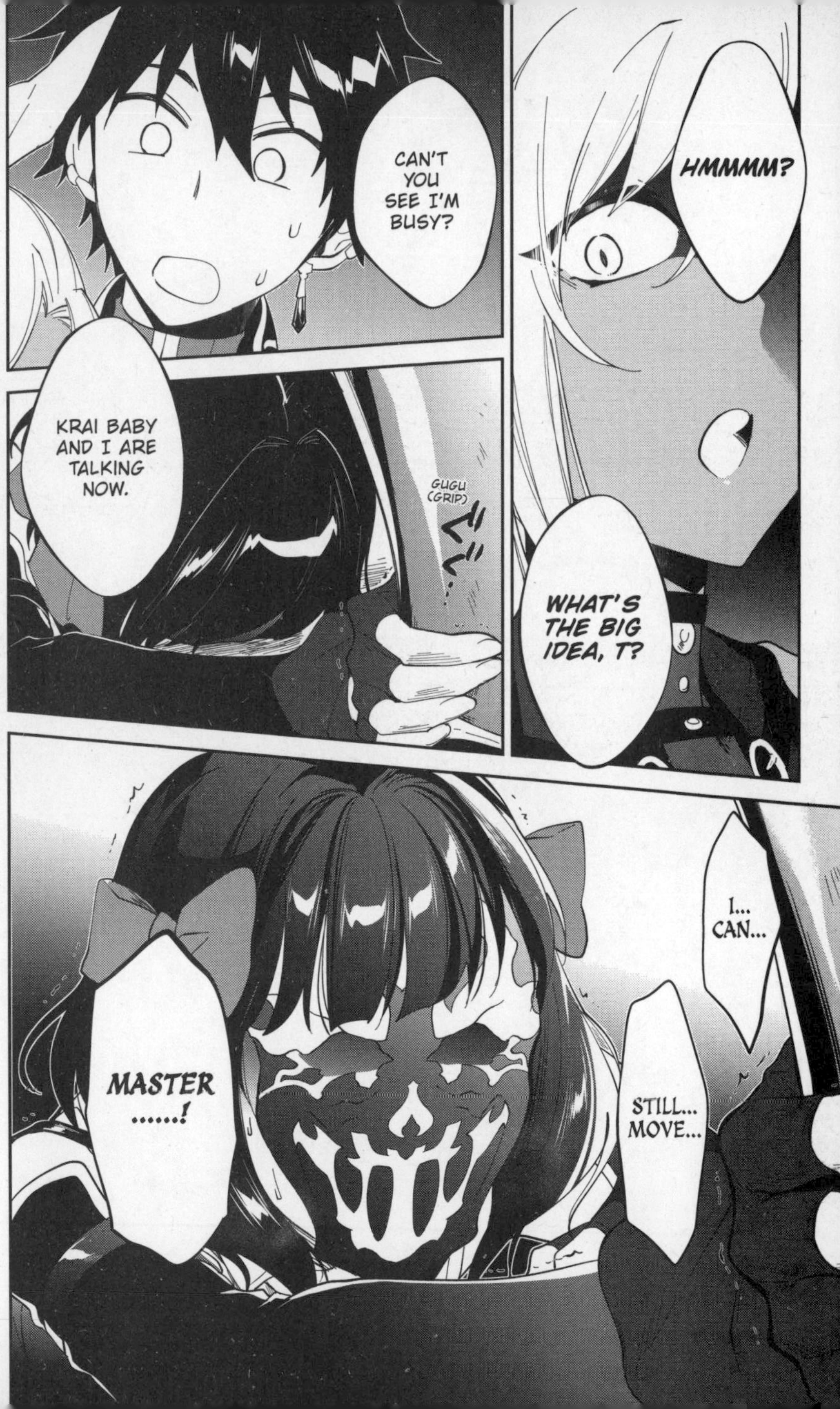
HMMMM?
WHAT'S THE BIG IDEA, T?
CAN'T YOU SEE I'M BUSY?
KRAI BABY AND I ARE TALKING NOW.
GUGU (GRIP)
I... CAN...
STILL... MOVE...
MASTER ......!

LET THIS
Grieving Soul Retire
WOE IS THE WEAKLING WHO LEADS THE STRONGEST PARTY

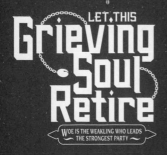

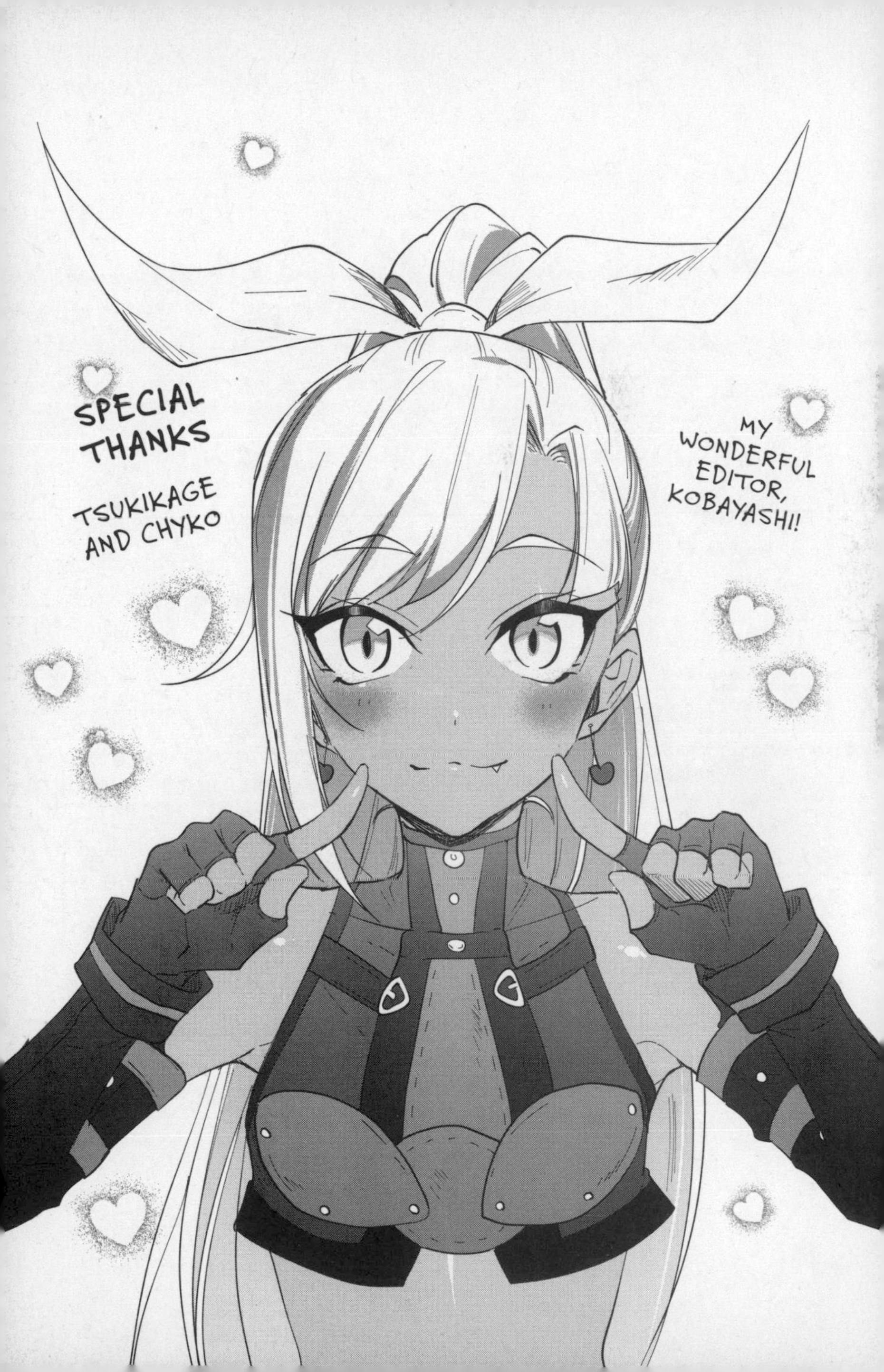
SPECIAL THANKS
TSUKIKAGE AND CHYKO
MY WONDERFUL EDITOR, KOBAYASHI!

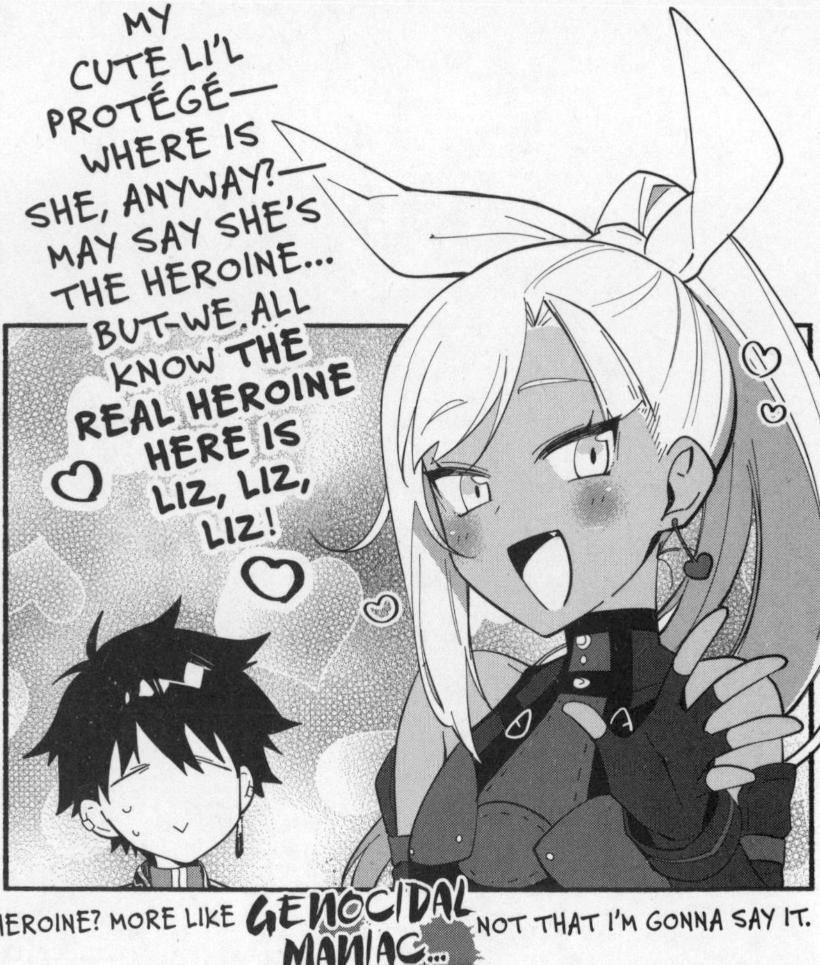
MY CUTE LI'L PROTÉGÉ—WHERE IS SHE, ANYWAY?—MAY SAY SHE'S THE HEROINE... BUT WE ALL KNOW THE REAL HEROINE HERE IS LIZ, LIZ, LIZ!

HEROINE? MORE LIKE GENOCIDAL MANIAC... NOT THAT I'M GONNA SAY IT.

Turn to the back of
the book for an
original short story by
Tsukikage, the author of
*Let This Grieving
Soul Retire!*

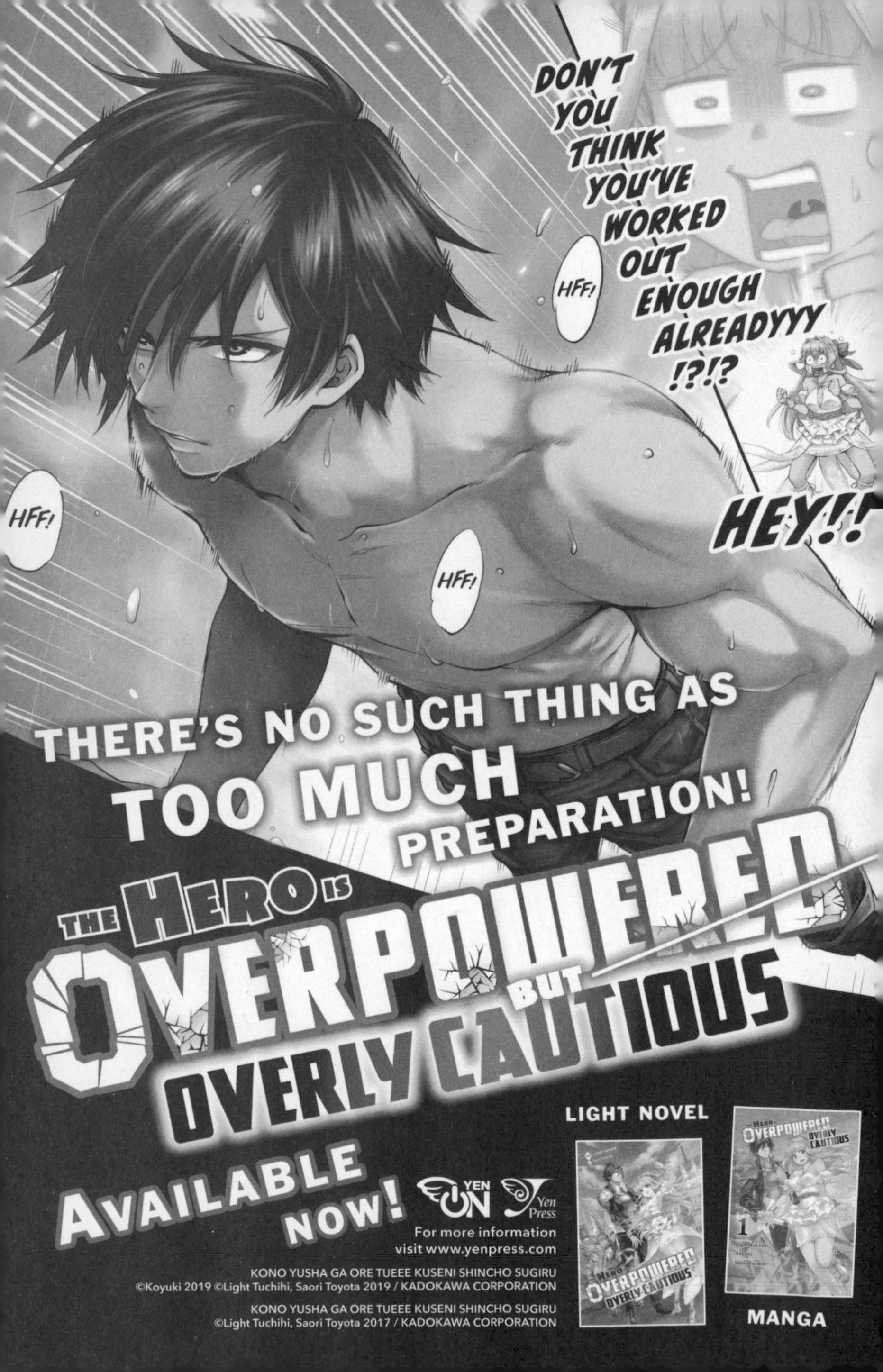
DON'T YOU THINK YOU'VE WORKED OUT ENOUGH ALREADYYY !?!?
HEY!!
HFF!
HFF!
HFF!
THERE'S NO SUCH THING AS TOO MUCH PREPARATION!
THE HERO IS OVERPOWERED BUT OVERLY CAUTIOUS
LIGHT NOVEL
MANGA
AVAILABLE NOW!
YEN ON
Yen Press
For more information visit www.yenpress.com
KONO YUSHA GA ORE TUEEE KUSENI SHINCHO SUGIRU
©Koyuki 2019 ©Light Tuchihi, Saori Toyota 2019 / KADOKAWA CORPORATION
KONO YUSHA GA ORE TUEEE KUSENI SHINCHO SUGIRU
©Light Tuchihi, Saori Toyota 2017 / KADOKAWA CORPORATION

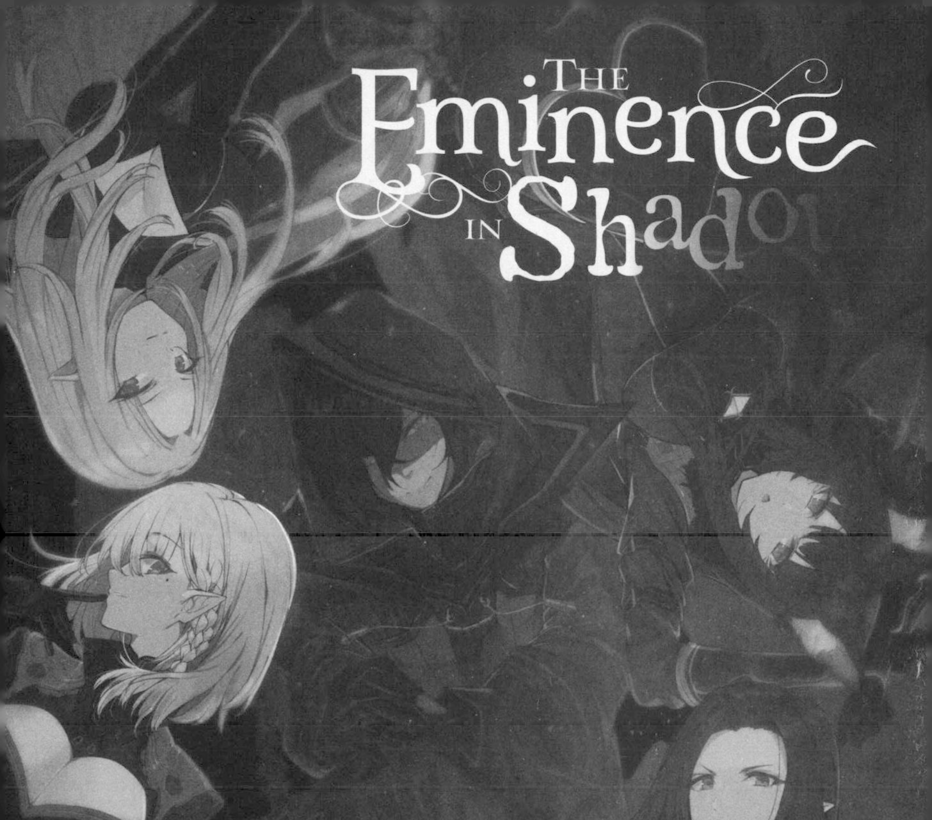
THE
Eminence
IN Shadow

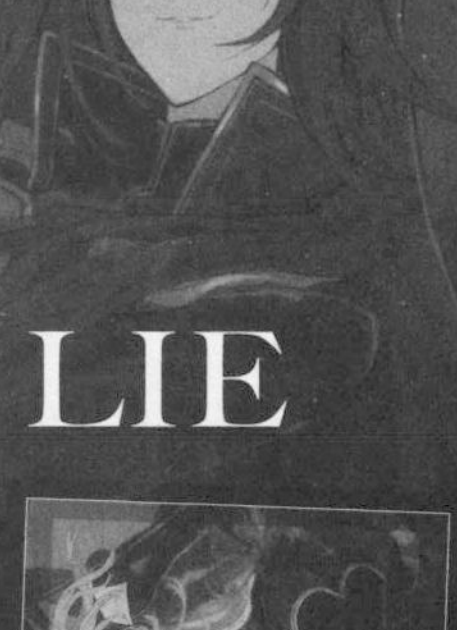
The
Eminence
in Shadow
Daisuke Aizawa
01

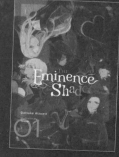

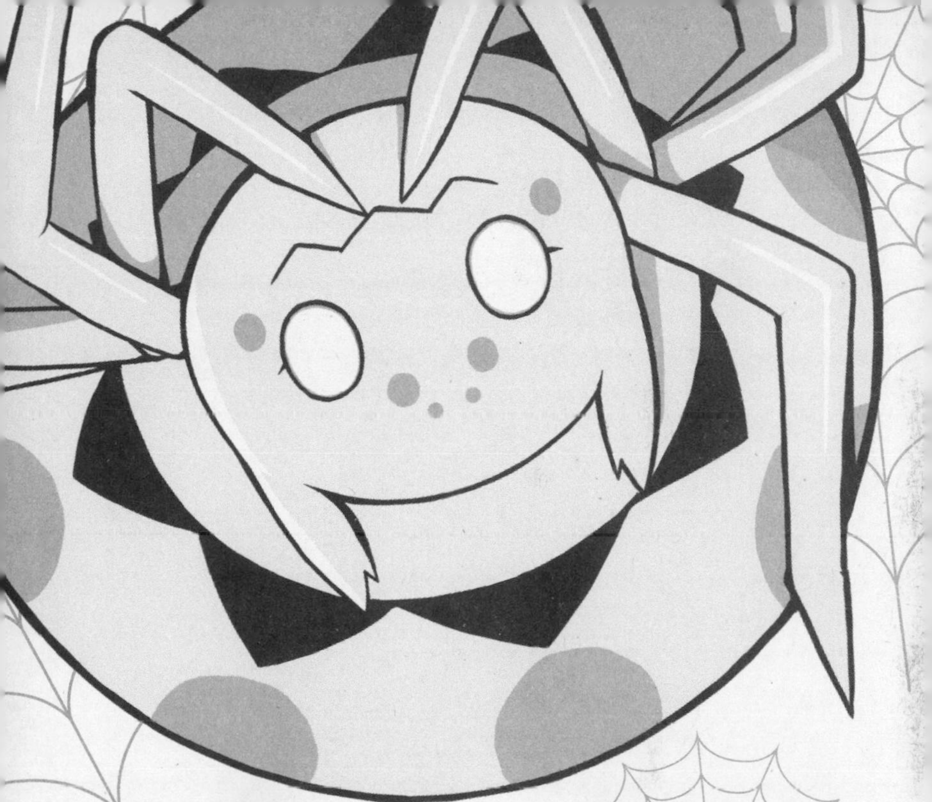

So I'm a Spider, So What?

MANGA VOL. 1-10

LIGHT NOVEL VOL. 1-14

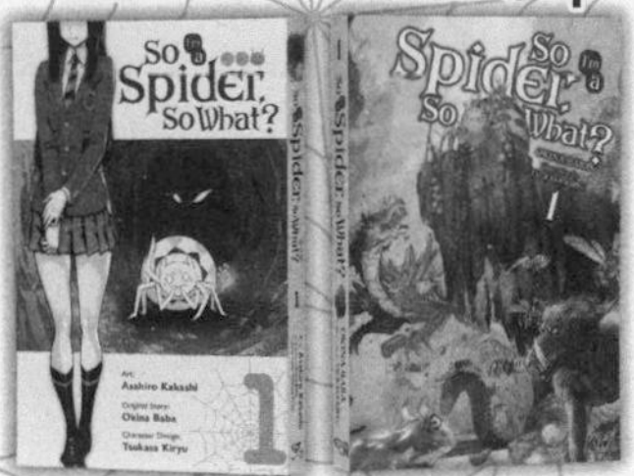
So I'm a Spider, So What?
Asahiro Kakashi
Okina Baba
Tsukasa Kiryu
1
Spider, So I'm a So What?

AVAILABLE NOW!

YOU CAN ALSO KEEP UP WITH THE MANGA SIMUL-PUB EVERY MONTH ONLINE!

I'M GONNA SURVIVE—JUST WATCH ME!

I was your average, everyday high school girl, but now I've been reborn in a magical world...as a spider?! How am I supposed to survive in this big, scary dungeon as one of the weakest monsters? I gotta figure out the rules to this QUICK, or I'll be kissing my short second life good-bye...

Yen Press

YenPress.com

YEN ON

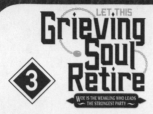

LET THIS
Grieving Soul Retire
3
WOE IS THE WEAKLING WHO LEADS THE STRONGEST PARTY

Rai Hebino

ORIGINAL STORY: **Tsukikage**

CHARACTER DESIGN: **Chyko**

TRANSLATION: **John Neal**

LETTERING: **Chiho Christie**

NAGEKI NO BOREI WA INTAI SHITAI ~SAIJAKU HUNTER NI YORU SAIKYO PARTY IKUSEIJUTSU~ Vol.3

First published in Japan in 2020 by KADOKAWA CORPORATION, Tokyo.
English translation rights arranged with KADOKAWA CORPORATION, Tokyo, through TUTTLE-MORI AGENCY, INC., Tokyo.

Yen Press
150 West 30th Street, 19th Floor
New York, NY 10001

Visit us at yenpress.com • facebook.com/yenpress • twitter.com/yenpress
yenpress.tumblr.com • instagram.com/yenpress

First Yen Press Edition: June 2022
Edited by Yen Press Editorial: Emily Gikas, Riley Pearsall
Designed by Yen Press Design: Jane Sohn

Yen Press is an imprint of Yen Press, LLC.
The Yen Press name and logo are trademarks of Yen Press, LLC.

The publisher is not responsible for websites (or their content) that are not owned by the publisher.

Library of Congress Control Number: 2021946317

ISBNs: 978-1-9753-3451-2 (paperback)
978-1-9753-3452-9 (ebook)

2 4 6 8 10 9 7 5 3 1

WOR

Printed in the United States of America

LET THIS
Grieving Soul Retire
~WOE IS THE WEAKLING WHO LEADS THE STRONGEST PARTY~

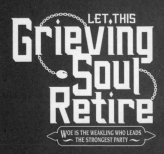

"You—! Ah, w-welcome back, Miss Smart." Liz's sudden appearance had caught vice clanmaster Eva off guard. The woman stood in the middle of the office, visibly shaken. "Mr. Krai is out at the moment. I believe he went to assist Tino at the White Wolf's Den."

It had been a very long run. The beasts, the phantoms, the bandits—none of them had posed much of a threat compared to the sheer distance Liz had covered. By the time she made it to the capital, the sun had completely set. It had been a very long run indeed, but she was satisfied knowing that she'd arrived several times faster than she would have if she'd waited for the carriage.

No way was Krai expecting this. Not in a million years.

Liz stopped for a moment to calm her ragged breathing. There was a public spout right in front of the gates into town; there, she doused herself to wash off all the blood and sweat. As the water flushed away the grime of her journey, Liz's mood took a total turn upward. All she had to do now was drop in and let Krai know she was back.

She gave her body a good, strong shake to dry off. Fighting back the urge to recklessly vault over the city wall, she submitted to the proper security inspection and entered the capital through the main gate. Since she'd gone to all that trouble to come back, she figured it'd be a shame to start off her time here by getting scolded. That would end the whole thing on a sour note.

As it was, Liz entered clan headquarters in squeaky-clean condition and opened the door to the clanmaster's chambers in high spirits.

"I'm back, Krai Baby! Didja miss me? …Wait, where the hell is Krai Baby?"

caravan despite its security detail. For a moment, Liz considered leaving the merchants to their plight—but then she realized how poorly it would reflect on her if word got out that a Grieving Soul had abandoned them in their time of need.

"Dammit, why noooooooow!? Get outta my way or die!"

Without dropping her speed for a moment, Liz took aim at the man who looked like the leader of the highwaymen. She rammed straight into him, knocking him back hard. Her momentum propelled her past bandit after bandit, striking them in their most vulnerable spots as she blew past with a war cry of "Die, die, die! Die, you damn roadblocks!" The merchants were spared her blows but not her ire. "And you! This is what you get for hiring shitty security! Now move it or lose it!"

Liz moved at such speed that not a drop of bandit blood landed on her as she struck. After about ten bandits fell, the rest of them lost their will to fight.

What a waste of precious time! Why's everyone trying to piss me off today of all days!?

Gotta get home. Gonna get home. Krai's waiting. He'll say "Welcome back, Liz!" and maybe even praise me for saving the caravan... That's gotta be worth a head pat or two for sure!

A chill ran through the caravan guards at the very sight of Liz, but she ignored them as she started running once again down the road to home.

"Haah... Haah... Finally...made it..."

C'moooooon!"

As expected, the Garest Mountains proved to be home to an abnormally high concentration of vicious beasts. Monster after monster appeared in Liz's path, only to be ripped to shreds and trampled underfoot as she pressed on with all her might. Her heart throbbed like it might burst out of her chest at any moment; her limbs practically screamed out in pain. However, Liz knew she could hardly call herself a hunter if she balked at this trial.

Survival of the fittest played out in real time in the Garest Mountains, and Liz remained at the top of the food chain.

Liz made her way down the far side of the mountains and returned to flat land. The grass underneath her feet again told her there was only a short way left to go until the capital.

Her heart pounded so intensely that she could hear the blood pulsing by her ears. Sweat cascaded down her skin to stain the ground below her. But even through the exhaustion, her thief's senses were on high alert. She smelled blood in the air and heard wailing and the unmistakable clashing of swords.

As the sun set over the road, a merchant caravan was under siege by bandits. From the sound of it, the merchants weren't exactly winning.

The Zebrudian empire was relatively safe in the grand scheme of things, but such attacks weren't especially rare. The bandits, with numbers on their side, were emboldened enough to strike at the around and spare themselves the considerable danger. On their way out to the Night Palace, the Grieving Souls had chosen to risk the steep and decrepit mountain roads and forced their carriage through the shortcut. Not that those were the only dangers of this path—the mountains were reportedly crawling with monsters the likes of which commanded considerable bounties for their viciousness. However, Liz had no choice but to take the shortcut on foot.

This is all a test, Liz thought. After another light stretch, she rushed off toward the mountains.

"I'm almost home, Krai Baby!"

Now, running in mountainous terrain is significantly more taxing than running on flat land, even in the best possible conditions. Liz could feel her legs, which had been so light and swift at the start of her journey, growing steadily heavier and heavier, but she pushed onward and upward, driving herself to tread treacherous footholds and dart around falling rocks and splintering branches. She'd run through her share of mountains long before, as part of her training. None of those mountains were anywhere near as steep as the Garest range—but then again, past Liz wasn't nearly as powerful as she was.

Gotta get home. Gonna get home! Krai's waiting to hear back from me! He's so busy running the clan that he can't have adventures of his own. That's why he needs to hear it from me! I usually gotta share the spotlight with Luke and Sitri, but this time, it'll be all Liz!

"Get outta my way, you stupid mountains!

a scream. The world around her was a blur as she sped through it.

Then, as her luck would have it, she came across a massive herd of magical beasts that just so happened to be crossing her exact path.

"Get the hell outta my waaaaaaay!"

"Mooooo—?!"

Naturally, stopping to let the herd pass was not an option. Either way, the creatures out in the open couldn't hold a candle to the ones she'd already fought in the vault. She charged forward, ramming the giant cattle—each one easily three times her size—into the air with every impact. One cow, two, three, four— she tackled her way through the herd, one bovine after the other. Finally, she made it to the other side, leaving the beasts to bleat and rage behind her. Liz pushed on, forcing herself to keep up the pace through the fields.

Eventually, she saw a huge mountain range looming before her. The Garest Mountains were home to all sorts of fiendish monsters; they were well-known throughout Zebrudia as dangerous ground. Despite her labored breathing, Liz managed to click her tongue in frustration yet again.

"Dammit! I forgot this, too!"

There was a shortcut to the capital that passed through the Garest Mountains. By taking the mountain pass, you could cut a full day off your travels—assuming, of course, that you survived. The vast majority of travelers chose to take the long way

"It's been a while since I've had a nice death-sprint anyway."

When it came down to it, Liz's strength lay more in her explosive power than in endurance, but she had no other choice if she wanted to get back to town quickly. After a small sigh and some light stretching, she took off running at ballistic speed.

With a firm kick off from the ground, Liz pushed herself forward, blitzing through fields crawling with monsters. No matter what kind of beast she happened across—monsters, phantoms, wild animals, other humans—none of them had a prayer of chasing Liz down once her spirit was truly fired up.

"Wait for me, Krai Babyyyyyyy!!"

Hunters' exposure to mana material allows them to grow and develop in any way they choose. Liz had used that power to boost the strength of her legs to well past that of a normal human. However, that didn't mean she wouldn't eventually tire out after running at full speed for an hour or two—maybe three.

Gotta get home. Gonna get home! I'll do whatever it takes if it gets me there one second faster! The clanmaster's eagerly waiting for me to tell him I'm back—I've gotta do it!

Liz knew that Krai wouldn't be too thrilled about her leaving the rest of the party behind and bolting home, but she also knew he'd give her the big hug hello that she wanted all the same. She kicked off from the ground again, blasting away her fatigue with phantoms like these before on the way in, but at the same time, they'd proven to be formidable enemies for the entire party fighting together. Each one of their ranks could be more than deadly enough on its own.

She blazed past, giving each one a good sideswiping thump with the back of her gauntlets. She felt her exposed skin heating up as the air beat against it, but she didn't let up speed.

The phantoms were tough and skilled. Even if the odds were overwhelmingly in her favor, it would still take plenty of time to defeat all of them. On the other hand, Liz was much faster.

Gotta get home. Gonna get home. I'm getting back alive, no matter what! Just like I promised!

"Hold on, Krai Baby!" Liz shouted. "And you guys get the hell outta my way! Move or die!"

With the pesky phantoms routed, Liz made her way out of the Night Palace. She clicked her tongue in frustration as she took in the scene that awaited her outside the vault.

"Tch! Shit, I totally forgot!"

The Night Palace was located on the Zebrudian frontier, and even with an excellent carriage to carry the Grieving Souls through the mountains and plains that separated the vault from the capital, it had taken them a full week to arrive. With the rest of the party still back in the Palace, Liz wouldn't have the luxury of taking the carriage home.

"Only one thing to do," Liz said to herself.

with newfound resolution. "Nah, I'm good. See you guys back at home!"

"H-hey, wait…"

Liz's heart pounded; her whole body pulsed with energy. Ignoring Sitri's admonishments, she bolted off with all her strength.

The Night Palace was relatively close to Zebrudia, but it was still known for being an especially difficult treasure vault to complete. The Grieving Souls aimed to be the strongest hunting party of all, so they were no strangers to high-level vaults. Compared to the phantoms Liz had previously encountered in her hunting career, the ones in the Palace were truly top-class. They were way beyond ordinary opponents, both in quality and quantity.

Since the party had supposedly beaten all the phantoms on the way in, Liz expected a smooth trip back out—but instead she found droves of variant phantom knights, all clad in jet-black armor, popping into view as she ran. They were fearsome foes indeed—far above mere humans in terms of both skill and sheer physical ability.

The phantom knights fired an enormous volley of arrows at her before she had time to breathe. Liz darted forward faster than a bullet and closed the huge distance between them without a moment's hesitation.

"Hyaaaaaaaaaaaah!"

Liz knew she couldn't afford to spare any strength in this fight. Her party had already knocked out lingo, these monsters are called "bosses." Typically, when a boss is defeated, it stays gone until enough mana material naturally gathers in the area to manifest it again. However, tough treasure vaults like the Night Palace don't see many successful hunters—meaning an excessive amount of mana material can build up all at once, creating a dangerous exception to the boss-reappearance rule. Having to take on boss after boss in these perilous vaults isn't something most hunters will ever have to deal with, but the Grieving Souls have experienced it so often that they have their own name for it: a "boss rush."

In a treasure-hunting party, thieves like Liz have two primary jobs: scouting for foes and cracking locks. Liz Smart was certainly a capable fighter, but it wasn't her actual forte.

"You sure, Liz?" Luke Sykol, one of Liz's fellow Grieving Souls—known as Thousand Swords—stood by idly swinging a giant sword he'd claimed from a fallen phantom as he spoke. "You don't even wanna see the bosses? I thought you were looking forward to this."

"Hmmm…?" Liz bit her lip and hummed as she mulled it over. Now she wasn't sure. But she knew that if she went on into the boss room and found the fierce battle to the death that surely awaited inside, she would definitely get caught up in the rush. And if that happened, who knows when she'd make it back to the capital?

Liz shook herself out of her hesitation and replied